WRITINGS IN INDIAN HISTORY, 1985–1990

THE D'ARCY MCNICKLE CENTER
BIBLIOGRAPHIES IN AMERICAN INDIAN HISTORY

WRITINGS IN INDIAN HISTORY, 1985–1990

Compiled by
JAY MILLER,
COLIN G. CALLOWAY,
and RICHARD A. SATTLER

UNIVERSITY OF OKLAHOMA PRESS : NORMAN AND LONDON

Book design by Bill Cason.

Library of Congress Cataloging-in-Publication Data

Miller, Jay, 1947–
    Writings in Indian history, 1985–1990 / compiled by Jay Miller, Colin G.
Calloway, and Richard A. Sattler.
        p.   cm. —(The D'Arcy McNickle Center bibliographies in American Indian
history ; v. 2)
    Includes index.
    ISBN 0–8061–2759–7 (alk. paper)
    1. Indians of North America—History—Bibliography. 2. North America—
History—Bibliography. I. Calloway, Colin G. (Colin Gordon), 1953–
II. Sattler, Richard A., 1952–   .   III. Title. IV. Series.
Z1206.M55   1995
[E77]
016.973'0497—dc20   95–8776
                                                                                              CIP

Writings in Indian History, 1985–1990 is Volume 2 of The D'Arcy McNickle Center
Bibliographies in American Indian History.

The paper in this book meets the guidelines for permanence and durability of the
Committee on Production Guidelines for Book Longevity of the Council on Library
Resources, Inc. ∞

1   2   3   4   5   6   7   8   9   10

Contents

Introduction to the Series

Frederick E. Hoxie, General Editor

DURING the 1960s and 1970s, the scholarly world witnessed a rapid expansion of interest in the history of Native Americans. Spurred by public sympathy, political pressure, and a recognition that the subject had been ignored for too long, authors from many disciplines began producing a flood of books and articles. Indian studies programs and journals began to appear, and a new generation of students received specialized training in the Native American past. By the middle of the 1980s the field of Indian history had begun to build its own infrastructure: organizations, networks of individuals, and institutions had come to support a variety of educational and publishing activities, from new survey courses to prizewinning monographs. This infrastructure also ensured the production of hundreds of scholarly publications each year.

When the Newberry Library established the Center for the History of the American Indian in 1972, director D'Arcy McNickle and his colleagues believed that a bibliography series was essential to the development of serious scholarship in the field. Researchers expressed substantial interest in Indian history at that time but lacked adequate knowledge of the existing scholarly literature, a literature that spreads across (and beyond) the traditional disciplines of history, anthropology, English, and religion. These researchers needed ready access to the work of past scholars. The product of McNickle's concern was the Newberry Library Center for the History of the American Indian Bibliographical Series, a collection of thirty short volumes published by Indiana University Press and designed to provide newcomers to the field with an introduction to selected topics in Indian history.

This series, together with two volumes of bibliographies on Indian-white relations by Francis Paul Prucha (which cover items published up to 1980), has enabled a generation of readers to translate their curiosity into serious scholarly endeavor. The Prucha volumes were published as *A Bibliographical Guide to the History of Indian-White Relations in the United States* by the University of Chicago Press (1977) and *Indian-White Relations in the United States: A Bibliography of Works Published 1975–1980* by the University of Nebraska Press (1982).

Despite this progress, however, the volume of new material being produced each year required the creation of yet another bibliographical tool. The D'Arcy McNickle Center Bibliographies in American Indian History provide comprehensive coverage of new scholarship in the field with two types of publications: volumes of bibliographical essays and indexed bibliographical lists organized by topic.

Prepared by a cross section of scholars from a variety of disciplinary and regional backgrounds, the bibliographic essays both review recent trends in historical scholarship and point to areas to which researchers should apply their efforts in the future. *New Directions in American Indian History,* edited by Colin G. Calloway (who was at that time the McNickle Center's assistant director) and published in 1988, was the first of these volumes. It was intended to provide students of the Native American past with a guide to recent research and a variety of suggestions for new areas of inquiry.

The second type of publication is a comprehensive bibliography of works on Indian history published in English during a specific period. These bibliographies, arranged topically, comprise publications in the disciplines of history, anthropology, sociology, literature, economics, religious studies, and linguistics. This volume, which is the first of this type in the series, covers material published from 1985 through 1990. In the future, we intend to alternate volumes of bibliographical essays and bibliographical citations.

The D'Arcy McNickle Center bibliographies should provide students at all levels with comprehensive, ongoing guides to a field that has established itself as a permanent part of American intellectual life. We hope they will contribute to wider dissemination of scholarship in American Indian history and to continued growth in the field.

Preface

AS this volume was going to press, one of its compilers received refereed comments on a paper he had submitted to a historical journal. "Frankly," confessed a reviewer in obvious dismay, "I had to check to see if he was a historian or an anthropologist." With a traditional British education in history and no formal training in anthropology, Colin Calloway took being mistaken for an anthropologist as something of a compliment.

This incident reflects more significant developments in the writing of Indian history. "Straight histories" of Indian wars and government policies still abound and are of considerable value, but they no longer represent the sum of Indian history. In recent years, more scholars have turned their attention to what might be called Indian social history, and to pursue their intellectual goals they have increasingly crossed the lines separating traditional academic disciplines. A fuller understanding of Native American life and experiences has required a variety of disciplinary perspectives. In their scholarly struggles, historians and anthropologists have been forced to talk to each other and to consult widely with members of native communities. Incorporating different methodologies does not necessarily constitute a shift in academic allegiance but is simply "a better way to write Indian history."

As this bibliography attests, Indian history is a mansion with many rooms. The titles in our lists range from military history to native linguistics to current legal issues. Writers in each of these fields contribute in their own way to a more complete picture of the history of Native American experience. The years between 1985 and 1990 witnessed a steady increase in scholarship devoted to American Indians, and much of the new work is multidisciplinary in its scope and approach. This bibliography records the scholarship in an attempt to make the diverse and growing literature accessible to an equally diverse readership of academic scholars, students, members of Indian communities, and others with an interest in general American history.

In 1985, the D'Arcy McNickle Center began to produce annual lists of publications in American Indian history. Colin G. Calloway completed the first list at the Newberry Library, but his departure for the University of Wyoming in 1987 and Jay Miller's arrival at the Newberry led to a new arrangement and a collaboration. Each has focused on his own interests. Miller primarily gathered anthropological works and Calloway historical ones, but each complemented the work of the other by seeking out more obscure references either in libraries and publications or by correspondence and conversation. Each year's list was circulated to over one hundred colleagues with requests for further suggestions and corrections. (People were very good at pointing out omissions of their own work.) Each year Miller undertook the primary responsibility for assembling all the citations, although Calloway had the right to approve the results. As we completed each list, we began work on the next year's compilation. This cumulative six-year listing was always the goal before us. As the work neared completion, Richard A. Sattler, an anthropologist and ethnohistorian, joined the project when Miller departed for Seattle. He added more works (mostly reflecting his own interests), scoured major journals for inadvertent omissions, and brought the manuscript into finished form. When the manuscript was complete, Frederick E. Hoxie served as a final editor, revising some categories and correcting assignments to ensure consistency.

Our intent in this volume was to be as thorough and comprehensive as possible. We strove to cover as wide a range of serial publications as we could find. We did not include titles deemed too theoretical or too specialized to relate generally to Indian history. Instead, we concentrated on diverse publications that illuminate the Native American past. Despite the fact that some of these titles were published outside of North America, only works in English have been included. Only a few dissertations have been included; these titles appear if the subject is otherwise slighted or is of special significance to the D'Arcy McNickle Center. Sometimes, the entry marks a new topic for Native American history. Every issue of *Meeting Ground,* the

McNickle Center's biennial newsletter, carried pleas for more citations or corrections of ones already included. In this way, our readers and colleagues aided our efforts.

The organization of categories for this volume began with the two volumes produced by Francis Paul Prucha, S.J. His works, cited above in the Introduction to the Series, represent the first effort to assemble exhaustive bibliographies in Indian history. As the field has grown, however, and new topics have arisen, we have felt the need to modify some of Prucha's categories. Several disciplines now feature a historical subarea. For example, literature has come to include titles in historical linguistics, and demography has expanded into an important field of inquiry for scholars of the Indian experience.

Two chapters seem to carry the burden of this bibliography. These are Chapter 3, "Indian-White Relations: Governmental Affairs, Military Relations, and the Interaction of Native and European Communities" and Chapter 7, "Ethnohistory: Historical Approaches to Indian Communities and Cultures."

Although we used our categories according to academic conventions, we did consult Native American opinions for the placement of some items. Thus, whereas most Native cultures would not separate the topic heading of Chapter 11, "Environments: Physical and Spiritual" from that of Section 11.3, "Religion," we defined religion as a subtopic under environment for the sake of organizational clarity; but out of respect for Native American opinions, we chose to list issues of repatriation and reburial under Section 11.3, "Religion," rather than Chapter 6.0, "Legal Relations Between Native Americans and Others."

For their help and encouragement over the years, we would like to thank Harvey Markowitz, George Grossman, John Sugden, Cecil King, Helen Tanner, Nancy Shoemaker, and John Aubrey. During the last three years, the listings were done with a bibliographic program provided by George Christakes and George Kren.

Most entries are given without comment. To those that proved confusing, we added a brief explanation to lessen ambiguity.

The primary purpose of this bibliography is to provide a reference tool for scholars and students of Indian history. But the volume has a wider significance. The number and range of publications produced in a six-year period reflect the many ways in which Native American civilization appeals to authors. The continuing vitality and richness of the field demonstrates the perennial fascination and challenges of the American Indian past.

JAY MILLER

Seattle, Washington

COLIN G. CALLOWAY

University of Wyoming

RICHARD A. SATTLER

Newberry Library

WRITINGS IN INDIAN HISTORY, 1985–1990

I
General Studies, Bibliographies, and Guides to Sources

1.1   GENERAL STUDIES

1.   **Arden, Harvey.** "Who Owns Our Past?" *National Geographic* 175 (March 1989): 376–92.

2.   **Bedini, Silvio,** ed. *The Columbus Encyclopedia.* New York: Simon and Schuster, 1990.

3.   **Bitterli, U.** *Cultures in Conflict: Encounters Between European and Non-European Cultures, 1492–1800.* Trans. Ritchie Robertson. Cambridge: Polity Press, 1989.

4.   **Churchill, Ward,** ed. *Critical Issues in Native North America.* Copenhagen, Denmark: International Work Group on Indigeneous Affairs, 1989.

5.   **Comeau, Pauline,** and **Aldo Santine.** *The First Canadians: A Profile of Canada's Native People Today.* Toronto: James Lorimer and Co., 1990.

6.   **Confederation of American Indians.** *Indian Reservations: A State and Federal Handbook.* Jefferson, N.C.: McFarland and Co., 1986.

7.   **Cox, Bruce A.,** ed. *Native People, Native Lands: Canadian Indians, Inuit, and Métis.* Ottawa: Carleton University Press, 1988.

8.   **Feest, Christian.** *Indians of North America.* Leiden, Holland: E. J. Brill Publishing Co., 1986.

9.   **Fisher, Robin,** and **Kenneth Coates,** eds. *Out of the Background: Readings on Canadian Native History.* Toronto: Copp Clark Pitman, 1988.

10.   **Fowler, Don D.** "Images of American Indians, 1492–1892." *Halcyon* 12 (1990): 75–100.

11.   **Gillis, Michael J.,** ed. *Essays in North American Indian History.* Dubuque, Iowa: Kendall/Hunt, 1990.

12.   **Harris, R. Cole,** ed. *Historical Atlas of Canada: From the Beginning to 1800.* Assisted by Geoffrey J. Mathews. Toronto: University of Toronto Press, 1987.

13.   **Hoxie, Frederick E.,** ed. *Indians in American History: An Introduction.* Arlington Heights, Ill.: Harlan Davidson, 1988.

14.   **Klein, Barry,** ed. *Reference Encyclopedia of the American Indian.* 2 vols. New York: Todd Publications, 1986.

15.   **Leacock, Eleanor Burke,** and **Nancy Oestrich Lurie,** eds. *North American Indians in Historical Perspective.* 1971. Reprint, Prospect Heights, Ill.: Waveland Press, 1988.

16.   **Prucha, Francis Paul.** *Atlas of*

American Indian Affairs. Lincoln: University of Nebraska Press, 1990.

17.   **Richardson, Malcolm.** "1992: Opportunities for Indian History." *History News* 45 (May/June 1990): 10–18.

18.   **Scheper-Hughes, Nancy.** "The Best of Two Worlds, the Worst of Two Worlds: Reflection on Culture and Fieldwork Among the Rural Irish and Pueblo Indians." *Comparative Studies in Society and History* 29 (1987): 56–75.

19.   **Snipp, C. Matthew.** *American Indians: The First of This Land.* New York: Russell Sage Foundation, 1990.

20.   **Stuart, Paul.** *Nations Within a Nation: Historical Statistics of American Indians.* Westport, Conn.: Greenwood Press/Praeger, 1987.

21.   **Tanner, Helen Hornbeck,** ed. *Atlas of Great Lakes Indian History.* With Adele Hast, Jacqueline Peterson, and Robert J. Surtees. Norman: University of Oklahoma Press, 1987.

22.   **Trenton, Patricia,** and **Patrick T. Houlihan.** *Native Americans: Five Centuries of Changing Images.* New York: Harry N. Abrams, 1989.

23.   **Viola, Herman.** *After Columbus: The Smithsonian Chronicle of the North American Indians.* Washington, D.C.: Smithsonian Institution Press, 1990.

24.   **Waldman, Carl.** *Atlas of the North American Indian.* Maps by Molly Braun. New York: Facts on File, 1985.

25.   ———. *Encyclopedia of Native American Tribes.* New York: Facts on File, 1988.

26.   ———. *Who Was Who in Native American History: Indians and Non-Indians from Early Contacts Through 1990.* New York: Facts on File, 1990.

27.   **Washburn, Wilcomb,** ed. *History of Indian-White Relations.* Vol. 4 of

Handbook of North American Indians, ed. W. Sturtevant. Washington, D.C.: Smithsonian Institution Press, 1988.

28.   **Weeks, Philip,** ed. *The American Indian Experience: A Profile, 1524 to the Present.* Arlington Heights, Ill.: Forum Press, 1988.

1.2   BIBLIOGRAPHIES

29.   **Beck, David.** *The Chicago American Indian Community, 1883–1988: Annotated Bibliography and Guide to Sources in Chicago.* Chicago: NAES College Press, 1988.

30.   **Blumer, Thomas J.** *Bibliography of the Catawba.* Metuchen, N.J.: Scarecrow Press, 1987.

31.   **Brewington, Lillian, Normie Bullard,** and **R. W. Reising.** "Writing in Love: An Annotated Bibliography of Critical Responses to the Poetry and Novels of Louise Erdrich and Michael Dorris." *American Indian Culture and Research Journal* 10, no. 4 (1986): 81–86.

32.   **Calloway, Colin G.,** ed. *New Directions in American Indian History.* Norman: University of Oklahoma Press, 1988.

33.   **Colonnese, Tom,** and **Louis Owens.** *American Indian Novelists: An Annotated Critical Bibliography.* New York: Garland, 1985.

34.   **Dempsey, Hugh A.,** and **Lindsay Moir.** *Bibliography of the Blackfeet.* Metuchen, N.J.: Scarecrow Press, 1989.

35.   **Edmunds, R. David.** *Kinsmen Through Time: An Annotated Bibliography of Potawatomi History.* Metuchen, N.J.: Scarecrow Press, 1987.

36.   **Frazier, Gregory W.** *American Indian Index.* Denver: Arrowstar, 1985.

37.   **Giordano Fedora.** "North American Indians in Italian (1950–1981): A

Bibliography of Books." In *Indians and Europe: An Interdisciplinary Collection of Essays*, ed. C. Feest, 491–503. Aachen, West Germany: Edition Herodot, 1987.

38. Heard, J. Norman. *The Northeastern Woodlands.* Vol. 2 of *Handbook of the American Frontier: Four Centuries of Indian-White Relationships.* Native American Resources Series, no. 1. Metuchen, N.J.: Scarecrow Press, 1990.

39. ———. *The Southeastern Woodlands.* Vol. 1 of *Handbook of the American Frontier: Four Centuries of Indian-White Relationships.* Native American Resources Series, no. 1. Metuchen, N.J.: Scarecrow Press, 1987.

40. Hoyt, Anne Kelley. *Bibliography of the Chickasaw.* Metuchen, N.J.: Scarecrow Press, 1987.

41. Hunter, Carol D. "A Bibliography of Writings Concerning the Big Horn Medicine Wheel, Big Horn National Forest." *Annals of Wyoming* 57, no. 1 (1985): 13–20.

42. Johnson, Bryan R. *The Blackfeet: An Annotated Bibliography.* New York: Garland, 1988.

43. Jorgensen, Delores. *Update to a Bibliography of Indian Law Periodical Articles, Published 1980–86: January 1987–December 1988.* Bibliography compiled by Delores Jorgensen and Barbara Heisinger. Vermillion, S.Dak.: McKusick Law Library, University of South Dakota, 1989.

44. Kersey, Harry A., Jr. *The Seminole and Miccosukee Tribes: A Critical Biography.* Bloomington: Indiana University Press for the D'Arcy McNickle Center, 1987.

45. Krech, Shepard, III. *Canadian Native Anthropology and History: A Bibliography.* Rupert's Land Research Centre, Occasional Paper no. 2. Winnipeg, 1986.

46. Littlefield, Daniel F., Jr., and James W. Parins. "The American Native Press: A Survey of Recent Scholarship." *Native Press Research Journal* 1 (1986): 6–9.

47. ———, eds. *American Indian and Alaska Native Newspapers and Periodicals, 1925–1970.* Westport, Conn.: Greenwood Press, 1986. [Companion volumes published 1983–1986]

48. ———. *A Bibliography of Native American Writers, 1772–1924: A Supplement.* Metuchen, N.J.: Scarecrow Press, 1985. [Supplement to 1981 original]

49. Lobb, Michael L., and Thomas D. Watts. *Native American Youth and Alcohol: An Annotated Bibliography.* New York: Greenwood Press, 1989.

50. Lydon, James G. *Struggle for Empire: A Bibliography of the French and Indian War.* Garland Reference Library of Social Science, no. 188. New York: Garland, 1986.

51. Meiklejohn, C., and D. A. Rokala, eds. *The Native Peoples of Canada: An Annotated Bibliography of Population Biology, Health, and Illness.* Mercury Series Paper, vol. 134. Ottawa: Canadian Museum of Civilization, 1987.

52. Merrell, James H. "Supplementary Reading List for Eastern Indians." In *The Impact of Indian History on the Teaching of United States History: Papers and Commentary from the 1985 Conference at the Smithsonian Institution, Washington, D.C.*, 241–60. D'Arcy McNickle Center for the History of the American Indian, Occasional Papers in Curriculum, no. 4. Chicago: Newberry Library, 1986.

53. Oppelt, Norman. *Southwestern Pottery: An Annotated Bibliography and List of Types and Wares.* Metuchen, N.J.: Scarecrow Press, 1988.

54. Parker, Dorothy. "D'Arcy

McNickle: An Annotated Bibliography of His Published Articles and Book Reviews in a Biographical Context." *American Indian Culture and Research Journal* 14, no. 2 (1990): 55–75.

55. Peterson, John H., Jr., ed. *A Choctaw Sourcebook.* New York: Garland, 1985.

56. Porter, Frank W., III. *Native American Basketry: An Annotated Bibliography.* Westport, Conn.: Greenwood Press, 1988.

57. Rock, Roger O., comp. *The Native American in American Literature: A Selectively Annotated Bibliography.* Westport, Conn.: Greenwood Press, 1985.

58. Rollings, Willard. "In Search of Multisided Frontiers: Recent Writing on the History of the Southern Plains." In *New Directions in American Indian History,* ed. C. G. Calloway, 79–96. Norman: University of Oklahoma Press, 1988.

59. Roscoe, Will. "Bibliography of Berdache and Alternative Gender Roles Among North American Indians." *Journal of Homosexuality* 14, no. 3 (1987): 81–171.

60. Ruoff, A. Lavonne Brown. "American Indian Literatures: Introduction and Bibliography." *American Studies International* 24, no. 2 (1986): 2–52.

61. ———. "Gerald Vizenor: Selected Bibliography." *American Indian Quarterly* 9 (1985): 75–78.

62. Salzmann, Zdenek, comp. *The Arapaho Indians: A Research Guide and Bibliography.* Westport, Conn.: Greenwood Press, 1988.

63. Sutton, Imre. "A Selected Bibliography of the California Indian, with Emphasis on the Past Decade." *American Indian Culture and Research Journal* 14, no. 2 (1988): 81–114.

64. Swagerty, William R. "Supplementary Bibliography for Audio-Visual Materials in Indian History." In *The Impact of Indian History on the Teaching of United States History: Papers and Commentary from the 1985 Conference at the Smithsonian Institution, Washington, D.C.,* 261–68. D'Arcy McNickle Center for the History of the American Indian, Occasional Papers in Curriculum, no. 4. Chicago: Newberry Library, 1986.

65. Tate, Michael L. *The Indians of Texas: An Annotated Research Bibliography.* Metuchen, N.J.: Scarecrow Press, 1986.

66. Weist, Katherine M., and **Susan R. Sharrock.** *An Annotated Bibliography of Northern Plains Ethnohistory.* University of Montana Department of Anthropology, Contributions to Anthropology, no. 8. Missoula, 1985.

67. Wiedman, Dennis. *Ethnohistory: A Researcher's Guide.* Anthropology Department, College of William and Mary, Studies in Third World Societies, no. 35. Williamsburg, Va., 1986.

68. Wiget, Andrew O. "Native American Literature: A Bibliographic Survey of American Indian Literary Traditions." *Choice* 23 (June 1986): 1503–12.

69. Wilson, Terry P. *Bibliography of the Osage.* Metuchen, N.J.: Scarecrow Press, 1985.

1.3   PUBLISHED DOCUMENTS, MANUSCRIPTS, AND GUIDES TO PRIMARY MATERIALS

70. Allen, Robert, and **Mary A. T. Tobin.** *Native Studies in Canada: A Research Guide.* Ottawa: Treaties and Historical Research Centre, Comprehensive

Claims, Indian and Northern Affairs Canada, 1989.

71. **Blackburn, Thomas C.,** and **Travis Hudson.** *Time's Flotsam: Overseas Collections of California Indian Material.* Menlo Park, Calif.: Ballena Press and Santa Barbara Museum of Natural History, 1990.

72. **Clarke Memorial Museum.** *The Hover Collection of Karuk Baskets.* Eureka, Calif.: Clarke Memorial Museum, 1985. [Karuk history]

73. **Davis, Robert Scott, Jr.** *A Guide to Native American Research Sources at the Georgia Department of Archives and History, 1985.* [Available from the author, Route 2, Box 67, Jasper, Ga. 30143]

74. **De Witt, Donald L.,** ed. *American Indian Resource Materials in the Western History Collections, University of Oklahoma.* Norman: University of Oklahoma Press, 1990.

75. **Feest, Christian.** "Some Eighteenth Century Specimens from Eastern North America in Collections in the German Democratic Republic." *Jahrbuch des Museums für Völkerkunde zu Leipzig* 37 (1987): 281–301.

76. **Garrow, Patrick H.** "Public Documents as Primary Sources for Ethnohistorical Research: The Mattamuskeet Model." In *Ethnohistory: A Researcher's Guide,* ed. D. Wiedman, 1–24. Williamsburg, Va.: College of William and Mary, 1986.

77. **Graymont, Barbara,** ed. *New York–New Jersey Treaties, 1609–1682.* Vol. 7 of *Early American Indian Documents, Treaties, and Laws, 1607–1789.* ed. A. T. Vaughan. Frederick, Md.: University Publications of America, 1985.

78. **Halpern, Katherine Spencer,** et al. *Guide to the Microfilm Edition of the*

Washington Matthews Papers. Albuquerque: University of New Mexico Press, 1985. [Matthews was an army surgeon who wrote on Hidatsa and Navajo]

79. **Hosen, Frederick E.,** ed. *Rifle, Blanket, and Kettle: Selected Indian Treaties and Laws.* Jefferson, N.C.: McFarland, 1985.

80. **Hoxie, Frederick E.** "The View from Eagle Butte: National Archives Field Branches and the Writing of American Indian History." *Journal of American History* 76 (1989): 172–80.

81. **Jennings, Francis, William Fenton, Mary A. Drucke,** and **David R. Miller,** eds. *Iroquois Indians: A Documentary History of the Diplomacy of the Six Nations and Their League: Guide to the Microfilm Collection.* Woodbridge, Conn.: Research Publications, 1985.

82. **Judkins, Russell A.,** ed. *Iroquois Studies: A Guide to Documentary and Ethnographic Resources from Western New York to the Genessee Valley.* Geneseo: Department of Anthropology, State University of New York at Geneseo, 1987.

83. **Juricek, John T.,** ed. *Georgia Treaties, 1733–1763.* Vol. 11 of *Early American Indian Documents, Treaties, and Laws, 1607–1789,* ed. A. T. Vaughan. Frederick, Md.: University Publications of America, 1987.

84. **Kutsche, Paul.** *A Guide to Cherokee Documents in the Northeastern United States.* Metuchen, N.J.: Scarecrow Press, 1986.

85. **Larner, John W., Jr.,** ed. *The Papers of the Society of American Indians, 1906–1946.* Wilmington, Del.: Scholarly Resources, 1986. [10 microfilm rolls]

86. **Lewis, G. Malcolm.** "Indian Maps: Their Place in the History of Plains Cartography." In *Mapping the*

North American Plains: Essays in the History of Cartography, ed. F. C. Luebke, F. W. Kaye, and G. E. Moulton, 63–80. Norman: University of Oklahoma Press, 1987.

87.   Moulton, Gary E., ed. *Journals of the Lewis and Clark Expedition.* Vol. 2, *August 30, 1803–August 24, 1804.* Lincoln: University of Nebraska Press, 1986.

88.   ———. *Journals of the Lewis and Clark Expedition.* Vol. 3, *August 25, 1804–April 6, 1805.* Lincoln: University of Nebraska Press, 1987.

89.   ———. *Journals of the Lewis and Clark Expedition.* Vol. 4, *April 7–July 14, 1805.* Lincoln: University of Nebraska Press, 1987.

90.   ———. *Journals of the Lewis and Clark Expedition.* Vol. 5, *July 28–November 1, 1805.* Lincoln: University of Nebraska Press, 1988.

91.   ———. *Journals of the Lewis and Clark Expedition.* Vol. 6, *November 2, 1805–March 22, 1806.* Lincoln: University of Nebraska Press, 1990.

92.   Nasitir, A. P., ed. *Before Lewis and Clark: Documents Illustrating the History of Missouri, 1785–1804.* 1952. Reprint, Lincoln: University of Nebraska Press, 1990.

93.   Panton, Leslie and Co. "The Papers of Panton, Leslie and Company." Microfilm. Woodbridge, Conn.: Research Publication, 1986.

94.   Porter, Frank W., III. *In Pursuit of the Past: An Anthropological and Bibliographic Guide to Maryland and Delaware.* Metuchen, N.J.: Scarecrow Press, 1986.

95.   Proulx, Jean-Rene, and Sylvie Vincent, comps. *Review of Ethnohistorical Research on the Native Peoples of Quebec.* 5 vols. Montreal: Ministere des Affairs Culturelles du Quebec, 1985.

96.   Robinson, W. Stitt, ed. *Maryland Treaties, 1632–1775.* Vol. 6 of *Early American Indian Documents, Treaties, and Laws, 1607–1789,* ed. A. T. Vaughan. Frederick, Md.: University Publications of America, 1987.

97.   Vane, Sylvia Brakke, and Lowell John Bean, eds. *California Indian Primary Sources: A Guide to Manuscripts, Artifacts, Documents, Serials, Music, and Illustrations.* Menlo Park, Calif.: Ballena Press, 1990.

98.   Vaughan, Alden T., ed. *Early American Indian Documents, Treaties, and Laws, 1607–1789.* 20 vols. Frederick, Md.: University Publications of America, 1985–1987. [Vols. 1, 2, 4, 5, 6, 7, 11 published]

99.   Wedel, Mildred Mott, ed. *A Jean Delanglez, S.J., Anthology: Selections Useful for Mississippi Valley and Trans-Mississippi American Indian Studies.* New York: Garland Publishing, 1985.

100.   Wehrkamp, Tim. "A Selected Guide to Sources on New Mexico Indians in the Modern Period." *New Mexico Historical Review* 60 (1985): 435–44.

II
Pre-Contact History

2.1 GENERAL STUDIES

101. **Baker, Brenda,** and **George Armelagos.** "The Origin and Antiquity of Syphilis: Paleopathological Diagnosis and Interpretation." *Current Anthropology* 29, no. 4 (1988): 703–38.

102. **Brown, James A.** "America Before Columbus." In *Indians in American History: An Introduction,* ed. F. E. Hoxie, 19–45. Arlington Heights, Ill.: Harlan Davidson, 1988.

103. **Dixon, E. James.** "The Origins of the First Americans." *Archaeology* 38 (January/February 1985): 22–28.

104. **Drennan, Robert D.,** and **Carlos A. Uribe,** eds. *Chiefdoms in the Americas.* Lanham, Md.: University Press of America, 1987. [Both regional and comparative]

105. **Edmunds, R. David.** "Pre-Columbian America Reconsidered." *Halcyon* 12 (1990): 1–18.

106. **Fagan, Brian.** *The Great Journey: The Peopling of Ancient America.* New York: Thames and Hudson, 1987.

107. **Ford, Richard I.,** ed. *Prehistoric Food Production in North America.* University of Michigan Museum of Anthropology, Anthropological Papers, no. 75. Ann Arbor, 1985.

108. **Greenberg, Joseph H., Christy G. Turner II,** and **Stephen L. Zegura.** "The Settlement of the Americas: A Comparison of the Linguistic, Dental, and Genetic Evidence." *Current Anthropology* 27, no. 5 (1986): 477–97.

109. **Grumet, Robert S.** "A New Ethnohistorical Model for North American Indian Demography." *North American Archaeologist* 11 (1990): 29–42.

110. **Hall, Robert L.** "Medicine Wheels, Sun Circles, and the Magic of World Center Shrines." *Plains Anthropologist* 30, no. 109 (1985): 181–95.

111. **Harris, S. L.** "American Indian Legends, I: The Bridge of the Gods." *American West* 22 (July 1985): 14–15.

112. **Kopper, Philip,** et al. *The Smithsonian Book of North American Indians Before the Coming of the Europeans.* Washington, D.C.: Smithsonian Books, 1986.

113. **Larson, Clark S.** *The Antiquity and Origin of Native Americans.* New York: Garland, 1985.

114. **Smith, Bruce D.,** ed. *The Mississippian Emergence.* Washington, D.C.: Smithsonian Institution Press, 1990.

115. **Snow, Dean R.** *Archaeology of North America.* New York: Chelsea House, 1989.

116.   Voigt, Vilmos. "Early Viking Sources About the New World." In *American Anthropological Studies,* vol. 1, ed. L. Boglar and G. K. Nagy, 269–95. Budapest: Eotvos Lorand University, 1985.

2.2   THE EAST

117.   Adovasio, J. M., and Ronald C. Carlisle. "Pennsylvania Pioneers." *Natural History* 95, no. 12 (1986): 20–24. [Meadowcroft Rock Shelter]

118.   Anderson, David, and Glen T. Hanson. "Early Archaic Settlement in the Southeastern United States: A Case Study from the Savannah River Valley." *American Antiquity* 53, no. 2 (1988): 262–86.

119.   "The Archaeology of the St. Lawrence Iroquoians." *Man in the Northeast* (special issue) 40 (fall 1990).

120.   Bartels, Dennis A., and Olaf Uwe Janzen. "Micmac Migration to Western Newfoundland." *Canadian Journal of Native Studies* 10 (1990): 71–94.

121.   Becker, Marshall J. "Lenape Population at the Time of European Contact: Estimating Native Numbers in the Lower Delaware Valley." *Proceedings of the American Philosophical Society* 133 (1989): 112–22.

122.   Blitz, John H. *An Archaeological Study of the Mississippi Choctaw Indians.* Jackson: Mississippi Department of Archives and History, 1985.

123.   Boyd, C. Clifford, and Gerald F. Schroedl. "In Search of Coosa." *American Antiquity* 52 (1987): 840–44.

124.   Bridges, Marilyn. "Above the Mounds: A Photographic Portfolio." *Timeline* 5 (1988): 37–47.

125.   Brose, David S., James A. Brown, and David W. Penny. *Ancient Art of the American Woodland Indians.* New York: Abrams, 1985.

126.   Brown, Ian W. "The Calumet Ceremony in the Southeast and Its Archaeological Manifestations." *American Antiquity* 54 (1989): 311–31.

127.   Byrne, Kevin, and David C. Parris. "Reconstruction of the Diet of the Middle Woodland Amerindian Population at Abbott Farm by Bone-Trace Analysis." *American Journal of Physical Anthropology* 74 (1987): 373–84.

128.   Conner, Michael D., ed. *The Hill Creek Homestead and the Late Mississippian Settlement in the Lower Illinois Valley.* Kampsville, Ill.: Center for American Archaeology, 1985.

129.   Custer, Jay F. "Coastal Adaptations on the Atlantic Coast of North America." *Archaeology of Eastern North America* 16 (1988): 79–186.

130.   ———. *Late Woodland Cultures in the Middle Atlantic Region.* Newark: University of Delaware Press, 1986.

131.   Dickens, Roy S., Jr., and H. Trawick Ward, eds. *Structure and Process in Southeastern Archaeology.* Tuscaloosa: University of Alabama Press, 1985.

132.   Dincauze, Dena F. "A Capsule Prehistory of Southern New England." In *The Pequots in Southern New England: The Fall and Rise of an American Indian Nation,* ed. L. M. Hauptman and J. D. Wherry, 19–32. Norman: University of Oklahoma Press, 1990.

133.   Dye, David H., and Cheryl A. Cox, eds. *Towns and Temples Along the Mississippi.* Tuscaloosa: University of Alabama Press, 1990.

134.   Engelbrecht, William. "Factors Maintaining Low Population Density

Among Prehistoric New York Iroquois."
American Antiquity 52 (1987): 13–27.

135.   Farnsworth, Kenneth B., and **Thomas E. Emerson,** eds. *Early Woodland Archaeology.* Kampsville, Ill.: Center for American Archaeology Press, 1986.

136.   Fiedel, Stuart. "Algonquian Origins: A Problem in Archaeological-Linguistic Correlation." *Archaeology of Eastern North America* 15 (1987): 1–12.

137.   Fowler, Melvin. *The Cahokia Atlas: A Historical Atlas of Cahokia Archaeology.* Studies in Illinois Archaeology, no. 6. Springfield: Illinois Historic Preservation Agency, 1989.

138.   Fritz, Gayle, and **Bruce Smith.** "Old Collections and New Technology: Documenting the Domestication of Chenopodium in Eastern North America." *Mid-continental Journal of Archaeology* 13, no. 1 (1988): 3–27.

139.   Galloway, Patricia, ed. *The Southeastern Ceremonial Complex: Artifacts and Analysis.* Lincoln: University of Nebraska Press, 1989.

140.   Halsey, John R. "Sanilac's Petroglyphs: Ancient Marks, Ancient Rituals." *Michigan History* 74 (July/August 1990): 10.

141.   Hatch, James W. "Mortuary Indicators of Organizational Variability Among the Late Prehistoric Chiefdoms in the Southeastern United States Interior." In *Chiefdoms in the Americas,* ed. R. D. Drennan and C. A. Uribe, 9–20. Lanham, Md.: University Press of America, 1987.

142.   Hudson, Charles M. "The Genesis of Georgia's Indians." *Journal of Southwest Georgia History* 3 (fall 1985): 1–16.

143.   Jamieson, J. B. "Trade and Warfare: The Disappearance of the Saint Lawrence Iroquoians." *Man in the Northeast* 39 (1990): 79–86.

144.   Jefferies, Richard W. *The Archaeology of Carrier Mills: Ten Thousand Years in the Saline Valley of Illinois.* Urbana: University of Illinois Press, 1987.

145.   Jeter, Marvin D., Jerome C. Rose, G. Ishmael Williams, Jr., and **Anna M. Harmon.** *Archeology and Bioarcheology of the Lower Mississippi Valley and Trans-Mississippi South in Arkansas and Louisiana.* Arkansas Archeological Survey Research Series, no. 37. Fayetteville: Arkansas Archeological Survey, 1989.

146.   Kaphches, Mima. "The Spatial Dynamics of Ontario Iroquoian Longhouses." *American Antiquity* 55 (1990): 49–68.

147.   Kerber, Jordan E. "Where Are the Late Woodland Villages?" *Bulletin of the Massachusetts Archaeological Society* 49 (1988): 44–84.

148.   Knight, Vernon, Jr. "Symbolism of Mississippian Mounds." In *Powhatan's Mantle: Indians in the Colonial Southeast,* ed. P. H. Wood, G. A. Waselkov, and M. T. Hatley, 279–91. Lincoln: University of Nebraska Press, 1989.

149.   Leone, Mark P., and **Parker B. Potter, Jr.,** eds. *The Recovery of Meaning: Historical Archaeology in the Eastern United States.* Washington, D.C.: Smithsonian Institution Press, 1988.

150.   Limp, W. Frederick, Ellen Zahn, and **James P. Harcourt.** *The Archeological Literature of the South-Central United States.* Arkansas Archeological Survey Research Series, no. 36. Fayetteville: Arkansas Archeological Survey, 1989.

151.   McGimsey, Charles R., and

Michael D. Conner, eds. *Deer Track: A Late Woodland Village in the Mississippi Valley.* Kampsville, Ill.: Center for American Archaeology, 1985.

152.   Mainfort, Robert C., Jr. "Middle Woodland Ceremonies at Pison Mounds, Tennessee." *American Antiquity* 53 (1988): 158–72.

153.   Nicholas, George P., ed. *Holocene Human Ecology in Northeastern North America.* New York: Plenum Press, 1988.

154.   Niemczycki, Mary Ann Palmer. "The Genesee Connection: The Origins of Iroquois Culture in West-Central New York." *North American Archaeologist* 7 (1986): 15–44.

155.   O'Brien, Patricia J., and William P. McHugh. "Mississippian Solstice Shrines and a Cahokia Calendar: A Hypothesis Based on Ethnohistory and Archaeology." *North American Archaeologist* 8 (1987): 227–47.

156.   Pauketat, Timothy. "A Burned Domestic Building at Cahokia." *Wisconsin Archaeologist* 68, no. 3 (1987): 212–37.

157.   Paul, R. Eli. "Faces of the First Nebraskans." *Nebraska History* 69, no. 2 (1988): 50–59.

158.   Peebles, Christopher S., and Glenn A. Black. "Moundville from 1000 to 1500 A.D. as Seen from 1840 to 1985 A.D." In *Chiefdoms in the Americas,* ed. R. D. Drennan and C. A. Uribe, 21–42. Lanham, Md.: University Press of America, 1987.

159.   Pendergast, James F. "Huron–St. Lawrence Relations in the Terminal Prehistoric Period." *Ontario Archaeology* 44 (1985): 23–39.

160.   Price, T. Douglas. "Late Archaic Subsistence in the Midwestern United States." *Journal of Human Evolution* 14 (1985): 449–59.

161.   Sherrod, P. Clay, and Martha Ann Rolingson. *Surveyors of the Ancient Mississippi Valley.* Arkansas Archeological Survey Research Series, no. 28. Fayetteville: Arkansas Archeological Survey, 1987.

162.   Silverberg, Robert. *The Mound Builders.* Athens: Ohio University Press, 1986.

163.   Skele, Mikels. *The Great Knob: Interpretations of Monks Mound.* Studies in Illinois Archaeology, no. 4. Springfield: Illinois Historic Preservation Agency, 1989.

164.   Smith, Bruce D. "Origins of Agriculture in Eastern North America." *Science* 246 (1989): 1566–71.

165.   Smith, Bruce D., and C. Wesley Cowan. "Domesticated Chenopodium in Prehistoric Eastern North America: New Accelerator Dates from Eastern Kentucky." *American Antiquity* 52 (1987): 355–57. [Date is 3400 B.P.]

166.   Smith, Marion F., Jr., and Scarry, John F. "Apalachee Settlement Distribution: The View from the Florida Master Site File." *Florida Anthropologist* 41 (1988): 351–64.

167.   Story, Dee Ann, Janice A. Guy, Barbara A. Burnett, Martha Doty Freeman, Jerome C. Rose, D. Gentry Steele, Ben W. Olive, and Karl J. Reinhard. *The Archeology and Bioarcheology of the Gulf Coastal Plain.* 2 vols. Arkansas Archeological Survey Research Series, no. 38. Fayetteville: Arkansas Archeological Survey, 1990.

168.   Voss, Jerome, and John Blitz. "Archeological Investigations in the Choctaw Homeland." *American Antiquity* 53, no. 1 (1988): 125–45.

169.   Warrick, Gary. "Estimating Ontario Iroquoian Village Duration." *Man in the Northeast* 36 (1988): 21–60.

170. Williams, Mark, and Gary Shapiro, eds. *Lamar Archaeology: Mississippian Chiefdoms in the Deep South.* Tuscaloosa: University of Alabama Press, 1990. [Late prehistoric and early historic archaeology of the Creeks and neighboring peoples]

171. Yerkes, Richard W. *Prehistoric Life on the Mississippi Flood Plain: Stone Tool Use, Settlement Organization, and Subsistence Practices at the Labras Lake Site, Illinois.* Chicago: University of Chicago Press, 1987.

2.3   THE SOUTHWEST

172. Brock, Sharon L., and Christopher B. Ruff. "Diachronic Patterns of Change in Structural Properties of the Femur in the Prehistoric American Southwest." *American Journal of Physical Anthropology* 75 (1988): 113–27.

173. Brody, J. J. *The Anasazi: Ancient Indian People of the American Southwest.* New York: Rizzoli, 1990.

174. Cole, Sally J. *Legacy on Stone: Rock Art of the Colorado Plateau and Four Corners Region.* Boulder, Colo.: Johnson Books, 1990.

175. Cordell, Linda S., and George J. Gumerman, eds. *Dynamics of Southwestern Prehistory.* Washington, D.C.: Smithsonian Institution Press, 1989.

176. Davis, William, ed. *Anasazi Subsistence and Settlement on White Mesa, San Juan County, Utah.* Lanham, Md.: University of Press of America, 1988.

177. Ferguson, William M., and Arthur H. Rohn. *Anasazi Ruins of the Southwest in Color.* Albuquerque: University of New Mexico Press, 1986.

178. Ford, Richard I., ed. *The Prehistoric American Southwest—A Source Book: History, Chronology, Ecology, and Technology.* New York: Garland, 1987.

179. Haskell, J. Loring. *Southern Athapaskan Migration, A.D. 200–1750.* Tsaile, Ariz.: Navajo Community College Press, 1987.

180. Lekson, Stephen H. "Great House Architecture of Chaco Canyon, New Mexico." *Archaeology* 40 (May/June 1987): 22–29.

181. ———. *Great Pueblo Architecture of Chaco Canyon, New Mexico.* Albuquerque: University of New Mexico Press, 1986.

182. Martin, John F. "The Prehistory and Ethnohistory of Havasupai-Hualapai Relations." *Ethnohistory* 32, no. 2 (1985): 135–53.

183. Matlock, Gary, and Scott Warren. *Enemy Ancestors: The Anasazi World with a Guide to Sites.* Flagstaff, Ariz.: Northland Press, 1988.

184. Merbs, Charles F. "Patterns of Health and Sickness in the Precontact Southwest." In *Columbian Consequences,* vol. 1, *Archaeological and Historical Perspectives on the Spanish Borderlands West,* ed. D. H. Thomas, 41–56. Washington, D.C.: Smithsonian Institution Press, 1989.

185. Patterson-Rudolph, Carol. "Water Jar Boy: A Petroglyph and Story from La Cienaga Pueblo." *American Indian Culture and Research Journal* 14, no. 1 (1990): 1–24.

186. Shafer, Harry. *Ancient Texans: Rock Art and Lifeways Along the Lower Pecos.* San Antonio: Texas Monthly Press for the Wittee Museum, 1986.

187. Smith, Watson. When Is a Kiva? and Other Questions About Southwestern Archaeology. Tucson: University of Arizona Press, 1990.

188. Upham, Steadman, and Lori Stephens Reed. "Regional Systems in

the Central and Northern Southwest: Demography, Economy, and Sociopolitics Preceding Contact." In *Columbian Consequences,* vol. 1, *Archaeological and Historical Perspectives on the Spanish Borderlands West,* ed. D. H. Thomas, 57–76. Washington, D.C.: Smithsonian Institution Press, 1989.

189.   Vivian, R. Gwinn. *The Chacoan Prehistory of the San Juan Basin.* New York: Academic Press, 1990.

2.4   THE PLAINS AND PLATEAU

190.   Baugh, Timothy G. "Culture History and Protohistoric Societies in the Southern Plains." *Plains Anthropologist* 31, no. 114 (1986): 167–87.

191.   ———. "Current Trends in Southern Plains Archaeology." *Plains Anthropologist* 31, no. 114, pt. 2 (1986): 1–187.

192.   Benn, David B. "Hawks, Serpents, and Bird-Men: Emergence of the Oneonta Mode of Production." *Plains Anthropologist* 34, no. 125 (1989): 233–60.

193.   Bryan, Liz. *Buffalo People: Archaeology on the Canadian Plains.* Edmonton: University of Alberta Press, 1990.

194.   Burley, David V., ed. *Contribution to Plains Prehistory: The 1984 Victoria Symposium.* Edmonton: Alberta Culture Historical Resources Division, 1985.

195.   Cassells, E. Steve. *Prehistoric Hunters of the Black Hills.* Boulder, Colo.: Johnson Books, 1986.

196.   Drass, Richard R. "Plains Village Settlements in Central Oklahoma: A Survey Along the Middle Course of the Washita River." *Plains Anthropologist* 31, no. 114, pt. 2 (1986): 155–66. [Intensive use A.D. 1000–1600]

197.   Gallagher, James P., and **Robert Sasso.** "Investigations into Oneonta Ridged Field Agriculture on the North-ern Margins of the Prairie Peninsula." *Plains Anthropologist* 32, no. 116 (1987): 141–51.

198.   Greiser, Sally Thompson. "Predictive Models of Hunter-Gatherer Subsistence Strategies on the Central High Plains." *Plains Anthropologist* 30, no. 110, pt. 2 (1985): 1–134.

199.   Haack, Steven C. "A Critical Evaluation of Medicine Wheel Astronomy." *Plains Anthropologist* 32, no. 115 (1987): 77–82.

200.   Habicht-Mauche, Judith A. "Southwestern Style Culinary Ceramics on the Southern Plains: A Case Study of Technological Innovation and Cross-Cultural Interaction" *Plains Anthropologist* 32, no. 116 (1987): 175–89.

201.   Hofman, Jack L., Robert L. Brooks, Joe S. Hays, Douglas W. Owsley, Richard L. Jantz, Murray K. Marks, and **Mary H. Manhein.** *From Clovis to Comanchero: Archeological Overview of the Southern Great Plains.* Arkansas Archeological Survey Research Series, no. 35. Fayetteville: Arkansas Archeological Survey, 1989.

202.   Keyser, James D. "A Lexicon for Historic Plains Indian Rock Art: Increasing Interpretive Potential." *Plains Anthropologist* 32, no. 115 (1987): 43–71.

203.   Krause, Richard. "Toward a History of Great Plains Systematics." *Plains Anthropologist* 34, no. 126 (1989): 281–92.

204.   McLaird, James D. "The Welsh, the Vikings, and the Lost Tribes of Israel on the Northern Plains: The Legend of the White Mandan." *South Dakota History* 18 (1988): 245–73.

205.   Michlovic, Michael G. "Cultural Evolutionism and Plains Archaeology." *Plains Anthropologist* 31, no. 113 (1986): 219–24.

206.   Vicker, J. Roderick. *Alberta Plains Prehistory: A Review.* Archaeological Survey of Alberta, Occasional Paper no. 27. Edmonton: Alberta Culture Historical Resources Division, 1986.

207.   Wedel, Waldo R. *Central Plains Prehistory: Holocene Environments and Culture Change in the Republican River Basin.* Lincoln: University of Nebraska Press, 1986.

208.   ———. *A Plains Archaeology Sourcebook: Selected Papers of the Nebraska State Historical Society.* New York: Garland, 1985.

209.   Wiley, Patrick S. *Prehistoric Warfare on the Great Plains: Skeletal Analysis of the Crow Creek Massacre Victims.* New York: Garland, 1990.

210.   Zimmerman, Larry J. *People of Prehistoric South Dakota.* Lincoln: University of Nebraska Press, 1985.

2.5   CALIFORNIA, THE GREAT BASIN, AND THE NORTHWEST COAST

211.   Condie, Carol J., and Don Fowler, eds. *Anthropology in the Desert West: Essays in Honor of Jesse D. Jennings.* Salt Lake City: University of Utah Press, 1986.

212.   Hattori, Eugene M. "The First Nevadans: Historical Themes of the Pleistocene Human Occupation in Nevada." *Halcyon* 7 (1985): 105–17.

213.   Jackson, Thomas L. "Reconstructing Migration in California Prehistory." *American Indian Quarterly* 13 (1989): 359–68.

214.   Mehringer, Peter J., Jr. "Prehistoric Environments." In *Great Basin,* ed. W. L. d'Azevedo, 31–50. Vol. 11 of *Handbook of North American Indians,* ed. W. Sturtevant. Washington, D.C.: Smithsonian Institution, 1986.

2.6   THE ARCTIC AND SUBARCTIC

215.   Aigner, Jean S. "Early Arctic Settlement in North America." *Scientific American* 253, no. 5 (1985): 160–69.

216.   Dumond, Don E. "A Reexamination of Eskimo-Aleut Prehistory." *American Anthropologist* 89 (1987): 32–56.

217.   Ives, John W. *A Theory of Northern Athapaskan Prehistory.* Calgary: University of Calgary Press, 1990.

218.   Murdoch, John. *Ethnological Results of the Point Barrow Expedition.* 1887–88. Reprint, Washington, D.C.: Smithsonian Institution Press, 1988.

III

Indian-White Relations: Governmental Affairs, Military Relations, and the Interaction of Native and European Communities

3.1   GENERAL STUDIES

219.   Axtell, James. *The Invasion Within: The Contest of Cultures in Colonial North America.* New York: Oxford University Press, 1985.

220.   Brandon, William. *New Worlds for Old: Reports from the New World and Their Effect on the Development of Social Thought in Europe, 1500–1800.* Athens: Ohio University Press, 1986.

221.   Burton, Bruce. "Literature, Paradigm, and Plunder in the New World, 1492–1610: Vespucci, Columbus, Sir Thomas More, Montaigne, and Shakespeare." *Northeast Indian Quarterly* 7 (1990): 56–65.

222.   Fagan, Brian. *Clash of Cultures.* New York: W. H. Freeman, 1985.

223.   Fitzhugh, William W., ed. and commentator. *Cultures in Contact: The Impact of European Contacts on Native American Cultural Institutions, A.D. 1000–1800.* Washington, D.C.: Smithsonian Institution Press, 1985.

224.   Gad, Finn. "Danish Greenland Policies." In *History of Indian-White Relations,* ed. W. Washburn, 110–18. Vol. 4 of *Handbook of North American Indians,* ed. W. Sturtevant. Washington, D.C.: Smithsonian Institution Press, 1988.

225.   Hall, Thomas D. "Native Americans and Incorporation: Patterns and Problems." *American Indian Culture and Research Journal* 11, no. 2 (1987): 1–30.

226.   Hoffer, Peter Charles, ed. *Indians and Europeans: Selected Articles on Indian-White Relations in Colonial North America.* New York: Garland, 1988.

227.   Kawashima, Yasuhide. "Forest Diplomats: The Role of Interpreters in Indian-White Relations on the Early American Frontiers." *American Indian Quarterly* 13 (1989): 1–14.

228.   Kelly, Lawrence C. *Federal Indian Policy.* New York: Chelsea House, 1990.

229.   Kvasnicka, Robert. "United States Indian Treaties and Agreements." In *History of Indian-White Relations,* ed. W. Washburn, 195–201. Vol. 4 of *Handbook of North American Indians,* ed. W. Sturtevant. Washington, D.C.: Smithsonian Institution Press, 1988.

230.   Lider, Gerald. "When Parrots Learn to Talk, and Why They Can't: Domination, Deception, and Self-Deception in Indian-White Relations." *Comparative Studies in Society and History* 29 (1987): 3–23.

231.   Limerick, Patricia Nelson. "Here to Stay." *Wilson Quarterly* 10, no. 1 (1986): 99–112.

232. McCord, David, and William Cleveland. *Black and Red: The Historical Meeting of Africans and Native Americans.* Atlanta: Dreamkeeper Press, 1990.

233. "Mormons and Native Americans." *Dialogue* (special edition) 18 (1985).

234. Muga, David A. "Native Americans and the Nationalities Question: Premises for a Marxist Approach to Ethnicity and Self-Determination." *Nature, Society, and Thought* 1 (1987): 7–26.

235. Nichols, Roger L., ed. *The American Indian: Past and Present.* Rev. ed. New York: Wiley, 1986.

236. O'Brien, Sharon. "The Government–Government and Trust Relationships: Conflicts and Inconsistencies." *American Indian Culture and Research Journal* 10, no. 4 (1986): 57–80.

237. Ortiz, Alfonso. "Indian/White Relations: A View from the Other Side of the 'Frontier.'" In *Indians in American History: An Introduction,* ed. F. E. Hoxie, 1–16. Arlington Heights, Ill.: Harlan Davidson, 1988.

238. Parry, Lindsay J. "Aborigines and Europeans." *Social Studies* 81 (May/June 1990): 106–12.

239. Pierce, Richard. "Russian and Soviet Eskimo Indian Policies." In *History of Indian-White Relations,* ed. W. Washburn, 119–27. Vol. 4 of *Handbook of North American Indians,* ed. W. Sturtevant. Washington, D.C.: Smithsonian Institution Press, 1988.

240. Prucha, Francis Paul. *The Great Father: The United States Government and the American Indians.* Abr. ed. Lincoln: University of Nebraska Press, 1986.

241. ———. *The Indians in American Society: From the Revolutionary War to the Present.* Berkeley: University of California Press, 1985.

242. ———. "Presents and Delegations." In *History of Indian-White Relations,* ed. W. Washburn, 238–44. Vol. 4 of *Handbook of North American Indians,* ed. W. Sturtevant. Washington, D.C.: Smithsonian Institution Press, 1988.

243. ———. "United States Indian Policies." In *History of Indian-White Relations,* ed. W. Washburn, 40–50. Vol. 4 of *Handbook of North American Indians,* ed. W. Sturtevant. Washington, D.C.: Smithsonian Institution Press, 1988.

244. Purdy, Barbara A. "American Indians After A.D. 1492: A Case Study of Forced Culture Change." *American Anthropologist* 90 (1988): 640–55.

245. Roberts, Charles E. "Choctaw Generations: From Removal in Mississippi to Relocation in California." In *Native Views of Indian-White Historical Relations,* ed. D. L. Fixico, 80–91. D'Arcy McNickle Center for the History of the American Indian, Occasional Papers in Curriculum, no. 7. Chicago: Newberry Library, 1989.

246. Rubertone, Patricia E. "Archaeology, Colonialism, and Seventeenth Century Native America: Towards an Alternative Interpretation." In *Conflict in the Archaeology of Living Traditions,* ed. R. Layton, 32–45. London: Unwin Hyman, 1989.

247. *The Struggle for Political Autonomy: Papers and Comments from the Second Newberry Conference on Themes in American Indian History.* D'Arcy McNickle Center for the History of the American Indian, Occasional Papers in Curriculum, no. 11. Chicago: Newberry Library, 1989.

248. Williams, Walter L. "American Imperialism and the Indians." Comments by Gary Nash. In *The Impact of*

Indian History on the Teaching of United States History: Papers and Commentary from the 1986 Conference at Los Angeles, 37–70. D'Arcy McNickle Center for the History of the American Indian, Occasional Papers in Curriculum, no. 5. Chicago: Newberry Library, 1987.

3.2   FRENCH COLONIAL RELATIONS

249.   **Allain, Mathe.** *Not Worth a Straw: French Colonial Policy and the Early Years of Louisiana.* Lafayette: University of Southwestern Louisiana, 1988.

250.   **Anderson, Karen.** *Chain Her by One Foot: The Subjugation of Women in Seventeenth-Century France.* London: Routledge, 1990.

251.   **Chasse, Paul.** "The D'Abbadie de Saint Castins and the Abenakis of Maine in the Seventeenth Century." In *Proceedings of the Tenth Meeting of the French Colonial Historical Society,* ed. P. P. Boucher, 59–74. Lanham, Md.: University Press of America, 1985.

252.   **Devens, Carol.** "Separate Confrontations: Gender as a Factor in Indian Adaptation to European Colonization in New France." *American Quarterly* 38 (1986): 461–80.

253.   **Dickason, Olive P.** "The French and the Abenaki: A Study in Frontier Politics." *Vermont History* 58 (1990): 82–98.

254.   **Dickerson, John A.** "French and British Attitudes to Native People in Colonial North America." *Storia Nordamericana* 4, no. 1/2 (1987): 41–56.

255.   **Faulkner, Alaric,** and **Gretchen Faulkner.** *The French at Pentagoet, 1635–1674: An Archaeological Portrait of the Acadian Frontier.* Augusta, Maine, and St. John, N.B.: The Maine Historic Preservation Commission and the New Brunswick Museum, 1987.

256.   **Foret, Michael J.** "War or Peace? Louisiana, the Choctaws and Chickasaws, 1733–1735." *Louisiana History* 31 (1990): 273–92.

257.   **Galloway, Patricia K.** "The Chief Who Is Your Father: Choctaw and French Views of the Diplomatic Relation." In *Powhatan's Mantle: Indians in the Colonial Southeast,* ed. P. H. Wood, G. A. Waselkov, and M. T. Hatley, 254–78. Lincoln: University of Nebraska Press, 1989.

258.   ———. "Talking with Indians: Interpreters and Diplomacy in French Louisiana." In *Race and Family in the Colonial South,* ed. W. D. Jordan and S. L. Skemp, 109–29. Jackson: University Press of Mississippi, 1987.

259.   **Jaenen, Cornelius J.** "Characteristics of French-Amerindian Contact in New France." *Essays on the History of North American Discovery and Exploration,* ed. S. H. Palmer and D. Reinhartz, 79–101. College Station: Texas A & M Press, 1989.

260.   ———. "French Sovereignty and Native Nationhood During the French Regime." *Native Studies Review* 2, no. 1 (1986): 83–113.

261.   ———. "The Role of Presents in French Amerindian Trade." In *Explorations in Canadian Economic History: Essays in Honor of Irene M. Spy,* ed. D. Cameron, 231–50. Ottawa: University of Ottawa Press, 1985.

262.   **Jones, Elizabeth.** *Gentlemen and Jesuits: Quests for Glory and Adventure in the Early Days of New France.* Toronto: University of Toronto Press, 1986.

263.   **Mohawk, John.** "And They Cut the Corn: Recounting the Attack of Marquis de Denonville." *Turtle Quarterly* 1, no. 1 (1986): 8–11.

264.   **Pendergast, James F.** "Native

Encounters with Europeans in the Sixteenth Century in the Region Now Known as Vermont." *Vermont History* 58 (1990): 99–124.

265. **Peyser, Joseph L.** "The Fate of the Fox Survivors: A Dark Chapter in the History of the French in the Upper Country, 1726–1737." *Wisconsin Magazine of History* 73 (winter 1989): 83–110.

266. ———. "The 1730 Siege of the Foxes: Two Maps by Canadian Participants Provide Additional Information on the Fort and Its Location." *Illinois Historical Journal* 80, no. 3 (1987): 147–54.

267. **Schlesinger, Roger.** "Andre Thevet on the Amerindians of New France." In *Proceedings of the Tenth Meeting of the French Colonial Historical Society,* ed. P. P. Boucher, 129–38. Lanham, Md.: University Press of America, 1985.

268. **Trigger, Bruce G.** *Natives and Newcomers: Canada's "Heroic Age" Reconsidered.* Montreal: McGill-Queen's University Press, 1985.

269. **Usner, Daniel H., Jr.** "The Deerskin Trade in French Louisiana." In *Proceedings of the Tenth Meeting of the French Colonial Historical Society,* ed. P. P. Boucher, 75–93. Lanham, Md.: University Press of America, 1985.

270. **Wade, Mason.** "French Indian Policies." In *History of Indian-White Relations,* ed. W. Washburn, 20–28. Vol. 4 of *Handbook of North American Indians,* ed. W. Sturtevant. Washington, D.C.: Smithsonian Institution Press, 1988.

271. **Waselkov, Gregory, and John Colltier.** "European Perceptions of Eastern Muskogean Ethnicity." In *Proceedings of the Tenth Meeting of the French Colonial Historical Society,* ed. P. P. Boucher, 23–46. Lanham, Md.: University Press of America, 1985.

272. **Wyezynski, Michel.** "The French-Iroquois Treaty of 1684." *Archivist* 16 (November/December 1989): 6–9.

3.3 SPANISH COLONIAL RELATIONS

273. **Adams, E. Charles.** "Passive Resistance: Hopi Responses to Spanish Contact and Conquest." In *Columbian Consequences,* vol. 1, *Archaeological and Historical Perspectives on the Spanish Borderlands West,* ed. D. H. Thomas, 77–92. Washington, D.C.: Smithsonian Institution Press, 1989.

274. **Anderson, H. Allen.** "The Encomienda in New Mexico, 1598–1680." *New Mexico Historical Review* 60 (1985): 353–77.

275. **Bushnell, Amy Turner.** "Ruling the Republic of Indians in Seventeenth-Century Florida." In *Powhatan's Mantle: Indians in the Colonial Southeast,* ed. P. H. Wood, G. A. Waselkov, and M. T. Hatley, 134–50. Lincoln: University of Nebraska Press, 1989.

276. **Carrico, Richard L.** "Spanish Crime and Punishment: The Native American Experience in Colonial San Diego, 1769–1830." *Western Legal History* 3 (1990): 21–33.

277. **Castillo, Edward D.** "The Native Response to the Colonization of Alta California." In *Columbian Consequences,* vol. 1, *Archaeological and Historical Perspectives on the Spanish Borderlands West,* ed. D. H. Thomas, 377–94. Washington, D.C.: Smithsonian Institution Press, 1989.

278. ———, trans. and ed. "The Assassination of Padre Andre's Quintana by the Indian of Mission Santa Cruz in 1812: The Narrative of Lorenzo Asisara." *California History* 68 (fall 1989): 117–25.

279. **Corbin, James E.** "Spanish-
Indian Interactions on the Eastern Frontier of Texas." In *Columbian Consequences,*
vol. 1, *Archaeological and Historical Perspectives on the Spanish Borderlands West,*
ed. D. H. Thomas, 269–76. Washington, D.C.: Smithsonian Institution
Press, 1989.

280. **Cordell, Linda S.** "Durango to
Durango: An Overview of the Southwest Heartland." In *Columbian Consequences,* vol. 1, *Archaeological and
Historical Perspectives on the Spanish Borderlands West,* ed. D. H. Thomas, 17–
40. Washington, D.C.: Smithsonian Institution Press, 1989.

281. **Costello, Julia G.** "Variability
Among the Alta California Missions:
The Economics of Agricultural Produc-
tion." In *Columbian Consequences,* vol. 1,
*Archaeological and Historical Perspectives on
the Spanish Borderlands West,* ed. D. H.
Thomas, 435–50. Washington, D.C.:
Smithsonian Institution Press, 1989.

282. **Costello, Julia G.,** and **David
Hornbeck.** "Alta California: An Over-
view." In *Columbian Consequences,* vol. 1,
*Archaeological and Historical Perspectives on
the Spanish Borderlands West,* ed. D. H.
Thomas, 303–32. Washington, D.C.:
Smithsonian Institution Press, 1989.

283. **Cuello, José.** "The Persistence
of Indian Slavery and Encomienda in the
Northeast of Colonial Mexico, 1577–
1723." *Journal of Social History* 21 (summer 1988): 683–706.

284. **Cutter, Charles R.** *The Protector
de Indios in Colonial New Mexico, 1659–
1821.* Albuquerque: University of New
Mexico Press, 1986.

285. **Deagan, Kathleen A.** "Accommodation and Resistance: The Process
and Impact of Spanish Colonization in
the Southeast." In *Columbian Conse-*

quences, vol. 2, *Archaeological and Historical Perspectives on the Spanish Borderlands
East,* ed. D. H. Thomas, 297–314.
Washington, D.C.: Smithsonian Institution Press, 1990.

286. ———. "Sixteenth-Century
Spanish-American Colonization in the
Southeastern United States and the Caribbean." In *Columbian Consequences,* vol.
2, *Archaeological and Historical Perspectives on the Spanish Borderlands East,* ed.
D. H. Thomas, 225–50.

287. ———. "Spanish-Indian Inter-
action in Sixteenth Century Florida and
Hispaniola." In *Cultures in Contact: The
Impact of European Contacts on Native
American Cultural Institutions, A.D.
1000–1800,* ed. W. W. Fitzhugh, 281–
318. Washington, D.C.: Smithsonian
Institution Press, 1985.

288. **de la Teja, Jesús F.** "Indians,
Soldiers, and Canary Islanders: The
Making of a Texas Frontier Commu-
nity." *Locus* 3 (fall 1990): 81–96.

289. **Dickinson, Sam.** "Arkansas's
Spanish Halberds." *Arkansas Archeologist*
25–26 (1987): 53–61. [Possible de Soto
link]

290. **Dobyns, Henry.** "Indians in the
Colonial Spanish Borderlands." In *Indians in American History: An Introduction,*
ed. F. E. Hoxie, 67–93. Arlington
Heights, Ill.: Harlan Davidson, 1988.

291. **Doyel, David E.** "The Transi-
tion to History in Northern Pimeria
Alta." In *Columbian Consequences,* vol. 1,
*Archaeological and Historical Perspectives on
the Spanish Borderlands West,* ed. D. H.
Thomas, 139–58. Washington, D.C.:
Smithsonian Institution Press, 1989.

292. **Dye, David H.** "Warfare in the
Sixteenth-Century Southeast: The de
Soto Expedition in the Interior." In *Co-
lumbian Consequences,* vol. 2, *Archaeologi-*

cal and Historical Perspectives on the Spanish Borderlands East, ed. D. H. Thomas, 211–22. Washington D.C.: Smithsonian Institution Press, 1990.

293. **Espinosa, J. Manuel.** *The Pueblo Indian Revolt of 1696 and the Franciscan Missions in New Mexico: Letters of the Missionaries and Related Documents.* Norman: University of Oklahoma Press, 1988.

294. **Ewen, Charles R.** "Soldier of Fortune: Hernando de Soto in the Territory of the Apalachee, 1539–1540." In *Columbian Consequences,* vol. 2, *Archaeological and Historical Perspectives on the Spanish Borderlands East,* ed. D. H. Thomas, 83–92. Washington, D.C.: Smithsonian Institution Press, 1990.

295. **Farris, Glenn J.** "The Russian Imprint on the Colonization of California." In *Columbian Consequences,* vol. 1, *Archaeological and Historical Perspectives on the Spanish Borderlands West,* ed. D. H. Thomas, 481–98. Washington, D.C.: Smithsonian Institution Press, 1989.

296. **Fox, Anne A.** "The Indians at Rancho de las Cabras." In *Columbian Consequences,* vol. 1, *Archaeological and Historical Perspectives on the Spanish Borderlands West,* ed. D. H. Thomas, 259–68. Washington, D.C.: Smithsonian Institution Press, 1989.

297. **Garner, Richard L.** "Long-Term Silver Mining Trends in Spanish America: A Comparative Analysis of Peru and Mexico." *American Historical Review* 93 (1988): 888–935.

298. **Gibson, Charles.** "Spanish Indian Policies." In *History of Indian-White Relations,* ed. W. Washburn, 96–102. Vol. 4 of *Handbook of North American Indians,* ed. W. Sturtevant. Washington, D.C.: Smithsonian Institution Press, 1988.

299. **Gilmore, Kathleen.** "The Indians of Mission Rosario: From the Books and from the Ground." In *Columbian Consequences,* vol. 1, *Archaeological and Historical Perspectives on the Spanish Borderlands West,* ed. D. H. Thomas, 231–44. Washington, D.C.: Smithsonian Institution Press, 1989.

300. **Greenwood, Roberta S.** "The California Ranchero: Fact and Fancy." In *Columbian Consequences,* vol. 1, *Archaeological and Historical Perspectives on the Spanish Borderlands West,* ed. D. H. Thomas, 451–66. Washington, D.C.: Smithsonian Institution Press, 1989.

301. **Guest, Francis F.** "Junípero Serra and His Approach to the Indians." *Southern California Quarterly* 67 (1985): 223–61.

302. **Hally, David J., Marvin T. Smith,** and **James B. Langford, Jr.** "The Archaeological Reality of de Soto's Coosa." In *Columbian Consequences,* vol. 2, *Archaeological and Historical Perspectives on the Spanish Borderlands East,* ed. D. H. Thomas, 121–38. Washington, D.C.: Smithsonian Institution Press, 1990.

303. **Hann, John H.** "Apalachee Counterfeiters in St. Augustine." *Florida Historical Quarterly* 67 (1988): 52–68.

304. ———. "St. Augustine's Fallout from the Yamasee War." *Florida Historical Quarterly* 68 (1989): 180–200.

305. ———. "Twilight of the Mocamo and Guale Aborigines as Portrayed in the 1695 Spanish Visitation." *Florida Historical Quarterly* 66 (1987): 1–24.

306. ———, ed. and trans. "Translation of Alonso de Leturiondo's Memorial to the King of Spain." *Florida Archaeology* 2 (1986): 165–225.

307. ———, ed. and trans. "Translation of Governor Rebolledo's 1657 Visi-

tation of Three Florida Provinces and Related Documents." *Florida Archaeology* 2 (1986): 81–145.

308. **Henige, David.** "The Context, Content, and Credibility of La Florida del Inca." *Americas* 43 (1986): 1–23.

309. **Hester, Thomas R.** "Perspectives on the Material Culture of the Indians of the Texas–Northeastern Mexico Borderlands." In *Columbian Consequences,* vol. 1, *Archaeological and Historical Perspectives on the Spanish Borderlands West,* ed. D. H. Thomas, 213–30. Washington, D.C.: Smithsonian Institution Press, 1989.

310. ———. "Texas and Northeastern Mexico: An Overview." In *Columbian Consequences,* vol. 1, *Archaeological and Historical Perspectives on the Spanish Borderlands West,* ed. D. H. Thomas, 191–212. Washington, D.C.: Smithsonian Institution Press, 1989.

311. **Hoffman, Paul E.** *A New Andalusia and a Way to the Orient: A History of the American Southeast During the Sixteenth Century.* Baton Rouge: Louisiana State University Press, 1990.

312. **Hoover, Robert L.** "Spanish-Native Interaction and Acculturation in the Alta California Missions." In *Columbian Consequences,* vol. 1, *Archaeological and Historical Perspectives on the Spanish Borderlands West,* ed. D. H. Thomas, 395–406. Washington, D.C.: Smithsonian Institution Press, 1989.

313. **Hornbeck, David.** "Economic Growth and Change at the Missions of Alta California, 1769–1846." In *Columbian Consequences,* vol. 1, *Archaeological and Historical Perspectives on the Spanish Borderlands West,* ed. D. H. Thomas, 423–34. Washington, D.C.: Smithsonian Institution Press, 1989.

314. **Hudson, Charles M.** *The Juan Pardo Expeditions: Explorations of the Carolinas and Tennessee, 1566–1568.* Washington, D.C.: Smithsonian Institution Press, 1990.

315. ———. "Juan Pardo's Excursion Beyond Chiaha." *Tennessee Anthropologist* 12 (1987): 74–87.

316. ———. "An Unknown South: Spanish Explorers and Southeastern Chiefdoms." In *Visions and Revisions: Ethnohistoric Perspectives on Southern Cultures,* ed. G. Sabo III and W. Schneider, 6–24. Proceedings of the Southern Anthropological Society, no. 20. Athens: University of Georgia Press, 1987.

317. **Hudson, Charles M., Marvin T. Smith, Chester DePratter, and Emilia Kelly.** "The Tristan de Luna Expedition, 1559–1561." *Southeastern Archaeology* 8 (1989): 31–45.

318. **Hudson, Charles M., John E. Worth, and Chester DePratter.** "Refinements in Hernando de Soto's Route Through Georgia and South Carolina." In *Columbian Consequences,* vol. 2, *Archaeological and Historical Perspectives on the Spanish Borderlands East,* ed. D. H. Thomas, 107–19. Washington, D.C.: Smithsonian Institution Press, 1990.

319. **Hutchinson, Dale L.** "Postcontact Biocultural Change: Mortuary Site Evidence." In *Columbian Consequences,* vol. 2, *Archaeological and Historical Perspectives on the Spanish Borderlands East,* ed. D. H. Thomas, 61–70. Washington, D.C.: Smithsonian Institution Press, 1990. [Southeast]

320. **John, Elizabeth A. H.** "Crusading in the Hispanic Borderlands." *Journal of the Southwest* 30 (1988): 190–99.

321. ———, ed. *Views from the Apache Frontier: Report on the Northern Provinces of New Spain, 1799, by José*

Cortés. Albuquerque: University of New Mexico Press, 1989.

322. **Kelsey, Harry.** "European Impact on the California Indians, 1530–1830." *Americas* 41 (1985): 494–511.

323. **Kessell, John L.** "Spaniards and Pueblos: From Crusading Intolerance to Pragmatic Accommodation." In *Columbian Consequences,* vol. 1, *Archaeological and Historical Perspectives on the Spanish Borderlands West,* ed. D. H. Thomas, 127–38. Washington, D.C.: Smithsonian Institution Press, 1989.

324. **Kessell, John L.,** et al., eds. *Remote Beyond Compare: Letters of Don Diego de Vargas to His Family from New Spain and New Mexico, 1675–1706.* Albuquerque: University of New Mexico Press, 1989.

325. **Landers, Jane.** "African Presence in Early Spanish Colonization of the Caribbean and the Southeastern Borderlands." In *Columbian Consequences,* vol. 2, *Archaeological and Historical Perspectives on the Spanish Borderlands East,* ed. D. H. Thomas, 315–28. Washington, D.C.: Smithsonian Institution Press, 1990.

326. **Langford, James B., Jr.** "The Coosawattee Plate: A Sixteenth-Century Catholic/Aztec Artifact from Northwest Georgia." In *Columbian Consequences,* vol. 2, *Archaeological and Historical Perspectives on the Spanish Borderlands East,* ed. D. H. Thomas, 139–52. Washington, D.C.: Smithsonian Institution Press, 1990.

327. **Levy, Janet E., J. Alan May,** and **David G. Moore.** "From Ysa to Joara: Cultural Diversity in the Catawba Valley from the Fourteenth to the Sixteenth Century." In *Columbian Consequences,* vol. 2, *Archaeological and Historical Perspectives on the Spanish Bor-*derlands East, ed. D. H. Thomas, 153–68. Washington, D.C.: Smithsonian Institution Press, 1990.

328. **Little, Keith,** and **Caleb Curren.** "Conquest Archaeology of Alabama." In *Columbian Consequences,* vol. 2, *Archaeological and Historical Perspectives on the Spanish Borderlands East,* ed. D. H. Thomas, 169–95. Washington, D.C.: Smithsonian Institution Press, 1990.

329. **Lomawaima, Hartman H.** "Hopification: A Strategy for Cultural Preservation." In *Columbian Consequences,* vol. 1, *Archaeological and Historical Perspectives on the Spanish Borderlands West,* ed. D. H. Thomas, 93–100. Washington, D.C.: Smithsonian Institution Press, 1989.

330. **Lycett, Mark T.** "Spanish Contact and Pueblo Organization: Long-Term Implications of European Colonial Expansion in the Rio Grande Valley, New Mexico." In *Columbian Consequences,* vol. 1, *Archaeological and Historical Perspectives on the Spanish Borderlands West,* ed. D. H. Thomas, 115–26. Washington, D.C.: Smithsonian Institution Press, 1989.

331. **Lyon, Eugene.** "The Enterprise of Florida." In *Columbian Consequences,* vol. 2, *Archaeological and Historical Perspectives on the Spanish Borderlands East,* ed. D. H. Thomas, 281–96. Washington, D.C.: Smithsonian Institution Press, 1990.

332. **McGuire, Randall H.,** and **Maria Elisa Villalpando.** "Prehistory and the Making of History in Sonora." In *Columbian Consequences,* vol. 1, *Archaeological and Historical Perspectives on the Spanish Borderlands West,* ed. D. H. Thomas, 159–78. Washington, D.C.: Smithsonian Institution Press, 1989.

333. **Marrinan, Rochelle A., John F. Scarry,** and **Rhonda L. Majors.**

"Prelude to de Soto: The Expedition of Pánfilo de Narváez." In *Columbian Consequences,* vol. 2, *Archaeological and Historical Perspectives on the Spanish Borderlands East,* ed. D. H. Thomas, 71–82. Washington, D.C.: Smithsonian Institution Press, 1990.

334. Mathes, W. Michael. "Baja California: A Special Area of Contact and Colonization, 1535–1697." In *Columbian Consequences,* vol. 1, *Archaeological and Historical Perspectives on the Spanish Borderlands West,* ed. D. H. Thomas, 407–22. Washington, D.C.: Smithsonian Institution Press, 1989.

335. Milanich, Jerald T. "The European Entrada into La Florida: An Overview." In *Columbian Consequences,* vol. 2, *Archaeological and Historical Perspectives on the Spanish Borderlands East,* ed. D. H. Thomas, 3–29. Washington, D.C.: Smithsonian Institution Press, 1990.

336. Milanich, Jerald T., and Susan Milbrath, eds. *First Encounters: Spanish Explorations in the Caribbean and the United States, 1492–1570.* Gainesville: University of Florida Press, 1989.

337. Mitchem, Jeffrey M. "Initial Spanish-Indian Contact in West Peninsular Florida: The Archaeological Evidence." In *Columbian Consequences,* vol. 2, *Archaeological and Historical Perspectives on the Spanish Borderlands East,* ed. D. H. Thomas, 49–59. Washington, D.C.: Smithsonian Institution Press, 1990.

338. Monroy, Douglas, ed. *Thrown Among Strangers: The Making of Mexican Culture in Frontier California.* Berkeley: University of California Press, 1990.

339. Morse, Dan F., and Phyllis A. Morse. "The Spanish Exploration of Arkansas." In *Columbian Consequences,* vol. 2, *Archaeological and Historical Perspectives on the Spanish Borderlands East,* ed.

D. H. Thomas, 197–211. Washington, D.C.: Smithsonian Institution Press, 1990.

340. Naylor, Thomas H., and Charles W. Polzer, eds. *The Presidio and Militia on the Northern Frontier of New Spain,* vol. 1, *1570–1700.* Tucson: University of Arizona Press, 1986.

341. Polzer, Charles W. "The Spanish Colonial Southwest: New Technologies for Old Documents." In *Columbian Consequences,* vol. 1, *Archaeological and Historical Perspectives on the Spanish Borderlands West,* ed. D. H. Thomas, 179–90. Washington, D.C.: Smithsonian Institution Press, 1989.

342. Poyo, Gerald E., and Gilberto Hinojosa. "Spanish Texas and Borderlands Historiography in Transition: Implications for United States History." *Journal of American History* 75 (1988): 393–416.

343. Price, Catherine. "The Comanche Threat to Texas and New Mexico in the Eighteenth Century and the Development of Spanish Indian Policy." *Journal of the West* 24 (April 1985): 34–45.

344. Ramenofsky, Ann F. "Loss of Innocence: Explanations of Differential Persistence in the Sixteenth-Century Southeast." In *Columbian Consequences,* vol. 2, *Archaeological and Historical Perspectives on the Spanish Borderlands East,* ed. D. H. Thomas, 31–48. Washington, D.C.: Smithsonian Institution Press, 1990.

345. Ramirez, Susan, ed. *Indian-Religious Relations in Colonial Spanish America.* Maxwell School of Citizenship and Public Affairs, Foreign and Comparative Studies, Latin American Series, no. 9. Syracuse, N.Y.: Syracuse University, 1989.

346.   Scarry, C. Margaret, and Elizabeth J. Reitz. "Herbs, Fish, Scum, and Vermin: Subsistence Strategies in Sixteenth-Century Spanish Florida." In *Columbian Consequences*, vol. 2, *Archaeological and Historical Perspectives on the Spanish Borderlands East,* ed. D. H. Thomas, 343–56. Washington, D.C.: Smithsonian Institution Press, 1990.

347.   Scarry, John F. "Beyond Apalachee Province: Assessing the Evidence for Early European-Indian Contact in Northwest Florida." In *Columbian Consequences*, vol. 2, *Archaeological and Historical Perspectives on the Spanish Borderlands East,* ed. D. H. Thomas, 93–106. Washington, D.C.: Smithsonian Institution Press, 1990.

348.   Shilz, Thomas E., and Donald E. Worcester. "The Spread of Firearms Among the Indian Tribes on the Northern Frontier of New Spain." *American Indian Quarterly* 11 (1987): 1–10.

349.   South, Stanley. "From Thermodynamics to a Status Artifact Model: Spanish Santa Elena." In *Columbian Consequences*, vol. 2, *Archaeological and Historical Perspectives on the Spanish Borderlands East,* ed. D. H. Thomas, 329–42. Washington, D.C.: Smithsonian Institution Press, 1990.

350.   Spicer, Edward. "Mexican Indian Policies." In *History of Indian-White Relations,* ed. W. Washburn, 103–9. Vol. 4 of *Handbook of North American Indians,* ed. W. Sturtevant. Washington, D.C.: Smithsonian Institution Press, 1988.

351.   Thomas, David Hurst, ed. *Columbian Consequences*, vol. 1, *Archaeological and Historical Perspectives on the Spanish Borderlands West*. Washington, D.C.: Smithsonian Institution Press, 1989.

352.   ———, ed. *Columbian Consequences,* vol. 2, *Archaeological and Historical Perspectives on the Spanish Borderlands East*. Washington, D.C.: Smithsonian Institution Press, 1990.

353.   Turpin, Solveig A. "The Iconography of Contact: Spanish Influences in the Rock Art of the Middle Rio Grande." In *Columbian Consequences*, vol. 1, *Archaeological and Historical Perspectives on the Spanish Borderlands West,* ed. D. H. Thomas, 277–302. Washington, D.C.: Smithsonian Institution Press, 1989.

354.   Tyler, S. Lyman. *Two Worlds: The Indian Encounter with the European, 1492–1509.* Salt Lake City: University of Utah Press, 1988.

355.   Walker, Phillip L., Patricia Lambert, and Michael J. DeNiro. "The Effects of European Contact on the Health of Alta California Indians." In *Columbian Consequences*, vol. 1, *Archaeological and Historical Perspectives on the Spanish Borderlands West,* ed. D. H. Thomas, 349–64. Washington, D.C.: Smithsonian Institution Press, 1989.

356.   Weber, David J. "Coronado and the Myth of Quivira." *Southwest Reviews* 7 (spring 1985): 230–41.

3.4   ENGLISH AND DUTCH COLONIAL RELATIONS TO 1775

357.   Auth, Stephen F. *The Ten Years' War: Indian-White Relations in Pennsylvania, 1757–1765.* New York: Garland, 1989.

358.   Axtell, James. "Colonial America Without the Indians: Counterfactual Reflection." *Journal of American History* 73 (1987): 981–96.

359.   ———. "Colonial America Without the Indians: A Counterfactual Scenario." In *Indians in American Histo-*

ry: An Introduction, ed. F. E. Hoxie, 47–65. Arlington Heights, Ill.: Harlan Davidson, 1988.

360. ———. "The Indian in American History: The Colonial Period." Comments by Francis Jennings and T. H. Breen. In *The Impact of Indian History on the Teaching of United States History: Proceedings of the 1984 Chicago Conference, Sessions 1–2,* 1–30. D'Arcy McNickle Center for the History of the American Indian, Occasional Papers in Curriculum, no. 2. Chicago: Newberry Library, 1985.

361. ———. "The Power of Print in the Eastern Woodlands." *William and Mary Quarterly* 44 (1987): 300–309.

362. **Baine, Rodney M.** "The Myth of the Creek Pictograph." *Atlanta History* 32 (summer 1988): 43–52. [1735 pictographs on bison robe of Cherokee chief's speech sent to London]

363. **Baker, Emerson W.** "New Evidence on the French Involvement in King Philip's War." *Maine Historical Society Quarterly* 27 (fall 1988): 85–91.

364. ———. "A Scratch with a Bear's Paw: Anglo-Indian Land Deeds in Early Maine." *Ethnohistory* 36, no. 3 (1989): 235–56.

365. **Barbour, Philip L.,** ed. *The Complete Works of Captain John Smith (1580–1631).* 3 vols. Chapel Hill: University of North Carolina Press, 1986.

366. **Bartocci, Clara.** "Puritans Versus Pequots: Four Eye-Witness Reports of the First War in Colonial New England." *Storia Nordamericana* 4, no. 1/2 (1987): 21–92.

367. **Bee, Robert L.** "Connecticut's Indian Policy: From Testy Arrogance to Benign Bemusement." In *The Pequots in Southern New England: The Fall and Rise of an American Indian Nation,* ed. L. M. Hauptman and J. D. Wherry, 194–212. Norman: University of Oklahoma Press, 1990.

368. **Bourne, Russell.** *The Red King's Rebellion: Racial Politics in New England, 1675–78.* New York: Atheneum, 1990.

369. **Bragdon, Kathleen J.** "The Material Culture of the Christian Indians of New England, 1650–1775." In *Documentary Archaeology and the New World,* ed. M. C. Beaudry, 126–31. New York: Cambridge University Press, 1988.

370. **Briceland, Alan V.** *Westward from Virginia: The Exploration of the Virginia Frontier, 1650–1710.* Charlottesville: University Press of Virginia, 1987.

371. **Ceci, Lynn.** "Squanto and the Pilgrims: On Planting Corn in the Manner of the Indians." In *The Invented Indian: Cultural Fictions and Government Policies,* ed. J. A. Clifton, 71–90. New Brunswick, N.J.: Transaction Publishers, 1990.

372. **Christoph, Peter R.,** and **Florence A. Christoph,** eds. *The Andros Papers, 1677–1678.* Translations from Dutch by Charles T. Gehring. Syracuse, N.Y.: Syracuse University Press, 1990.

373. **Crosby, Constance A.** "From Myth to History, or Why King Philip's Ghost Walks Abroad." In *The Recovery of Meaning: Historical Archaeology in the Eastern United States,* ed. M. P. Leone and P. B. Potter, Jr., 183–209. Washington, D.C.: Smithsonian Institute Press, 1989.

374. **Daudelin, Don.** "Numbers and Tactics at Bushy Run." *Western Pennsylvania Historical Magazine* 68 (1985): 153–79.

375. Dickason, Olive P. "Amerindians Between French and English in Nova Scotia, 1713–1763." *American Indian Culture and Research Journal* 10, no. 4 (1986): 31–56.

376. Dowd, Gregory Evans. "The French King Wakes Up in Detroit: 'Pontiac's War' in Rumor and History." *Ethnohistory* 37, no. 3 (1990): 254–78.

377. Eid, Leroy V. "Their Rules of War: The Fallacy of James Smith's Summary of Indian Woodland War." *Register of the Kentucky Historical Society* 86 (1988): 4–23. [1660s–1670s]

378. Fausz, J. Frederick. "An 'Abundance of Blood Shed on Both Sides': England's First Indian War, 1609–1614." *Virginia Magazine of History and Biography* 98 (1990): 3–56.

379. ———. "Merging and Emerging Worlds: Anglo-Indian Interest Groups in the Development of the Seventeenth Century Chesapeake." In *Colonial Chesapeake Society,* ed. L. G. Carr, P. D. Morgan, and J. B. Russo, 47–98. Chapel Hill: University of North Carolina Press, 1988.

380. ———. "Middlemen in Peace and War: Virginia's Earliest Indian Interpreters, 1608–1632." *Virginia Magazine of History and Biography* 95 (1987): 41–64.

381. ———. "Patterns of Anglo-Indian Aggression and Accommodation Along the Mid-Atlantic Coast, 1564–1634." In *Cultures in Contact: The Impact of European Contacts on Native American Cultural Institutions, A.D. 1000–1800,* ed. W. W. Fitzhugh, 225–68. Washington, D.C.: Smithsonian Institution Press, 1985.

382. Francis, Peter, Jr. "The Beads That Did Not Buy Manhattan Island." *New York History* 67, no. 1 (1986): 1–22. [Corrects misconceptions of Dutch purchase]

383. Garratt, John G. *The Four Indian Kings/Les Quatre Rois Indiens.* Assisted by Bruce Robertson. Ottawa: Public Archives, distributed by the Canadian Government Publishing Center, 1985.

384. Gehring, Charles T., and Robert S. Grumet. "Observations of the Indians from Jasper Danckaerts' Journal, 1679–1680." *William and Mary Quarterly* 44 (1987): 104–20.

385. Gehring, Charles T., and William A. Starna. *A Journey into Mohawk and Oneida Country, 1634–1635: The Journal of Harmen Meyndertaz Van Der Bogaert.* Syracuse, N.Y.: Syracuse University Press, 1988.

386. Gehring, Charles T., William A. Starna, and William N. Fenton. "The Tawagonski Treaty of 1613: The Final Chapter." *New York History* 68, no. 4 (1987): 373–94. [Bogus first Indian treaty]

387. Grumet, Robert S. "The Selling of Lenapehaking." *Bulletin of the Archaeological Society of New Jersey* 44 (1989): 1–6.

388. Haan, Richard L. "Covenant and Consensus: Iroquois and English, 1676–1760." In *Beyond the Covenant Chain: The Iroquois and Their Neighbors in Indian North America, 600–1800,* ed. D. K. Richter and J. H. Merrell, 41–52. Syracuse, N.Y.: Syracuse University Press, 1987.

389. Hagedorn, Nancy L. "'A Friend to Go Between Them': The Interpreter as Cultural Broker During Anglo-Iroquois Councils, 1740–70." *Ethnohistory* 35, no. 1 (1988): 60–80.

390. Harrington, Faith. "Sea Tenure in Seventeenth-Century New Hamp-

shire: Native Americans and Englishmen in the Sphere of Coastal Resources." *Historical New Hampshire* 40 (1985): 18–33.

391. **Hatley, Marvin T.** "The Dividing Paths: The Encounters of the Cherokees and the South Carolinians in the Southern Mountains, 1670–1785." Ph.D. dissertation, Duke University, 1989.

392. ———. "The Three Lives of Keowee: Loss and Recovery in Eighteenth-Century Cherokee Villages." In *Powhatan's Mantle: Indians in the Colonial Southeast,* ed. P. H. Wood, G. A. Waselkov, and M. T. Hatley, 223–48. Lincoln: University of Nebraska Press, 1989.

393. **Hauptman, Laurence M.** "The Pequot War and Its Legacies." In *The Pequots in Southern New England: The Fall and Rise of an American Indian Nation,* ed. L. M. Hauptman and J. D. Wherry, 69–80. Norman: University of Oklahoma Press, 1990.

394. **Henry, Jackie.** "The Proclamation of 1763." *Archivist* 16 (November/December 1989): 10–11.

395. **Hirsch, Adam J.** "The Collision of Military Cultures in Seventeenth Century New England." *Journal of American History* 74 (1988): 1187–1212.

396. **Hulton, Paul.** "First Views from the New World: John White in America, 1584." *American History Illustrated* 19 (January 1985): 22–29.

397. ———, ed. *America, 1585: The Complete Drawings of John White.* Chapel Hill: University of North Carolina Press, 1985.

398. **Jacobs, Wilbur.** "British Indian Policies to 1783." In *History of Indian-White Relations,* ed. W. Washburn, 5–12. Vol. 4 of *Handbook of North American Indians,* ed. W. Sturtevant. Washington, D.C.: Smithsonian Institution Press, 1988.

399. **Jennings, Francis.** "Dutch and Swedish Indian Policies." In *History of Indian-White Relations,* ed. W. Washburn, 13–19. Vol. 4 of *Handbook of North American Indians,* ed. W. Sturtevant. Washington, D.C.: Smithsonian Institution Press, 1988.

400. ———. *Empire of Fortune: Crowns, Colonies, and Tribes in the Seven Years War in America.* New York: W. W. Norton, 1988.

401. **Jennings, Francis,** and **William N. Fenton,** eds. *The History and Culture of Iroquois Diplomacy: An Interdisciplinary Guide to the Treaties of the Six Nations and Their League.* Syracuse, N.Y.: Syracuse University Press, 1985.

402. **Jones, Dorothy.** "British Colonial Indian Treaties." In *History of Indian-White Relations,* ed. W. Washburn, 185–94. Vol. 4 of *Handbook of North American Indians,* ed. W. Sturtevant. Washington, D.C.: Smithsonian Institution Press, 1988.

403. **Judy, Mark A.** "Powder Keg on the Upper Missouri: Sources of Blackfeet Hostility, 1730–1810." *American Indian Quarterly* 11 (1987): 31–48.

404. **Kawashima, Yashuhide.** "Colonial Government Agencies." In *History of Indian-White Relations,* ed. W. Washburn, 245–54. Vol. 4 of *Handbook of North American Indians,* ed. W. Sturtevant. Washington, D.C.: Smithsonian Institution Press, 1988.

405. ———. *Puritan Justice and the Indian: White Man's Law in Massachusetts, 1630–1763.* Middletown, Conn.: Wesleyan University Press, 1986.

406. **Kenny, Herbert A.** "The Mas-

conomo Statue." *Essex Institute Historical Collections* 122 (1986): 61–68. [Statue of Agawam Sachem in Manchester, Mass., town hall]

407.   La Fantasie, Glenn W., ed. *The Correspondence of Roger Williams.* 2 vols. Hanover, N.H.: University Presses of New England, 1988.

408.   Leach, Douglas. "Colonial Indian Wars." In *History of Indian-White Relations,* ed. W. Washburn, 128–43. Vol. 4 of *Handbook of North American Indians,* ed. W. Sturtevant. Washington, D.C.: Smithsonian Institution Press, 1988.

409.   McLoughlin, William C. "Georgia's Role in Instigating Compulsory Indian Removal." *Georgia Historical Quarterly* 70 (1986): 605–37.

410.   Merrell, James H. "Minding the Business of the Nation: Hagler as Catawba Leader." *Ethnohistory* 31, no. 1 (1986): 55–70.

411.   Mullin, Michael J. "The Albany Congress and Colonial Confederation." *Mid-America* 72 (April/July 1990): 93–105.

412.   Patterson, Lisa. "Errant Peace Treaty." *Archivist* 16 (November/December 1989): 14–15. [Fragments of 1764 treaty between Hurons and Sir William Johnson in the University of Western Ontario Library]

413.   Prins, Harald E. L., and Bruce J. Bourque. "Norridgewock: Village Translocation on the New England–Acadian Frontier." *Man in the Northeast* 33 (1987): 137–58.

414.   Puglisi, Michael J. "An Unsupportable Burden: Paying for King Philip's War on the Massachusetts Frontier." *Historical Journal of Massachusetts* 16 (1988): 187–203.

415.   Ranlet, Philip. "Another Look at the Causes of King Philip's War." *New England Quarterly* 61 (1988): 79–100.

416.   Richter, Daniel K. "Cultural Brokers and Intercultural Politics: New York–Iroquois Relations, 1664–1701." *Journal of American History* 75 (1988): 40–67.

417.   ———. "War, Peace, and Politics in Seventeenth Century Huronia (Iroquoia)." In *Cultures in Conflict: Current Archaeological Perspectives,* ed. D. C. Tkaczuk and B. C. Vivian, 283–89. Proceedings of the Twentieth Annual Meeting of the Archaeological Association of the University of Calgary. Calgary: University of Calgary Archaeological Association, 1989.

418.   Robinson, W. S. "Conflicting Views on Landholding: Lord Baltimore and the Experiences of Colonial Maryland with Native Americans." *Maryland Historical Magazine* 83 (summer 1988): 85–97.

419.   Salisbury, Neal. "The Colonizing of Indian New England." *Massachusetts Review* 26, no. 2/3 (1985): 447–60.

420.   ———. "Indians and Colonists in Southern New England After the Pequot War: An Uneasy Balance." In *The Pequots in Southern New England: The Fall and Rise of an American Indian Nation,* ed. L. M. Hauptman and J. D. Wherry, 81–95. Norman: University of Oklahoma Press, 1990.

421.   ———. "Indians in Colonial History." In *The Impact of Indian History on the Teaching of United States History: Papers and Commentary from the 1985 Conference at the Smithsonian Institution, Washington, D.C.,* 1–42. D'Arcy McNickle Center for the History of the American Indian, Occasional Papers in

Curriculum, no. 4. Chicago: Newberry Library, 1986.

422. ———. "Social Relationships on a Moving Frontier: Natives and Settlers in Southern New England, 1638–1675." *Man in the Northeast* 33 (1987): 89–99.

423. ———. "Toward the Covenant Chain: Iroquois and Southern New England Algonquians, 1637–1684." In *Beyond the Covenant Chain: The Iroquois and Their Neighbors in Indian North America, 600–1800,* ed. D. K. Richter and J. H. Merrell, 61–73. Syracuse, N.Y.: Syracuse University Press, 1987.

424. **Shriver, Philip.** "The Beaver Wars and the Destruction of the Erie Nation." *Timeline* 1 (1985): 29–41.

425. **Smith, Dwight L.** "A North American Neutral Indian Zone: Persistence of a British Idea." *Northwest Ohio Quarterly* 61 (1989): 46–63.

426. **Smits, David D.** "'Abominable Mixture': Toward the Repudiation of Anglo-Indian Intermarriage in Seventeenth-Century Virginia." *Virginia Magazine of History and Biography* 95 (1987): 157–92.

427. ———. "'We Are Not to Grow Wild': Seventeenth-Century New England's Repudiation of Anglo-Indian Intermarriage." *American Indian Culture and Research Journal* 11, no. 4 (1987): 1–32.

428. **Steele, Ian K.** *Betrayals: Fort William Henry and the "Massacre."* New York: Oxford University Press, 1990.

429. **Stevens, Paul L.** "The Indian Diplomacy of Captain Richard B. Lernoult, British Military Commandant of Detroit, 1774–1775." *Michigan Historical Review* 13 (spring 1987): 47–82.

430. **Strong, John.** "Tribal Systems and Land Alienation: A Case Study." In *Papers of the Sixteenth Algonquian Conference,* ed. W. Cowan, 183–200. Ottawa: Carleton University Press, 1985.

431. **Thomas, Peter A.** "Cultural Change on the Southern New England Frontier, 1630–1665." In *Cultures in Contact: The Impact of European Contacts on Native American Cultural Institutions, A.D. 1000–1800,* ed. W. W. Fitzhugh, 131–61. Washington, D.C.: Smithsonian Institution Press, 1985.

432. **van Gestal, Ada.** "Van Der Donck's Description of the Indians: Additions and Corrections." *William and Mary Quarterly* 47 (1990): 411–21.

433. **van Longkhuyzen, Harold W.** "A Reappraisal of the Praying Indians: Acculturation, Conversion, and Identity at Natick, Massachusetts, 1646–1730." *New England Quarterly* 63 (1900): 396–428.

434. **Vaughan, Alden T.** "Frontier Banditti and the Indians: The Paxton Boy's Legacy, 1763–1775." *Pennsylvania History* 51 (1984): 1–29.

435. **White, Richard.** "The 'Middle Ground' for Indians in the Great Lakes." In *The Struggle for Political Autonomy: Papers and Comments from the Second Newberry Conference on Themes in American Indian History,* 22–32. D'Arcy McNickle Center for the History of the American Indian, Occasional Papers in Curriculum, no. 11. Chicago: Newberry Library, 1989.

436. **Wickwire, Franklin B.** "Go on and Be Brave: The Battle of Point Pleasant." *Timeline* 4 (1987): 2–19. [Shawnee participation in Lord Dunmore's War in Virginia, 1774]

437. **Wood, Peter.** "Indian Servitude in the Southeast." In *History of Indian-White Relations,* ed. W. Washburn, 407–

9. Vol. 4 of *Handbook of North American Indians,* ed. W. Sturtevant. Washington, D.C.: Smithsonian Institution Press, 1988.

438.   Young, James R. "Colonial-Indian Treaty Relations in the Northeast: An Overview." In *Native Views of Indian-White Historical Relations,* ed. D. L. Fixico, 55–67. D'Arcy McNickle Center for the History of the American Indian, Occasional Papers in Curriculum, no. 7. Chicago: Newberry Library, 1989.

3.5   INDIAN-WHITE RELATIONS IN THE U.S.A., 1775–1865

439.   Allen, Michael. "Justice for the Indians: The Federalist Quest, 1783–1796." *Essex Institute Historical Collections* 122 (1986): 124–41.

440.   Allen, Robert S. "His Majesty's Indian Allies: Native Peoples, the British Crown, and the War of 1812." *Michigan Historical Review* 14 (fall 1988): 1–24.

441.   Arndt, Katherine L. "Russian Relations with the Stikine Tlingit, 1833–1867." *Alaska History* 3 (spring 1988): 27–44.

442.   Bahos, Charles. "On Opothleyahola's Trail: Locating the Battle of Round Mountain." *Chronicles of Oklahoma* 63 (1985): 58–89.

443.   Barber, Douglas. "Council Government and the Genesis of the Creek War (1812–13)." *Alabama Review* 38 (July 1985): 163–84.

444.   Barreiro, Jose. "Indian Roots of American Democracy." *Northeast Indian Quarterly* (special issue) 4/5 (winter/spring 1988/89).

445.   Bennett, Richard Edmond. "Cousin Laman in the Wilderness: The Beginnings of Brigham Young's Indian Policy." *Nebraska History* 67, no. 1 (1986): 69–82. [Young's policies were first applied among Plains Indians on the banks of the Missouri River]

446.   Berkhofer, Robert F., Jr. "Americans Versus Indians: The Northwest Ordinance, Territory Making, and Native Americans." *Indiana Magazine of History* 84 (1988): 90–108.

447.   Bieder, Robert E. *Science Encounters the Indian, 1820–1880: The Early Years of American Ethnology.* Norman: University of Oklahoma Press, 1986.

448.   Black Horse. "The Gratten Massacre, as Drawn from the Indian Point of View." *American West* 22 (December 1985): 46–51.

449.   Brandt, Penny S. "A Letter of Dr. John Sibley, Indian Agent." *Louisiana History* 29 (1988): 365–87.

450.   Calloway, Colin G. *Crown and Calumet: British-Indian Relations, 1783–1815.* Norman: University of Oklahoma Press, 1987.

451. ———. "The End of an Era: British-Indian Relations in the Great Lakes Region After the War of 1812." *Michigan Historical Review* 12 (fall 1986): 1–20.

452. ———. "Neither White nor Red: White Renegades on the American Indian Frontier." *Western Historical Quarterly* 17 (1986): 43–66.

453. ———. "Sentinels of the Revolution: Bedel's New Hampshire Rangers and the Abenaki Indians on the Upper Connecticut." *Historical New Hampshire* 45 (1990): 271–95.

454. ———. "Suspicion and Self-Interest: British-Indian Relations and the Peace of Paris." *Historian* 48 (1985): 41–60.

455.   Campisi, Jack. "The Oneida

Treaty Period, 1783–1838." In *The Oneida Indian Experience: Two Perspectives,* ed. J. Campisi and L. M. Hauptman, 48–64. Syracuse, N.Y.: Syracuse University Press, 1988.

456.   **Carrico, Richard L.** *Strangers in a Stolen Land: American Indians in San Diego, 1850–1880.* San Diego State University, Publications in American Indian Studies, no. 2. San Diego: San Diego State University, 1986.

457.   **Carroll, George H.** "Indian Captivities of the Upper Ohio Valley, 1755–1795." In *Selected Papers from the 1987 and 1988 George Rogers Clark Trans-Appalachian Frontier History Conferences,* ed. R. J. Holden, 17–34. Vincennes, Ind.: Vincennes University, 1990.

458.   **Castillo, Edward.** "An Indian Account of the Decline and Collapse of Mexico's Hegemony over the Missionized Indians of California." *American Indian Quarterly* 13 (1989): 391–408.

459.   **Cave, Alfred E.** "Canaanites in a Promised Land: The American Indian and the Providential Theory of Empire." *American Indian Quarterly* 12 (1988): 277–97.

460.   **Christianson, James R.** "Removal: A Foundation for the Formation of Federalized Indian Policy." *Journal of Cherokee Studies* 10 (1985): 215–29.

461.   **Clark, Jerry L.** "Thus Spoke Chief Seattle: The Story of an Undocumented Speech." *Prologue* 17 (spring 1985): 58–67.

462.   **Clemmer, Richard O.** "The Tail of the Elephant: Indians in Emigrant Diaries, 1844–1862." *Nevada Historical Society Quarterly* 30 (1987): 269–90.

463.   **Coker, Edward C.,** and **Daniel L. Schafer.** "A West Point Graduate in the Second Seminole War: William Warren Chapman and the View from Fort Foster." *Florida Historical Quarterly* 68 (1990): 447–75.

464.   **Cutrer, Thomas W.** "The Tallapoosa Might Truly Be Called the 'River of Blood': Major Alexander McCulloch and the Battle of Horseshoe Bend, March 27, 1813." *Alabama Review* 43 (1990): 35–39.

465.   **Danker, Donald.** "A High Price for a Lame Cow." *Kansas History* 10 (1987): 111–17.

466.   **Darling, Ernest F.** "Lincoln's Message to Indian Territory." *Chronicles of Oklahoma* 63 (1985): 186–91.

467.   **Davis, Lee.** "Tracking Jedediah Smith Through Hupa Territory." *American Indian Quarterly* 13 (1989): 369–89.

468.   **DeMallie, Raymond J.** "Early Kiowa and Comanche Treaties: The Treaties of 1835 and 1837." *American Indian Journal* 9, no. 2 (1986): 16–22.

469.   **Denham, James M.** "'Some Prefer the Seminoles': Violence and Disorder Among Soldiers and Settlers in the Second Seminole War, 1835–42." *Florida Historical Quarterly* 70 (1990): 38–54.

470.   **Diedrich, Mark.** "Chief Hole-in-the-Day and the 1862 Chippewa Distubance: A Reappraisal." *Minnesota History* 50 (1987): 193–203.

471.   **Dillon, Rodney E., Jr.** "Seminole Indians in the Florida War: The Soldier's View." *Broward Legacy* 8 (summer/fall 1985): 31–34.

472.   **Dorman, Robert L.** "Thomas Jefferson's Letter to the Indians: Fate of a Frontier Artifact." *Chronicles of Oklahoma* 63 (1985/86): 341–59.

473.   **Earle, Thomas.** *Sir John Johnson: The Exile.* Toronoto: Dundurn Press, 1986.

474.   **Edmunds, R. David.** "American Expansion in the Nineteenth Century: A Second Look." In *The Impact of Indian History on the Teaching of United States History: Papers and Commentary from the 1985 Conference at Smithsonian Institution, Washington, D.C.*, 43–94. D'Arcy McNickle Center for the History of the American Indian, Occasional Papers in Curriculum, no. 4. Chicago: Newberry Library, 1986.

475.   ———. "'Evil Men Who Add to Our Difficulties': Shawnees, Quakers, and William Wells, 1807–1808." *American Indian Culture and Research Journal* 14, no. 4 (1990): 1–14.

476.   ———. "The Indian in American History: American Expansion in the Nineteenth Century." Comments by Mary Young and James A. Henretta. In *The Impact of Indian History on the Teaching of United States History: Proceedings of the 1984 Chicago Conference, Sessions 1–2*, 49–77. D'Arcy McNickle Center for the History of the American Indian, Occasional Papers in Curriculum, no. 2. Chicago: Newberry Library, 1985.

477.   ———. "Indians as Pioneers: Potawatomis on the Frontier." *Chronicles of Oklahoma* 65 (1988): 340–53.

478.   ———. "Indian-White Warfare: A Look at Both Sides." *Northwest Ohio Quarterly* 61 (1989): 35–45.

479.   ———. "Walking the Corn Road: Shawnees and Quakers in the Ohio Country, 1807–1808." In *Native Views of Indian-White Historical Relations*, ed. D. L. Fixico, 69–78. D'Arcy McNickle Center for the History of the American Indian, Occasional Papers in Curriculum, no. 7. Chicago: Newberry Library, 1989.

480.   **Egan, Ferol.** *Sand in a Whirlwind: The Paiute Indian War of 1860.* Reno: University of Nevada Press, 1985.

481.   **Eid, Leroy V.** "'A Kind of Running Fight': Indian Battlefield Tactics in the Late Eighteenth Century." *Western Pennsylvania Historical Magazine* 71 (1988): 147–71.

482.   ———. "'National' War Among Indians of Northeastern North America." *Canadian Review of American Studies* 16, no. 2 (1985): 125–54.

483.   **Ellenberg, George B.** "An Uncivil War of Words: Indian Removal in the Press, 1830." *Atlanta History* 33 (spring 1989): 48–59.

484.   **Ezell, John S.** "'Demon Rum' and the Five Civilized Tribes, 1754–1861." *Mid-America* 72 (January 1990): 3–24.

485.   **Ferguson, Robert B.** "Treaties Between the United States and the Choctaw Nation." In *The Choctaw Before Removal*, ed. C. K. Reeves, 214–30. Jackson: University Press of Mississippi, 1985.

486.   **Fierst, John T.** "Return to 'Civilization': John Tanner's Troubled Years at Sault Ste. Marie." *Minnesota History* 50 (1986): 23–36. [The final years of the former captive]

487.   **Flanagan, Sharon.** "The Georgia Cherokees Who Remained: Race, Status, and Property in the Chattahoochee Community." *Georgia Historical Quarterly* 73 (1989): 584–609.

488.   **Fredericksen, John C.,** ed. "Kentucky at the Thames, 1813: A Rediscovered Narrative by William Greathouse." *Register of the Kentucky Historical Society* 82 (1985): 93–107.

489.   **Gaines, W. Craig.** *The Confederate Cherokees: John Drew's Regiment of Mounted Rifles.* Baton Rouge: Louisiana State University Press, 1989.

490.   *Georgia Historical Quarterly* (special issue commemorating the sesquicentennial of Cherokee removal, 1838–39) 73 (fall 1989).

491.   **Gibson, Arrell M.** "Indian Land Transfers." In *History of Indian-White Relations,* ed. W. Washburn, 211–329. Vol. 4 of *Handbook of North American Indians,* ed. W. Sturtevant. Washington, D.C.: Smithsonian Institution Press, 1988.

492.   ———. "Native Americans and the Civil War." *American Indian Quarterly* 9 (1985): 385–410.

493.   **Gilbert, Bil.** *God Gave Us This Country: Tekamthi and the First American Civil War.* New York: Atheneum, 1989.

494.   **Graves, William H.** "The Five Civilized Tribes and the Beginning of the Civil War." *Journal of Cherokee Studies* 10 (1985): 205–14.

495.   **Graymont, Barbara.** "The Oneidas and the American Revolution." In *The Oneida Indian Experience: Two Perspectives,* ed. J. Campisi and L. M. Hauptman, 31–42. Syracuse, N.Y.: Syracuse University Press, 1988.

496.   **Green, Joan.** "Civilize the Indian: Government Policies, Quakers, and Cherokee Education." *Journal of Cherokee Studies* 10 (1985): 192–204.

497.   **Griffen, William B.** *Apaches at War and Peace: The Janos Presidio, 1750–1858.* Albuquerque: University of New Mexico Press, 1988.

498.   ———. *Utmost Good Faith: Patterns of Apache-Mexican Hostilities in Northern Chihuahua Border Warfare, 1821–1848.* Albuquerque: University of New Mexico Press, 1989.

499.   **Grinde, Donald A.,** and **Bruce Johansen.** *Exemplar of Liberty: Native America and the Evolution of Democracy.*
Los Angeles: American Indian Studies Center, University of California—Los Angeles, 1990.

500.   **Grove, B. D.** "Edwin Forrest, Metamora, and the Indian Removal Act of 1830." *Theatre Journal* 37 (1985): 181–91.

501.   **Hagan, William T.** "The Black Hawk War." In *An Anthology of Western Great Lakes Indian History,* ed. D. L. Fixico, 271–94. Milwaukee: American Indian Studies, University of Wisconsin—Milwaukee, 1987.

502.   **Hamilton, Allen Lee.** "The Warren Wagon Train Raid: Frontier Indian Policy at the Crossroads." *Arizona and the West* 28 (1986): 201–24.

503.   **Hammon, Neal,** and **James Russell Harris,** eds. "'In a Dangerous Situation': Letters of Col. John Floyd, 1774–1783." *Register of the Kentucky Historical Society* 83 (1985): 202–36.

504.   **Harrison, Lowell H.** "Nat Crain and the Battle of the Thames." *Filson Club History Quarterly* 64 (July 1990): 377–83.

505.   **Hawes, Leland M., Jr.** "The Dade Massacre: Adding New Insights." *Sunland Tribune* 11 (1985): 2–6.

506.   **Henri, Florette.** *The Southern Indians and Benjamin Hawkins, 1796–1816.* Norman: University of Oklahoma Press, 1986.

507.   **Herring, Joseph B.** "Cultural and Economic Resilience Among the Kickapoo Indians of the Southwest." *Great Plains Quarterly* 6 (1986): 263–75.

508.   ———. "Indian Intransigency in Kansas: Government Bureaucracy Versus Mokohoko's Sacs and Foxes." *Western Historical Quarterly* 17 (1986): 185–200.

509.   ———. "The Vermillion Kickapoos of Illinois: The Prophet Kenekuk's

Peaceful Resistance to Indian Removal." In *Selected Papers of the Fourth Illinois History Symposium,* 28–38. Springfield: Illinois State Historical Society, 1985.

510.   Holmes, Jack D. L. "Benjamin Hawkins and United States Attempts to Teach Farming to Southern Indians." *Agricultural History* 60 (1986): 216–32.

511.   Holmes, Tony. "Early Cherokee Ferry Crossings of the Eastern Tennessee River Basin." *Journal of Eastern Tennessee History* 62 (1990): 54–79. [1790s]

512.   Hood, Garfield W. "Return of the Laughing Whitefish: An Account of the Establishment of the Keewenaw Bay Indian Community." *Michigan Bar Journal* 64 (May 1985): 400–407.

513.   Horsman, Reginald. "The Origins of Oneida Removal to Wisconsin, 1815–1822." In *An Anthology of Western Great Lakes Indian History,* ed. D. L. Fixico, 203–32. Milwaukee: American Indian Studies, University of Wisconsin—Milwaukee, 1987.

514.   ———. "United States Indian Policies, 1776–1815." In *History of Indian-White Relations,* ed. W. Washburn, 29–39. Vol 4 of *Handbook of North American Indians,* ed. W. Sturtevant. Washington, D.C.: Smithsonian Institution Press, 1988.

515.   Hunter, Juanita. "The Indians and the Michigan Road." *Indiana Magazine of History* 83 (1987): 244–66.

516.   Hurtado, Albert L. "California Indians and the Workaday West: Labor, Assimilation, and Survival." *California History* 69 (1990): 2–11.

517.   ———. "Indians in Town and Country: The Nisenan Indians' Changing Economy and Society as Shown in John A. Sutter's 1856 Correspondence." *American Indian Culture and Research Journal* 12, no. 2 (1988): 31–52.

518.   ———. *Indian Survival on the California Frontier.* New Haven, Conn.: Yale University Press, 1988.

519.   Johansen, Bruce E. "William James Sidis' 'Tribes and States': An Unpublished Exploration of Native American Contributions to Democracy." *Northeast Indian Quarterly* 4 (1989): 24–29.

520.   Johansen, Bruce E., and Donald A. Grinde, Jr. "The Debate Regarding Native American Precedents for Democracy: A Recent Historiography." *American Indian Culture and Research Journal* 14, no. 1 (1990): 61–88.

521.   Johansen, Bruce E., and Elisabeth Tooker. "Commentary on the Iroquois and the United States Constitution." *Ethnohistory* 37, no. 3 (1990): 279–97.

522.   King, Jeff S. " 'Do Not Execute Chief Pocatello': President Lincoln Acts to Save the Shoshoni Chief." *Utah Historical Quarterly* 53, no. 3 (1985): 236–47.

523.   Klos, George. "Blacks and the Seminole Removal Debate, 1821–1835." *Florida Historical Quarterly* 68 (1989): 55–78.

524.   Knepper, George W. "Breaching the Ohio Boundary: The Western Tribes in Retreat." In *The American Indian Experience: A Profile, 1524 to the Present,* ed. P. Weeks, 81–95. Arlington Heights, Ill.: Forum Press, 1988.

525.   Kopperman, Paul E. "The Captive's Return: Bouquets's Victory." *Timeline* 7 (1990): 2–15.

526.   Lankford, George E. "Losing the Past: Draper and the Ruddell Indian Captivity." *Arkansas Historical Quarterly* 49 (autumn 1990): 214–39. [Lyman Draper and Isaac and George Ruddell families]

527.   Lehman, L. David. "The End of the Iroquois Mystique: The Oneida Land Cessation Treaties of the 1780s." *William and Mary Quarterly* 47 (October 1990): 523–47).

528.   Lurie, Nancy O. "In Search of Chaetar: New Findings on Black Hawk's Surrender." *Wisconsin Magazine of History* 71 (spring 1988): 163–83.

529.   McClurken, James. "Ottawa Adaptive Strategies to Indian Removal." *Michigan Historical Review* 12 (spring 1986): 29–56.

530.   McLoughlin, William G. *Cherokee Renascence in the New Republic.* Princeton, N.J.: Princeton University Press, 1987.

531.   Madsen, Brigham D. *Glory Hunter: A Biography of Patrick Edward O'Connor.* Salt Lake City: University of Utah Press, 1990.

532.   ———. *The Shoshoni Frontier and the Bear River Massacre.* Salt Lake City: University of Utah Press, 1985.

533.   Mahon, John K. "Indian–United States Military Situation." In *History of Indian-White Relations,* ed. W. Washburn, 144–62. Vol. 4 of *Handbook of North American Indians,* ed. W. Sturtevant. Washington, D.C.: Smithsonian Institution Press, 1988.

534.   Malouf, Carling I., and John Findlay. "Euro-American Impact Before 1870." In *Great Basin,* ed. W. L. d'Azevedo, 499–516. Vol. 11 of *Handbook of North American Indians,* ed. W. Sturtevant. Washington, D.C.: Smithsonian Institution Press, 1986.

535.   Mancall, Peter C. "The Revolutionary War and the Indians of the Upper Susquehanna Valley." *American Indian Culture and Research Journal* 12, no. 1 (1988): 39–58.

536.   Manzo, Joseph T. "Women in Indian Removal." In *A Cultural Geography of North American Indians,* ed. T. E. Ross and T. G. Moore, 213–26. Boulder, Colo.: Westview Press, 1987.

537.   Mardock, Robert. "Indian Rights Movement Until 1887." In *History of Indian-White Relations,* ed. W. Washburn, 301–4. Vol. 4 of *Handbook of North American Indians,* ed. W. Sturtevant. Washington, D.C.: Smithsonian Institution Press, 1988.

538.   Matsen, William E. "The Battle of Sugar Point: A Re-Examination." *Minnesota History* 50 (1987): 269–75.

539.   Merrell, James H. "Declarations of Independence: Indian-White Relations in the New Nation." In *The American Revolution: Its Character and Limits,* ed. J. P. Greene, 197–223. New York: New York University Press, 1987.

540.   Milligan, James C., and L. David Norris. "A Connecticut Yankee in the Indian Territory." *Chronicles of Oklahoma* 68 (1990): 266–75. [Charles H. Sawyer]

541.   Miriani, Ronald. "Against the Wind: The Shawnee at Wapakoneta." *Queen City Heritage* 48 (spring 1990): 33–47.

542.   Mormino, Gary R., ed. "'The Firing of Guns and Crackers Continued Till Light': A Diary of the Billy Bowlegs War." *Tequesta* 45 (1985): 48–72.

543.   Morrison, Kenneth M. "Native Americans and the American Revolution." Comments by Gary Nash. In *The Impact of Indian History on the Teaching of United States History: Papers and Commentary from the 1986 Conference at Los Angeles,* 1–36. D'Arcy McNickle Center for the History of the American Indian, Occasional Papers in Curriculum, no. 5. Chicago: Newberry Library, 1987.

544. ————. "Native Americans and the American Revolution: Historic Stories and Shifting Frontier Conflict." In *Indians in American History: An Introduction*, ed. F. E. Hoxie, 95–115. Arlington Heights, Ill.: Harlan Davidson, 1988.

545. **Murrin, John M.** "Self-Interest Conquers Patriotism: Republicans, Liberals, and Indians Reshape the Nation." In *The American Revolution: Its Character and Limits*, ed. J. P. Greene, 224–29. New York: New York University Press, 1987.

546. **Nelson, Paul David.** *Anthony Wayne, Soldier of the Early Republic.* Bloomington: Indiana University Press, 1985.

547. ————. "'Mad' Anthony Wayne and the Kentuckians of the 1790s." *Register of the Kentucky Historical Society* 84 (1986): 1–17.

548. **Nielson, Donald M.** "The Mashpee Indian Revolt of 1833." *New England Quarterly* 58 (1985): 400–420.

549. **O'Donnell, Terence.** "The Cayuse Indian War." *Idaho Yesterdays* 31 (1987): 57–63.

550. **Owsley, Frank L., Jr.** "Ambrister and Arbuthnot: Adventurers or Martyrs for British Honor?" *Journal of the Early Republic* 5 (1985): 289–308.

551. **Perdue, Theda.** "The Conflict Within: The Cherokee Power Structure and Removal." *Georgia Historical Quarterly* 73 (1989): 467–91.

552. ————. "Indians in Southern History." In *The Impact of Indian History on the Teaching of United States History: Papers and Commentary from the 1985 Conference at the Smithsonian Institution, Washington, D.C.,* 213–40. D'Arcy McNickle Center for the History of the American Indian, Occasional Papers in Curriculum, no. 4. Chicago: Newberry Library, 1986.

553. ————. "Indians in Southern History." In *Indians in American History: An Introduction*, ed. F. E. Hoxie, 137–57. Arlington Heights, Ill.: Harlan Davidson, 1988.

554. ————. "John Ross and the Cherokee Indians: A Review Essay." *Georgia Historical Quarterly* 70 (1986): 456–76.

555. ————. "The Trail of Tears: Removal of the Southern Indians." In *The American Indian Experience: A Profile, 1524 to the Present*, ed. P. Weeks, 96–117. Arlington Heights, Ill.: Forum Press, 1988.

556. **Phillips, George.** "The Alcaldes: Indian Leadership in the Spanish Missions of California." In *The Struggle for Political Autonomy: Papers and Comments from the Second Newberry Conference on Themes in American Indian History*, 83–89. D'Arcy McNickle Center for the History of the American Indian, Occasional Papers in Curriculum, no. 11. Chicago: Newberry Library, 1989.

557. **Satz, Ronald N.** "Cherokee Traditionalism, Protestant Evangelism, and the Trail of Tears." Parts 1 and 2. *Tennessee Historical Quarterly* 44, nos. 2–3 (1985): 285–301, 380–401.

558. ————. "The Cherokee Trail of Tears: A Sesquicentennial Perspective." *Georgia Historical Quarterly* 73 (1989): 431–66.

559. **Schaaf, Gregory.** "From the Great Law of Peace to the Constitution of the United States: A Revision of America's Democratic Roots." *American Indian Law Review* 14 (1989): 323–32.

560. ————. *Wampum Belts and Peace Trees: George Morgan, Native Americans, and Revolutionary Diplomacy.* Golden, Colo.: Fulcrum Press, 1990.

561. **Schultz, Duane.** *Month of the*

Freezing Moon: The Creek Massacre, November 1864. New York: St. Martin's Press, 1990.

562.   **Secrest, William.** "Jarboe's War." *Californians* 6 (1988): 16–22.

563.   **Shea, Peter.** "A New and Accurate Map of Philip's Grant." *Vermont History* 53 (1985): 36–42.

564.   **Sheehan, Bernard W.** "Concord Bridge and the 'Savage' Indians." In *The Impact of Indian History on the Teaching of United States History: Papers and Commentary from the 1985 Conference at the Smithsonian Institution, Washington, D.C.,* 171–212. D'Arcy McNickle Center for the History of the American Indian, Occasional Papers in Curriculum, no. 4. Chicago: Newberry Library, 1986.

565.   ———. "The Problem of the Indian in the Revolution." In *The American Indian Experience: A Profile, 1524 to the Present,* ed. P. Weeks, 66–80. Arlington Heights, Ill.: Forum Press, 1988.

566.   **Smith, F. Todd.** "After the Treaty of 1835: The United States and the Kadohadacho Indians." *Louisiana History* 30 (1989): 157–72.

567.   **Smith, Nicholas N.** "The Long Shot: Fact and Tradition." In *Papers of the Twenty-First Algonquian Conference,* ed. W. Cowan, 337–44. Ottawa: Carleton University Press, 1990.

568.   **Sprague, Stuart S.** "The Death of Tecumseh and the Rise of Rumpsey Dumpsey: The Making of a Vice President." *Filson Club History Quarterly* 59, no. 4 (1985): 455–61.

569.   **Stevens, Paul L.** "'To Invade the Frontiers of Kentucky?' The Indian Diplomacy of Philippe de Rocheblave, Britain's Acting Commandant at Kaskaskia, 1776–1778." *Filson Club History Quarterly* 64 (April 1990): 205–46.

570.   ———. "'To Keep the Indians of the Wabache in His Majesty's Interest': The Indian Diplomacy of Edward Abbott, British Lieutenant Governor of Vincennes, 1776–1778." *Indiana Magazine of History* 83 (1987): 141–72.

571.   ———. "Wabasha Visits Governor Carleton, 1776: New Light on a Legendary Episode of Dakota-British Diplomacy on the Great Lakes Frontier." *Michigan Historical Review* 16 (spring 1990): 21–48.

572.   **Sugden, John.** "Early Pan-Indianism: Tecumseh's Tour of the Indian Country, 1811–1812." *American Indian Quarterly* 10 (1986): 273–304.

573.   ———. *Tecumseh's Last Stand.* Norman: University of Oklahoma Press, 1985.

574.   **Sunseri, Alvin R.** "Revolt in Taos, 1846–47: Resistance to U.S. Occupation." *El Palacio* 96 (fall 1990): 38–47.

575.   **Sword, Wiley.** *President Washington's Indian War: The Struggle for the Old Northwest, 1790–1795.* Norman: University of Oklahoma Press, 1985.

576.   **Tooker, Elisabeth.** "The United States Constitution and the Iroquois League." *Ethnohistory* 35, no. 4 (1988): 305–36.

577.   ———. "The United States Constitution and the Iroquois League." In *The Invented Indian: Cultural Fictions and Government Policies,* ed. J. A. Clifton, 107–48. New Brunswick, N.J.: Transaction Publishers, 1990.

578.   **Trafzer, Clifford E.,** ed. *Indians, Superintendents, and Councils: Northwestern Indian Policy, 1850–1855.* Lanham, Md.: University Press of America, 1985.

579. Turcheneske, John A. "Federal Indian Policy and the Brotherton Indians." In *Papers of the Sixteenth Algonquian Conference*, ed. W. Cowan, 201–9. Ottawa: Carleton University Press, 1985.

580. Usner, Daniel H., Jr. "American Indians on the Cotton Frontier: Changing Economic Relations with Citizens and Slaves in the Mississippi Territory." *Journal of American History* 72 (1985): 297–317.

581. Utley, Robert. "Indian–United States Military Situation, 1848–1881." In *History of Indian-White Relations,* ed. W. Washburn, 163–84. Vol. 4 of *Handbook of North American Indians,* ed. W. Sturtevant. Washington, D.C.: Smithsonian Institution Press, 1988.

582. Vipperman, Carl J. "The Bungled Treaty of New Echota: The Failure of Cherokee Removal, 1836–38." *Georgia Historical Quarterly* 73 (1989): 540–58.

583. Warner, Michael S. "General Josiah Harmar's Campaign Reconsidered: How the Americans Lost the Battle of Kekionga." *Indiana Magazine of History* 83 (1987): 43–64.

584. Webber, Bert. *Indians Along the Oregon Trail: The Tribes of Nebraska, Idaho, Oregon, and Washington Identified.* Medford, Oreg.: Pacific Northwest Books Co., 1989.

585. Weeks, Philip. *Farewell, My Nation: The American Indian and the United States, 1820–1890.* Arlington Heights, Ill.: Harlan Davidson, 1990.

586. Wells, Samuel J. "Federal Indian Policy: From Accommodation to Removal." In *The Choctaw Before Removal,* ed. C. K. Reeves, 181–213. Jackson: University Press of Mississippi, 1985.

587. ———. "International Causes of the Treaty of Mount Dexter, 1805."

Journal of Mississippi History 48 (1986): 177–85.

588. Wickman, Patricia R. "'A Trifling Affair': Loomis Lyman Langdon and the Third Seminole War." *Florida Historical Quarterly* 63 (1985): 303–17.

589. Wienker, Curtis W. "Archaeological Evidence of a Second Seminole War Autopsy." *Florida Anthropologist* 40 (1987): 229–32.

590. Williams, Carol. "My First Indian: Interaction Between Women and Indians on the Trail, 1845–1865." *Overland Journal* 4 (1986): 13–18.

591. Williams, Harold David. "Gambling Away the Inheritance: The Cherokee Nation and Georgia's Gold and Land Lotteries of 1832–1833." *Georgia Historical Quarterly* 73 (1989): 519–39.

592. ———. "The North Georgia Gold Rush." Ph.D. dissertation, Auburn University, 1989.

593. Wright, Robin. "The Traveling Exhibition of Captain Samuel Hadlock, Jr.: Eskimos in Europe, 1822–1826." In *Indians and Europe: An Interdisciplinary Collection of Essays,* ed. C. Feest, 215–33. Aachen, West Germany: Edition Herodot, 1987.

594. Wrone, David R. "Indian Treaties and the Democratic Idea." *Wisconsin Magazine of History* 70 (winter 1986): 83–106.

595. Young, Mary. "The Exercise of Sovereignty in Cherokee Georgia." *Journal of the Early Republic* 10 (spring 1990): 43–64.

596. ———. "Tribal Reorganization in the Southeast, 1800–1840." In *The Struggle for Political Autonomy: Papers and Comments from the Second Newberry Conference on Themes in American Indian History,*

59–82. D'Arcy McNickle Center for the History of the American Indian, Occasional Papers in Curriculum, no. 11. Chicago: Newberry Library, 1989.

3.6 INDIAN-WHITE RELATIONS IN THE U.S.A., 1865–1900

597. Barney, Gerald D. *Mormons, Indians, and the Ghost Dance of 1890.* Lanham, Md.: University Press of America, 1986.

598. Bendall, Herman. "The Superintendent of Indian Affairs, Arizona Territory, Annual Report, 1871 and 1872." *Western States Jewish History* 22 (April 1990): 195–206.

599. Bender, Norman J. *New Hope for the Indians: The Grant Peace Policy and the Navajos in the 1870s.* Albuquerque: University of New Mexico Press, 1989.

600. Berthrong, Donald J. "The Bitter Years: Western Indian Reservation Life." In *The American Indian Experience: A Profile, 1524 to the Present,* ed. P. Weeks, 153–73. Arlington Heights, Ill.: Forum Press, 1988.

601. ———. "Nineteenth-Century United States Government." In *History of Indian-White Relations,* ed. W. Washburn, 255–63. Vol. 4 of *Handbook of North American Indians,* ed. W. Sturtevant. Washington, D.C.: Smithsonian Institution Press, 1988.

602. Blackstone, Sarah J. *Buckskins, Bullets, and Business: A History of Buffalo Bill's Wild West.* Westport, Conn.: Greenwood Press, 1986.

603. Blaine, Martha Royce. *Pawnee Passage, 1870–1875.* Norman: University of Oklahoma Press, 1990.

604. Bolt, Christine. *American Indian Policy and American Reform: Case Studies of the Campaign to Assimilate the American Indians.* London: Allen and Unwin, 1987.

605. Boxberger, Daniel L. "The Lummi Indians and the Canadian/American Pacific Treaty." *American Indian Quarterly* 12 (1988): 299–311.

606. Brice, Danaly. *The Great Comanche Raid: Boldest Indian Attack of the Texas Republic.* Austin, Tex.: Eakin Press, 1987.

607. Buecker, Thomas R., ed. "The Journals of James S. McClellan, 1st Sgt., Company H, 3rd Cavalry." *Annals of Wyoming* 57, no. 1 (1985): 21–34.

608. Buecker, Thomas R., and **R. Eli Paul.** "Pawnee Scouts: Auxiliary Troops in the U.S. Cavalry, 1864–1877." *Military Images* 7 (July–August 1985): 16–19.

609. ———, eds. "Go South and Be Free." *Chronicles of Oklahoma* 65 (1987): 132–57. [John Williamson and 1,400 Pawnee forced to Indian Territory in 1874]

610. Calloway, Colin G. "Sword Bearer and the 'Crow Outbreak' of 1887." *Montana* 36 (fall 1986): 38–51.

611. Camp, Gregory S. "Working Out Their Own Salvation: The Allotment of Land in Severalty and the Turtle Mountain Chippewa Band, 1870–1920." *American Indian Culture and Research Journal* 14, no. 2 (1990): 19–38.

612. Carroll, John M., ed. *Indian Wars Campaign Medal: Its History and Its Recipients.* Mattituek, N.Y.: Amereon, 1985.

613. Carter, Kent. "Federal Indian Policy: The Dawes Commission, 1887–1889." *Prologue* 22 (winter 1990): 339–42.

614. Chalfant, William Y. *Cheyennes and Horse Soldiers: The 1857 Expedition* *and the Battle of Solomon's Fork.* Norman: University of Oklahoma Press, 1989.

615.   Christianson, James R. "The Kansas-Osage Border War of 1874: Fact or Wishful Thinking?" *Chronicles of Oklahoma* 63 (1985): 292–311. [Kansas settlers attack an Osage hunting party]

616.   Clark, Wahne C. "The Grand Celebration: An Indian Delegation to Washington." *Chronicles of Oklahoma* 64 (1988): 192–205.

617.   Clow, Richmond L. "General William S. Harney on the Northern Plains." *South Dakota History* 16 (1986): 229–48.

618.   Cole, D. C. *The Chiricahua Apache, 1846–1876: From War to Reservation.* Albuquerque: University of New Mexico Press, 1988.

619.   Connelly, Herbert H. "The Battle of Wounded Knee, as Told by Sergeant James F. Connelly." *Persimmon Hill* 16 (winter 1990): 16–21.

620.   Culbertson, Joseph. *Indian Scouts: Memoirs, 1876–1895.* Edited by M. D. Trout. Rev. ed., San Diego: Van Allen Publications, 1985.

621.   Danker, Donald F. "Big Bat Pourier's Version of the Sibley Scout." *Nebraska History* 66, no. 2 (1985): 129–44.

622.   Darling, Roger. *A Sad and Tragic Blunder: Generals Terry and Custer at the Little Big Horn—New Discoveries.* Vienna, Va.: Potomac-Western Press, 1990.

623.   Delo, David M. "The Little Known Battle of Snake Mountain." *Annals of Wyoming* 59, no. 2 (1987): 28–35. [Northern Arapaho and Sioux versus Shoshones and U.S., 1874]

624.   DeMontravel, Peter R. "General Nelson A. Miles and the Wounded Knee Controversy." *Arizona and the West* 23 (1986): 23–44.

625.   Dewing, Rolland. *Wounded Knee: The Meaning and Significance of the Second Incident.* New York: Irvington Publishing, 1985.

626.   Dinges, Bruce J. "The Victorio Campaign of 1880: Cooperation and Conflict on the United States–Mexico Border." *New Mexico Historical Review* 62 (1987): 81–94.

627.   Doyle, Susan Badger. "Indian Perspectives of the Bozeman Trail, 1864–1868." *Montana* 40 (winter 1990): 56–67.

628.   Fincher, Jack. "The Grisly Drama of the Modoc War and Captain Jack." *Smithsonian* 15, no. 11 (1985): 134–54.

629.   Gatewood, Charles B. "The Surrender of Geronimo." *Journal of Arizona History* 27 (1986): 53–70.

630.   Gibbon, John. *From Where the Sun Now Stands: A Manuscript of the Nez Perce War.* College Station: Texas A & M Press, 1988.

631.   Gibson, Arrell M. "The Centennial Legacy of the General Allotment Act." *Chronicles of Oklahoma* 65 (1987): 228–51.

632.   Hacker, Peter A. "Confusion and Conflict: A Study of Atypical Responses to Nineteenth Century Federal Indian Policies by the Citizen Band Potawatomies." *American Indian Culture and Research Journal* 13, no. 1 (1989): 79–95.

633.   Hagan, William T. "How the West Was Lost." Comments by Peter Iverson. In *The Impact of Indian History on the Teaching of United States History: Papers and Commentary from the 1986 Conference at Los Angeles,* 71–110. D'Arcy

McNickle Center for the History of the American Indian, Occasional Papers in Curriculum, no. 5. Chicago: Newberry Library, 1987.

634. ———. "How the West Was Lost." In *Indians in American History: An Introduction,* ed. F. E. Hoxie, 179–202. Arlington Heights, Ill.: Harlan Davidson, 1988.

635. ———. *The Indian Right Association: The Herbert Welsh Years, 1882–1904.* Tucson: University of Arizona Press, 1985.

636. ———. "Reformers' Images of the Native Americans: The Late Nineteenth Century." In *The American Indian Experience: A Profile, 1524 to the Present,* ed. P. Weeks, 207–17. Arlington Heights, Ill.: Forum Press, 1988.

637. ———. "United States Indian Policies, 1860–1900." In *History of Indian-White Relations,* ed. W. Washburn, 51–65. Vol. 4 of *Handbook of North American Indians,* ed. W. Sturtevant. Washington, D.C.: Smithsonian Institution Press, 1988.

638. **Hamilton, Allen Lee.** *Sentinel of the Southern Plains: Fort Richardson and the Northwest Texas Frontier, 1866–1878.* Dallas: Texas Christian University, 1988.

639. **Hardorff, Richard.** *The Custer Battle Casualties: Burials, Exhumations, and Reinterments.* El Segundo, Calif.: Upton and Sons, 1989.

640. **Hays, Lavern.** "The Panhandle Indian Scare of 1891." *True West* 34, no. 4 (1987): 44–49.

641. **Hedren, Paul L.** "Fort Laramie and the Sioux War of 1876." *South Dakota History* 17 (1987): 223–40.

642. ———. *Fort Laramie in 1876: Chronicles of a Frontier Post at War.* Lincoln: University of Nebraska Press, 1988.

643. ———. *With Crook in the Black Hills: Stanley J. Morrow's 1876 Photographic Legacy.* Boulder, Colo.: Pruett Publishing, 1985.

644. **Henriksson, Markku.** *The Indian on Capitol Hill: Indian Legislation and the United States Congress, 1862–1907.* Studia Historica, no. 25. Helsinki: Finnish Historical Society (Suomen Historiallien Seura), 1988.

645. **Hill, Michael D.,** and **Ben Innis,** eds. "The Fort Buford Diary of Private Sanford, 1876–1877." *North Dakota History* 52, no. 4 (1985): 2–40.

646. **Hoover, Herbert T.** "The Sioux Agreement of 1889 and Its Aftermath." *South Dakota History* 19 (1989): 56–94.

647. **Hosmer, Brian C.** "'Rescued from Extinction?': The Civilizing Program in Indian Territory." *Chronicles of Oklahoma* 48 (1990): 138–53.

648. **Hoxie, Frederick E.** "Crow Leadership Amidst Reservation Oppression." In *The Struggle for Political Autonomy: Papers and Comments from the Second Newberry Conference on Themes in American Indian History,* 94–106. D'Arcy McNickle Center for the History of the American Indian, Occasional Papers in Curriculum, no. 11. Chicago: Newberry Library, 1989.

649. **Huntzicker, William E.** "The 'Sioux Outbreak' in the Illustrated Press." *South Dakota History* 20 (1990): 299–322.

650. **Hutton, Paul,** ed. *Soldiers West: Biographies from the Military Frontier.* Lincoln: University of Nebraska Press, 1987.

651. **Jensen, Richard E.** "Agent to the Oto: The Recollections of Albert

Lamborn Green." *Nebraska History* 69, no. 4 (1988): 169–81.

652. ———. "Big Foot's Followers at Wounded Knee." *Nebraska History* 71, no. 4 (1990): 194–212.

653. Jones, Robert H. "Industrial Society and the Opening of the West: The American Indian in the Trans-Mississippi West and the Impact of the American Civil War." In *The American Indian Experience: A Profile, 1524 to the Present,* ed. P. Weeks, 121–35. Arlington Heights, Ill.: Forum Press, 1988.

654. Josephy, Alvin, Jr., Trudy Thomas, and Jeanne Eder. *Wounded Knee: Lest We Forget.* Cody, Wyo.: Buffalo Bill Historical Center, 1990.

655. Kenoi, Samuel E. "A Chiricahua Apache's Account of the Geronimo Campaign of 1886." *Journal of Arizona History* 27 (1986): 71–90. [Recorded by Morris E. Opler]

656. King, W. Kent. *Massacre: The Custer Cover-Up, the Original Maps of Custer's Battlefield.* El Segundo, Calif.: Upton and Sons, 1989.

657. Lang, William L. "Where Did the Nez Perces Go in Yellowstone in 1877?" *Montana* 40 (winter 1990): 14–29.

658. Lathrop, Alan K. "Another View of Wounded Knee." *South Dakota History* 16 (1986): 249–68.

659. Lekson, Stephen. *Nana's Raid: Apache Warfare in Southern New Mexico, 1881.* El Paso: Texas Western Press/ University of Texas, 1987.

660. McDonald, J. Douglas, A. L. McDonald, Bill Tallbull, and Ted Risingsun. "The 'Cheyenne Outbreak' Revisited: The Employment of Archaeological Methodology in the Substantia-

tion of Oral History." *Plains Anthropologist* 34, no. 145 (1989): 265–69.

661. McPherson, Robert S. "Boundaries, Bonanzas, and Bickering: Consolidation of the Northern Navajo Frontier, 1870–1905." *New Mexico Historical Review* 62 (1987): 169–90.

662. ———. *The Northern Navajo Frontier, 1860–1900: Expansion Through Adversity.* Albuquerque: University of New Mexico Press, 1988.

663. Mangum, Neil C. *Battle of the Rosebud: Prelude to the Little Big Horn.* El Segundo, Calif.: Upton and Sons, 1987.

664. Mark, Joan. *A Stranger in Her Native Land: Alice Fletcher and the American Indians.* Lincoln: University of Nebraska Press, 1988.

665. Mathes, Valerie Sherer. "Helen Hunt Jackson: A Legacy of Indian Reform." *Essays and Monographs in Colorado History* 4 (1986): 25–58.

666. ———. "Helen Hunt Jackson and the Campaign for Ponca Restitution, 1880–1881." *South Dakota History* 17 (1987): 23–41.

667. ———. *Helen Hunt Jackson and Her Indian Reform Legacy.* Austin: University of Texas Press, 1990.

668. ———. "Helen Hunt Jackson and the Ponca Controversy." *Montana* 39 (winter 1989): 42–53.

669. ———. "Nineteenth Century Women and Reform: The Women's National Indian Association." *American Indian Quarterly* 14 (1990): 1–18.

670. Metcalf, Warren. "A Precarious Balance: The Northern Utes and the Black Hawk War." *Utah Historical Quarterly* 57 (winter 1989): 24–35.

671. Munkres, Robert L. "Congress and the Indian: The Politics of Con-

quest." *Annals of Wyoming* 60, no. 1 (1988): 22–31.

672.   Nichols, Richard. "The United States, Canada, and the Indians, 1865–1876." *Social Science Journal* 26 (1989): 249–64.

673.   Nowicka, Ewa. "The 'Polish Movement Friends of the American Indians.'" In *Indians and Europe: An Interdisciplinary Collection of Essays,* ed. C. Feest, 599–608. Aachen, West Germany: Edition Herodot, 1987.

674.   Ogden, Annegret. "A Lady Tours the Wigwams: The Voice of Ida Pfeiffer, Amateur Ethnologist and Globe Trotter from Austria." *Californians* 7 (1990): 14–16.

675.   Osburn, Katherine Marie Birmingham. "The Navajo at the Bosque Redondo: Cooperation, Resistance, and Initiative, 1864–1868." *New Mexico Historical Review* 60 (1985): 399–413.

676.   Overfield, Lloyd J., II. *The Little Big Horn, 1876: The Official Communications, Documents, and Reports.* Lincoln: University of Nebraska Press, 1990.

677.   Pomerance, Bernard. *We Need to Dream All This Again: An Account of Crazy Horse, Custer, and the Battle for the Black Hills.* New York: Viking Press, 1987.

678.   Prucha, Francis Paul. "Rutherford B. Hayes Indian Peace Medal." *Hayes Historical Journal* 7 (spring 1988): 37–39.

679.   Robrock, David P. "The Seventh Cavalry and the Plains Indians Wars, 1861–66." *Montana* 39 (spring 1989): 2–17.

680.   Salisbury, Robert S. "William Windom, the Sioux, and Indian Affairs." *South Dakota History* 17 (1987): 202–22.

681.   Schilz, Thomas F. "Plight of the Tonkawas, 1875–1898." *Chronicles of Oklahoma* 64 (1987): 68–87.

682.   Schroenberger, Dale, ed. "A Trooper with Custer: Augustus de Voto's Account of the Little Big Horn." *Montana* 40 (winter 1990): 68–71.

683.   Scott, Douglas D., and Melissa A. Connor. "Post-mortem at the Little Bighorn." *Natural History* 95, no. 6 (1986): 46–55.

684.   Scott, Douglas D., and Richard A. Fox, Jr. *Archaeological Insights into the Custer Battle: An Assessment of the 1984 Field Season.* Norman: University of Oklahoma Press, 1987.

685.   Scott, Douglas D., Richard A. Fox, Jr., Melissa A. Connor, and Dick Hamon. *Archaeological Perspectives on the Battle of the Little Big Horn: The Final Report.* Norman: University of Oklahoma Press, 1989.

686.   Smith, Burton M. "Business, Politics, and Indian Land Settlements in Montana, 1882–1904." *Canadian Journal of History* 20, no. 1 (1985): 45–64.

687.   ———. "Politics and the Crow Indian Land Cessions, 1851–1904." *Montana* 36 (fall 1986): 24–37.

688.   Smith, Sherry L. *Sagebrush Soldier: Private William Earl Smith's View of the Sioux War of 1876.* Norman: University of Oklahoma Press, 1989.

689.   ———. *The View from Officers' Row: Army Perceptions of Western Indians.* Tucson: University of Arizona Press, 1990.

690.   ———. "A Window on Themselves: Perceptions of Indians by Military Officers and Their Wives." *New Mexico Historical Review* 64 (1989): 447–61.

691.   Sonnichsen, C. L. *Geronimo and*

the End of the Apache Wars. Tucson: Arizona Historical Society, 1987.

692. ——— ed. *Journal of Arizona History* (special issue commemorating the surrender of Geronimo and Naiche) 27 (spring 1986).

693. Stefon, Frederick J. "Richard Henry Pratt and His Indians." *Journal of Ethnic Studies* 15, no. 2 (1987): 86–114.

694. Steinbach, Robert H. "The Red River War of 1874–1875: Selected Correspondence Between Lieutenant Frank Baldwin and His Wife, Alice." *Southwestern Historical Quarterly* 93 (1990): 497–518.

695. Svaldi, David. *Sand Creek and the Rhetoric of Extermination: A Case Study in Indian-White Relations.* Lincoln: University of Nebraska Press, 1989.

696. Sweeney, Edwin R. "Cochise and the Prelude to the Bascom Affair." *New Mexico Historical Review* 64 (1989): 427–46.

697. Trafzer, Clifford E. *Northwest Tribes in Exile: Modoc, Nez Perce, and Palouse Removal to the Indian Territory.* Sacramento, Calif.: Sierra Oaks Publishing, 1987.

698. Trafzer, Clifford E., and Richard D. Scheuerman. "'This Land Is Your Land and You Are Being Robbed of It': Dispossession of Palouse Indian Land, 1860–1880." *Idaho Yesterdays* 29 (1986): 2–14.

699. Trennert, Robert A. "John H. Stout and the Grant Peace Policy Among the Pimas." *Arizona and the West* 28 (1986): 45–66.

700. Unrau, William E., and H. Craig Miner. *Tribal Dispossession and the Ottawa Indian University Fraud.* Norman: University of Oklahoma Press, 1985.

701. Utley, Robert M. *Cavalier in Buckskin: George Armstrong Custer and the Western Military Frontier.* Norman: University of Oklahoma Press, 1988.

702. ———. "Oliver Otis Howard." *New Mexico Historical Review* 62 (1987): 55–63.

703. ———. "War Houses in the Sioux Country." *Montana* 35 (fall 1985): 19–25.

704. Van West, Carroll. "Acculturation by Design: Architectural Determination and the Montana Indian Reservation, 1870–1930." *Great Plains Quarterly* 7 (1987): 91–102.

705. ——— ed. "Roughing It up the Yellowstone to Wonderland: An Account of a Trip Through the Yellowstone in 1878, by Colgate Hoyt." *Montana* 36, no. 2 (1986): 22–35. [Brother-in-law of Nelson A. Miles; tour included Custer battlefield with Northern Cheyenne]

706. Warde, Mary Jane. "Fight for Survival: The Indian Response to the Boomer Movement." *Chronicles of Oklahoma* 67 (1989): 30–51.

707. Wilfong, Cherry L. *Following the Nez Perce Trail: A Guide to the Nee-Me-Poo National Historical Trail with Eyewitness Accounts.* Corvallis: Oregon State University Press, 1990.

708. Winkler, Albert. "The Circleville Massacre: A Brutal Incident in Utah's Black Hawk War." *Utah Historical Quarterly* 55, no. 1 (1987): 4–21.

709. ———. "From War to Peace: Rutherford B. Hayes and the Administration of Indian Affairs, 1877–1881." *Old Northwest* 11 (1986): 149–72.

710. Wooster, Robert. "The Army and the Politics of Expansion: Texas and the Southwestern Borderlands, 1870–

1886." *Southwestern Historical Quarterly* 93 (1989): 151–68.

711. ———. *The Military and United States Indian Policy, 1865–1903.* New Haven, Conn.: Yale University Press, 1988.

712. **Young, Mary.** "Quakers, Wolves, and Make-Believe White Men: Assimilationist Indian Policy and Its Critics." *Journal of American Ethnic History* 4 (spring 1985): 92–97.

3.7   INDIAN-WHITE RELATIONS IN THE U.S.A., 1900–1945

713. **Anderson, H. Allen.** "Ernest Thompson Seton and the Woodcraft Indians." *Journal of American Culture* 8 (spring 1985): 43–50.

714. **Berthrong, Donald J.** "Legacies of the Dawes Act: Bureaucrats and Land Thieves at the Cheyenne-Arapaho Agencies of Oklahoma." In *The Plains Indians of the Twentieth Century,* ed. P. Iverson, 31–53. Norman: University of Oklahoma Press, 1985.

715. **Biolsi, Thomas.** "The IRA and the Politics of Acculturation: The Sioux Case." *American Anthropologist* 87 (1985): 656–59.

716. **Cash, Joseph,** and **Herbert T. Hoover.** "The Indian New Deal and the Years That Followed: Three Interviews." In *The Plains Indians of the Twentieth Century,* ed. P. Iverson, 107–32. Norman: University of Oklahoma Press, 1985.

717. **Chauduri, Joyotpaul.** "American Indian Policy: An Overview." In *American Indian Policy in the Twentieth Century,* ed. V. Deloria, Jr., 15–33. Norman: University of Oklahoma Press, 1985.

718. **Clayton, Lawrence A.** "The Columbian Exchange Five Hundred

Years Later." *Bulletin of the Society for Spanish and Portuguese Studies* 10 (January 1985): 4–8.

719. **Clow, Richmond L.** "Cattlemen and Tribal Rights: The Standing Rock Leasing Conflict of 1902." *North Dakota History* 54, no. 2 (1987): 23–30.

720. ———. "The Indian Reorganization Act and the Loss of Tribal Sovereignty: Constitutions on the Rosebud and Pine Ridge Reservations." *Great Plains Quarterly* 7 (1987): 125–34.

721. ———. "The Lakota Ghost Dance After 1890." *South Dakota History* 20 (1990): 323–33.

722. **Covington, James W.** "Formation of the State of Florida Indian Reservation." *Florida Historical Quarterly* 64 (1985): 62–75.

723. **Deloria, Vine, Jr.** "The Evolution of Federal Indian Policy Making." In *American Indian Policy in the Twentieth Century,* ed. V. Deloria, Jr., 239–56. Norman: University of Oklahoma Press, 1985.

724. ——— ed. *American Indian Policy in the Twentieth Century.* Norman: University of Oklahoma Press, 1985.

725. **Dinwoodie, David H.** "Indians, Hispanos, and Land Reform: New Deal Struggle in New Mexico." *Western Historical Quarterly* 17 (1986): 291–323.

726. **Finger, John.** "Conscription, Citizenship, and 'Civilization': World War I and the Eastern Band of the Cherokee." *North Carolina Historical Review* 63 (1986): 283–307.

727. **Franco, Jere.** "Bringing Them in Alive: Selective Service and Native Americans." *Journal of Ethnic Studies* 18, no. 3 (1990): 1–28.

728. ———. "Loyal and Heroic Ser-

vice: The Navajos and World War II."
Journal of Arizona History 27 (1986):
391–406.

729. **Fritz, Henry E.** "The Last Hurrah of Christian Humanitarian Indian Reform: The Board of Indian Commissioners, 1909–1918." *Western Historical Quarterly* 16 (1985): 147–62.

730. **Gibson, Arrell M.** "To Kill a Nation: Liquidation of the Five Indian Republics." In *The American Indian Experience: A Profile, 1524 to the Present,* ed. P. Weeks, 189–203. Arlington Heights, Ill.: Forum Press, 1988.

731. **Hafford, William E.** "The Navajo Code Talkers." *Arizona Highways* 65 (February 1989): 36–45.

732. **Hagan, William T.** "Adjusting to the Opening of the Kiowa, Comanche, and Kiowa-Apache Reservations." In *The Plains Indians of the Twentieth Century,* ed. P. Iverson, 11–30. Norman: University of Oklahoma Press, 1985.

733. **Hampton, Carol.** "The American Indian Religious Freedom Act: Its Antecedents and Its Future." In *Native Views of Indian-White Historical Relations,* ed. D. L. Fixico, 128–42. D'Arcy McNickle Center for the History of the American Indian, Occasional Papers in Curriculum, no. 7. Chicago: Newberry Library, 1989.

734. **Harring, Sidney L.** "Crazy Snake and the Creek Struggle for Sovereignty: Native American Legal Culture and American Law." In *The Struggle for Political Autonomy: Papers and Comments from the Second Newberry Conference on Themes in American Indian History,* 107–24. D'Arcy McNickle Center for the History of the American Indian, Occasional Papers in Curriculum, no. 11. Chicago: Newberry Library, 1989.

735. **Hauptman, Laurence M.** "Africa View: John Collier, the British Colonial Service, and American Indian Policy, 1933–1945." *Historian* 48 (1986): 53–59.

736. **Haycox, Stephen.** "Alaska Native Brotherhood Conventions: Sites and Grand Officers, 1914–1959." *Alaska History* 4 (fall 1989): 38–46.

737. **Hillman, James R.** *History of the Michigan Commission of Indian Affairs.* Clinton, Ohio: Hillman Publishers, 1986.

738. **Holm, Tom.** "Fighting a White Man's War: The Extent and Legacy of Indian Participation in World War II." In *The Plains Indians of the Twentieth Century,* ed. P. Iverson, 149–68. Norman: University of Oklahoma Press, 1985.

739. **Hoxie, Frederick E.** "The Curious Story of Reformers and the American Indians." In *Indians in American History: An Introduction,* ed. F. E. Hoxie, 205–28. Arlington Heights, Ill.: Harlan Davidson, 1988.

740. ———. "From Prison to Homeland: The Cheyenne River Reservation Before World War I." In *The Plains Indians of the Twentieth Century,* ed. P. Iverson, 55–75. Norman: University of Oklahoma Press, 1985.

741. **Kelly, Lawrence.** "United States Indian Policies, 1900–1980." In *History of Indian-White Relations,* ed. W. Washburn, 66–80. Vol. 4 of *Handbook of North American Indians,* ed. W. Sturtevant. Washington, D.C.: Smithsonian Institution Press, 1988.

742. **Kersey, Harry A., Jr.** *The Florida Seminoles and the New Deal: 1933–1942.* Boca Raton: Florida Atlantic University Press, 1989.

743. ———. "Florida Seminoles in the Depression and New Deal, 1933–1942: An Indian Perspective." *Florida Historical Quarterly* 65 (1986): 175–95.

744. ———. "The New Red Atlantis: John Collier's Encounter with the Florida Seminoles in 1935." *Florida Historical Quarterly* 66 (1987): 131–51.

745. ———. "The Tony Tommie Letter, 1916: A Transitional Seminole Document." *Florida Historical Quarterly* 64 (1986): 301–14.

746. Kidwell, Clara Sue. "The Choctaw Struggle for Land and Identity in Mississippi, 1830–1918." In *After Removal: The Choctaw in Mississippi,* ed. S. J. Wells and R. Tubby, 64–93. Jackson: University Press of Mississippi, 1985.

747. Lacy, Michael G. "The United States and American Indians: Political Relations." In *American Indian Policy in the Twentieth Century,* ed. V. Deloria, Jr., 83–104. Norman: University of Oklahoma Press, 1985.

748. Lawson, Michael L. "Federal Water Projects and Indian Lands: The Pick-Sloan Plan, a Case Study." In *The Plains Indians of the Twentieth Century,* ed. P. Iverson, 169–85. Norman: University of Oklahoma Press, 1985.

749. Lopach, James J., Margery H. Brown, and Richmond L. Clow. *Tribal Government Today: Politics on Montana Indian Reservations.* Boulder, Colo.: Westview Press, 1990.

750. McPherson, Robert S. "Navajos, Mormons, and Henry L. Mitchell: Cauldron of Conflict on the San Juan." *Utah Historical Quarterly* 55, no. 1 (1987): 50–65.

751. Martin, Jill E. "'Neither Fish, Flesh, Fowl, nor Good Red Herring': The Citizenship Status of American Indians, 1830–1924." *Journal of the West* 29 (July 1990): 75–87.

752. Matsen, William E. "The Battle of Sugar Point: A Re-examination." *Minnesota History* 50 (1987): 269–75.

753. Meyer, Melissa L. "Signature and Thumbprints: Ethnicity Among the White Earth Anishinaabeg, 1889–1920." *Social Science History* 14, no. 3 (1990): 305–45.

754. Murray, Paul T. "Who Is an Indian? Who Is a Negro? Virginia Indians in the World War II Draft." *Virginia Magazine of History and Biography* 95 (1987): 215–31.

755. Nash, Philleo. "Twentieth-Century United States Government Agencies." In *History of Indian-White Relations,* ed. W. Washburn, 264–75. Vol. 4 of *Handbook of North American Indians,* ed. W. Sturtevant. Washington, D.C.: Smithsonian Institution Press, 1988.

756. Nelson, Robert A., and Joseph F. Sheley. "Bureau of Indian Affairs Influence on Indian Self-Determination." In *American Indian Policy in the Twentieth Century,* ed. V. Deloria, Jr., 177–96. Norman: University of Oklahoma Press, 1985.

757. Ortiz, Gilbert. "Acoma Pueblo Lands and the Railroads in the Southwest." In *Native Views of Indian-White Historical Relations,* ed. D. L. Fixico, 105–17. D'Arcy McNickle Center for the History of the American Indian, Occasional Papers in Curriculum, no. 7. Chicago: Newberry Library, 1989.

758. Roberts, Charles. "The Second Choctaw Removal, 1903." In *After Removal: The Choctaw in Mississippi,* ed. S. J. Wells and R. Tubby, 94–110. Jackson: University Press of Mississippi, 1985.

759. Rusco, Elmer R. "Formation of the Reno-Sparks Tribal Council, 1934–

1939." *Nevada Historical Society Quarterly* 30 (1987): 316–39.

760. ———. "Purchasing Lands for Nevada Indian Colonies, 1916–17." *Nevada Historical Society Quarterly* 32 (1989): 1–22.

761. **Samek, Hana.** *The Blackfoot Confederacy, 1880–1920: A Comparative Study of Canadian and U.S. Indian Policy.* Albuquerque: University of New Mexico Press, 1987.

762. **Shoemaker, Nancy.** "Urban Indians and Ethnic Choices: American Indian Organizations in Minneapolis, 1920–1950." *Western Historical Quarterly* 19 (1988): 431–47.

763. **Smith, Ralph A.** "The Comanches' Foreign War: Fighting Head Hunters in the Tropics." *Great Plains Journal* 24/25 (1985/86): 21–44.

764. **Stuart, Paul.** "Administrative Reform in Indian Affairs." *Western Historical Quarterly* 16, no. 2 (1985): 133–46.

765. **Svingen, Orlan J.** "Jim Crow, Indian Style." *American Indian Quarterly* 11 (1987): 275–86.

766. **Tate, Michael L.** "From Scout to Doughboy: The National Debate over Integrating American Indians into the Military, 1891–1918." *Western Historical Quarterly* 17 (1986): 417–43.

767. ———. "Pershing's Pets: Apache Scouts in the Mexican Punitive Expedition of 1916." *New Mexico Historical Review* 66 (1990): 49–71.

768. **Taylor, Graham D.** "The Divided Heart: The Indian New Deal." In *The American Indian Experience: A Profile, 1524 to the Present,* ed. P. Weeks, 240–59. Arlington Heights, Ill.: Forum Press, 1988.

769. **Weil, Richard H.** "Destroying a Homeland: White Earth, Minnesota." *American Indian Culture and Research Journal* 13, no. 2 (1989): 69–96.

770. **Wilson, Terry P.** "Scarred Earth, Scarred People: The Osages and Oil on Allotted Lands." In *Native Views of Indian-White Historical Relations,* ed. D. L. Fixico, 93–103. D'Arcy McNickle Center for the History of the American Indian, Occasional Papers in Curriculum, no. 7. Chicago: Newberry Library, 1989.

771. ———. *The Underground Reservation: Osage Oil.* Lincoln: University of Nebraska Press, 1985.

772. **Zanjani, Sally S.** "'Totell Disregard to the Welfair of the Indians': The Longstreet-Bradfute Controversy at Moapa Reservation." *Nevada Historical Society Quarterly* 29 (1986): 241–53.

3.8   INDIAN-WHITE RELATIONS IN THE U.S.A., 1945–1990

773. "American Indian Governments in the Reagan Era." *American Indian Culture and Research Journal* (special issue) 10, no. 2 (1986).

774. **Anders, Gary C.** "The Alaska Native Experience with the Alaska Native Claims Settlement Act." In *The Struggle for the Land: Indigenous Insight and Industrial Empire in the Semiarid World,* ed. P. A. Olson, 127–45. Lincoln: University of Nebraska Press, 1990.

775. **Bronitsky, Gordon.** "Indian Assimilation in the El Paso Area." *New Mexico Historical Review* 62 (1987): 151–68.

776. ———. "Isleta's Unsung Hero: Veteran's Toughest Fight Earns Voting Rights." *New Mexico Magazine* 67, no. 8 (1989): 85–91. [Miguel Trujillo]

777. **Burt, Larry W.** "Nowhere Left to Go: Montana's Crees, Métis, and Chippewas and the Creation of Rocky Boy's Reservation." *Great Plains Historical Quarterly* 7 (1987): 195–209.

778. ———. "Roots of the Native American Urban Experience: Relocation Policy in the 1950s." *American Indian Quarterly* 10 (1986): 85–99.

779. **Churchill, Ward,** and **Vander Wall, Jim.** *Agents of Repression: The FBI's Secret Wars Against the Black Panther Party and the American Indian Movement.* Boston: South End Press, 1988.

780. **Clark, Carter Blue.** "Bury My Heart in Smog: Urban Indians." In *The American Indian Experience: A Profile, 1524 to the Present,* ed. P. Weeks, 279–91. Arlington Heights, Ill.: Forum Press, 1988.

781. **Clemmer, Richard O.** "Hopis, Western Shoshones, and Southern Utes: Three Different Responses to the Indian Reorganization Act of 1934." *American Indian Culture and Research Journal* 10, no. 2 (1986): 15–40.

782. **Cornell, George L.** "American Indian Influences on the Formation of the Modern Conservation Ethic." In *Native Views of Indian-White Historical Relations,* ed. D. L. Fixico, 178–89. D'Arcy McNickle Center for the History of the American Indian, Occasional Papers in Curriculum, no. 7. Chicago: Newberry Library, 1989.

783. **Cornell, Stephen.** "American Indians, American Dreams, and the Meaning of Success." *American Indian Culture and Research Journal* 11, no. 4 (1987): 59–70.

784. ———. "The New Indian Politics." *Wilson Quarterly* 10, no. 1 (1986): 113–31.

785. ———. *The Return of the Native:*
American Indian Political Resurgence. New York: Oxford University Press, 1988.

786. **Covington, James M.** "Formation of the State of Florida Indian Reservation." *Florida Historical Quarterly* 64 (1985): 62–75.

787. **De La Cruz, Joseph.** "Indian Self-Determination: The Real and Indian Self-Government: The Reality." In *The Struggle for Political Autonomy: Papers and Comments from the Second Newberry Conference on Themes in American Indian History,* 162–70. D'Arcy McNickle Center for the History of the American Indian, Occasional Papers in Curriculum, no. 11. Chicago: Newberry Library, 1989.

788. **Deverell, William F.** "The Return of Blue Lake to the Taos Pueblo." *Princeton University Library Chronicle* 49, no. 1 (1987): 57–73.

789. **Dewing, Rolland.** *Wounded Knee: The Meaning and Significance of the Second Incident.* New York: Irvington, 1985.

790. **Drinnon, Richard.** *Keeper of Concentration Camps: Dillon S. Myer and American Racism.* Berkeley: University of California Press, 1986.

791. **Elston, Catherine Feher.** *Children of Sacred Ground: America's Last Indian War.* Flagstaff, Ariz.: Northland Publishing, 1988. [Navajo/Hopi]

792. **Fenton, William N.** "Return of Eleven Wampum Belts to the Six Nations Iroquois Confederacy on Grand River, Canada." *Ethnohistory* 36, no. 4 (1989): 329–410.

793. **Fixico, Donald L.** "Dislocated: The Federal Policy of Termination and Relocation, 1945–60." In *The American Indian Experience: A Profile, 1524 to the Present,* ed. P. Weeks, 260–77. Arlington Heights, Ill.: Forum Press, 1988.

794. ———. "The Muskogee Creeks: A Nativistic People." In *Between Two Worlds: The Survival of Twentieth Century Indians,* ed. A. M. Gibson, 30–43. Oklahoma City: Oklahoma Historical Society, 1986.

795. ———. *Termination and Relocation: Federal Indian Policy, 1945–1960.* Albuquerque: University of New Mexico Press, 1986.

796. ———. "Tribal Governments and the Struggle Against Termination." In *The Struggle for Political Autonomy: Papers and Comments from the Second Newberry Conference on Themes in American Indian History,* 137–45. D'Arcy McNickle Center for the History of the American Indian, Occasional Papers in Curriculum no. 11. Chicago: Newberry Library, 1989.

797. ———. "Tribal Leaders and the Demand for Natural Energy Resources on Reservation Lands." In *The Plains Indians of the Twentieth Century,* ed. P. Iverson, 219–35. Norman: University of Oklahoma Press, 1985.

798. Gibson, Arrell M., ed. *Between Two Worlds: The Survival of Twentieth Century Indians.* Oklahoma City: Oklahoma Historical Society, 1986.

799. Glenn, J. L. "Dr. Glenn Struggles for Seminole Improvement." *Broward Legacy* 8 (summer/fall 1985): 36–44. [1935 Florida Seminole Agency report]

800. Greenbaum, S. D. "In Search of Lost Tribes: Anthropology and the Federal Acknowledgement Process." *Human Organization* 44 (1985): 361–67.

801. Gross, Emma R. *Contemporary Federal Policy Toward American Indians.* New York: Greenwood Press, 1989.

802. Hansen, Ramona Soza. "Native American Fishing Industry Under the Alaska Reorganization Act, 1936–1960." In *Native Views of Indian-White Historical Relations,* ed. D. L. Fixico, 142–56. D'Arcy McNickle Center for the History of the American Indian, Occasional Papers in Curriculum, no. 7. Chicago: Newberry Library, 1989.

803. Hauptman, Laurence M. "Circle the Wagons." *Capital Region* 2 (1987): 29–31, 52–53. [New York State versus the Indians]

804. ———. *Contemporary Iroquois and the Struggle for Survival: From World War II to the Emergence of Red Power.* Syracuse, N.Y.: Syracuse University Press, 1985.

805. ———. *Forming American Indian Policy in New York State, 1970–1986.* Albany: SUNY Press, 1988.

806. ———. "Learning the Lessons of History: The Oneidas of Wisconsin Reject Termination, 1943–1956." *Journal of Ethnic Studies* 14, no. 3 (1986): 31–52.

807. Hauptman, Laurence M., and Jack Campisi. "The Voice of Eastern Indians: The American Indian Chicago Conference of 1961 and the Movement for Federal Recognition." *Proceedings of the American Philosophical Society* 132 (1988): 316–29.

808. Hendricks, Charles. "The Eskimos and the Defense of Alaska." *Pacific Historical Review* 54 (1985): 271–95.

809. Hertzberg, Hazel Whitman. "Indian Rights Movement, 1887–1973." In *History of Indian-White Relations,* ed. W. Washburn, 305–23. Vol. 4 of *Handbook of North American Indians,* ed. W. Sturtevant. Washington, D.C.: Smithsonian Institution Press, 1988.

810. Hoffman, Thomas J. "Native Americans and Contemporary Politics: The General Social Survey, 1972–1984."

Free Inquiry in Creative Sociology 15 (1987): 151–55.

811.   Holm, Tom. "The Crisis in Tribal Government." In *American Indian Policy in the Twentieth Century,* ed. V. Deloria, Jr., 135–54. Norman: University of Oklahoma Press, 1985.

812.   ———. "Mechanistic Versus Organic Human-Land Relationships: The Navajo-Hopi Joint Use Area Dispute as a Case Study." In *Native Views of Indian-White Historical Relations,* ed. D. L. Fixico, 167–76. D'Arcy McNickle Center for the History of the American Indian, Occasional Papers in Curriculum, no. 7. Chicago: Newberry Library, 1989.

813.   Iverson, Peter. "Building and Self-Determination: Plains and Southwestern Indians in the 1940s and 1950s." *Western Historical Quarterly* 16 (1985): 163–73.

814.   ———. "Cowboys and Indians, Stockman and Aborigines: The Rural American West and the Northern Territory of Australia Since 1945." *Social Science Journal* 26 (1989): 1–14.

815.   ———. "Cowboys, Indians, and the Modern West." *Arizona and the West* 28 (1986): 107–44.

816.   ———. "Knowing the Land, Leaving the Land: Navajos, Hopis, and Relocation in the American West." *Montana* 38 (winter 1988): 67–70.

817.   Jaimes, M. Annette. "The Hollow Icon: An American Indian Analysis of the Kennedy Myth and Federal Indian Policy." *Wicazo Sa Review* 4 (spring 1990): 34–44.

818.   Joe, Jennie R. "Forced Relocation and Assimilation: Dillon Myer and the Native American." *Amerasia Journal* 13, no. 2 (1986/87): 161–65.

819.   ——— ed. *American Indian Policy and Cultural Values: Conflict and Accommodation.* Los Angeles: American Indian Study Center, University of California—Los Angeles, 1986.

820.   Jorgensen, Joseph G. "Federal Policies, American Indian Polities, and the 'New Federalism.'" *American Indian Culture and Research Journal* 10, no. 2 (1986): 1–14.

821.   ———. "Sovereignty and the Structure of Dependency at Northern Ute." *American Indian Culture and Research Journal* 10, no. 2 (1986): 75–83.

822.   Josephy, Alvin M., Jr. "The Impacts of Recent American Indian History." Comments by Robert L. Bee and William H. Tuttle. In *The Impact of Indian History on the Teaching of United States History: Proceedings of the 1984 Chicago Conference, Sessions 3–4,* 1–37. D'Arcy McNickle Center for the History of the American Indian, Occasional Papers in Curriculum, no. 3. Chicago: Newberry Library, 1985.

823.   ———. "Modern America and the Indian." In *Indians in American History: An Introduction,* ed. F. E. Hoxie, 251–72. Arlington Heights, Ill.: Harlan Davidson, 1988.

824.   Kersey, Harry A., Jr. "'Give Us Twenty-Five Years': Florida Seminoles from near Termination to Self-Determination, 1953–1957." *Florida Historical Quarterly* 67 (January 1989): 290–309.

825.   Kloberdanz, Timothy J. "In the Land of the 'Inyan Woslata': Plains Indian Influences on Reservation Whites." *Great Plains Quarterly* 7 (1987): 69–82.

826.   Landsman, Gail H. "Ganienkeh: Symbol and Politics in an Indian-

White Conflict." *American Anthropologist* 87, no. 4 (1985): 826–39.

827. ———. "Indian Activism and the Press: Coverage of the Conflict at Ganienkeh." *Anthropological Quarterly* 60 (1988): 101–13.

828. ———. *Sovereignty and Symbol: Indian-White Conflict at Ganienkeh.* Albuquerque: University of New Mexico Press, 1988.

829. **Lopach, James,** et al. *Tribal Government Today: Politics on Montana Indian Reservations.* Boulder, Colo.: Westview Press, 1990.

830. **Lurie, Nancy O.** "The Contemporary American Indian Scene." In *North American Indians in Historical Perspective,* ed. E. B. Leacock and N. O. Lurie, 418–80. Prospect Heights, Ill.: Waveland Press, 1988.

831. **McCool, Daniel.** "Indian Voting." In *American Indian Policy in the Twentieth Century,* ed. V. Deloria, Jr., 105–33. Norman: University of Oklahoma Press, 1985.

832. **McGuire, Thomas R.** "Federal Indian Policy: A Framework for Evaluation." *Human Organization* 49 (1990): 206–16.

833. **McNabb, Steven.** "Impacts of Federal Policy Decisions on Alaska Natives." *Journal of Ethnic Studies* 18, no. 1 (1990): 111–26.

834. **McNickle, D'Arcy.** "Americans Called Indians." In *North American Indians in Historical Perspective,* ed. E. B. Leacock and N. O. Lurie, 29–63. Prospect Heights, Ill.: Waveland Press, 1988.

835. **Minugh, Carol J., Glen T. Morris,** and **Rudolf C. Ryser.** *Indian Self Governance: Perspective on the Political Status of Indian Nations in the United States of America.* Kenmore, Wash.: Center for World Indigenous Studies, 1989.

836. **Nichols, Roger L.** "Indians in the Post-termination Era." *Storia Nordamericana* 5, no. 1 (1988): 71–88.

837. ———. "Native American Survival in an Integrationist Society." *Journal of American Ethnic History* 10 (fall 1990): 87–93.

838. ———. "Something Old, Something New: Indians Since World War II." In *The American Indian Experience: A Profile, 1524 to the Present,* ed. P. Weeks, 292–312. Arlington Heights, Ill.: Forum Press, 1988.

839. **O'Brien, Sharon.** *American Indian Tribal Governments.* Norman: University of Oklahoma Press, 1989.

840. ———. "Federal Indian Policies and the International Protection of Human Rights." In *American Indian Policy in the Twentieth Century,* ed. V. Deloria, Jr., 35–61. Norman: University of Oklahoma Press, 1985.

841. **Parlow, Anita.** *Cry, Sacred Ground: Big Mountain, USA.* Washington, D.C.: Christic Institute, 1988.

842. **Parman, Donald L.** "Indians in the Twentieth Century." In *The Impact of Indian History on the Teaching of United States History: Papers and Commentary from the 1985 Conference at the Smithsonian Institution, Washington, D.C.,* 95–134. D'Arcy McNickle Center for the History of the American Indian, Occasional Papers in Curriculum, no. 4. Chicago: Newberry Library, 1986.

843. **Peyer, Bernd C.** "Who Is Afraid of AIM?" In *Indians and Europe: An Interdisciplinary Collection of Essays,* ed. C. Feest, 551–64. Aachen, West Germany: Edition Herodot, 1987.

844. **Philp, Kenneth R.** "Dillon S.

Meyer and the Advent of Termination: 1950–1953." *Western Historical Quarterly* 19 (1988): 37–60.

845. ———. *Indian Self-Rule: First-hand Accounts of Indian-White Relations from Roosevelt to Reagan.* Salt Lake City, Utah: Howe Brothers, 1986.

846. ———. "Stride Toward Freedom: The Relocation of Indians to Cities, 1952–1960." *Western Historical Quarterly* 16 (1985): 175–90.

847. **Porter, Frank W., III.** "In Search of Recognition: Federal Indian Policy and the Landless Tribes of Western Washington." *American Indian Quarterly* 14 (1990): 113–32.

848. **Preston, Douglas.** "Skeletons in Our Museums' Closets." *Harpers* 278 (February 1989): 66–70.

849. **Quinn, William W., Jr.** "The Southwest Syndrome: Notes on Indian Descendant Recruitment Organizations and Their Perceptions of Native American Culture." *American Indian Quarterly* 14 (1990): 147–56.

850. **Ragsdale, Fred L.** "The Deception of Geography." In *American Indian Policy in the Twentieth Century,* ed. V. Deloria, Jr., 63–82. Norman: University of Oklahoma Press, 1985.

851. ———. "A Non-fly in Amber: The Modes of Tribal Government." In *The Struggle for Political Autonomy: Papers and Comments from the Second Newberry Conference on Themes in American Indian History,* 146–58. D'Arcy McNickle Center for the History of the American Indian, Occasional Papers in Curriculum, no. 11. Chicago: Newberry Library, 1989.

852. **Redhouse, John.** *The Forgotten Long Walk: When the Navajos Had Too Many People.* Albuquerque, N.Mex.: Redhouse/Wright Productions, 1986.

853. ———. *Geopolitics of the Navajo-Hopi Land Dispute.* Albuquerque, N.Mex.: Redhouse/Wright Productions, 1985.

854. ———. *Holy Land: A Navajo Pilgrimage Back to Dinetah.* Albuquerque, N.Mex.: Redhouse/Wright Productions, 1985.

855. **Robbins, Lynn A.** "Upper Skagit (Washington) and Gambell (Alaska) Indian Reorganization Act Governments: Struggles with Constraints, Restraints, and Power." *American Indian Culture and Research Journal* 10, no. 2 (1986): 61–75.

856. **Robbins, Rebecca L.** "The Forgotten American: A Foundation for Contemporary Indian Self-Determination." *Wicazo Sa Review* 4 (spring 1990): 27–33.

857. **Rudnicki, Walter.** "The Politics of Aggression: Indian Termination in the 1980s." *Native Studies Review* 3, no. 1 (1987): 81–94.

858. **Schroeder, Aribert.** "'They Lived Together with Their Dogs and Horses': 'Indian Copy' in West German Newspapers, 1968–1982." In *Indians and Europe: An Interdisciplinary Collection of Essays,* ed. C. Feest, 527–50. Aachen, West Germany: Edition Herodot, 1987.

859. **Sills, Marc.** "Relocation Reconsidered: Competing Explanations of the Navajo-Hopi Land Settlement Act of 1974." *Journal of Ethnic Studies* 14, no. 3 (1986): 53–83.

860. **Sklansky, Jeff.** "Rock, Reservation, and Prison: The Native American Occupation of Alcatraz Island." *American Indian Culture and Research Journal* 13, no. 1 (1989): 29–68.

861. **Stuart, Paul H.** "Financing Self-Determination: Federal Indian Ex-

penditures, 1975–88." *American Indian Culture and Research Journal* 14, no. 2 (1990): 1–18.

862. **Stull, Donald D., Jerry A. Schultz, and Ken Cadue, Sr.** "Rights Without Resources: The Rise and Fall of the Kansas Kickapoo." *American Indian Culture and Research Journal* 10, no. 2 (1986): 41–60.

863. **United States Senate.** "A Report of the Special Committee on Investigations of the Select Committee on Indian Affairs." *Final Report and Legislative Recommendations.* Washington, D.C.: U.S. Government Printing Office, 1989. [Review of policy and a call for "New Federalism"]

864. **Weber, Kenneth.** "Demographic Shifts in Eastern Montana Reservation Counties: An Emerging Native American Political Base?" *Journal of Ethnic Studies* 16, no. 4 (1989): 101–16.

865. **Welch, Michael E.** "Community, the West, and the American Indian." *Journal of the Southwest* 31 (1989): 141–58.

866. **West, W. Richard, Jr., and Kevin Gover.** "Indians in United States Civil Rights History." In *The Impact of Indian History on the Teaching of United States History: Papers and Commentary from the 1985 Conference at the Smithsonian Institution, Washington, D.C.,* 135–70. D'Arcy McNickle Center for the History of the American Indian, Occasional Papers in Curriculum, no. 4. Chicago: Newberry Library, 1986.

867. ———. "The Struggle for Indian Civil Rights." In *Indians in American History: An Introduction,* ed. F. E. Hoxie, 275–93. Arlington Heights, Ill.: Harlan Davidson, 1988.

868. **Willard, C. William.** "The Comparative Political History of Two Tribal Governments." *Wicazo Sa Review* 6 (spring 1990): 56–62.

3.9 INDIAN-WHITE RELATIONS IN CANADA, 1775–1990

869. **Abel, Kerry M.** "Lost Tribes?" *Canadian Review of American Studies* 18, no. 3 (1987): 407–12.

870. **Angus, James T.** "How the Dokis Indians Protected Their Timber." *Ontario History* 81 (1989): 181–200.

871. **Barron, F. L., and James B. Waldram,** eds. *1885 and After: Native Society in Transition.* Regina, Sask.: Canadian Plains Research Center, University of Regina, 1986.

872. **Barsh, Russell L.** "Europe's Role in Displacing Native Canadians." In *Indians and Europe: An Interdisciplinary Collection of Essays,* ed. C. Feest, 565–83. Aachen, West Germany: Edition Herodot, 1987.

873. **Bartlett, Richard H.** *Indian Reserves and Aboriginal Lands in Canada: A Homeland.* Saskatoon: University of Saskatchewan Native Law Centre, 1990.

874. **Burnat, Jim.** "Native-European Relations, Indian Treaties, and Surrenders." *Archivist* 16 (November/December 1989): 2–3.

875. **Carter, Sarah.** "A Fate Worse than Death." *Beaver* 68 (April/May 1988): 21–28.

876. ———. *Lost Harvests: Prairie Indian Reserve Farmers and Government Policy.* Montreal: McGill-Queens University Press, 1990.

877. ———. "Two Acres and a Cow: 'Peasant' Farming for the Indians of the Northwest, 1889–97." *Canadian Historical Review* 70 (1989): 27–52.

878. **Clancy, Peter.** "The Making of Eskimo Policy in Canada, 1952–62: The

Life and Times of the Eskimo Affairs Committee." *Arctic* 40 (1987): 191–97.

879. **Clark, Bruce.** *Native Liberty, Crown Sovereignty: The Existing Aboriginal Right of Self-Government in Canada.* Montreal: McGill-Queens University Press, 1990.

880. **Cole, Douglas, and Ira Chaikin.** *An Iron Hand upon the People: The Law Against the Potlatch on the Northwest Coast.* Seattle: University of Washington Press, 1990.

881. **Coon-coon, Gran Chief Matthew.** "Indian Rights in Canada: An International Issue." *Saskatchewan Indian Federated College Journal* 4, no. 2 (1988): 91–98.

882. **Cozzetto, Don.** "Governance and Aboriginal Claims in Northern Canada." *American Indian Culture and Research Journal* 14, no. 2 (1990): 39–53.

883. **Cumming, Peter.** *Native People's Rights.* Toronto: Edmond Montgomery Publications, 1986.

884. **Cuthand, Stan.** "Poundmaker's Surrender." *Saskatchewan Indian* 16 (September 1988): 14–15.

885. **Daniels, Douglas.** "The Coming Crisis in the Aboriginal Rights Movement: From Colonialism to Neo-Colonialism to Renaissance." *Native Studies Review* 2, no. 2 (1986): 97–116.

886. **Dempsey, Hugh A.,** ed. "Calgary and the Riel Rebellion." *Alberta History* 33, no. 2 (1985): 7–18.

887. **Dempsey, James.** "Problems of Western Canadian Indian War Veterans After World War One." *Native Studies Review* 5, no. 2 (1989): 1–18.

888. **Dickason, Olive P.** "Frontiers in Transition: Nova Scotia, 1713–1763, Compared to the North-West, 1869–

1885." In *1885 and After: Native Society in Transition,* ed. F. L. Barron and J. B. Waldram, 23–38. Regina, Sask.: Canadian Plains Reserach Center, University of Regina, 1986.

889. **Driben, Paul.** "Revisiting the RCNE: An Evaluation of the Recommendations Made by the Royal Commission on the Northern Environment Concerning the Native People in Northern Ontario." *Native Studies Review* 2, no. 1 (1986): 45–67.

890. **Duffy, R. Quinn.** *The Road to Nunavut: The Progress of the Eastern Arctic Inuit Since the Second World War.* Montreal: McGill-Queens University Press, 1988.

891. **Elias, P. D.** "Aboriginal Rights and Litigation: History and Future of Court Decisions in Canada." *Polar Record* 25 (1989): 1–9.

892. **Fisher, Robin, and Kenneth Coates,** eds. *Out of the Background: Readings on Canadian Native History.* Toronto: Copp, Clark, Pitman Ltd., 1988.

893. **Flanagan, Thomas.** "Louis Riel and the Dispersion of the American Métis." *Minnesota History* 49 (1985): 179–90.

894. ———. "Louis Riel: Was He Really Crazy?" In *1885 and After: Native Society in Transition,* ed. F. L. Barron and J. B. Waldram, 105–40. Regina, Sask.: Canadian Plains Research Center, University of Regina, 1986.

895. ———. "The Sovereignty and Nationhood of Canadian Indians: A Comment on Boldt and Long." *Canadian Journal of Political Science* 18 (June 1985): 367–74.

896. **Full, Peter.** "Building Nunavut: A Story of Inuit Self-Government." *Northern Review* 1 (1988): 59–72.

897.   Gaffen, Fred. *Forgotten Soldiers: An Illustrated History of Canada's Native Peoples in Both World Wars.* Penticition, B.C.: Theytus Books, 1985.

898.   Gooderham, George M. "The Gypsy Indians and the Last Treaty." *Alberta History* 34, no. 3 (1986): 15–19. [Crees and Ojibwa in Saskatchewan]

899.   Grescher, Donna. "Introduction" and "Selected Documents from the Assembly of Manitoba Chiefs of the Meech Lake Accord." *Native Studies Review* 6, no. 1 (1990): 119–52.

900.   Hildebrandt, Walter. *The Battle of Batoche: British Small Warfare and the Entrenched Métis.* Ottawa: Parks Canada, 1985.

901.   Hudson, D. R. "Fraser River Fisheries: Antrhopology, the State, and First Nations." *Native Studies Review* 6, no. 2 (1990): 31–42.

902.   Idiens, Dale. "Eskimos in Scotland, Circa 1682–1924." In *Indians and Europe: An Interdisciplinary Collection of Essays,* ed. C. Feest, 161–74. Aachen, West Germany: Edition Herodot, 1987.

903.   "Indian Separatism: Canada's Native People Demand Their Sovereignty." *Alberta Report,* March 30, 1987.

904.   Jobson, Valerie. "The Blackfoot and the Rationing System." *Alberta History* 33, no. 4 (1985): 13–17.

905.   Johansen, Bruce E. "Mohawks, Axes, and Taxes." *History Today* 35 (April 1985): 10–16.

906.   Johansen, Gregory J. "'To Make Some Provision for Their Half Breeds': The Nemaha Half-Breed Reserve, 1830–66." *Nebraska History* 67, no. 1 (1986): 8–29.

907.   Johnson, Leo A. "The Mississauga–Lake Ontario Land Surrender of 1805." *Ontario History* 83 (1990): 233–54.

908.   Johnston, Darlene. *Taking of the Indian Lands in Canada: Consent or Coercion?* Saskatoon: University of Saskatchewan Press, 1989.

909.   Keller, Robert. "Haida Indian Land Claims and South Moresby National Park." *American Review of Canadian Studies* 20 (1990): 7–30.

910.   Kennedy, Patricia. "Tracking the Treaty Texts." *Archivist* 16 (November/December 1989): 12–13.

911.   Klutschak, Heinrich. *Overland to Starvation Cove: With the Inuit in Search of Franklin, 1878–1880.* Translated and edited by William Barr. Toronto: University of Toronto Press, 1987.

912.   Krotz, Larry. *Indian Country: Inside Another Canada.* Toronto: McClelland and Stewart, 1990.

913.   Kulchyski, Peter. "A Considerable Unrest: F. O. Loft and the League of Indians." *Native Studies Review* 4, no. 1/2 (1988): 95–118.

914.   Lal Ravi. "Watershed Year, 1878: New Policy in Indian Affairs." In *Papers of the Twenty-First Algonquian Conference,* ed. W. Cowan, 172–80. Ottawa: Carleton University Press, 1990.

915.   Lester, Tanya. "How Manitoba's Aboriginal People Stopped Meech." *Canadian Dimension* 24 (September 1990): 6–9.

916.   Long, J. Anthony, and Menno Boldt. *Governments in Conflict? Provinces and Indian Nations in Canada.* University of Toronto Press, 1988.

917.   ———. "Leadership Selection in Canadian Indian Communities: Reforming the Present and Incorporating the Past." *Great Plains Quarterly* 7 (1987): 103–15.

918.   Long, John S. "'No Basis for Argument': The Signing of Treaty Nine in Northern Ontario, 1905–1906." *Native Studies Review* 5, no. 2 (1989): 19–54.

919.   McDonald, James A. "Bleeding Day and Night: The Construction of the Grand Trunk Pacific Railway Across Tsimshian Reserve Lands." *Canadian Journal of Native Studies* 10 (1990): 33–70.

920.   McKenzie, Wayne. "Métis Self-Government in Saskatchewan." In *1885 and After: Native Society in Transition,* ed. F. L. Barron and J. B. Waldram, 297–306. Regina, Sask.: Canadian Plains Research Center, University of Regina, 1986.

921.   McLean, Don. *1885: Métis Rebellion or Government Conspiracy?* Winnipeg: Pemmican Publications, 1985.

922.   Metzger, Lynn R. *Cleveland American Indian Center: Urban Survival and Adaptation.* Ph.D. dissertation, Case Western Reserve University, 1989.

923.   Miller, J. R. "Owen Glendower, Hotspur, and Canadian Indian Policy." *Ethnohistory* 37, no. 4 (1990): 386–415.

924.   ———. *Skyscrapers Hide the Heavens: A History of Indian-White Relations in Canada.* Toronto: University of Toronto Press, 1989.

925.   Morrison, R. Bruce, and R. C. Wilson, eds. *Native Peoples: The Canadian Experience.* Toronto: McClelland and Stewart, 1986.

926.   Mossman, Manfred. "The Charismatic Pattern: Canada's Riel Rebellion of 1885." *Prairie Forum* 10 (1985): 307–25.

927.   Nock, David A. *A Victorian Missionary and Canadian Indian Policy: Cultural Synthesis Versus Cultural Replacement.* Waterloo, Ont.: Wilfrid Laurier University Press, 1987.

928.   Pointing, J. Rick. *Arduous Journey: Canadian Indians and Decolonization.* Toronto: McClelland and Stewart, 1986.

929.   Price, John A. "Ethical Advocacy Versus Propaganda: Canada's Indian Support Groups." In *The Invented Indian: Cultural Fictions and Government Policies,* ed. J. A. Clifton, 255–70. New Brunswick, N.J.: Transaction Publishers, 1990.

930.   Price, Richard, ed. *The Spirit of Alberta Indian Treaties.* Edmonton: Pica Pica Books and University of Alberta Press, 1987. [Updated]

931.   Purich, Donald. *Our Land: Native Rights in Canada.* Toronto: James Lorimar and Co., 1986.

932.   Raudsepp, Enn. "The Native Press in Canada." *Saskatchewan Indian Federated College Journal* 2, no. 1 (1986): 69–84.

933.   Regular, Keith. "On Public Display." *Alberta History* 34, no. 1 (1986): 1–10.

934.   Robertson, Heather, ed. *I Fought Riel: A Military Memoir.* Toronto: James Lorimar, 1985.

935.   Rocan, Claude. "Louis Riel: Turmoil in the Nineteenth Century." *Rotunda* 18, no. 3 (1985/86): 44–49.

936.   Rostkowski, Joelle. "The Redman's Appeal for Justice: Deskaheh and the League of Nations." In *Indians and Europe: An Interdisciplinary Collection of Essays,* ed. C. Feest, 435–53. Aachen, West Germany: Edition Herodot, 1987.

937.   Ryan, Joan. "Aboriginal Peoples in Canada: Contemporary Dimensions of Political Dominance." *American Indian Quarterly* 11 (1987): 315–23.

938.   Sanders, Douglas. "Govern-

ment Indian Agencies in Canada." In *History of Indian-White Relations,* ed. W. Washburn, 276–83. Vol. 4 of *Handbook of North American Indians,* ed. W. Sturtevant. Washington, D.C.: Smithsonian Institution Press, 1988.

939. **Silver, A. I.** "Ontario's Alleged Fanaticism in the Riel Affair." *Canadian Historical Review* 64 (1988): 21–56.

940. **Sprague, Douglas N.** *Canada and the Métis, 1869–85.* Waterloo, Ont.: Wilfrid Laurier University Press, 1988.

941. **Sprague, Douglas N., and P. R. Maihot.** "Persistent Settlers: The Dispersal and Resettlement of the Red River Métis, 1870–85." *Canadian Ethnic Studies* 17 (1985): 1–30.

942. **Stanley, George F. G.,** ed. "The Last Word on Louis Riel—The Man of Several Faces." In *1885 and After: Native Society in Transition,* ed. F. L. Barron and J. B. Waldram, 3–23. Regina, Sask.: Canadian Plains Research Center, University of Regina, 1986.

943. **Stonechild, Blair.** "The Indian View of the 1885 Uprising." *Saskatchewan Indian Federated College Journal* 2, no. 1 (1986): 49–68.

944. ———. *Saskatchewan Indians and the Resistance of 1885: Two Case Studies.* Regina: Saskatchewan Education, 1986.

945. **Strain, Laurel A., and Neena L. Chappell.** "Social Networks of Urban Native Elders: A Comparison with Non-Natives." *Canadian Ethnic Studies* 21 (1989): 104–17.

946. **Surtees, Robert J.** "Canadian Indian Policies." In *History of Indian-White Relations,* ed. W. Washbrun, 81–95. Vol. 4 of *Handbook of North American Indians,* ed. W. Sturtevant. Washington, D.C.: Smithsonian Institution Press, 1988.

947. ———. "Canadian Indian Treaties." In *History of Indian-White Relations,* ed. W. Washburn, 202–10. Vol. 4 of *Handbook of North American Indians,* ed. W. Sturtevant. Washington, D.C.: Smithsonian Institution Press, 1988.

948. **Tagutsiak, Anna A.** "The Murder of Robert Janes Told by a Witness." *Eskimo* (n.s.) 35 (1988): 5–10.

949. **Tennant, Paul.** *Aboriginal Peoples and Politics: The Indian Land Question in British Columbia, 1849–1889.* Vancouver: University of British Columbia Press, 1990.

950. **Titley, E. B.,** ed. *A Narrow Vision: Duncan Campbell Scott and the Administration of Indian Affairs.* Vancouver: University of British Columbia Press, 1986.

951. **Tobias, J. L.** "Indian Reserves in Western Canada: Indian Homelands or Devices for Assimilation?" In *Native People, Native Lands: Canadian Indians, Inuit, and Métis,* ed. B. A. Cox, 148–57. Ottawa: Carelton University Press, 1988.

952. **Waiser, W. A.** "Surveyors at War: A. O. Wheeler's Diary of the Northwest Rebellion." *Saskatchewan History* 38 (1985): 41–52.

953. **Walker, James W.** "Race and Recruitment in World War I: Enlistment of Visible Minorities in the Canadian Expeditionary Force." *Canadian Historical Review* 70 (1989): 1–26.

954. **Waterston, Jane.** "Gilbert Parker and the Rebellion of 1837." *Journal of Canadian Studies* 20, no. 1 (1985): 80–89.

955. **Weaver, Sally M.** "Indian Policy in the New Conservative Government, Part 1: The Nielsen Task Force of 1985." *Native Studies Review* 2, no. 1 (1986): 1–43.

956. ———. "Indian Policy in the New Conservative Government, Part 2: The Nielsen Task Force in the Context of Recent Policy Initiatives." Comments by Noel Dyck, George Erasmus, Richard Price, and Sally M. Weaver. *Native Studies* 2, no. 2 (1986): 1–84.

957. **Wiebe, Rudy,** and **Bob Beal,** eds. *War in the West: Voices of the 1885 Rebellion.* Toronto: McClelland and Stewart, 1985.

958. **Wonders, William C.** "The Changing Role and Significance of Native Peoples in Canada's Northwest Territories." *Polar Record* 23 (1987): 661–72.

959. ———. "Overlapping Native Land Claims in the Northwest Territories." *American Review of Canadian Studies* 18 (1988): 359–68.

960. "World War Volunteers from Saskatchewan." *Native Studies Review* 5, no. 2 (1989): 95–112.

IV
Economic Life, Trade, and Traders

4.1 GENERAL STUDIES

961. **Ambler, Marjane.** *Breaking the Iron Bonds: Indian Control of Energy Development.* Lawrence: University of Kansas Press, 1990.

962. **Bahe, Billy.** "Comments About the Decline of Indian Involvement in Agriculture in the United States." In *Overcoming Economic Dependency: Papers and Comments from the First Newberry Conference on Themes in American Indian History,* 173–77. D'Arcy McNickle Center for the History of the American Indian, Occasional Papers in Curriculum, no. 9. Chicago: Newberry Library, 1988.

963. **Carlson, Leonard.** "Property Rights and American Indians: American Indian Farmers and Ranchers in the Late Nineteenth and Early Twentieth Centuries." In *Overcoming Economic Dependency: Papers and Comments from the First Newberry Conference on Themes in American Indian History,* 107–41. D'Arcy McNickle Center for the History of the American Indian, Occasional papers in Curriculum, no. 9. Chicago: Newberry Library, 1988.

964. **Churchill, Ward.** "American Indian Lands: The Native Ethnic Amid Resource Development." *Environment* 28, no. 6 (1986): 14–17, 28–34.

965. **Clow, Richmond L.** "Taxing the Omaha and Winnebago Trust Lands, 1910–1971: An Infringement of the Tax Immune Status of Indian Country." *American Indian Culture and Research Journal* 9, no. 4 (1985): 1–22.

966. **Cornell, Stephen,** and **Joseph P. Kalt.** "Pathways from Poverty: Economic Development and Institution-Building on American Indian Reservations." *American Indian Culture and Research Journal* 14, no. 1 (1990): 89–145.

967. **Gudeman, Stephen F.** "Dependency: A View of the North from the South." In *Overcoming Economic Dependency: Papers and Comments from the First Newberry Conference on Themes in American Indian History,* 8–26. D'Arcy McNickle Center for the History of the American Indian, Occasional Papers in Curriculum, no. 9. Chicago: Newberry Library, 1988.

968. **Iverson, Peter.** "Indians and Cattle Ranching: Identity, Symbol, and Style in the American West." In *Overcoming Economic Dependency: Papers and Comments from the First Newberry Conference on Themes in American Indian History,* 178–87. D'Arcy McNickle Center for the History of the American Indian, Occasional papers in Curriculum, no. 9. Chicago: Newberry Library, 1988.

969.   Kay, Jeanne. "Native Americans in the Fur Trade and Wildlife Depletion." *Environmental Review* 9, no. 2 (1985): 118–30.

970.   Kinley, Larry. "The Northwest Salmon Fishery." In *Overcoming Economic Dependency: Papers and Comments from the First Newberry Conference on Themes in American Indian History,* 207–21. D'Arcy McNickle Center for the History of the American Indian, Occasional Papers in Curriculum, no. 9. Chicago: Newberry Library, 1988.

971.   Krech, Shepard, III. "The Hudson's Bay Company and Dependence Among Subarctic Tribes Before 1900." In *Overcoming Economic Dependency: Papers and Comments from the First Newberry Conference on Themes in American Indian History,* 62–70. D'Arcy McNickle Center for the History of the American Indian, Occasional Papers in Curriculum, no. 9. Chicago: Newberry Library, 1988.

972.   Lewis, David Rich. "Farming and the Northern Ute Experience, 1850–1940." In *Overcoming Economic Dependency: Papers and Comments from the First Newberry Conference on Themes in American History,* 142–64. D'Arcy McNickle Center for the History of the American Indian, Occasional Papers in Curriculum, no. 9. Chicago: Newberry Library, 1988.

973.   Lohse, E. S. "Trade Goods." In *History of Indian-White Relations,* ed. W. Washburn, 396–403. Vol. 4 of *Handbook of North American Indians,* ed. W. Sturtevant. Washington, D.C.: Smithsonian Institution Press, 1988.

974.   Martin Phillip. "Comments on Economic Dependency in Indian Communities." In *Overcoming Economic Dependency: Papers and Comments from the First Newberry Conference on Themes in American Indian History,* 58–61. D'Arcy McNickle Center for the History of the American Indian, Occasional Papers in Curriculum, no. 9. Chicago: Newberry Library, 1988.

975.   Miller, Christopher L., and George R. Hamell. "A New Perspective on Indian-White Contact: Cultural Symbols and Colonial Trade." *Journal of American History* 73 (1986): 311–28.

976.   Miner, H. Craig. "'All These Things I Shall Give You': The American Indian and American Business." In *Overcoming Ecnomic Dependency: Papers and Comments from the First Newberry Conference on Themes in American Indian History,* 27–37. D'Arcy McNickle Center for the History of the American Indian, Occasional Papers in Curriculum, no. 9. Chicago: Newberry Library, 1988.

977.   Olsen, Kaaren. "Native Women and the Fur Trade." *Canadian Women Studies* 10 (1989): 55–58.

978.   O'Neil, Floyd. "Overcoming Economic Dependency." In *Overcoming Economic Dependency: Papers and Comments from the First Newberry Conference on Themes in American Indian History,* 222–28. D'Arcy McNickle Center for the History of the American Indian, Occasional Papers in Curriculum, no. 9. Chicago: Newberry Library, 1988.

979.   *Overcoming Economic Dependency: Papers and Comments from the First Newberry Conference on Themes in American Indian History.* D'Arcy McNickle Center for the History of the American Indian, Occasional Papers in Curriculum, no. 9. Chicago: Newberry Library, 1988.

980.   Page, Vicki. "Reservation Development in the United States: Peripherality in the Core." *American Indian Culture and Research Journal* 9, no. 3 (1985): 21–36.

981. Potvin, Joseph. *Fur and First Canadians.* Ottawa: Canadian Arctic Resources Committee, 1988.

982. Ray, Arthur J. *The Canadian Fur Trade in the Industrial Age.* Toronto: University of Toronto Press, 1990.

983. ———. "Economic Dependency: Searching for the Evidence." In *Overcoming Economic Dependency: Papers and Comments from the First Newberry Conference on Themes in American Indian History,* 95–100. D'Arcy McNickle Center for the History of the American Indian, Occasional papers in Curriculum, no. 9. Chicago: Newberry Library, 1988.

984. Roberts, Robert B. *Encyclopedia of Historic Forts: The Military, Pioneer, and Trading Posts of the United States.* New York: MacMillan, 1988.

985. Rothenberg, Diane. "Indian Agricultural Response." In *Overcoming Economic Dependency: Papers and Comments from the First Newberry Conference on Themes in American Indian History,* 165–72. D'Arcy McNickle Center for the History of the American Indian, Occasional Papers in Curriculum, no. 9. Chicago: Newberry Library, 1988.

986. Snipp, C. Matthew. "American Indians and Natural Resource Development: Indigenous Peoples' Land, Now Sought After, Has Produced New Indian-White Problems." *American Journal of Economics and Sociology* 45 (1986): 457–74.

987. ———. "The Changing Political and Economic Status of the American Indians: From Captive Nations to Internal Colonies." *American Journal of Economics and Sociology* 45 (1986): 143–57.

988. ———. "Old and New Views of Economic Development in Indian Country." In *Overcoming Economic Dependency: Papers and Comments from the First Newberry Conference on Themes in American Indian History,* 53–57. D'Arcy McNickle Center for the History of the American Indian, Occasional Papers in Curriculum, no. 9. Chicago: Newberry Library, 1988.

989. Swagerty, William R. "Relations Between Northern Plains Indians and the American Fur Trade Company to 1867." In *Overcoming Economic Dependency: Papers and Comments from the First Newberry Conference on Themes in American Indian History,* 71–94. D'Arcy McNickle Center for the History of the American Indian, Occasional Papers in Curriculum, no. 9. Chicago: The Newberry Library, 1988.

990. Trigger, Bruce G., Toby Morantz, and Louise Dechene, eds. *Le Castor Fait Tout: Selected Papers of the Fifth North American Fur Trade Conference, 1985.* Montreal: Lake St. Louis Historical Society, 1987.

991. Trosper, Ronald L. "Powerlessness Causes Dependence." In *Overcoming Economic Dependency: Papers and Comments from the First Newberry Conference on Themes in American Indian History,* 200–206. D'Arcy McNickle Center for the History of the American Indian, Occasional Papers in Curriculum, no. 9. Chicago: Newberry Library, 1988.

992. ———. "That Other Discipline: Economics and American Indian History." In *New Directions in American Indian History,* ed. C. G. Calloway, 199–222. Norman: University of Oklahoma Press, 1988.

993. Usner, Daniel H., Jr. "A New Direction in the Economic History of American Indians." In *Overcoming Economic Dependency: Papers and Comments from the First Newberry Conference on Themes in American Indian History,* 229–

38. D'Arcy McNickle Center for the History of the American Indian, Occasional Papers in Curriculum, no. 9. Chicago: Newberry Library 1988.

994. **Vinje, David L.** "Cultural Values and Economic Development on Reservations." In *American Indian Policy in the Twentieth Century,* ed. V. Deloria, Jr., 155–75. Norman: University of Oklahoma Press, 1985.

995. ———. "Economic Development on Reservations in the Twentieth Century." In *Overcoming Economic Dependency: Papers and Comments from the First Newberry Conference on Themes in American Indian History,* 38–52. D'Arcy McNickle Center for the History of the American Indian, Occasional Papers in Curriculum, no. 9. Chicago: Newberry Library, 1988.

996. **Weick, Edward.** "Northern Native People and the Larger Canadian Society: Emerging Relations." *American Review of Canadian Studies* 18 (1988): 317–30.

997. **Wheeler, Robert C.** *A Toast to the Fur Trade: A Picture Essay on Its Material Culture.* St. Paul, Minn.: Wheeler Productions, 1985.

998. **White, Robert H.** *Tribal Assets: The Rebirth of Native America.* New York: Henry Holt, 1990.

999. **Ziontz, Alvin.** "The Case of the Pacific Northwest Indian Fishing Tribes: Benefits and Costs of Overcoming Dependency." In *Overcoming Economic Dependency: Papers and Comments from the First Newberry Conference on Themes in American Indian History,* 188–99. D'Arcy McNickle Center for the History of the American Indian, Occasional papers in Curriculum, no. 9. Chicago: Newberry Library, 1988.

4.2 ECONOMIC LIFE AND TRADE EAST OF THE MISSISSIPPI AND AT HUDSON'S BAY

1000. **Anderson, Karen.** "Commodity Exchange and Subordination: Montagnais-Naskapi and Huron Women, 1600–1650." *Signs* 11 (1985): 48–62.

1001. **Arthur, Elizabeth.** "An Outpost of Empire: The Martin Fall Post of the Hudson's Bay Company, 1821–78." *Ontario History* 78 (1986): 5–23.

1002. **Beattie, Judith Hudson.** "Indian Maps on the Hudson's Bay Company Archives: A Comparison of Five Area Maps Recorded by Peter Fidler, 1801–1802." *Archivaria* 21 (1985/86): 166–75.

1003. **Black-Rogers, Mary.** "Varieties of 'Starving': Semantics and Survival in the Subarctic Fur Trade, 1750–1850." *Ethnohistory* 33, no. 4 (1986): 353–83.

1004. **Bourque, Bruce J.,** and **Ruth Holmes Whitehead.** "Tarrantines and the Introduction of European Trade Goods in the Gulf of Maine." *Ethnohistory* 32, no. 4 (1985): 327–41.

1005. **Bradley, James W.** "Native Exchange and European Trade: Cross-Cultural Dynamics in the Sixteenth Century." *Man in the Northeast* 33 (1987): 31–46.

1006. **Calloway, Colin G.** "Foundations of Sand: The Fur Trade and British-Indian Relations, 1783–1815." In *Le Castor Fait Tout: Selected Papers of the Fifth North American Fur Trade Conference, 1985,* ed. B. G. Trigger, T. Morantz, and L. Dechene, 144–63. Montreal: Lake St. Louis Historical Society, 1987.

1007. **Ceci, Lynn.** "Native Wampum as a Peripheral Resource in the Seventeenth-Century World-System." In *The Pequots in Southern New England: The Fall and Rise of an American Indian Nation,* ed. L. M. Hauptman and J. D. Wherry, 48–63. Norman: University of Oklahoma Press, 1990.

1008.   **Coker, William S., and Thomas D. Wilson.** *Indian Traders of the Southeastern Spanish Borderlands: Panton, Leslie and Company and John Forbes and Company, 1783–1847.* Gainesville: University Presses of Florida, 1985.

1009.   **Cooper, Matthew.** "Relations of Modes of Production in Nineteenth Century America: The Shakers and Oneida." *Ethnology* 26, no. 1 (1987): 1–16.

1010.   **Copland, Dudley.** *Copalook: Chief Trader, Hudson's Bay Company, 1923–1939.* Winnipeg: Watson and Dwyer, 1986.

1011.   **Cranmer, Leon E.** *Cushnoc: The History and Archaeology of Plymouth Colony Traders on the Kennebec.* Occasional Publications in Maine Archaeology, no. 7. Augusta: Maine Archaeological Society, 1990.

1012.   **Dickinson, John A.** "Old Routes and New Wares: The Advent of European Goods in the St. Lawrence Valley." In *Le Castor Fait Tout: Selected Papers of the Fifth North American Fur Trade Conference, 1985,* ed. B. G. Trigger, T. Morantz, and L. Dechene, 25–41. Montreal: Lake St. Louis Historical Society, 1987.

1013.   **Eccles, William.** "The Fur Trade in the Colonial Northeast." In *History of Indian-White Relations,* ed. W. Washburn, 324–34. Vol. 4 of *Handbook of North American Indians,* ed. W. Sturtevant. Washington, D.C.: Smithsonian Institution Press, 1988.

1014.   **Eckert, Irma.** "The Early Fur Trade at York and Chruchill: Implications for the Native People of the North Central Subarctic." In *Le Castor Fait Tout: Selected Papers of the Fifth North American Fur Trade Conference, 1985,* ed. B. G. Trigger, T. Morantz, and L. Dechene, 223–35. Montreal: Lake St. Louis Historical Society, 1987.

1015.   **Ens, Gerhard.** "The Political Exogamy of the 'Private Trade' on the Hudson Bay: The Example of Moose Factory, 1741–1744." In *Le Castor Fait Tout: Selected Papers of the Fifth North American Fur Trade Conference, 1985,* ed. B. G. Trigger, T. Morantz, and L. Dechene, 382–440. Montreal: Lake St. Louis Historical Society, 1987.

1016.   **Fausz, J. Frederick.** "'To Draw Thither the Trade of Beavers': The Strategic Significance of the English Fur Trade in the Chesapeake, 1620–1660." In *Le Castor Fait Tout: Selected Papers of the Fifth North American Fur Trade Conference, 1985,* ed. B. G. Trigger, T. Morantz, and L. Dechene, 42–71. Montreal: Lake St. Louis Historical Society, 1987.

1017.   **Feder, Kenneth L.** "Of Stone and Metal: Trade and Warfare in Southern New England." *New England Social Studies Bulletin* 44, no. 1 (1986): 27–30.

1018.   **Foster, J. E.** "The Home Guard Cree and the Hudson's Bay Company: The First Hundred Years." In *Native People, Native Lands: Canadian Indians, Inuit, and Métis,* ed. B. A. Cox, 107–16. Ottawa: Carleton University Press, 1988.

1019.   **Gallay, Alan.** "The Search for an Alternate Source of Trade: The Creek Indians and Jonathan Bryan." *Georgia Historical Quarterly* 73 (1989): 209–30.

1020.   **Gibson, James.** "The Maritime Trade in the Colonial Northeast." In *History of Indian-White Relations,* ed. W. Washburn, 324–34. Vol. 4 of *Handbook of North American Indians,* ed. W. Sturtevant. Washington, D.C.: Smithsonian Institution Press, 1988.

1021.   Gradie, Charlotte M. "Spanish Jesuits in Virginia: The Mission That Failed." *Virginia Magazine of History and Biography* 96 (1988): 131–56.

1022.   Gullov, Hans Christian. "Whales, Whalers, and Eskimos: The Impact of European Whaling on the Demography and Economy of Eskimo Society in West Greenland." In *Cultures in Contact: The Impact of European Contacts on Native American Cultural Institutions, A.D. 1000–1800,* ed. W. W. Fitzhugh, 71–96. Washington, D.C.: Smithsonian Institution Press, 1985.

1023.   Hagerty, Gilbert W. *Wampum, War, and Trade Goods of the Hudson.* Interlaken, N.Y.: Heart of the Lakes Publishing Co, 1985.

1024.   Hedican, Edward J. "Modern Economic Trends Among the Northern Ojibwa." *Man in the Northeast* 30 (1985): 1–25.

1025.   Holzkamm, Tim E. "Fur Trade Dependency and the Pillager Ojibway of Leach Lake, 1825–1842." *Minnesota Archaeologist* 45, no. 2 (1986): 9–18.

1026.   Holzkamm, Tim E., Victor P. Lytwyn, and Leo G. Waisberg. "Rainy River Sturgeon: An Ojibway Resource in the Fur Trade Economy." *Canadian Geographer* 32 (1988): 194–205.

1027.   Kaplan, Susan A. "European Goods and Socio-Economic Change in Early Labrador Inuit Society." In *Cultures in Contact: The Impact of European Contacts on Native American Cultural Institutions, A.D. 1000–1800,* ed. W. W. Fitzhugh, 45–70. Washington, D.C.: Smithsonian Institution Press, 1985.

1028.   Kardulias, P. Nick. "Fur Production as a Specialized Activity in a World System: Indians in the North American Fur Trade." *American Indian Culture and Research Journal* 14, no. 1 (1990): 25–60.

1029.   Kraft, Herbert C. "Evidence of Contact and Trade in the Middle Atlantic Region and with the Minisink Indians of the Upper Delaware River Valley." *Journal of Middle Atlantic Archaeology* 5 (1989): 77–102.

1030.   ———. "Sixteenth and Seventeenth Century Indian-White Trade Relations in the Middle Atlantic and Northeast Regions." *Archaeology in Eastern North America* 17 (1989): 1–29.

1031.   Kuhn, Robert D. "Trade and Exchange Among the Mohawk-Iroquois: A Trace Element Analysis of Ceramic Smoking Pipes." *North American Archaeologist* 8 (1987): 305–15.

1032.   Little, Elizabeth A. "Nantucket Whaling in the Early Eighteenth Century." In *Papers of the Nineteenth Algonquian Conference,* ed. W. Cowan, 111–31. Ottawa: Carleton University Press, 1988.

1033.   Littlefield, Loraine. "Women Traders in the Maritime Fur Trade." In *Native People, Native Lands: Canadian Indians, Inuit, and Métis,* ed. B. A. Cox, 173–85. Ottawa: Carleton University Press, 1988.

1034.   Lytwyn, Victor P. *The Fur Trade of the Little North: Indians, Pedlars, and Englishmen East of Lake Winnipeg, 1760–1821.* Winnipeg: Rupert's Land Research Centre, 1986.

1035.   McKee, Jesse O., and Steve Murray. "Economic Progress and Development of the Choctaw Since 1945." In *After Removal: The Choctaw in Mississippi,* ed. by S. J. Wells and R. Tubby, 122–36. Jackson: University Press of Mississippi, 1985.

1036.   Marquart, William H. "Politics and Production Among the Calusa of South Florida." In *Hunters and Gatherers,* part 1, *History, Evolution, and Social Change,* ed. T. Ingold, D. Riches, and J. Woodburn, 161–88. Oxford, England: Berg, 1988.

1037.   Merrell, James, "'Our Bond of Peace': Patterns of Intercultural Exchange in the Carolina Piedmont, 1650–1750." In *Powhatan's Mantle: Indians in the Colonial Southeast,* ed. P. H. Wood, G. A. Waselkov, and M. T. Hatley, 196–222. Lincoln: University of Nebraska Press, 1989.

1038.   Nash, Ronald J., and Virginia P. Miller. "Model Building and the Case of the Micmac Economy." *Man in the Northeast* 34 (1987): 41–56.

1039.   Newman, Peter C. *The Story of the Hudson's Bay Company.* Vol. 1, *Company of Adventurers.* New York: Viking-Penguin, 1987.

1040.   ———. *The Story of the Hudson's Bay Company.* Vol. 2, *Caesars of the Wilderness.* New York: Viking-Penguin, 1987.

1041.   Olien, Michael. "After the Indian Slave Trade: Cross-Cultural Trade in the Western Caribbean Rimland, 1816–1820." *Journal of Antropological Research* 44, no. 1 (1988): 41–66.

1042.   Pastore, Ralph. "Fishermen, Furriers, and Beothuks: The Economy of Extinction." *Man in the Northeast* 33 (1987): 47–62.

1043.   Potter, Stephen R. "Early English Effects on Virginia Algonquian Exchange and Tribute in the Tidewater Potomac." In *Powhatan's Mantle: Indians in the Colonial Southeast,* ed. P. H. Wood, G. A. Waselkov, and M. T. Hatley, 151–72. Lincoln: University of Nebraska Press, 1989.

1044.   Ray, Arthur J. "The Hudson's Bay Company and Native People." In *History of Indian-White Realtions,* ed. W. Washburn 335–50. Vol. 4 of *Handbook of North American Indians,* ed. W. Sturtevant. Washington, D.C.: Smithsonian Institution Press, 1988.

1045.   Richling, Barnett. "Without Compromise: Hudson's Bay Company and Moravian Mission Trade Rivalry in Nineteenth Century Labrador." In *Le Castor Fait Tout: Selected Papers of the Fifth North American Fur Trade Conference, 1985,* ed. B. G. Trigger, T. Morantz, and L. Dechene, 456–84. Montreal: Lake St. Louis Historical Society, 1987.

1046.   Rogers, Edward S. "Paul Kane and the Spirit Chief at Norway House." *Rotunda* 18, no. 3 (1985/86): 34–39.

1047.   Searcy, Margaret Zehmer. "Choctaw Subsistence, 1540–1830: Hunting, Fishing, Farming, and Gathering." In *The Choctaw Before Removal,* ed. C. K. Reeves, 32–54. Jackson: University Press of Mississippi, 1985.

1048.   Starna, William A. "Seventeenth-Century Dutch-Indian Trade: A Perspective from Iroquoia." *De Halve Maen* 59, no. 3 (1986): 5–8, 21.

1049.   Strong, John A. "Shinnecock Whalers: A Case Study in the Seventeenth Century Assimilation Patterns." In *Acts of the Seventeenth Algonquian Conference,* ed. W. Cowan, 327–42. Ottawa: Carleton University Press, 1986.

1050.   Usner, Daniel H., Jr. "American Indians in Colonial New Orleans." In *Powhatan's Mantle: Indians in the Colonial Southeast,* ed. P. H. Wood, G. A. Waselkov, and M. T. Hatley, 104–27. Lincoln: University of Nebraska Press, 1989.

1051.   ———. "Economic Relations in the Southeast Until 1783." In *History of Indian-White Relations,* ed. W. Washburn, 391–95. Vol. 4 of *Handbook of North American Indians,* ed. W. Sturtevant. Washington, D.C.: Smithsonian Institution Press, 1988.

1052. ———. "The Frontier Exchange Economy of the Lower Mississippi Valley in the Eighteenth Century." *William and Mary Quarterly* 44 (1987): 165–92.

1053. van West, John J. "Ojibwa Fisheries, Commercial Fisheries Development, and Fisheries Administration, 1873–1915: An Examination of Conflicting Interest and the Collapse of the Sturgeon Fisheries of the Lake of the Woods." *Native Studies Review* 6, no. 1 (1990): 31–66.

1054. Waldram, James B. *As Long as the Rivers Run: Hydroelectric Development and Native Communities in Western Canada.* Winnipeg: University of Manitoba Press, 1988.

1055. ———. "Native Employment and Hydroelectric Development in Northern Manitoba." *Journal of Canadian Studies* 22, no. 3 (1987): 62–77.

1056. White, Bruce M. "A Skilled Game of Exchange: Ojibway Fur Trade Protocol." *Minnesota History* 50 (1987): 229–40.

1057. Wills, Richard H. *Conflicting Perceptions: Western Economics and the Great Whale River Cree.* Chicago: Tutorial Press, 1985.

4.3   ECONOMIC LIFE AND TRADE WEST OF THE MISSISSIPPI AND IN ALASKA

1058. Algier, Keith. "Robert Meldrum and the Crow Peltry Trade." *Montana* 36 (summer 1986): 36–47.

1059. Anfinson, John "Transitions in the Fur Trade: Transformations in Mandan Culture." In *Le Castor Fait Tout:*

Selected Papers of the Fifth North American Fur Trade Conference, 1985, ed. B. G. Trigger, T. Morantz, and L. Dechene, 311–34. Montreal: Lake St. Louis Historical Society, 1987.

1060. Austerman, Wayne R. "Cotas de Mallas and the Western Tribes." *Museum of the Fur Trade Quarterly* 22 (summer 1986): 6–12.

1061. Barsh, Russell L. "The Substitution of Cattle for Bison on the Great Plains." *The Struggle for the Land: Indigenous Insight and Industrial Empire in the Semiarid World,* ed. P. A. Olson, 103–26. Lincoln: University of Nebraska Press, 1990.

1062. Bishop, Charles. "Coast-Interior Exchange: The Origins of Stratification in Northwestern North America." *Arctic Anthroplogy* 24 (1987): 72–83.

1063. Boxberger, Daniel L. "In and Out of the Labor Force: The Lummi Indians and the Development of the Commerical Salmon Fishery of North Puget Sound, 1880–1900." *Ethnohistory* 35, no. 2 (1988): 161–90.

1064. Burrows, James K. "'A Much-Needed Class of Labour': The Economy and Income of the Southern Interior Plateau Indians, 1897–1910." *BC Studies* 71 (spring 1986): 27–46.

1065. Coates, Kenneth. "On the Outside in Their Homeland: Native People and the Evolution of the Yukon Economy." *Northern Review* 1 (1988): 73–89.

1066. Donald, Leland. "Slave Raiding on the North Pacific Coast." In *Native People, Native Lands: Canadian Indians, Inuit, and Métis,* ed. B. A. Cox, 161–72. Ottawa: Carleton University Press, 1988.

1067. Elias, Peter Douglas. "Wage

Labour, Aboriginal Rights, and the Cree of the Churchill River Basin, Saskatchewan." *Native Studies Review* 6, no. 2 (1990): 43–64.

1068.   Faiman-Silva, Sandra L. "Tribal Land to Private Land: A Century of Oklahoma Choctaw Timberland Alienation from the 1880s to the 1980s." *Journal of Forest History* 32 (October 1988): 191–204.

1069.   Farris, Glenn J. "Recognizing Indian Folk History as Real History: A Fort Ross Example." *American Indian Quarterly* 13 (1989): 471–80.

1070.   Flanders, Nicholas E. "The Alaska Native Corporation as Conglomerate: The Problem of Profitability." *Human Organization* 48 (1989): 299–314.

1071.   Flores, Dan. *Journal of an Indian Trader: Anthony Glass and the Texas Trading Frontier, 1790–1810.* College Station: Texas A & M Press, 1985.

1072.   Foote, Cheryl. "Spanish-Indian Trade Along New Mexico's Frontier in the Eighteenth Century." *Journal of the West* 24 (April 1985): 22–33.

1073.   George, Peter J., and Richard Preston. "'Going in Between': The Impact of European Technology on the Work Patterns of the West Main Cree of Northern Ontario." *Journal of Economic History* 47 (1987): 447–60.

1074.   Gough, Barry M., ed. *Journal of Alexander Henry the Younger.* 2 vols. Toronto: Champlain Society, 1988.

1075.   Hales, David A., and Tamara P. K. Lincoln. "Newsletters and Publications of Alaska Native Corporations: A Profile of Changing Concerns." *Native Press Research Journal* 2 (1986): 9–14.

1076.   Hannon, James L. "Rendezvous Re-evaluated." In *Le Castor Fait Tout: Selected Papers of the Fifth North*

American Fur Trade Conference, 1985, ed. B. G. Trigger, T. Morantz, and L. Dechene, 411–37. Montreal: Lake St. Louis Historical Society, 1987.

1077.   Huelsbeck, David R. "Whaling in the Precontact Economy of the Central Northwest Coast." *Arctic Anthropology* 25 (1988): 1–15.

1078.   Hughs, Richard E., and James A. Bennyhoff. "Early Trade." In *Great Basin,* ed. W. L. d'Azevedo, 238–55. Vol. 11 of *Handbook of North American Indians,* ed. W. Sturtevant. Washington, D.C.: Smithsonian Institution, 1986.

1079.   Humins, John H. "Furs, Astor, and Indians: The American Fur Company in the Old North-West Territory." *Michigan History* 69 (March 1985): 24–31.

1080.   Iverson, Peter. "The Cowboys Are Indians: Indian Cattle Ranching in the American West." *Storia Nordamericana* 5, no. 1 (1988): 115–24.

1081.   Kamber, Peter Heinrich. "Timber and Termination: The Klamath Case." *European Review of Native American Studies* 3, no. 3 (1989): 43–47.

1082.   Ketz, James A., and Katherine L. Arndt. "The Russian-American Company and Development of Alaskan Copper River Fur Trade." In *Le Castor Fait Tout: Selected Papers of the Fifth North American Fur Trade Conference, 1985,* ed. B. G. Trigger, T. Morantz, and L. Dechene, 438–55. Montreal: Lake St. Louis Historical Society, 1987.

1083.   Knack, Martha. "The Role of Credit in Native Adaptation to the Great Basin Ranching Economy." *American Indian Culture and Research Journal* 11, no. 1 (1987): 43–66.

1084.   Krech, Shepard, III. "The Early Fur Trade in the Northwestern

Subarctic: The Kutchin and the Trade in Beads." In *Le Castor Fait Tout: Selected Papers of the Fifth North American Fur Trade Conference, 1985,* ed. B. G. Trigger, T. Morantz, and L. Dechene, 236–77. Montreal: Lake St. Louis Historical Society, 1987.

1085.   **Makahonuk, Glen.** "Wage-Labor in the Northwest Fur Trade Economy, 1760–1849." *Saskatchewan History* 41 (winter 1988): 1–18.

1086.   **Malloy, Mary.** "Souvenirs of the Fur Trade, 1799–1832: The Northwest Coast Indian Collection of the Salem East India Marine Society." *American Indian Art Magazine* 11 (autumn 1986): 30–35.

1087.   **Mitchell, Donald,** and **Leland Donald.** "Some Economic Aspects of Tlingit, Haida, and Tsimshian Slavery." *Journal of Economic Anthropology* 7 (1985): 19–35.

1088.   **Myers, Thomas P.** "An Examination of Central Plains Moccasins: Evidence of Adaptation to a Reservation Economy." *Plains Anthropologist* 32, no. 115 (1987): 29–41.

1089.   **Nicks, Trudy.** "Native Response to the Early Fur Trade at Lesser Slave Lake." In *Le Castor Fait Tout: Selected Papers of the Fifth North American Fur Trade Conference, 1985,* ed. B. G. Trigger, T. Morantz, and L. Dechene, 278–310. Montreal: Lake St. Louis Historical Society, 1987.

1090.   **Notzke, Claudia.** Indian Reserves in Canada: Development Problems of the Stoney and Piegan Reserves in Alberta. Ottawa: Marburg-Lahn, 1985.

1091.   **Parker, James.** *Emporium of the North: Fort Chipewyan and the Fur Trade to 1835.* Regina, Sask.: Canadian Plains Research Center, University of Regina, 1987.

1092.   **Patterson, E. Palmer.** "The Nishga and the Fur Trade, 1834–42." *Native Studies Review* 6, no. 1 (1990): 67–82.

1093.   **Perttula, Timothy K.,** and **Bob D. Skiles.** "Another Look at an Eighteenth-Century Archaeological Site in Wood County, Texas." *Southwestern Historical Quarterly* 92 (1989): 417–35. [Le Dout French trading post]

1094.   **Pottinger, Richard.** "Indian Reservation Labor Markets: A Navajo Assessment and Challenge." *American Indian Culture and Research Journal* 9, no. 3 (1985): 1–21.

1095.   **Rogers, J. Daniel.** *Objects of Change: The Archaeology and History of Arikara Contact with Europeans.* Washington, D.C.: Smithsonian Institution Press, 1990.

1096.   **Ronda, James P.** *Astoria.* Lincoln: University of Nebraska Press, 1990.

1097.   ———. "Astoria and the Birth of Empire." *Montana* 36, no. 3 (1986): 22–35.

1098.   **Schilz, Thomas F.** "The Gros Ventres and the Canadian Fur Trade, 1754–1831." *American Indian Quarterly* 12 (1988): 41–56.

1099.   ———. "Robes, Rum, and Rifles: Indian Middlemen in the Northern Plains Fur Trade." *Montana* 40 (winter 1990): 2–13.

1100.   **Schilz, Thomas F.,** and **Jodye Lynn Dickson Schilz.** "Beads, Bangles, and Buffalo Robes: The Rise and Fall of the Indian Fur Trade Along the Missouri and Des Moines Rivers, 1200–1820." *Annals of Iowa* 49 (summer/fall 1987): 5–25.

1101.   **Swagerty, William R.** "Indian Trade in the Trans-Mississippi West to

1870." In *History of Indian-White Relations,* ed. W. Washburn, 374–75. Vol. 4 of *Handbook of North American Indians,* ed. W. Sturtevant. Washington, D.C.: Smithsonian Institution Press, 1988.

1102.   **Thistle, Paul C.** *Indian-European Trade Relations in the Lower Saskatchewan River Region to 1840.* Winnipeg: University of Manitoba Press, 1986.

1103.   **Thompson, Erwin N.** *Fort Union Trading Post: Fur Trade Empire on the Upper Missouri.* Medora, N.Dak.: Theodore Roosevelt Nature and History Association, 1986.

1104.   **Thurman, Melburn D.** "Blue Color and Shawnee Cloth: A Possible Example of a Localized Component of a Horizon Style." *Plains Anthropologist* 31, no. 113 (1986): 219–24.

1105.   **Tough, Frank.** "Changes to the Native Economy of Northern Manitoba in the Post-Treaty Period: 1870–1900." *Native Studies Review* 1, no. 1 (1985): 40–66.

1106.   ———. "Indian Economic Behavior, Exchange, and Profits in Northern Manitoba During the Decline of the Monopoly, 1870–1930." *Journal of Historical Geography* 16 (October 1990): 385–401.

1107.   **Tower, Michael.** "Traders Along the Washita: A Short History of the Shirley Trading Company." *Chronicles of Oklahoma* 65 (1987): 4–15.

[South-central Indian Territory, 1858–1880s]

1108.   **Van Kirk, Sylvia.** "The Role of Native Women in the Creation of Fur Trade Society in Western Canada, 1620–1830." In *The Women's West,* ed. S. Armitage and E. Jameson, 53–62. Norman: University of Oklahoma Press, 1987.

1109.   **Volk, Robert W.** "Barter, Blankets, and Bracelets: The Role of the Trader in the Navajo Textile and Silverwork Industries, 1868–1930." *American Indian Culture and Research Journal* 12, no. 4 (1988): 39–64.

1110.   **Wenzel, Geroge W.** "Canadian Inuit in a Mixed Economy: Thoughts on Seals, Snowmobiles, and Animal Rights." *Native Studies Review* 2, no. 1 (1986): 69–82.

1111.   **Wood, W. Raymond,** and **Thomas D. Thiessen,** eds. *Early Fur Trade on the Northern Plains: Canadian Traders Among the Mandan and Hidatsa Indians, 1738–1818.* Norman: University of Oklahoma Press, 1985.

1112.   **Wyatt, Victoira.** "Alaskan Indian Wage Earners in the Nineteenth Century: Economic Choices and Ethnic Identity on Southeast Alaska's Frontier." *Pacific Northwest Quarterly* 78 (1987): 43–49.

1113.   **Yerbury, J. Colin.** *The Subarctic Indians and the Fur Trade, 1680–1860.* Vancouver: University of British Columbia Press, 1986.

V
Missions and Missionaries

5.1 GENERAL WORKS

1114. Archer, John H. "The Anglican Church and the Indian in the Northwest." *Journal of the Canadian Church Historical Society* 28, no. 1 (1986): 19–30.

1115. "Missions and Native Americans." *American Presbyterians* (special issue) 65 (fall 1987).

1116. Whiteman, Darrell. "Using Missionary Documents in Ethnohistorical Research." In *Ethnohistory: A Researcher's Guide,* ed. D. Wiedman, 25–60. Williamsburg, Va.: College of William and Mary, 1986.

5.2 MISSIONS AND MISSIONARIES BEFORE 1775

1117. Axtell, James. "White Legend: The Jesuit Missions in Maryland." *Maryland Historical Magazine* 81 (spring 1986): 1–7.

1118. Bonvillain, Nancy. "The Iroquois and the Jesuits: Strategies of Influence and Resistance." *American Indian Culture and Research Journal* 10, no. 1 (1986): 29–42.

1119. ———. "Missionary Role in French Colonial Expansion: An Examination of the Jesuit Relations." *Man in the Northeast* 29 (1985): 1–14.

1120. Brooks, Katherine J. "The Effect of the Catholic Missionaries on the Micmac Indians of Nova Scotia, 1610–1986." *Nova Scotia Historical Review* 6, no. 1 (1986): 63–74.

1121. Bushnell, Amy Turner. "The Sacramental Imperative: Catholic Ritual and Indian Sedentism in the Provinces of Florida." In *Columbian Consequences,* vol. 2, *Archaeological and Historical Perspectives on the Spanish Borderlands East,* ed. D. H. Thomas, 475–90. Washington, D.C.: Smithsonian Institution Press, 1990.

1122. Campeau, Lucien. "Roman Catholic Missions in New France." In *History of Indian-White Relations,* ed. W. Washburn, 464–71. Vol. 4 of *Handbook of North American Indians,* ed. W. Sturtevant. Washington, D.C.: Smithsonian Institution Press, 1988.

1123. Carlson, Catherine C., et al. *Archival and Archaeological Research Report on the Configuration of the Seven Original Seventeenth Century Praying Indian Towns of the Massachusetts Bay Colony.* Amherst: University of Massachusetts Aracheological Services, produced for the Massachusetts Historical Commission, 1986.

1124. Cogley, Richard W. "John Eliot in Recent Scholarship." *American*

Indian Culture and Research Journal 14, no. 2 (1990): 77–92.

1125.   Cook, Sherburne, and Cesare Marino. "Roman Catholic Missions in California and the Southwest." In *History of Indian-White Relations,* ed. W. Washburn, 472–80. Vol. 4 of *Handbook of North American Indians,* ed. W. Sturtevant. Washington, D.C.: Smithsonian Institution Press, 1988.

1126.   Daivtolo, Robert, Jr. "The Role of the Quakers in Indian Affairs During the French and Indian Wars." *Quaker History* 77 (1988): 1–30.

1127.   Eaton, Jack D. "The Gateway Missions of the Lower Rio Grande." In *Columbian Consequences,* vol. 1, *Archaeological and Historical Perspectives on the Spanish Borderlands West,* ed. D. H. Thomas, 245–58. Washington, D.C.: Smithsonian Institution Press, 1989.

1128.   Erickson, Vincent O. "Passamaquoddies and Protestants: Deacon Sockabason and the Reverend Kellogg of the Society for Propagating the Gospel." *Man in the Northeast* 29 (1985): 87–107.

1129.   Fontana, Bernard L. "Santa Ana de Cuiguiburitac: Pimeria Alta's Northernmost Mission." *Journal of the Southwest* 19 (1987): 133–59.

1130.   Gannon, Michael V. "Defense of Native American and Franciscan Rights in the Florida Missions." In *Columbian Consequences,* vol. 2, *Archaeological and Historical Perspectives on the Spanish Borderlands East,* ed. D. H. Thomas, 449–58. Washington, D.C.: Smithsonian Institution Press, 1990.

1131.   Griffin, John W. "Changing Perspectives on the Spanish Missions of La Florida." In *Columbian Consequences,* vol. 2, *Archaeological and Historical Perspectives on the Spanish Borderlands East,* ed. D. H. Thomas, 399–408. Washing-

ton, D.C.: Smithsonian Institution Press, 1990.

1132.   Harkins, Conrad, O.F.M. "On Franciscans, Archaeology, and Old Missions." In *Columbian Consequences,* vol. 2, *Archaeological and Historical Perspectives on the Spanish Borderlands East,* ed. D. H. Thomas, 459–74. Washington, D.C.: Smithsonian Institution Press, 1990.

1133.   Johnson, John R. "The Chumash and the Missions." In *Columbian Consequences,* vol. 1, *Archaeological and Historical Perspectives on the Spanish Borderlands West,* ed. D. H. Thomas, 365–76. Washington, D.C.: Smithsonian Institution Press, 1989.

1134.   Jones, B. Calvin, and Gary N. Shapiro. "Nine Mission Sites in Apalachee." In *Columbian Consequences,* vol. 2, *Archaeological and Historical Perspectives on the Spanish Borderlands East,* ed. D. H. Thomas, 491–510. Washington D.C.: Smithsonian Institution Press, 1990.

1135.   Lapomarda, Vincent A. "The Jesuit Missions of Colonial New England." *Essex Institute Historical Collections* 126 (1990): 91–109.

1136.   Lewis, Clifford. "Roman Catholic Missions in the Southeast and Northeast." In *History of Indian-White Relations,* ed. W. Washburn, 481–93. Vol. 4 of *Handbook of North American Indians,* ed. W. Sturtevant. Washington, D.C.: Smithsonian Institution Press, 1988.

1137.   Matter, Robert Allen. *Pre-Seminole Florida: Spanish Soldiers, Friars, and Indian Missions, 1513–1763.* New York: Garland, 1990.

1138.   Morrison, Kenneth. "Montagnais Missionization in Early New France: The Syncretic Imperative." *American Indian Culture and Research Journal* 10, no. 3 (1986): 1–23.

1139. **Naeher, Robert James.** "Dialogue in the Wilderness: John Eliot and the Indian Exploration of Puritanism as a Source of Meaning, Comfort, and Ethnic Survival." *New England Quarterly* 62 (1989): 346–68.

1140. **O'Brien, Jean M.** "The Praying Indians of Natick, Massachusetts, in New England, 1650–1677." In *Native Views of Indian-White Historical Relations,* ed. D. L. Fixico, 39–53. D'Arcy McNickle Center for the History of the American Indian, Occasional Papers in Curriculum, no. 7. Chicago: Newberry Library, 1989.

1141. **O'Neill, Sean.** "French Jesuits: Motives for Baptizing Indians on the Frontier of New France." *Mid-America* 71 (October 1989): 123–36.

1142. **Pettit, Norman,** ed. *Jonathan Edwards' The Life of David Brainerd.* New Haven, Conn.: Yale University Press, 1985 [1749]

1143. **Pomedli, Michael.** "Beyond Unbelief: Early Jesuit Interpretations of Native Religions." *Studies in Religion* 16 (1987): 275–87.

1144. **Reid, John.** "Mission to the Micmacs." *Beaver* 70 (October–November 1990): 15–23.

1145. **Reitz, Elizabeth J.** "Zooarchaeological Evidence for Subsistence at La Florida Missions." In *Columbian Consequences,* vol. 2, *Archaeological and Historical Perspectives on the Spanish Borderlands East,* ed. D. H. Tomas, 543–54. Washington, D.C.: Smithsonian Institution Press, 1990.

1146. **Richling, Barnett.** "'Very Serious Reflections': Inuit Dreams About Salvation and Loss in Eighteenth-Century Labrador." *Ethnohistory* 36, no. 2 (1989): 148–69.

1147. **Richter, Daniel.** "Iroquois Versus Iroquois: Jesuit Missions and Christianity in Village Politics, 1642–1686." *Ethnohistory* 32, no. 1 (1985): 1–16.

1148. **Ronda, James P.** "Black Robes and Boston Men: Indian-White Relations in New France and New England,1524–1701." In *The American Indian Experience: A Profile, 1524 to the Present,* ed. P. Weeks, 3–34. Arlington Heights, Ill.: Forum Press, 1988.

1149. **Ruhl, Donna L.** "Spanish Mission Paleoethnobotany and Culture Change: A Survey of the Archaeobotanical Data and Some Speculations on Aboriginal and Spanish Interactions in La Florida." In *Columbian Consequences,* vol. 2, *Archaeological and Historical Perspectives on the Spanish Borderlands East,* ed. D. H. Thomas, 555–80. Washington, D.C.: Smithsonian Institution Press, 1990.

1150. **Ruiz de Alarcón, Hernando.** *Treatise on the Heathen Superstitions That Today Live Among the Indians Native to This New Spain, 1629.* Translated by J. Richard Andrews and Ross Hassig. Norman: University of Oklahoma Press, 1987.

1151. **Saunders, Rebecca.** "Ideal and Innovation: Spanish Mission Architecture in the Southeast." In *Columbian Consequences,* vol. 2, *Archaeological and Historical Perspectives on the Spanish Borderlands East,* ed. D. H. Thomas, 527–42. Washington, D.C.: Smithsonian Institution Press, 1990.

1152. **Shapiro, Gary N.,** and **John H. Hann.** "The Documentary Image of the Council Houses of Spanish Florida Tested by Excavations at the Mission of San Luis de Talimali." In *Columbian Consequences,* vol. 2, *Archaeological and Historical Perspectives on the Spanish Borderlands East,* ed. D. H. Thomas, 511–26. Washington, D.C.: Smithsonian Institution Press, 1990.

1153. Thomas, David Hurst. "The Spanish Missions of La Florida: An Overview." In *Columbian Consequences,* vol. 2, *Archaeological and Historical Perspectives on the Spanish Borderlands East,* ed. D. H. Thomas, 357–98. Washington, D.C.: Smithsonian Institution Press, 1990.

1154. Trepp, Annette D. "The Churchman and the Indians: The Role of the Missionaries in the Indian War (1790–1795)." *Queen City Heritage* 48 (spring 1990): 20–31.

1155. Weber, David J. "Blood of Martyrs, Blood of Indians: Toward a More Balanced View of Spanish Missions in Seventeenth Century North America." In *Columbian Consequences,* vol. 2, *Archaeological and Historical Perspectives on the Spanish Borderlands East,* ed. D. H. Thomas, 429–48. Washington, D.C.: Smithsonian Institution Press, 1990.

1156. ———. "Blood of Martyrs, Blood of Indians: Toward a More Balanced View of the Spanish Missions in Seventeenth Century North America." In *The Struggle for Political Autonomy: Papers and Comments from the Second Newberry Conference on Themes in American Indian History,* 33–48. D'Arcy McNickle Center for the History of the American Indian, Occasional Papers in Curriculum, no. 11. Chicago: Newberry Library, 1989.

5.3   MISSIONS AND MISSIONARIES, 1775–1900

1157. Bahr, Donald. "Pima-Papago Christianity." *Journal of the Southwest* 30 (1988): 133–67.

1158. Bahr, Donald, and Susan Fenger. "Indians and Missions: Homage to and Debate with Rupert Costo and Jeanette Henry." *Journal of the Southwest* 31, no. 3 (1989): 300–321.

1159. Baird, W. David. "Cyrus By-ington and the Presbyterian Choctaw Mission." In *Churchmen and the Western Indians, 1820–1920,* ed. C. A. Milner II and F. O'Neil, 5–40. Norman: University of Oklahoma Press, 1985.

1160. Beaver, R. Pierce. "Protestant Churches and the Indians." ed. W. Washburn, 430–58. Vol. 4 of *Handbook of North American Indians,* ed. W. Sturtevant. Washington, D.C.: Smithsonian Institution Press, 1988.

1161. Buckley, Cornelius, S.J. *Nicholas Point, S.J.: His Life and Northwest Indian Chronicles.* Chicago: Loyola University Press, 1989.

1162. Burns, Robert. "Roman Catholic Missions in the Northwest." In *History of Indian-White Relations,* ed. W. Washburn, 494–500. Vol. 4 of *Handbook of North American Indians,* ed. W. Sturtevant. Washington, D.C.: Smithsonian Institution Press, 1988.

1163. Carriker, Robert C. "Joseph M. Cataldo, S.J.: Courier of Catholicism to the Nez Perces." In *Churchmen and the Western Indians, 1820–1920,* ed. C. A. Milner II and F. O'Neil, 109–42. Norman: University of Oklahoma Press, 1985.

1164. Carter, Max L. "John Johnston and the Friends: A Midwestern Indian Agent's Relationship with Quakers in the Early 1800s." *Quaker History* 78 (1989): 37–47.

1165. Coates, Lawrence G. "The Spalding, Whitman, and Lemhi Missions: A Comparison." *Idaho Yesterdays* 31 (spring/summer 1987): 38–46.

1166. Cole, Jean Murray. "Success or Survival? The Progress and Problems of the Tshimakain Mission." *Idaho Yesterdays* 31 (spring/summer 1987): 86–94.

1167. Colemn, Louis. "Cyrus Byington: Missionary to the Choctaws."

Chronicles of Oklahoma 62 (winter 1984/85): 360–87.

1168.   Coleman, Michael C. *Presbyterian Missionary Attitudes Toward American Indians, 1837–1895.* Jackson: University Press of Mississippi, 1985.

1169.   ———. "Problematic Panacea: Presbyterian Missionaries and the Allotment of Indian Lands in the Late Nineteenth Century." *Pacific Historical Review* 54 (1985): 143–60.

1170.   ———. "The Responses of American Indian Children to Presbyterian Schooling in the Nineteenth Century: An Analysis Through Missionary Sources." *History of Education Quarterly* 27 (winter 1987): 473–98.

1171.   Costo, Rupert, and Jeanette Henry, eds. *The Missions of California: A Legacy of Genocide.* San Francisco: Indian Historian Press of the American Indian Historical Society, 1987.

1172.   Deloria, Vine, Sr. "The Establishment of Christianity Among the Sioux." In *Sioux Indian Religion: Tradition and Innovation,* ed. R. J. DeMallie and D. Parks, 91–112. Norman: University of Oklahoma Press, 1987.

1173.   Dorais, Louis-Jacques, and Bernard Saladin d'Anglure. "Roman Catholic Missions in the Arctic." In *History of Indian-White Relations,* ed. W. Washburn, 501–5. Vol. 4 of *Handbook of North American Indians,* ed. W. Sturtevant. Washington, D.C.: Smithsonian Institution Press, 1988.

1174.   Fienup-Riordan, Ann. "The Martyrdom of Brother Hooker: Conflict and Conversion on the Kuskokwim." *Alaska History* 3 (winter 1988): 1–26.

1175.   Forbes, Bruce David. "John Jasper Methvin, Methodist 'Missionary to the Western Tribes' (Oklahoma)." In *Churchmen and the Western Indians,*

1820–1920, ed. C. A. Milner II and F. O'Neil, 41–73. Norman: University of Oklahoma Press, 1985.

1176.   Herring, Joseph B. "Presbyterian Ethnologists Among the Iowa and Sac Indians, 1837–1853." *American Presbyterians: Journal of Presbyterian History* 65 (1987): 195–203.

1177.   Herring, Rebecca Jane. "Their Work Was Never Done: Women Missionaries on the Kiowa-Comanche Reservation." *Chronicles of Oklahoma* 64 (1986): 68–83.

1178.   Hoover, Roy. "'To Stand Alone in the Wilderness': Edmund F. Ely, Missionary." *Minnesota History* 47 (1985): 265–80.

1179.   Jeffrey, Julie Roy. "The Making of a Missionary: Narcissa Whitman and Her Vocation." *Idaho Yesterdays* 31 (spring/summer 1987): 75–85.

1180.   Johnson, John. "Mission Registers as Anthropological Questionnaires: Understanding the Limitations of the Data." *American Indian Culture and Research Journal* 12, no. 2 (1988): 9–30. [California]

1181.   Kan, Sergei. "Russian Orthodox Brotherhoods Among the Tlingit: Missionary Goals and Native Response." *Ethnohistory* 32, no. 3 (1985): 196–223.

1182.   ———. "The Russian Orthodox Church in Alaska." In *History of Indian-White Relations,* ed. W. Washburn, 506–21. Vol. 4 of *Handbook of North American Indians,* ed. W. Sturtevant. Washington, D.C.: Smithsonian Institution Press, 1988.

1183.   ———, ed. "Native Cultures and Christianity in Northern North America: Selected Papers." *Arctic Anthropology* 24 (1987): 1–114.

1184.   Karlberg, Patricia E., and

Robert H. Keller. "Oregon Clergy and Indian War in the Northwest: Home Missionary Correspondence, 1855–57." *Pacific Northwest Quarterly* 79 (1988): 26–34.

1185. Keller, Robert H. "Episcopal Reformers and Affairs at Red Cloud Agency, 1870–1876." *Nebraska History* 68, no. 3 (1987): 116–26.

1186. ———. "The Gospel Comes to Northwest Washington." *Pacific Northwest Forum* 10, no. 1 (1985): 2–6.

1187. ———. "A Missionary Tour of Washington Territory: T. Dwight Hunt's 1855 Report." *Pacific Northwest Quarterly* 76 (1985): 148–55.

1188. ———. "Shrewd, Able, and Dangerous Men: Presbyterian and Dutch Reformed Indian Agents of the Southwest, 1870–1882." *Journal of Arizona History* 26 (1985): 243–58.

1189. Kidwell, Clara Sue. "Choctaws and Missionaries in Mississippi Before 1830." *American Indian Culture and Research Journal* 11, no. 2 (1987): 51–72.

1190. Kugel, Rebecca. "Religion Mixed with Politics: The 1836 Conversion of Mang'asid of Fond Du Lac." *Ethnohistory* 37, no. 2 (1990): 126–57.

1191. Long, John S. "*Manitu,* Power, Books, and *Wiihtikow:* Some Factors in the Adoption of Christianity by Nineteenth Century Western James Bay Cree." *Native Studies Review* 3, no. 1 (1987): 1–30.

1192. ———. "Rev. Edwin Watkins: Missionary to the Cree, 1852–1857." In *Papers of the Sixteenth Algonquian Conference,* ed. W. Cowan, 91–117. Ottawa: Carleton University Press, 1985.

1193. ———. "The Reverend George Barnley, Wesleyan Methodism, and the Fur Trade Company Families of James Bay." *Ontario History* 77 (1985): 43–64.

1194. McKevitt, Gerald. "Jesuit Missionary Linguistics in the Pacific Northwest: A Comparative Study." *Western Historical Quarterly* 21 (1990): 281–304.

1195. McLoughlin, William G. *Chapmions of the Cherokees: Evan and John B. Jones.* Princeton, N.J.: Princeton University Press, 1989.

1196. ———. "The Missionary Dilemma." *Canadian Review of American Studies* 16, no. 4 (1985): 395–409.

1197. ———. "The Murder Trial of the Reverend Evan Jones, Baptist Missionary to the Cherokee in North Carolina, 1833." *North Carolina Historical Review* 62 (1985): 157–78.

1198. ———. "The Reverend Evan Jones and the Cherokee Trail of Tears, 1838–39." *Georgia Historical Quarterly* 73 (1989): 559–83.

1199. Magnaghi, Russell M. "The Jesuits in the Lake Superior Country." *Inland Seas* 41, no. 3 (1985): 190–203.

1200. Mahnken, Norbert. "Old Baptist Mission and Evan Jones." *Chronicles of Oklahoma* 67 (1989): 174–93.

1201. Markowitz, Harvey. "Catholic Mission and the Sioux: A Crisis in the Early Paradigm." In *Sioux Indian Religion: Tradition and Innovation,* ed. R. J. DeMallie and D. Parks, 113–37. Norman: University of Oklahoma Press, 1987.

1202. Meighan, Clement W. "Indians and California Missions." *Southern California Quarterly* 69, no. 3 (1987): 187–201.

1203. Miles, Ray. " 'Give Us Our Catholic Priests': The Osage Plea for Freedom of Religion." *Chronicles of Oklahoma* 66 (1988): 52–63.

1204. Miller, Christopher L. *Pro-*

phetic Worlds: Indians and Whites on the Columbia Plateau. New Brunswick, N.J.: Rutgers University Press, 1985.

1205. Miller, Jay. "The Early Years of Watomika (James Bouchard): Delaware and Jesuit." American Indian Quarterly 13 (1989): 165–88.

1206. Milner, Clyde A., II. "Albert K. Smiley: Friend to Friends of the Indians." In Churchmen and the Western Indians, 1820–1920, ed. C. A. Milner II and F. O'Neil, 143–75. Norman: University of Oklahoma Press, 1985.

1207. Milner, Clyde A., II, and Floyd O'Neil, eds. Churchmen and the Western Indians, 1820–1920. Norman: University of Oklahoma Press, 1985.

1208. Mulhall, David. Will to Power: The Missionary Career of Father A. G. Morice. Vancouver: University of British Columbia Press, 1986.

1209. "Nineteenth Century Images of Native Clergy and Indian Missions." Native Studies Review 4, no. 1/2 (1988): 167–82.

1210. Nock, David. A Victorian Missionary and Canadian Indian Policy: Cultural Synthesis Versus Cultural Replacement. Waterloo, Ont.: Wilfrid Laurier University Press, 1988.

1211. Oleska, Michael, ed. Alaskan Missionary Spirituality. Sources of American Spirituality Series. New York: Paulist Press, 1987.

1212. O'Neil, Floyd A. "The Mormons, the Indians, and George Washington Bean." In Churchmen and the Western Indians, 1820–1920, ed. C. A. Milner II and F. O'Neil, 77–106. Norman: University of Oklahoma Press, 1985.

1213. Orr, Joan Greene. "Civilize the Indian: Government Policies, Quak-

ers, and Cherokee Educaton." Southern Friend 10 (1988): 27–38.

1214. Patterson, E. Palmer. "Native Missionaries of the North Pacific Coast: Philip McKay and Others." Pacific Historian 30 (1986): 22–37.

1215. Pease, Margaret. A Worthy Work in a Needy Time: The Montana Industrial School for Indians (Bond's Mission) 1886–1897. Boise, Idaho: [Privately published by the author], 1986.

1216. Peterson, Susan C. "Doing 'Women's Work': The Grey Nuns at Fort Totten Indian Reservation, 1874–1900." North Dakota History 52, no. 3 (1985): 18–25.

1217. Pillar, James R. "The Catholic Church's Ministry to the Choctaws of Mississippi in the Nineteenth Century." Journal of Mississippi History 50 (1988): 287–315.

1218. Potter, Gail Debuse. "A Note on the Samuel Allis Family: Missionaries to the Pawnees, 1834–46." Nebraska History 67, no. 1 (1986): 1–7.

1219. Price, John A. "Mormon Missions to the Indians." In History of Indian-White Relations, ed. W. Washburn, 459–63. Vol. 4 of Handbook of North American Indians, ed. W. Sturtevant, Washington, D.C.: Smithsonian Institution Press, 1988.

1220. Ronda, James P. "Reverend Samuel Kirkland and the Oneida Indians." In The Oneida Indian Experience: Two Perspectives, ed. J. Campisi and L. Hauptman, 23–30. Syracuse, N.Y.: Syracuse University Press, 1988.

1221. Sandos, James A. "Junípero Serra's Canonization and the Historical Record." American Historical Review 93 (1988): 1453–69.

1222. ———. "Levantamiento! The

1824 Chumash Uprising Reconsidered."
Southern California Quarterly 67 (summer 1985): 109–33

1223. **Schmutterer, Gerhard M.**
Tomahawk and Cross: Lutheran Missionaries Among the Northern Plains Tribes, 1858–1866. Sioux Falls, S.Dak.: Center for Western Studies, Augustana College, 1989.

1224. **Schoenberg, Wilfred P.** "The Bishops Blanchet and Their Role in the Whitman Massacre." *Idaho Yesterdays* 31 (spring/summer 1987): 3–7.

1225. **Shipek, Florence C.** "California Indian Reactions to the Franciscans." *Americas* 41 (1985): 480–94.

1226. **Simonson, Gayle.** "The Prayer Man: Ojibwa Henry Bird Steinhauer Brought Religion to the Cree." *Beaver* 68 (October/November 1988): 28–33.

1227. **Slickpoo, Allen P., Sr.** "The Nex Perce Attitude Toward the Missionary Experience." *Idaho Yesterdays* 31 (spring/summer 1987): 35–37.

1228. **Smith, Donald.** "The Life of George Copway or Kah-ge-ga-gah-bowh (1818–1869) and a Review of His Writings." *Journal of Canadian Studies* 23, no. 3 (1988): 8–38.

1229. **Sprague, Roderick.** "Plateau Shamanism and Marcus Whitman." *Idaho Yesterdays* 31 (spring/summer 1987): 55–56.

1230. **Stevens, Leland R.** "Mission to the Chippewa, 1857–1868." *Concordia Historical Institute Quarterly* 58 (fall 1985): 117–35.

1231. **Stevenson, J. C.** "Metlakatla: William Duncan on the North Coast Bring Jesus to the Tsimshians." *Beaver* 66 (August/September 1986): 35–41.

1232. **Stevenson, Winona.** "The Red River Indian Mission School and John West's 'Little Charges,' 1820–1833." *Native Studies Review* 4 no. 1/2 (1988): 129–66.

1233. **Walker, Willard.** "The Roles of Samuel A. Worcester and Elias Boudinot in the Emergence of a Printed Cherokee Syllabic Literature." *International Journal of American Linguistics* 51 (1985): 610–12.

1234. **Weber, Francis J.** *The California Missions: Bibliography.* Hong Kong: Libra for Archdiocese of Los Angeles, 1987.

1235. **Webster, Jonathan H.** "The Oregon Mission and the ABCFM." *Idaho Yesterdays* 31 (spring/summer 1987): 24–34.

1236. **Whitehead, Margaret,** ed. *They Call Me Father: The Memoirs of Father Nicolas Coccola.* Vancouver: University of British Columbia Press, 1988.

1237. **Zanger, Martin N.** "'Straight Tongue's Heath Word': Bishop Whipple and the Episcopal Mission to the Chippewas." In *Churchmen and the Western Indians, 1820–1902,* ed. C. A. Milner II and F. O'Neil, 177–214. Norman: University of Oklahoma Press, 1985.

5.4   MISSIONS AND MISSIONARIES, 1900–1990

1238. **Amoss, Pamela T.** "The Indian Shaker Church." In *Northwest Coast,* ed. W. Suttles, 633–39. Vol. 7 of *Handbook of North American Indians,* ed. W. Sturtevant. Washington, D.C.: Smithsonian Institution, 1990.

1239. **Barney, Gerald D.** *Mormons, Indians, and the Ghost Dance Religion of 1890.* Lanham, Md.: University Press of America, 1986.

1240. **Carson, Mary Eisenman.** *Blackrobe for the Yankton Sioux: Fr. Sylves-*

ter Eisenman, OSB (1891–1948). Chamberlain, S.Dak.: Tipit Press, 1989.

1241.   **Clow, Richmond L.** "Mary Clementine Collins: Missionary at Standing Rock." *North Dakota History* 52, no. 2 (1985): 10–17.

1242.   **Hilbert, Robert, S.J.** "Contemporary Catholic Mission Work Among the Sioux." In *Sioux Indian Religion: Tradition and Innovation,* ed. R. J. DeMallie and D. Parks, 139–47. Norman: University of Oklahoma Press, 1987.

1243.   **Langford, Sister John Christopher, M.S.B.T.** "Holy Rosary Indian Mission: The Mississippi Choctaw and the Catholic Church." In *After Removal: The Choctaw in Mississippi,* ed. S. J. Wells and R. Tubby, 112–21. Jackson: University Press of Mississippi, 1985.

1244.   **Moore, Edgar W.** "The Bierkempers, Navajos, and the Ganado Presbyterian Mission, 1901–1912." *American Presbyterians: Journal of Presbyterian History* 64 (1986): 125–38.

1245.   **Poor Man, Mercy.** "Christian Life Fellowship Church." In *Sioux Indian Religion: Tradition and Innovation,* ed. R. J. DeMallie and D. Parks, 149–55. Norman: University of Oklahoma Press, 1987.

VI
Legal Relations Between Native Americans and Others

6.1 LEGAL HISTORY

1246. "The Alaska Native Claims Settlement Act: An Illustration in the Quest for Native Self-Determination." *Oregon Law Review* 66 (1987): 195–218.

1247. Anderson, Steven B. "Native American Law and the Burger Court: A Shift in Judicial Methods." *Hamline Law Review* 8 (1985): 671–712.

1248. Baca, Lawrence. "The Legal Status of American Indians." In *History of Indian-White Relations,* ed. W. Washburn, 230–37. Vol. 4 of *Handbook of North American Indians,* ed. W. Sturtevant. Washington, D.C.: Smithsonian Institution Press, 1988.

1249. Ball, Milner. "Constitution, Court, Indian Tribes." *American Bar Foundation Research Journal* 1987 (winter 1987): 1–140.

1250. Bodayla, Stephen D. "Can an Indian Vote? *Elk v. Wilkins,* a Setback for Indian Citizenship." *Nebraska History* 67, no. 4 (1986): 372–80.

1251. Brodeur, Paul. *Restitutions: The Land Claims of the Mashpee, Passamaquoddy, and Penobscot Indians of New England.* Hanover, N.H.: University Press of New England, 1985.

1252. Campisi, Jack. "From Stanwix to Canandaigua: National Policy, States

Rights, and Indian Land." In *Iroquois Land Claims,* ed. C. Vecsey and W. A. Starna, 49–65. Syracuse, N.Y.: Syracuse University Press, 1988.

1253. ———. "The New England Tribes and Their Quest for Justice." In *The Pequots in Southern New England: The Fall and Rise of an American Indian Nation,* ed. L. M. Hauptman and J. D. Wherry, 179–93. Norman: University of Oklahoma Press, 1990.

1254. Carroll, Jane Lamm. "Dams and Damages: The Ojibway, the United States, and the Mississippi Headwaters Reservoirs." *Minnesota History* 52 (1990): 2–15.

1255. Churchill, Ward. "The Black Hills are not for Sale: A Summary of the Lakota Struggle for the 1868 Treaty Territory." *Journal of Ethnic Studies* 18, no. 1 (1990): 127–42.

1256. Clifton, James A. "Simon Pokagon's Sandbar: Potawatomi Claims to Chicago's Lakefront." *Michigan History* 71 (September 1987): 14–17.

1257. Cohen, Fay G. *Treaties on Trial: The Continuing Controversy over Northwest Indian Fishing Rights.* Seattle: University of Washington Press, 1986.

1258. Daniel, Michelle. "From Blood Feud to Jury System: The Metamorphosis of Cherokee Law from 1750 to 1840." *American Indian Quarterly* 11 (1987): 1–30.

1259. **Deloria, Vine, Jr.** "The Distinctive Status of Indian Rights." In *The Plains Indians of the Twentieth Century,* ed. P. Iverson, 237–48. Norman: University of Oklahoma Press, 1985.

1260. **Dickason, Olive P.** "Old World Law, New World Peoples, and the Concepts of Sovereignty." In *Essays on the History of North American Discovery and Exploration,* ed. S. H. Palmer and D. Reinhartz, 52–78. College Station: Texas A & M Press, 1988.

1261. **Diubaldo, Richard J.** "Canada's Inuit and Whiteman's Justice, 1900–1945: The Law Paramount." *Storia Nordamericana* 5, no. 1 (1988): 125–36.

1262. **Doherty, Robert.** *Disputed Waters: Native Americans and the Great Lakes Fishery.* Knoxville: University Press of Kentucky, 1900.

1263. **Fixico, Donald L.** "Chippewa Fishing and Hunting Rights and the Voight Decision." In *An Anthology of Western Great Lakes Indian History,* ed. D. L. Fixico, 481–519. Milwaukee: American Indian Studies, University of Wisconsin—Milwaukee, 1987.

1264. **Gibson, Arrell.** "Philosophical, Legal, and Social Rationales for Appropriating the Tribal Estate, 1607–1980." *American Indian Law Review* 12 (1985): 3–37.

1265. **Gover, Kevin,** and **Robert Lawrence.** "Avoiding *Santa Clara Pueblo v. Martinez:* The Litigation in Federal Court of Civil Actions Under the Indian Civil Rights Act." *Hamline Law Review* 8 (1985): 497–542.

1266. **Green, L. C.,** and **Olive P. Dickason.** *The Law of Nations and the New World.* Edmonton: University of Alberta Press, 1989.

1267. **Grossman, George S.** "Indians and the Law." In *New Directions in American Indian History,* ed. C. G. Calloway, 97–126. Norman: University of Oklahoma Press, 1988.

1268. **Hagan, William T.** "To Correct Certain Evils: The Indian Land Claims Cases." In *Iroquois Land Claims,* ed. C. Vecsey and W. A. Starna, 17–30. Syracuse, N.Y.: Syracuse University Press, 1988.

1269. **Harman, Sasha.** "Writing History by Litigation: The Legacy and Limitation of Northwest Indian Rights Cases." *Columbia* 4 (winter 1990): 5–15.

1270. **Harring, Sidney L.** "Crazy Snake and the Creek Struggle for Sovereignty: The Native American Legal Culture and American Law." *American Journal of Legal History* 34 (1990): 365–80.

1271. ———. "Crow Dog's Case: A Chapter in the Legal History of Tribal Sovereignty." *American Indian Law Review* 14 (1989): 191–240.

1272. ———. "The Incorporation of Alaskan Nations Under American Law: United States and Tlingit Sovereignty, 1867–1900." *Arizona Law Review* 31, no. 2 (1989): 279–328.

1273. **Hauptman, Laurence M.** "The Historical Background to the Present-Day Seneca Nation–Salamanca Lease Controversy." In *Iroquois Land Claims,* ed. C. Vecsey and W. A. Starna, 101–22. Syracuse, N.Y.: Syracuse University Press, 1988.

1274. ———. "Iroquois Land Issues: At Odds with the 'Family of New York.'" In *Iroquois Land Claims,* ed. C. Vecsey and W. A. Starna, 67–86. Syracuse, N.Y.: Syracuse University Press, 1988.

1275.   Hecht, Robert. "Taos Pueblo and the Struggle for Blue Lake." *American Indian Culture and Research Magazine* 13, no. 1 (1989): 53–77.

1276.   Hopkins, Kenneth M. "Henry S. Johnston: Attorney for the Otoe-Missourias." *Chronicles of Oklahoma* 83 (spring 1985): 28–47.

1277.   Hoxie, Frederick E. "Towards a 'New' North American Indian Legal History." *American Journal of Legal History* 30 (1986): 351–57.

1278.   Hundley, Norris, Jr. "The Winters Decision and Indian Water Rights: A Mystery Reexamined." In *The Plains Indians of the Twentieth Century,* ed. P. Iverson, 77–106. Norman: University of Oklahoma Press, 1985.

1279.   Jaimes, M. Annette. "The Pit River Indian Land Claim Disputes in Northern California." *Journal of Ethnic Studies* 14, no. 4 (1987): 47–64.

1280.   Keller, Robert H. "America's Native Sweet: Chippewa Treaties and the Right to Harvest Maple Sugar." *American Indian Quarterly* 13 (1989): 117–35.

1281.   ———. "Washington State and Tribal Sovereignty." *Pacific Northwest Quarterly* 79 (1988): 98–108.

1282.   Knack, Martha. "Federal Jurisdiction over Indian Water Rights in Nevada." In *Battle Born: Federal-State Conflict in Nevada During the Twentieth Century,* ed. A. C. Titus, 121–36. Dubuque, Iowa: Kendall-Hunt Co., 1989.

1283.   Lacey, Linda J. "The White Man's Law and the American Indian Family in the Assimilation Era." *Arkansas Law Review* 40, no. 2 (1987): 327–80.

1284.   Lavin, Chris. "Responses to the Cayuga Land Claim." In *Iroquois Land Claims,* ed. C. Vecsey and W. A. Starna, 87–100. Syracuse, N.Y.: Syracuse University Press, 1988.

1285.   Lawson, Paul E., and Jennifer Scholes. "Jurisprudence, Peyote, and the Native American Church." *American Indian Culture and Research Journal* 10, no. 1 (1986): 13–28.

1286.   Locklear, Arlinda. "The Allotment of the Oneida Reservation and Its Legal Ramifications." In *The Oneida Indian Experience: Two Perspectives,* ed. J. Campisi and L. M. Hauptman, 83–93. Syracuse, N.Y.: Syracuse University Press, 1988.

1287.   ———. "The Oneida Land Claims: A Legal Overview." In *Iroquois Land Claims,* ed. C. Vecsey and W. A. Starna, 141–53. Syracuse, N.Y.: Syracuse University Press, 1988.

1288.   Loftin, John D. "Anglo-American Jurisprudence and the Native American Tribal Quest for Religious Freedom." *American Indian Culture and Research Journal* 13, no. 1 (1989): 1–52.

1289.   McCool, Daniel. *Command of the Waters: Iron Triangles, Federal Water Development, and Indian Water.* Berkeley: University of California Press, 1987.

1290.   ———. "Precedent for the Winters Doctrine: Seven Legal Principles." *Journal of the Southwest* 29 (1987): 164–78.

1291.   MacLean, Brian D., and R. S. Ratner. "An Historical Analysis of Bills C-67 and C-68: Implications for the Native Offender." *Native Studies Review* 3, no. 1 (1987): 31–58.

1292.   McNabb, Steven, and Lynn A. Robbins. "Native Institutional Responses to the Alaska Native Claims to Settlement Act: Room for Optimism." *Journal of Ethnic Studies* 13, no. 1 (1985): 13–27.

1293.   Margolis, R. T. "The White Man's Law." *Wilson Quarterly* 10, no. 1 (1986): 125.

1294.   Massie, Michael. "The Cultural Roots of Indian Water Rights." *Annals of Wyoming* 59, no. 1 (1987): 15–28.

1295.   Mikkanen, Arvo Q. *"Rice v. Rehner:* A Limitation on the Exercise of Tribal Governmental Powers Based on Historical Factors?" *American Indian Journal* 9, no. 2 (1986): 2–15.

1296.   Miller, Bruce G. "After the FAP: Tribel Reorganization After Federal Recognition." *Journal of Ethnic Studies* 17, no. 2 (1989): 89–102. [Upper Skagit]

1297.   Norgren, Jill. "Protection of What Rights They Have: Original Principles of Federal Indian Law." *North Dakota Law Review* 64 (1988): 73–120.

1298.   Parker, Linda S. *Native American Estate: The Struggle over Indian and Hawaiian Lands.* Honolulu: University of Hawaii Press, 1989.

1299.   Peterson, Susan C. "Discrimination and Jurisdiction: Seven Civil Rights Cases in South Dakota, 1976–1982." *Journal of the West* 25 (October 1986): 44–48.

1300.   Peterson, Thomas F. *"Oregon Department of Fish and Wildlife v. Klamath Indian Tribe:* Diminishing Treaty Rights." *Oregon Law Review* 64 (1986): 701–26.

1301.   Petosky, John. "Indians and the First Amendment." In *American Indian Policy in the Twentieth Century,* ed. V. Deloria, Jr., 221–38. Norman: University of Oklahoma Press, 1985.

1302.   Phelps, Glenn A. "Representation Without Taxation: Citizenship and Suffrage in Indian Country." *American Indian Quarterly* 9, no. 2 (1985): 135–48.

1303.   Porter, Frank W., III. "Non-recognized American Indian Tribes in the Eastern United States: An Historical Overview." In *Strategies for Survival: American Indians in the Eastern United States,* ed. F. W. Porter III, 1–42. Westport, Conn.: Greenwood Press, 1986.

1304.   Potter, Constance, and Jean West. "Indian Depredation Cases Under the Acts of 1891 and 1915." *Prologue 22* (winter 1990): 369–99.

1305.   Powless, Irving, Jr. "The Sovereignty and Land Rights of the Houdenosaunee." In *Iroquois Land Claims,* ed. C. Vecsey and W. A. Starna, 155–61. Syracuse, N.Y.: Syracuse University Press, 1988.

1306.   Quinn, William W., Jr. "Federal Acknowledgement of American Indian Tribes: The Historical Development of a Legal Concept." *American Journal of Legal History* 34 (1990): 331–64.

1307.   Ragsdale, John W., Jr. "The Movement to Assimilate the American Indians: A Jurisprudential Study." *UMKC Law Review* [University of Missouri at Kansas City] 57, no. 3 (1989): 399–436.

1308.   Ray, Arthur J. "Creating the Image of the Savage in Defense of the Crown: The Ethnohistorian in Court." *Native Studies Review* 6, no. 2 (1990): 13–30.

1309.   Roessel, Faith. "Federal Recognition—A Historical Twist of Fate." *NARF Legal Review* 14 (summer 1989): 1–9.

1310.   Rusco, Elmer R. "Early Nevada and Indian Law." *Western Legal History* 2 (1989): 163–90.

1311.   ———. "Purchasing Lands for Nevada Indian Colonies." *Nevada Historical Society Quarterly* 32 (1989): 1–22.

1312.   Shipek, Florence C. "Mission Indians and Indians of California Land Claims." *American Indian Quarterly* 13, no. 4 (1989): 409–20.

1313.   Slagle, Al Logan. "Unfinished Justice: Completing the Restoration and Acknowledgement of California Indian Tribes." *American Indian Quarterly* 13, no. 4 (1989): 325–45.

1314.   Springer, James Warren. "American Indians and the Law of Real Property in Colonial New England." *American Journal of Legal History* 30 (1986): 25–38.

1315.   Sutton, Imre, ed. *Irredeemable America: The Indians' Estate and Land Claims.* Albuquerque: University of New Mexico Press, 1985.

1316.   Talbot, Steve. "Desecration and American Indian Religious Freedom." *Journal of Ethnic Studies* 12, no. 4 (1985): 1–18.

1317.   Tarlock, A. D. "One River, Three Sovereigns: Indian and Interstate Water Rights." *Land and Water Law Review* 22 (1987): 631–71.

1318.   Tellinghuisen, Roger A. "The Indian Child Welfare Act of 1978: A Practical Guide with [Limited] Commentary." *South Dakota Law Review* 34, no. 3 (1989): 660–99.

1319.   Thomas, Monica E. "The Alaska Native Claims Settlement Act: Conflict and Controversy." *Polar Record* 23 (1986): 27–36.

1320.   Turner, Shelley. "The Native American's Right to Hunt and Fish: An Overview of the Aboriginal Spiritual and Mystical Belief System, the Effect of European Contact, and the Continu-ing Fight to Observe a Way of Life." *New Mexico Law Review* 19 (1989): 377–423.

1321.   Ulmer, Mark. "Tribal Property: Defining the Parameters of the Federal Trust Relationship Under the Nonintercourse Act: Catawba Indians." *American Indian Law Review* 12 (1985): 109–74.

1322.   Vecsey, Christopher. "The Issues Underlying Iroquois Land Claims." In *Iroquois Land Claims,* ed. C. Vecsey and W. A. Starna, 1–16. Syracuse, N.Y.: Syracuse University Press, 1988.

1323.   Vecsey, Christopher, and William A. Starna, eds. *Iroquois Land Claims.* Syracuse, N.Y.: Syracuse University Press, 1988.

1324.   Vetter, William V. "Of Tribal Courts and 'Territories': Is Full Faith and Credit Required?" *California Western Law Review* 23, no. 2 (1987): 219–72.

1325.   Volk, Paul S. "The Legal Trail of Tears: Supreme Court Removal of Tribal Court Jurisdiction over Crimes by and Against Reservation Indians." *New England Law Review* 20 (1985): 247–83.

1326.   Wallace, Mary. "The Supreme Court and Indian Water Rights." In *American Indian Policy in the Twentieth Century,* ed. V. Deloria, Jr., 197–220. Norman: University of Oklahoma Press, 1985.

1327.   Walsh, John F. "Settling the Alaska Native Claims Settlement Act." *Stanford Law Review* 38 (1985): 227–63.

1328.   Whitson, Hollis A. "A Policy Review of the Federal Government's Relocation of Navajo Indians Under P.L. 93-531 and P.L. 96-305." *Arizona Law Review* 27, no. 2 (1985): 371–414.

1329.   Wilkinson, Charles F. *American Indians, Time, and the Law: Historical*

Rights at the Bar of the Supreme Court. New Haven, Conn.: Yale University Press, 1987.

1330. ———. "Indian Tribes and the American Constitution." In *Indians in American History: An Introduction,* ed. F. E. Hoxie, 117–34. Arlington Heights, Ill.: Harlan Davidson, 1988.

1331. ———. "The Old Quest to Enforce the Old Promises: Indian Law in the Modern Era." *NARF Legal Review* 10 (summer 1985): 5–22.

1332. ———. "The Place of Indian Law in Constitutional Law and History." Comments by Deana Harragarra Waters and Paul L. Murphy. In *The Impact of Indian History on the Teaching of United States History: Proceedings of the 1984 Chicago Conference, Sessions 1–2,* 103–29. D'Arcy McNickle Center for the History of the American Indian, Occasional Papers in Curriculum, no. 2. Chicago: Newberry Library, 1985.

1333. **Williams, Robert A., Jr.** *The American Indian in Western Legal Thought: The Discourses of Conquest.* New York: Oxford University Press, 1989.

1334. ———. "Documents of Barbarism: The Contemporary Legacy of European Racism and Colonialism in the Narrative Traditions of Federal Indian Law." *Arizona Law Review* 31, no. 2 (1989): 237–78.

1335. ———. "Jefferson, the Norman Yoke, and American Indian Lands." *Arizona Law Review* 29, no. 2 (1987): 165–94.

1336. ———. "Small Steps on the Long Road to Self-Sufficiency for Indian Nations: The Indian Tribal Governmental Tax Status Act of 1982." *Harvard Journal of Legislation* 22 (1985): 335–97.

1337. **Wishart, David L.** "Compensation for Dispossession: Payments to the Indians for Their Lands on the Central and Northern Great Plains in the Nineteenth Century." *National Geographic Research* 6 (winter 1990): 94–109.

1338. **Work, Shannon D.** "The Alaska Native Claims Settlement Act: An Illusion in the Quest for Native Self-Determination." *Oregon Law Review* 66 (1987): 195–218.

1339. **Zion, James W.** "The Navajo Peacemaker Court: Deference to the Old and Accommodation to the New." *American Indian Law Review* 11 (1985): 89–109.

6.2 LEGAL TREATISES AND COMMENTARIES

1340. **American Indian Law Center.** *Indian Family Law and Child Welfare: A Text.* Washington, D.C.: National American Indian Court Judges Association, 1986.

1341. **American Indian Lawyer Training Program.** *Indian Tribes as Sovereign Governments: A Sourcebook on Federal-Tribal History, Law and Policy.* Oakland, Calif.: AIRI Press, 1988.

1342. "American Indian Sacred Religious Sites and Government Development: A Conventional Analysis in an Unconventional Setting." Notes. *Michigan Law Review* 85, no. 4 (1987): 771–808.

1343. "American Indians and the First Amendment: Site-Specific Religion and Public Religion and Public Land Management." *Utah Law Review* 1987 (1987): 673–702.

1344. **Anders, Gary C.** "A Critical Analysis of the Alaska Native Land Claims and Native Corporate Development." *Journal of Ethnic Studies* 13, no. 1 (1985): 1–12.

1345.   Anders, Gary C., and Kathleen K. Anders. "Incompatible Goals in Unconventional Organization: The Politics of Alaska Native Corporations." *Organization Studies* 7 (1986): 213–33.

1346.   Anderson, Bob, and Lare Aschenbrenner. "Alaska Native Tribes Battle Discrimination." *NARF Legal Review* 12 (winter 1986): 1–7.

1347.   Atkinson, Karen J. "The Alaska National Interest Lands Conservation Act: Striking the Balance in Favor of 'Customary and Traditional' Subsistence Uses by Alaska Natives." *Natural Resources Journal* 27 (1987): 421–40.

1348.   Atwood, Barbara Ann. "Fighting over Indian Children: The Uses and Abuses of Jurisdictional Ambiguity." *UCLA Law Review* 36, no. 6 (1989): 1051–1108.

1349.   Barlett, Richard H. "Hydroelectric Power and Indian Water Rights on the Prairies." *Prairie Forum* 14 (1989): 177–94.

1350.   Barsh, Russell L. "The Ethnocidal Character of the State and International Law." *Journal of Ethnic Studies* 16, no. 4 (1989): 1–30.

1351.   Berger, Thomas. "Alaska Native Lands." *American Land Forum* 6 (1986): 46–49.

1352.   ———. *Village Journey: The Report of the Native Review Commission.* New York: Hill & Wang, 1985.

1353.   Black, Kathryn, David Bundy, Cynthia Pickering Christianson, and Cabot Christianson. "When Worlds Collide: Alaska Native Corporation and the Bankruptcy Code." *Alaska Law Review* 6 (1989): 73–131.

1354.   Blumm, Michael C. "A Trilogy of Tribes v. FERC: Reforming the Federal Role in Hydropower Licensing." *Harvard Environmental Law Review* 10 (1986): 1–59.

1355.   Bowman, Margaret B. "The Reburial of Native American Skeletal Remains: Approaches to the Resolution of a Conflict." *Harvard Environmental Law Review* 13, no. 1 (1989): 147–208.

1356.   Burton, Lloyd. *American Indian Water Rights and the Limits of Law.* Lawrence: University of Kansas Press, 1990.

1357.   Carter, Nancy Carol. *American Indian Law: Research and Sources.* New York: Haworth Press, 1985.

1358.   Chartier, Clem. "Aboriginal Rights and Land Issues: The Métis Perspective." In *The Quest for Justice: Aboriginal Peoples and Aboriginal Rights,* ed. M. Boldt and J. A. Long, 54–61. Toronto: University of Toronto Press, 1985.

1359.   Cleland, Charles E. "Indian Treaties and American Myths: Roots of Social Conflict over Treaty Rights." *Native Studies Review* 6 (1990): 81–87.

1360.   Clinton, Robert N. "The Curse of Relevance: An Essay on the Relationship of Historical Research to Federal Indian Litigation." *Arizona Law Review* 18, no. 1 (1986): 29–46.

1361.   ———. "Reservation Specificity and Indian Adjudication: An Essay on the Importance of Limited Contextualism in Indian Law." *Hamline Law Review* 8 (1985): 493–543.

1362.   ———. "The Right of Indigenous Peoples as Collective Group Rights." *Arizona Law Review* 32, no. 4 (1990): 739–47.

1363.   Cole, D. H. "A Signal Conflict Between Equal Footing and Aboriginal Indian Title." *Environmental Law* 16 (1985): 163–74.

1364. Collins, Richard B. "The Future Course of the Winters Doctrine." *University of Colorado Law Review* 56 (1985): 481–94.

1365. ———. "Indian Consent to American Government." *Arizona Law Review* 31, no. 2 (1989): 365–88.

1366. ———. "Indians' Allotment Water Rights." *Land and Water Law Review* 20 (1985): 421–57.

1367. Commanda, Mary Jane. "Significance of the Indian Treaties." *Archivist* 16 (November/December 1989): 4–5.

1368. Coulter, Robert T., and Steven M. Tullberg. "Indian Land Rights." *Antioch Law Journal* 3 (1985): 153–82.

1369. Crawford, Katherine B. "State Authority to Tax Non-Indian Oil and Gas Production on Reservations: *Cotton Petroleum Corporation v. New Mexico.*" *Utah Law Review* 1989 (1989): 495–519.

1370. Dahl, Eric William. "Native American Religious Freedom and Federal Land Management." *Northeast Indian Quarterly* 7 (1990): 14–23.

1371. Deloria, Vine, Jr. "Laws Founded in Justice and Humanity: Reflections on the Content and Character of Federal Indian Law." *Arizona Law Review* 32, no. 2 (1989): 203–24.

1372. ———. "A Simple Question of Humanity: The Moral Dimensions of the Reburial Issue." *NARF Legal Review* 14 (spring 1989): 1–14.

1373. Doremus, Christine A. "Jurisdiction over Adjudications Involving the Abenaki Indians of Vermont." *Vermont Law Review* 10 (1985): 417–35.

1374. Echo-Hawk, Walter R. "Museum Rights Versus Indian Rights: Guidelines for Assessing Competing Legal Interests in Native Cultural Resources." *New York University Review of Law and Social Change* 14 (1986): 437–53.

1375. Emory, Meade, and Robert A. Warden. "Income Taxation of Distributions: An Ambiguity in Need of Clarification." *Washington Law Review* 64, no. 3 (1989): 551–80.

1376. Feit, Harvey A. "James Bay Cree Self-Government and Land Management." In *We Are Here: Politics of Aboriginal Land Tenure,* ed. E. N. Wilmsen, 68–98. Berkeley: University of California Press, 1989.

1377. Feldman, Stephen M. "Preemption and the Dormant Commerce Clause: Implications for Federal Indian Law." *Oregon Law Review* 64 (1986): 667–700.

1378. Feraca, Stephen E. "Inside the BIA: Or, 'We're Getting Rid of All These Honkies.'" In *The Invented Indian: Cultural Fictions and Government Policies,* ed. J. A. Clifton, 271–90. New Brunswick, N.J.: Transaction Publishers, 1990.

1379. Flushman, Bruce S., and Joe Barbieri. "Aboriginal Title: The Special Case of California." *Pacific Law Journal* 17 (1986): 391–460.

1380. Folk-Williams, John A. "The Use of Negotiated Agreements to Resolve Water Disputes Involving Indian Rights." *Natural Resources Journal* 28 (1988): 63–103.

1381. Freidmund, Jeffery. "An Indian Victory on Sovereignty Grounds." *Williamette Law Review* 22, no. 1 (1986): 201–8.

1382. Getches, David H. "Competing Demands for the Colorado River." *University of Colorado Law Review* 56 (1985): 413.

1383. Gordon, Sarah B. "Indian Religious Freedom and Governmental Development of Public Lands." *Yale Law Review* 94 (1985): 1447–71.

1384. Gould, Diane Brazen. "The First Amendment and the American Indian Religious Freedom Act: An Approach to Protecting Native American Religion." *Iowa Law Review* 71 (1986): 869–91.

1385. Gross, Emma. *Contemporary Federal Policy Toward American Indians.* Contributions in Ethnic Studies, no. 25. New York: Greenwood Press, 1989.

1386. Hedger, Jeff. "Indian Law—The Validity of Tribal Severance Taxes Without Secretarial Approval." *Land and Water Law Review* 20 (1985): 121–29.

1387. Holland, Lauren. "The Use of Litigation in Indian Natural Resource Disputes." *Journal of Energy Law and Policy* 10, no. 1 (1989): 33–35.

1388. Hollinger, Joan. "Beyond the Best Interests of the Tribe: The Indian Child Welfare Act and the Adoption of Indian Children." *University of Detroit Law Review* 66, no. 3 (1989): 451–502.

1389. Holt, H. Barry. "Archaeological Preservation on Indian Lands: Conflicts and Dilemmas in Applying the National Historic Preservation Act." *Environmental Law* 15 (1985): 413–53.

1390. ———. "Can Indians Hunt in National Parks? Determinable Indian Treaty Rights and *United States v. Hicks*." *Environmental Law* 16 (1986): 207–54.

1391. Houghton, Richard H., III. "An Argument for Indian Status for Native Hawaiians—The Discovery of a Lost Tribe." *American Indian Law Review* 14 (1989): 1–55.

1392. Hoxie, Frederick E. "War of the Worlds: History Versus the Law in Charles Wilkinson's *American Indians, Time, and the Law.*" *Law and Social Enquiry* 13, no. 4 (1988): 791–99.

1393. Johnson, Ralph W., and James M. Madden. "Sovereign Immunity in Indian Tribal Law." *American Indian Law Review* 12, no. 2 (1987): 153–94.

1394. Jones, Camille. "Towards Equal Rights and Amendment of Section 12 (1) (b) of the Indian Act: A Postscript to *Lovelace v. Canada.*" *Harvard Women's Law Journal* 8 (1985): 195–213.

1395. Keller, Robert, ed. "Washington State and Tribal Sovereignty." *Pacific Northwest Quarterly* 79 (1988): 98–108.

1396. Kienetz, Alvin. "Decolonization in the North: Canada and the United States." *Canadian Review of Studies of Nationalism* 13 (1986): 57–77

1397. Kisken, Sybil R. "The Uncertain Legal Status of Alaskan Natives After *Native Village of Stevens v. Alaska.* Management and Planning: Exposing the Fallacious Distinctions Between Alaska Natives and Lower Forty-Eight Indians." *Arizona Law Review* 31, no. 2 (1989): 405–22.

1398. Kronowitz, Rachel San, Joanne Lichtman, Steven Paul McSloy, and Matthew G. Olson. "Toward Consent and Cooperation: Reconsidering the Political Status of Indian Nations." *Harvard Civil Rights–Civil Liberties Law Review* 22 (1987): 509–14.

1399. Kunstler, William M., and Stephen B. Young. "Symposium on Indian Law." *Hamline Law Review* 8 (1985): 493–96.

1400. Lacy, Paul E. "Implications of Summa Corporation on the Property Rights of the Eastern American Indians." *California Western Law Review* 22 (1986): 385–402.

1401. **Laurence, Robert.** "The Bald Eagle, the Florida Panther, and the Nation's Word: An Essay on the 'Quiet' Abrogation of Indian Treaties and the Proper Reading of *United States v. Dion.*" *Journal of Land Use and Environmental Law* 4 (1988): 1–21.

1402. ———. "Indian Treaties and Their Abrogation by Statutes on General Applicability: A Not Entirely Nonpartisan Essay on 'Quiet' Abrogations, 'Actual' Consideration, and the Unhappy Reception Given *U.S. v. Dion.*" *BYU Law Review* 1989 (1989): 853–75.

1403. ———. "Learning to Live with the Plenary Power of Congress over the Indian Nations." *Arizona Law Review* 30 (1988): 459–65.

1404. **Lester, Gregory.** *Aboriginal Land Rights: Some Notes on the Historiography of English Claims in North America.* Ottawa: Canadian Arctic Resources Committee, 1988.

1405. **Leventhal, Larry B.** "American Indians — The Trust Responsibility: An Overview." *Hamline Law Review* 8 (1985): 493–625.

1406. **Lichtenfels, Christine.** "Indian Reserved Water Rights: An Argument for the Right to Export and Sell." *Land and Water Law Review* 24 (1989): 131–51.

1407. **Lightstone, Marie.** "Indian Water Law: The Continuing Jurisdictional Nightmare." *Natural Resources Journal* 25 (1985): 841–56.

1408. **Lomawaima, Hartman H.** "Native American Collections: Legal and Ethical Concerns." *History News* 45 (May/June 1990): 6–7.

1409. **London, J. Tate.** "The 1991 Amendments to the Alaska Native Claims Settlement Act: Protection for Native Lands?" *Stanford Environmental Law Journal* 8 (1989): 200–228.

1410. **Long, J. Anthony,** and **Menno Boldt.** "Self-Determination and Extra-Legal Action: The Foundations of Native American Protest." *Canadian Review of Studies in Nationalism* 15 (1988): 111–20.

1411. **Lorbiecki, Stefanie A.** "Indian Sovereignty Versus Oklahoma's Gambling Laws." *Tulsa Law Journal* 20 (1985): 605–33.

1412. **Lord, William B.,** and **Mary G. Wallace,** eds. *Symposium Proceedings on Indian Water Rights and Water Resource Management.* Bethesda, Md.: American Water Resources Association, 1989.

1413. **McDonald, Michael.** "Indian Status: Colonialism or Sexism?" *Canadian Community Law Journal* 9 (1987): 23–48.

1414. **McDonnell, Dale L.** "Federal and State Regulation of Gambling and Liquor Sales Within Indian Country." *Hamline Law Review* 8 (1985): 493–599.

1415. **McElroy, Scott.** "Tribal Water Rights: 1986." *NARF Legal Review* 11 (fall 1986): 1–6.

1416. **McGuire, Thomas R.** "Operations on the Concept of Sovereignty: A Case Study of Indian Decision-Making." *Urban Anthropology* 17 (1988): 75–86.

1417. **MacIntyre, Donald D.** "Quantification of Indian Reserved Water Rights in Montana: State ex. rel. Greeley in the Footsteps of 'San Carlos Apache Tribe.'" *Public Land Law Review* 8 (1987): 33–60.

1418. **McKanna, Clare, Jr.** "Life Hangs in the Balance: The U.S. Supreme Court's Review of *Ex Parte Gon-*

Shay-Ee." Western Legal History 3 (1990): 197–211.

1419. McLish, Thomas P. "Tribal Sovereign Immunity: Searching for Sensible." *Columbia Law Review* 88 (1988): 173–93.

1420. McNeil, Kent. *Common Law/ Aboriginal Title.* Oxford: Clarendon Press, 1989.

1421. McSloy, Steven Paul. "American Indians and the Constitution: An Argument for Nationhood." *American Indian Law Review* 14 (1989): 139–90.

1422. Marston, Lester J., and **David A. Fink.** "The Indian Commerce Clause: The Reports of Its Death Have Been Greatly Exaggerated." *Golden Gate Law Review* 16 (1986): 205–43.

1423. Maynes, Frank E. "Indian Water Rights: Then and Now." *Colorado Lawyer* 15 (1986): 1–7.

1424. Mills, Antonia. "A Comparison of Wet'suwet'en Cases of the Reincarnation Type with Gitksan and Beaver." *Journal of Anthropological Research* 44, no. 4 (1988): 385–416.

1425. Montgomery, Andrew S. "Tribal Sovereignty and Congressional Dominion: Rights-of-Way for Gas Pipelines on Indian Reservations." *Stanford Law Review* 38 (1985): 195–225.

1426. Moore, Michael R. "Native American Water Rights: Efficiency and Fairness." *Natural Resources Journal* 29 (1989): 763–91.

1427. Morgan, Edward M. "Self-Government and the Constitution: A Comparative Look at Native Canadians and American Indians." *American Indian Law Review* 12 (1986): 39–56.

1428. Native American Rights Fund. "Indian Gaming: Law and Regulation." *NARF Legal Review* 10 (fall 1985): 1–5.

1429. Nelson, John Stuart. "Native American Religious Freedom and the Peyote Sacrament: The Precarious Balance Between State Interests and the Free Exercise Clause." *Arizona Law Review* 31, no. 2 (1989): 423–46.

1430. Neumann, Rita. "Taxation of Natural Resources Production on Tribal Lands." *Taxes* 63 (1985): 813–19.

1431. Noble, Heather. "Tribal Powers to Regulate Hunting in Alaska." *Alaska Law Review* 4 (1987): 223–76.

1432. Ott, Brian Richard. "Indian Fishing Rights in the Pacific Northwest: The Need for Federal Intervention." *Boston College Environmental Affairs Law Review* 14, no. 2 (1987): 313–43.

1433. Parlow, Anita. "Cry, Sacred Ground: Big Mountain, U.S.A." *American Indian Law Review* 14 (1989): 301–22.

1434. Pemberton, Richard, Jr. "'I Saw That It Was Holy': The Black Hills and the Concept of Sacred Land." *Law and Inequality* 3 (1985): 287–342.

1435. Peterson, John E., II. "Dance of the Dead: A Legal Tango for Control of Native American Skeletal Remains." *American Indian Law Review* 15 (1990): 115–50.

1436. Pommersheim, Frank. "The Crucible of Sovereignty: Analyzing Issues of Tribal Jurisdiction." *Arizona Law Review* 31, no. 2 (1989): 329–64.

1437. ———. "The Reservation as Place: A South Dakota Essay." *South Dakota Law Review* 34, no. 2 (1989): 246–70.

1438. Pryer, Anita Clark, and **Gypsy Cowherd Bailey.** "An Indian Site-

Specific Religious Claim Again Trips Over Judeo-Christian Stumbling Blocks." *Journal of Land Use and Environmental Law* 5 (1989): 193–322.

1439.   **Resnick, Judith.** "Dependent Sovereigns: Indian Tribes, States, and the Federal Courts." *University of Chicago Law Review* 56 (1989): 671–759.

1440.   **Rosenberg, Erica.** "Native Americans' Access to Religious Sites: Underprotected Under the Free Exercise Clause?" *Boston College Law Review* 26 (1985): 463–96.

1441.   **Rotenberg, Daniel.** "American States and Indian Tribes: Power Conflicts in the Supreme Court." *Dickinson Law Review* 92, no. 1 (1987): 81–103.

1442.   **Royster, Judith,** and **Rory SnowArrow Fausett.** "Control of Reservation Environment: Tribal Primacy, Federal Delegation, and the Limits of State Intrusion." *Washington Law Review* 64, no. 3 (1989): 581–659.

1443.   **Rusco, Elmer R.** "Civil Liberties Guarantees Under Tribal Law: A Survey of Civil Rights Provisions in Tribal Constitutions." *American Indian Law Review* 14 (1989): 269–300.

1444.   **Sanders, Douglas.** *Aboriginal Self-Government in the United States.* Kingston, Ont.: Institute of Intergovernmental Relations, Queens University, 1985.

1445.   **Schneebeck, Richard.** "Constitutional Law—Religious Freedom and Public Land Use." *Land and Water Law Review* 20 (1985): 109–19.

1446.   **Shapiro, Karen M.** "An Argument for the Marketability of Indian Reserved Water Rights: Tapping the Untapped Reservoir." *Idaho Law Review* 23, no. 2 (1987): 277–92.

1447.   **Shupe, Steven J.** "Indian Tribes in the Water Marketing Area." *American Indian Law Review* 15 (1990): 185–205.

1448.   ———. "Water in Indian Country: From Paper Rights to a Managed Resource." *University of Colorado Law Review* 57 (1986): 561–92.

1449.   **Sly, Peter W.** *Reserved Water Rights Settlement Manual.* Washington, D.C., and Covelo, Calif.: Island Press, 1988.

1450.   **Smith, Eric,** and **Mary Kancewick.** "The Tribal Status of Alaska Natives." *University of Colorado Law Review* 61 (1990): 455–516.

1451.   **Starna, William A.** "Aboriginal Title and Traditional Iroquois Land Use: An Anthropological Perspective." In *Iroquois Land Claims,* ed. C. Vecsey and W. A. Starna, 31–48. Syracuse, N.Y.: Syracuse University Press, 1988.

1452.   "*State v. Cutler:* Limitation on Indians' Hunting Rights in Idaho." Notes. *Idaho Law Review* 23, no. 2 (1987): 327–42.

1453.   **Stevens, Anastasia.** "Pueblo Water Rights in New Mexico." *Natural Resources Journal* 28 (1988): 535–83.

1454.   **Swaney, Karen Lee.** "Waiver of Indian Tribal Sovereign Immunity in the Context of Economic Development." *Arizona Law Review* 31, no. 2 (1989): 389–404.

1455.   **Togerson, James E.** "Indians Against Immigrants—Old Rivals, New Rules: A Brief Review and Comparison of Indian Law in the Contiguous United States, Alaska, and Canada." *American Indian Law Review* 14 (1989): 57–104.

1456.   **Trentadue, Jesse C.** "Tribal Court Jurisdiction over Collection Suits by Local Merchants and Lenders: An Obstacle to Credit for Reservation Indians." *American Indian Law Review* 13 (1987): 1–58.

1457.   Tso, Tom. "The Process of Decision Making in Tribal Courts." *Arizona Law Review* 31, no. 2 (1989): 225–36.

1458.   Ubelaker, Douglas, and Lauryn Guttenplan Grant. "Human Skeletal Remains: Preservation or Reburial?" *Yearbook of Physical Anthropology* 32 (1989): 249–87.

1459.   van Gestel, Allan. "The New York Indian Land Claims: The Modern Landowner as Hostage." In *Iroquois Land Claims,* ed. C. Vecsey and W. A. Starna, 123–39. Syracuse, N.Y.: Syracuse University Press, 1988.

1460.   Vetter, William V. "The Four Decisions in *Three Affiliated Tribes* and Pre-emption by Policy." *Land and Water Law Review* 23 (1988): 43–112.

1461.   Vollman, Tim, and M. Sharon Blackwell. "'Fatally Flawed': State Court Approval of Conveyances by Indians of the Five Civilized Tribes — Time for Legislative Reform." *Tulsa Law Journal* 25 (1989): 1–62.

1462.   Wagoner, Robert J. "The Subject Matter Jurisdiction of New Mexico District Courts over Civil Cases Involving Indians." *New Mexico Law Review* 15 (1985): 75–96.

1463.   Walker, Jana L. "On-Reservation Treaty Hunting Rights: Abrogation Versus Regulation by Federal Conservation Statutes — What Standard?" *Natural Resources Journal* 26 (1986): 187–96.

1464.   Walz, B. Eliot. "*State ex. rel. Joseph v. Redwing:* A Dictionary Definition Rationale for the Infringement of Tribal Self-Government." *South Dakota Law Review* 34, no. 3 (1989): 701–20.

1465.   Weatherford, Gary D., and F. Lee Brown, eds. *New Courses for the Colorado: Major Issues for the Next Century.* Albuquerque: University of New Mexico Press, 1986.

1466.   Wilkinson, Charles F. "The Idea of Sovereignty: Native Peoples, Their Lands, and Their Dreams." *NARF Legal Review* 13 (1988): 1–11.

1467.   Wright, Gordon K. "Recognition of Tribal Decisions in State Courts." *Stanford Law Review* 37 (1985): 1397–1424.

1468.   Yanagida, Joy A. "The Pacific Salmon Treaty." *American Journal of International Law* 81, no. 3 (1987): 577–92.

1469.   Young, Stephen Y. "Indian Tribal Sovereignty and American Fiduciary Undertakings." *Whittier Law Review* 8, no. 4 (1987): 825–915.

7

Ethnohistory: Historical Approaches to Indian Communities and Cultures

7.1 CULTURAL OVERVIEWS OF NORTH AMERICA

1470. **Axtell, James.** *After Columbus: Essays in the Ethnohistory of Colonial North America.* New York: Oxford University Press, 1988.

1471. **Barsh, Russell L.** "The Nature and Spirit of North American Political Systems." *American Indian Quarterly* 10 (1986): 181–98.

1472. **Bee, Robert L.** "The Predicament of the Native American Leader." *Human Organization* 49 (1990): 56–63.

1473. **Bonvillain, Nancy.** "Gender Relations in Native North America." *American Indian Culture and Research Journal* 13, no. 2 (1989): 1–28.

1474. **Colson, Elizabeth.** "Political Organizations in Tribal Societies: A Cross-Cultural Comparison." *American Indian Quarterly* 10 (1986): 5–19.

1475. **Cornell, Stephen.** "The Transformation of the Tribe: Organization and Self-Concept in Native American Ethnicities." *Ethnic and Racial Studies* 11 (January 1988): 27–47.

1476. **Cox, Bruce Alden,** ed. *Native People, Native Lands: Canadian Indians, Inuit, and Métis.* New York: Oxford University Press, 1988.

1477. **Edmunds, R. David.** "Two Cases Studies." *Wilson Quarterly* 10, no. 1 (1986): 132–42. [Overview of contemporary Hopi and Oklahoma Potawatomi]

1478. **Feest, Christian,** ed. *Indians and Europe: An Interdisciplinary Collection of Essays.* Aachen, West Germany: Edition Herodot, 1987.

1479. **French, Laurence.** *Psychocultural Change and the American Indian: An Ethnohistorical Analysis.* New York: Garland, 1987.

1480. **Harmon, Alexandra.** "When Is an Indian Not an Indian? Friends of the Indian and the Problems of Indian Identity." *Journal of Ethnic Studies* 18, no. 2 (1990): 95–123.

1481. **Hoxie, Frederick E.,** ed. "The History of American Indian Leadership." *American Indian Quarterly* (special issue) 10, no. 1 (1986).

1482. **Isaac, Barbara,** ed. *Hall of the North American Indian.* Cambridge, Mass.: Harvard University Press, 1990.

1483. **Katz, William.** *Black Indians: A Hidden Heritage.* New York: Atheneum, 1986. [Young adult]

1484. **Kupferer, Harriet J.** *Ancient Drums, Other Moccasins: Native North American Cultural Adaptation.* Englewood Cliffs, N.J.: Prentice Hall, 1988.

1485. Lewis, G. Malcolm. "Indian Delimitations of Primary Biogeographic Regions." In *A Cultural Geography of North American Indians,* ed. T. E. Ross and T. G. Moore, 93–106. Boulder, Colo.: Westview Press, 1987.

1486. Lurie, Nancy O. "Money, Semantics, and Indian Leadership." *American Indian Quarterly* 10 (1986): 47–63.

1487. McMillan, Alan D. *Native Peoples and Cultures of Canada: An Anthropological Overview.* Vancouver, B.C.: Douglas and McIntyre, 1989.

1488. Navakov, Peter, and **Robert Easton.** *Native American Architecture.* New York: Oxford University Press, 1989.

1489. Oxendine, Joseph B. *American Indian Sports Heritage.* Champaign, Ill.: Human Kinetics Books, 1988.

1490. Parman, Donald. "Indians of the Modern West." In *The Twentieth-Century West: Historical Interpretations,* ed. G. D. Nash and R. W. Etulain, 147–72. Albuquerque: University of New Mexico Press, 1989.

1491. Powers, William K. "And Then There Were None: Pan-Indianism Reconsidered." *Storia Nordamericana* 5, no. 1 (1988): 49–70.

1492. Ross, Thomas E., and **Tyrel G. Moore,** eds. *A Cultural Geography of the North American Indian.* Boulder, Colo.: Westview Press, 1987.

1493. Saum, Lewis O. "'Astonishing the Natives': Bringing the Wild West to Los Angeles." *Montana* 38 (1988): 2–13.

1494. "Southwest Museum: Native Cultures of the Americas." *Masterkey* (special issue) 61, no. 2/3 (1987): 1–48.

1495. Swentzell, Rina. "The Process of Culture—The Indian Perspective." *El Palacio* 93 (summer/fall 1987): 31–37.

1496. Tsosie, Rebecca. "Changing Women: The Cross-Currents of American Indian Feminine Identity." *American Indian Culture and Research Journal* 12, no. 1 (1988): 1–38.

1497. Walker, Deward E., Jr., and **David Carrasco.** *Witchcraft and Sorcery of the North American Native Peoples.* Reprint, Moscow: University of Idaho Press, 1988.

1498. Weatherford, Jack. *Indian Givers: How the Indians of the Americas Transformed the World.* New York: Crown Publishers, 1988.

1499. Weibel-Orlando, Joan. "Elders and Elderlies: Well-Being in Indian Old Age." *American Indian Culture and Research Journal* 13, no. 3–4 (1989): 149–70.

7.2 CULTURES OF THE NORTHEAST

1500. Abler, Thomas S. "Micmacs and Gypsies: Occupation of the Peripatetic Niche." In *Papers of the Twenty-First Algonquian Conference,* ed. W. Cowan, 1–11. Ottawa: Carleton University Press, 1990.

1501. Abler, Thomas S., and **Michael H. Logan.** "The Florescence and Demise of Iroquoian Cannibalism: Human Sacrifice and Malinowski's Hypothesis." *Man in the Northeast* 35 (1988): 1–26.

1502. Allen, John L. "The Illy-Smelling Sea: Indians, Information, and the Early Search for the Passage." *Man in the Northeast* 33 (1987): 127–35.

1503. Anderson, H. Allen. "The Delaware and Shawnee Indians and the Republic of Texas, 1820–45." *Southwestern Historical Quarterly* 94 (1990): 231–60.

1504. Arden, Harvey. "The Iroquois: Keepers of the Fire." *National Geographic* 172 (September 1987): 374–403.

1505. Aubert de Gaspé, Philippe Joseph. *Yellow Wolf and Other Tales of the St. Lawrence.* Translated by Jane Brierly. Montreal: Vehicule Press, 1990. [1786–1871]

1506. Bartels, Dennis A. "Kta-qmkuk Ilnui Sagimawoutie: Aboriginal Rights and the Myth of the Micmac Mercenaries in Newfoundland." In *Native People, Native Lands: Canadian Indians, Inuit, and Métis,* edited by B. A. Cox, 32–36. Ottawa: Carleton University Press, 1988.

1507. Becker, Marshall J. "Native Settlements in the Forks of the Delaware in the Eighteenth Century: Archaeological Implications." *Pennsylvania Archaeologist* 58 (1988): 42–60.

1508. ———. "The Okehocking Band of Lenape: Cultural Continuities and Accommodations in Southeastern Pennsylvania." In *Strategies for Survival: American Indians in the Eastern United States,* ed. F. W. Porter III, 43–84. Westport, Conn.: Greenwood Press, 1986.

1509. ———. "A Summary of Lenape Socio-Political Organization and Settlement Pattern at the Time of European Contact: The Evidence for Collecting Bands." *Journal of Middle Atlantic Archaeology* 4 (1988): 79–83.

1510. Bonvillain, Nancy. *The Huron.* New York: Chelsea House, 1989.

1511. Bourque, Bruce J. "Ethnicity on the Maritime Peninsula, 1600–1759." *Ethnohistory* 36, no. 3 (1989): 257–84.

1512. Boyce, Douglas C. "'As the Wind Scatters the Smoke': The Tuscaroras in the Eighteenth Century." In *Beyond the Covenant Chain: The Iroquois and Their Neighbors in Indian North America, 600–1800,* ed. D. K. Richter and J. H. Merrell, 151–63. Syracuse, N.Y.: Syracuse University Press, 1987.

1513. Bradley, James W. *Evolution of the Onondaga Iroquois: Accommodating Change, 1500–1655.* Syracuse, N.Y.: Syracuse University Press, 1987.

1514. Bragdon, Kathleen J. "'Emphatical Speech and Great Actions': An Analysis of Seventeenth Century Native Speech Events Described in Early Sources." *Man in the Northeast* 33 (1987): 101–111.

1515. Branstner, Susan. "Tinonontate Huron Indians at Michilimackinac." *Michigan History* 73 (November/December 1989): 24–31.

1516. Brashler, Janet C. "A Middle Sixteenth-Century Susquehannock Village in Hampshire County, West Virginia." *West Virginia Archaeologist* 2 (1983): 1–30.

1517. Brasser, T. J. C. "The Coastal Algonkians: People of the First Frontier." In *North American Indians in Historical Perspective,* ed. E. B. Leacock and N. O. Lurie, 64–91. Prospect Heights, Ill.: Waveland Press, 1988.

1518. Brenner, Elsie. "Sociological Implications of Mortuary Ritual Remains in the Seventeenth Century Native Southern New England." In *The Recovery of Meaning: Historical Archaeology in the Eastern United States,* ed. M. P. Leone and P. B. Potter, Jr., 147–81. Washington, D.C.: Smithsonian Institution Press, 1988.

1519. Caduto, Michael J. "Abenaki Myths: Living Legends of the People of the Dawn." *Vermont Life* 40 (winter 1986): 37–40.

1520. Calloway, Colin G. *The Abenaki*. New York: Chelsea House, 1989.

1521. ———. "Green Mountain Diaspora: Indian Population Movements in Vermont, Circa 1600–1800." *Vermont History* 54 (1986): 197–228.

1522. ———. *The Western Abenakis of Vermont, 1600–1800: War, Migration, and the Survival of an Indian People*. Norman: University of Oklahoma Press, 1990.

1523. Campbell, Richard D. *The People of the Land of Flint*. Lanham, Md.: University Press of America, 1985.

1524. Campisi, Jack. "The Emergence of the Mashantucket-Pequot Tribe, 1637–1975." In *The Pequots in Southern New England: The Fall and Rise of an American Indian Nation,* ed. L. M. Hauptman and J. D. Wherry, 117–40. Norman: University of Oklahoma Press, 1990.

1525. Campisi, Jack, and Laurence M. Hauptman, eds. *The Oneida Indian Experience: Two Perspectives.* Syracuse, N.Y.: Syracuse University Press, 1988.

1526. Cardy, Michael. "The Iroquois in the Eighteenth Century: A Neglected Source." *Man in the Northeast* 38 (1989): 1–20.

1527. Carlson, Richard G., ed. *Rooted Like the Ash Trees: New England Indians and the Land.* Naugatude, Conn.: Eagle Wing Press, 1987.

1528. Castellano, Marlene Brant. "Women in Huron and Ojibwa Societies." *Canadian Women Studies* 10 (summer/fall 1989): 45–49.

1529. Champagne, Duane. "The Delaware Revitalization Movement of the Early 1760s: A Suggested Reinterpretation." *American Indian Quarterly* 12 (1988): 107–26.

1530. Conner, Dennis, ed. *Onondaga: Portrait of a Native People.* Foreword by Laurence M. Hauptman, introduction by Ramon Gonyea. Syracuse, N.Y.: Syracuse University Press, 1985.

1531. Engelbrecht, William. "New York Iroquois Political Development." In *Cultures in Contact: The Impact of European Contacts on Native American Cultural Institutions, A.D. 1000–1800,* ed. W. W. Fitzhugh, 163–83. Washington, D.C.: Smithsonian Institution Press, 1985.

1532. Faux, David K. "Iroquoian Occupation of the Mohawk Valley During and After the Revolution." *Man in the Northeast* 34 (1987): 27–39.

1533. Feest, Christian. *The Powhatan Tribes.* New York: Chelsea House, 1990.

1534. Fenton, William N. *The False Faces of the Iroquois.* Norman: University of Oklahoma Press, 1987.

1535. ———. "A Further Note on Iroquois Suicide." *Ethnohistory* 33, no. 4 (1986): 448–57.

1536. ———. "The Iroquois in History." In *North American Indians in Historical Perspective,* ed. E. B. Leacock and N. O. Lurie, 129–68. Prospect Heights, Ill.: Waveland Press, 1988.

1537. ———. "Leadership in the Northeastern Woodlands of North America." *American Indian Quarterly* 10 (1986): 21–45.

1538. Friederici, Georg, Gabriel Nadeau, and Nathaniel Knowles. *Scalping and Torture: Warfare Practices Among North American Indians.* Ohsweken, Ont.: Irocrafts, 1986.

1539. Given, Brian J. "The Iroquois Wars and Native Arms." In *Native People, Native Lands: Canadian Indians, In-*

uit, and Métis, ed. B. A. Cox, 3–13. Ottawa: Carleton University Press, 1988.

1540. Graymont, Barbara. *The Iroquois.* New York: Chelsea House, 1988.

1541. Grumet, Robert S. *The Lenape.* New York: Chelsea House, 1990.

1542. Halbritter, Gloria, Loretta Metoxen, Judy Cornelius, Gerald Hill, Robert Smith, and **Purcell Powless.** "Oneida Traditions." In *The Oneida Indian Experience: Two Perspectives,* ed. J. Campisi and L. M. Hauptman, 145–52. Syracuse, N.Y.: Syracuse University Press, 1988.

1543. Hale, Duane Kendall. *Peacemakers of the Frontier: A History of the Delaware Tribe of Western Oklahoma.* Anadarko, Okla.: Western Delaware Tribal Press, 1987.

1544. Hamell, George R. "Mythical Realities and European Contact in the Northeast During the Sixteenth and Seventeenth Centuries." *Man in the Northeast* 33 (1987): 63–87.

1545. Hantman, Jeffrey L. "Between Powhatan and Quirank: Reconstructing Monacan Culture and History in the Context of Jamestown." *American Anthropologist* 92 (1990): 676–90.

1546. ———. "Monacan History and the Contact Era in Virginia." *Society for American Archaeology Bulletin* 8 (1990): 14.

1547. Hauptman, Laurence M., and **James D. Wherry,** eds. *The Pequots in Southern New England: The Fall and Rise of an American Indian Nation.* Norman: University of Oklahoma Press, 1990.

1548. Jennings, Francis. "'Pennsylvania Indians' and the Iroquois." In *Beyond the Covenant Chain: The Iroquois and Their Neighbors in Indian North America, 600–1800,* ed. D. K. Richter and J. H. Merrell, 75–91. Syracuse, N.Y.: Syracuse University Press, 1987.

1549. Josephy, Alvin M., Jr. "New England Indians, Then and Now." In *The Pequots in Southern New England: The Fall and Rise of an American Indian Nation,* ed. L. M. Hauptman and J. D. Wherry, 5–16. Norman: University of Oklahoma Press, 1990.

1550. Katzer, Bruce. "The Caughnawaga Mohawks: The Other Side of Ironwork." *Journal of Ethnic Studies* 15, no. 4 (1988): 39–55.

1551. Kelley, Marc A., Paul S. Sledzik, and **Sean P. Murphy.** "Health, Demographics, and Physical Constitution in Seventeenth-Century Rhode Island Indians." *Man in the Northeast* 34 (1987): 1–25.

1552. Konrad, Victor. "The Iroquois Return to Their Homeland: Military Retreat or Cultural Adjustment?" In *A Cultural Geography of North American Indians,* ed. T. E. Ross and T. G. Moore, 191–212. Boulder, Colo.: Westview Press, 1987.

1553. Kraft, Herbert. *The Lenape: Archaeology, History, and Ethnography.* Newark: New Jersey Historical Society, 1987.

1554. Krusche, Rolf. "The Origin of the Mask Concept in the Eastern Woodlands of North America." Translated by Annemarie Shimony and William C. Sturtevant. *Man in the Northeast* 31 (1986): 1–47.

1555. Kugel, Rebecca. "Factional Alignment Among the Minnesota Ojibwe, 1850–1880." *American Indian Culture and Research Journal* 9, no. 4 (1985): 23–48.

1556. Latta, Martha. "Iroquoian Stemware." *American Antiquity* 52 (1987): 717–24. [Native ceramics with European forms]

1557. Lenik, Edward J. "New Evidence on the Contact Period in Northeastern New Jersey and Southeastern New York." *Journal of Middle Atlantic Archaeology* 5 (1989): 103–20.

1558. Lynch, James. "The Iroquois Confederacy and the Adoption and Administration of Non-Iroquoian Individuals and Groups Prior to 1756." *Man in the Northeast* 30 (1985): 83–99.

1559. McBride, Kevin A. "Historical Archaeology of the Mashantucket Pequots, 1637–1900." In *The Pequots in Southern New England: The Fall and Rise of an American Indian Nation,* ed. L. M. Hauptman and J. D. Wherry, 96–116. Norman: University of Oklahoma Press, 1990.

1560. McConnell, Michael N. "Peoples 'In Between': The Iroquois and the Ohio Indians, 1720–1768." In *Beyond the Covenant Chain: The Iroquois and Their Neighbors in Indian North America, 600–1800,* ed. D. K. Richter and J. H. Merrell, 93–112. Syracuse, N.Y.: Syracuse University Press, 1987.

1561. McLester, Thelma Cornelius. "Oneida Women Leaders." In *The Oneida Indian Experience: Two Perspectives,* ed. J. Campisi and L. M. Hauptman, 108–25. Syracuse, N.Y.: Syracuse University Press, 1988.

1562. Mailhot, Jose. "Beyond Everyone's Horizon Stand the Naskapi." *Ethnohistory* 33, no. 4 (1986): 384–418.

1563. Marshall, Ingeborg. *Beothuks of Newfoundland: A Vanished People.* St. Johns, Nfld.: Breakwater Books, 1988.

1564. ———. "Beothuk and Micmac: Re-examining the Relationships." *Acadiensis* 17 (1988): 52–82.

1565. ———. *Reports and Letters by George Christopher Pulling Relating to the Beothuk of Newfoundland.* St. Johns, Nfld.: Breakwater Books, 1989.

1566. Martin, Charles A. "Innu (Montagnais) in Newfoundland." In *Papers of the Twenty-First Algonquian Conference,* ed. W. Cowan, 227–46. Ottawa: Carleton University Press, 1990.

1567. Mavor, James W., Jr., and Byron E. Dix. *Manitou: The Sacred Landscape of New England's Native Civilization.* Rochester, Vt.: Inner Traditions International, 1989.

1568. Merrell, James H. " 'Their Very Bones Shall Fight': The Catawba-Iroquois Wars." In *Beyond the Covenant Chain: The Iroquois and Their Neighbors in Indian North America, 600–1800,* ed. D. K. Richter and J. H. Merrell, 115–33. Syracuse, N.Y.: Syracuse University Press, 1987.

1569. Michelson, Gunther. "An Account of an Iroquois Condolence Council." *Man in the Northeast* 36 (1988): 61–75.

1570. Morrison, Alvin H. "Dawnland Dog-Feast: Wabanaki Warfare, Circa 1600–1760." In *Papers of the Twenty-First Algonquian Conference,* ed. W. Cowan, 258–78. Ottawa: Carleton University Press, 1990.

1571. Morrison, Alvin H., and David A. Ezzo. "Dawnland Dualism in Northeastern Regional Context." In *Papers of the Sixteenth Algonquian Conference,* ed. W. Cowan, 131–49. Ottawa: Carleton University Press, 1985.

1572. Niemczycki, Mary Ann. "Seneca Tribalization: An Adaptive Strategy." *Man in the Northeast* 36 (1988): 77–87.

1573. **Pearson, Bruce L.** "Savannah and Shawnee: The End of a Micro-controversy." *International Journal of American Linguistics* 53 (1987): 183–93.

1574. **Perdue, Theda.** "Cherokee Relations with the Iroquois in the Eighteenth Century." In *Beyond the Covenant Chain: The Iroquois and Their Neighbors in Indian North America, 600–1800*, ed. D. K. Richter and J. H. Merrell, 135–49. Syracuse, N.Y.: Syracuse University Press, 1987.

1575. **Peters, Russell M.** *The Wampanoags of Mashpee: An Indian Perspective on American History.* Jamaica Plains, N.Y.: [Privately printed], 1987.

1576. **Porter, Frank W., III.** *The Nanticoke.* New York: Chelsea House, 1987.

1577. ———. "The Nanticoke Indians in a Hostile World." In Strategies for Survival: American Indians in the Eastern United States, ed. F. W. Porter III, 139–71. Westport, Conn.: Greenwood Press, 1986.

1578. ———. *Strategies for Survival: American Indians in the Eastern United States.* Westport, Conn.: Greenwood Press, 1986.

1579. **Prins, Harald E. L.** "Micmacs and Maliseets in the St. Lawrence River Valley." In *Acts of the Seventeenth Algonquian Conference*, ed. W. Cowan, 263–78. Ottawa: Carleton University Press, 1986.

1580. **Richter, Daniel K.** "Ordeals of the Longhouse: The Five Nations in Early American History." In *Beyond the Covenant Chain: The Iroquois and Their Neighbors in Indian North America, 600–1800*, ed. D. K. Richter and J. H. Merrell, 11–27. Syracuse, N.Y.: Syracuse University Press, 1987.

1581. **Richter, Daniel K.,** and **James H. Merrell,** eds. *Beyond the Covenant Chain: The Iroquois and Their Neighbors in Indian North America, 600–1800.* Syracuse, N.Y.: Syracuse University Press, 1987.

1582. **Rogers, Edward S.,** ed. *A Northern Algonquian Source Book: Papers by Frank G. Speck.* New York: Garland, 1985.

1583. **Rountree, Helen C.** "Ethnicity Among the Citizen Indians of Tidewater Virginia, 1800–1930." In *Strategies for Survival: American Indians in the Eastern United States,* ed. F. W. Porter III, 173–209. Westport, Conn.: Greenwood Press, 1986.

1584. **Rudes, Blair,** and **Dorothy Crouse.** *The Tuscarora Legacy of J. N. B. Hewitt: Materials for the Study of the Tuscarora Language and Culture.* Mercury Series Paper, vol. 108. Hull, Queb.: Canadian Museum of Civilization, 1987.

1585. **Rumrill, Donald A.** "An Interpretation and Analysis of the Seventeenth Century Mohawk Nation: Its Chronology and Movements." *Bulletin and Journal of Archaeology for New York State* 90 (1985): 1–39.

1586. **Ruskin, Thelma.** *Indians of the Tidewater Country of Maryland, Delaware, Virginia, and North Carolina.* Lanham, Md.: Maryland History Press, 1985.

1587. **Shriver, Philip R.** "The Beaver Wars and the Destruction of the Erie Nation." *Timeline* 1 (1985): 29–41.

1588. **Simmons, William S.** "From Fakelore to Folklore: A Consideration of Some Wampanoag Texts." *Man in the Northeast* 30 (1985): 45–58.

1589. ———. "The Mystic Voice: Pequot Folklore from the Seventeenth Century to the Present." In *The Pequots in Southern New England: The Fall and Rise of an American Indian Nation,* ed. L.

M. Hauptman and J. D. Wherry, 141–75. Norman: University of Oklahoma Press, 1990.

1590. ———. *The Narragansett*. New York: Chelsea House, 1989.

1591. ———. *Spirit of the New England Tribes: Indian History and Folklore, 1620–1984*. Hanover, N.H.: University Press of New England, 1986.

1592. **Starna, William A.** "The Oneida Homeland in the Seventeenth Century." In *The Oneida Indian Experience: Two Perspectives,* ed. J. Campisi and L. M. Hauptman, 9–22. Syracuse, N.Y.: Syracuse University Press, 1988.

1593. ———. "The Pequot in the Early Seventeenth Century." In *The Pequots in Southern New England: The Fall and Rise of an American Indian Nation,* ed. L. M. Hauptman and J. D. Wherry, 33–47. Norman: University of Oklahoma Press, 1990.

1594. **Steckley, John L.** "An Ethnolinguistic Look at the Huron Longhouse." *Ontario Archaeology* 47 (1987): 19–32.

1595. ———. "How the Huron Became Wyandot: Onomastic Evidence." *Onomastica Canadiana* 70, no. 2 (1988): 59–70.

1596. ———. "The Huron Mat of War." *Archaeological Notes* 89, no. 6 (1989): 5–11.

1597. **Taylor, J. Garth.** "Labrador Inuit Use During the Early Contact Period." *Arctic Anthropology* 25 (1988): 120–35.

1598. **Tomkins, Edward.** "Photo Reveals Ancient Micmac Presence." *Archivist* 16 (November/December 1989): 16–17.

1599. **Usner, Daniel H., Jr.** "An American Indian Gateway: Some Thoughts on the Migration and Settlement of Eastern Indians Around Early St. Louis." *Gateway Heritage* 3 (winter 1990): 42–51.

1600. **Weinstein, Laurie.** "We're Still Living on Our Traditional Homeland: The Wampanoag Legacy in New England." In *Strategies for Survival: American Indians in the Eastern United States,* ed. F. W. Porter III, 85–112. Westport, Conn.: Greenwood Press, 1986.

1601. **Weinstein-Farson, Laurie.** *The Wampanoag*. New York: Chelsea House, 1989.

1602. **West, J. Martin.** "The Henry Hamilton Sketches: Visual Images of Woodland Indians." In *Selected Papers from the 1987 and 1988 George Rogers Clark Trans-Appalachian Frontier History Conferences,* ed. R. J. Holden, 35–53. Vincennes, Ind.: Vincennes University, 1990.

1603. **Wojelechowski, Franz.** *The Pauguset Tribes*. Nijmegen, Holland: Catholic University of Nijmegen, 1985.

7.3 CULTURES
OF THE SOUTHEAST

1604. **Alexander, Maxine.** "We Are Here Forever: Indians of the South." *Southern Exposure* 13 (1985): 12–15.

1605. ———, eds. *Indians of the South*. Durham, N.C.: Institute for Southern Studies, 1985.

1606. **Baird, W. David.** *The Quapaws*. New York: Chelsea House, 1989.

1607. **Bell, Amelia Rector.** "Separate People: Speaking of Creek Men and Women." *American Anthropologist* 92 (1990): 332–45.

1608. **Billie, James.** "Fighting Hun Tashuk Teek." *Southern Exposure* 13 (1985): 17–20.

1609. Blumer, Thomas J. "Wild Indians and the Devil: The Contemporary Catawba Indian Spirit World." *American Indian Quarterly* 9 (1985): 149–68.

1610. Bolton, Herbert Eugene. *The Hasinais: Southern Caddoans as Seen by the Earliest Europeans.* Edited by Russell M. Magnaghi. Norman: University of Oklahoma Press, 1987.

1611. Brain, Jeffrey P. *The Tunica-Biloxi.* New York: Chelsea House, 1988.

1612. Braund, Kathryn E. Holland. "Guardian of Tradition and Handmaidens of Change: Women's Roles in Creek Economic and Social Life During the Eighteenth Century." *American Indian Quarterly* 14 (1990): 239–58.

1613. Brescia, William. "Choctaw Oral Tradition Relating to Tribal Origin." In *The Choctaw Before Removal,* ed. C. K. Reeves, 3–16. Jackson: University Press of Mississippi, 1985.

1614. Brown, Virginia Pounds, ed. *Creek Indian History: A Historical Narrative of the Geneology, Traditions, and Downfall of the Muscoge or Creek Indian Tribe of Indians by One of the Tribe, George Stiggins (1788–1845).* Introduction and notes by William Stokes Wyman. Birmingham, Ala.: Birmingham Public Library Press, 1989.

1615. Champagne, Duane. "Cherokee Social Movements: A Response to Thornton." *American Sociological Review* 50 (February 1985): 127–30.

1616. Coleman, Louis. "Twenty-Five Days to the Choctaw Nation." *Chronicles of Oklahoma* 64 (1987): 4–15.

1617. Drechsel, Emanuel. "The Natchez Way." *Chronicles of Oklahoma* 65 (1987): 174–81.

1618. ———. "On Determining the Role of Chickasaw in the History and Origin of Mobilian Jargon." *International Journal of American Linguistics* 53 (1987): 21–29.

1619. ———. "Speaking 'Indian' in Louisiana." *Natural History* 95, no. 7 (1986): 4–13.

1620. Everett, Dianna. *The Texas Cherokees: A People Between Two Fires.* Norman: University of Oklahoma Press, 1990.

1621. Fogelson, Raymond D. "On the 'Petticoat Government' of the Eighteenth-Century Cherokee." In *Personality and the Cultural Construction of Society,* ed. D. K. Jordan and M. J. Swartz, 161–81. Tuscaloosa: University of Alabama Press, 1990.

1622. Franco, Jere. "The Alabama-Coushatta and Their Texas Friends." *East Texas Historical Journal* 27, no. 1 (1989): 31–43.

1623. Galloway, Patricia K. "Choctaw Factionalism and Civil War, 1746–1750.: In *The Choctaw Before Removal,* ed. C. K. Reeves, 120–56. Jackson: University Press of Mississippi, 1985.

1624. Garbarino, Merwyn S. *The Seminole.* New York: Chelsea House, 1989.

1625. "Georgia's Legacy of Native Indian Culture." *Early Georgia* (special issue) 35 (December 1985).

1626. Gettys, Marshall. "Historic Choctaw Pottery." *Chronicles of Oklahoma* 67 (1989): 414–25.

1627. Green, Michael D. *The Creeks.* New York: Chelsea House, 1990.

1628. Gregory, Hiram F. *The Southern Caddo: An Anthology.* New York: Garland, 1986.

1629. Griffith, Carolanne. "From Cherokee to Gatlinburg." *Southern Living* 20 (September 1986): 72–77.

1630. Grinde, Donald A. "Prelude to the Yamasee War: Environmental Adaptation of a Native People in the Southeast." In *Native Views of Indian-White Historical Relations,* ed. D. L. Fixico, 20–37. D'Arcy McNickle Center for the History of the American Indian, Occasional Papers in Curriculum, no. 7. Chicago: Newberry Library, 1989.

1631. Guice, John D. W. "Face to Face in Mississippi Territory." In *The Choctaw Before Removal,* ed. C. K. Reeves, 157–80. Jackson: University Press of Mississippi, 1985.

1632. Halliburton, R., Jr. "Chief Greenwood Leflore and His Mal Maison Plantation." In *After Removal: The Choctaw in Mississippi,* ed. S. J. Wells and R. Tubby, 56–63. Jackson: University Press of Mississippi, 1985.

1633. Hann, John H. *Apalachee: The Land Between the Rivers.* Gainesville: University Presses of Florida, 1988.

1634. Herring, Joseph B. "Cultural and Economic Resilience Among the Kickapoo Indians of the Southwest." *Great Plains Quarterly* 6 (1986): 263–75.

1635. Howard, James H., and Victoria Lindsay Levine. *Choctaw Music and Dance.* Norman: University of Oklahoma Press, 1990.

1636. Hudson, Charles M. "Some Thoughts on the Early Social History of the Cherokees." In *Conference on Cherokee Prehistory,* ed. D. G. Moore, 139–53. Swannanoa, N.C.: Warren Wilson College, 1986.

1637. ———. "The Spanish-Coosa Alliance in Sixteenth Century Georgia." *Georgia Historical Quarterly* 72 (1988): 599–626.

1638. Hudson, Charles M., Marvin Smith, David Hally, Richard Polhemus, and Chester DePratter. "Coosa: A Chiefdom in the Sixteenth-Century Southeastern United States." *American Antiquity* 50 (1985): 723–37.

1639. Jacobson, Daniel. "Alabama and Coushatta in Louisiana." *Southern Studies* 26 (summer 1987): 137–53.

1640. Kimball, Geoffrey. "Men's and Women's Speech in Koasati: A Reappraisal." *International Journal of American Linguistics* 53 (1987): 30–38.

1641. Kniffen, Fred B., Hiram F. Gregory, and George A. Stokes. *The Historic Indian Tribes of Louisiana, from 1542 to the Present.* Baton Rouge: Louisiana State University Press, 1987.

1642. Lankford, George E. *Native American Legends: Southeastern Legends: Tales from the Natchez, Caddo, Biloxi, Chickasaw, and Other Nations.* Little Rock, Ark.: August House, 1987.

1643. McAlexander, Hubert H. "The Saga of a Mixed-Blood Chickasaw Dynasty." *Journal of Mississippi History* 49 (1987): 288–300.

1644. McKee, Jesse O. *The Choctaw.* New York: Chelsea House, 1989.

1645. Magnaghi, Russell M., ed. *The Hasinais: Southern Caddoans as Seen by the Earliest Europeans.* Assembled by Herbert Eugene Bolton. Norman: University of Oklahoma Press, 1987.

1646. Merrell, James H. *The Catawbas.* New York: Chelsea House, 1989.

1647. ———. *The Indians' New World: Catawbas and Their Neighbors from European Contact Through the Era of Removal.* Chapel Hill: University of North Carolina Press, 1989.

1648. Moore, Alexander. *Nairne's Muskhogean Journals: The 1708 Expedition to the Mississippi River.* Jackson: University Press of Mississippi, 1988.

1649.   Moore, John H. "The Mvskoke National Question in Oklahoma." *Science and Society* 52 (1988): 163–90.

1650.   Moulton, Gary E., ed. *The Papers of Chief John Ross.* Vol. 1, *1807–1839.* Norman: University of Oklahoma Press, 1985.

1651.   ———. *The Papers of Chief John Ross.* Vol. 2, *1840–1866.* Norman: University of Oklahoma Press, 1985.

1652.   Newkumet, Vynola Beaver, and Howard Meredith. *Hasinai: A Traditional History of the Caddo Confederacy.* College Station: Texas A & M Press, 1988.

1653.   ———. "Into the Light: Origins of the Hasinai People." *Chronicles of Oklahoma* 66 (1988): 282–93.

1654.   Noley, Grayson. "The Early 1700s: Education, Economics, and Politics." In *The Choctaw Before Removal,* ed. C. K. Reeves, 73–119. Jackson: University Press of Mississippi, 1985.

1655.   ———. "1540: The First European Contact." In *The Choctaw Before Removal,* ed. C. K. Reeves, 55–72. Jackson: University Press of Mississippi, 1985.

1656.   Perdue, Theda. *The Cherokee.* New York: Chelsea House, 1989.

1657.   ———. *Native Carolinians: The Indians of North Carolina.* Raleigh, N.C.: Division of Archives and History, 1985.

1658.   ———. "Southern Indians and the Cult of True Womanhood." In *The Web of Southern Social Relations: Essays on Family Life, Education, and Women,* ed. W. J. Fraser, R. F. Saunders, Jr., and J. L. Wakelyn. 35–51. Athens: University of Georgia Press, 1985.

1659.   Potter, Eloise F., and John B. Funderburg. *Native Americans: The People and How They Lived.* Raleigh: North Carolina State Museum of Natural Sciences, 1986. [For young adults]

1660.   Reeves, Carolyn Keller. "Some Observations About the Choctaw Language of the Early Nineteenth Century." In *The Choctaw Before Removal,* ed. C. K. Reeves, 17–31.

1661.   ———, ed. *The Choctaw Before Removal.* Jackson: University Press of Mississippi, 1985.

1662.   Rountree, Helen C. *Pocahontas's People: The Powhatan Indians of Virginia Through Four Centuries.* Norman: University of Oklahoma Press, 1990.

1663.   ———. "The Termination and Dispersal of the Nottoway Indians of Virginia." *Virginia Magazine of History and Biography* 95 (1987): 193–214.

1664.   ———. *The Powhatan Indians of Virginia: The Traditional Culture.* Norman: University of Oklahoma Press, 1989.

1665.   Satz, Ronald N. "The Mississippi Choctaw: From the Removal Treaty to the Federal Agency." In *After Removal: The Choctaw in Mississippi,* ed. S. J. Wells and R. Tubby, 3–32. Jackson: University Press of Mississippi, 1985.

1666.   Smith, Marvin T. "Aboriginal Population Movements in the Early Historic Period Interior Southeast." In *Powhatan's Mantle: Indians in the Colonial Southeast,* ed. P. H. Wood, G. A. Waselkov, and M. T. Hatley, 21–34. Lincoln: University of Nebraska Press, 1989.

1667.   ———. *Archaeology of Aboriginal Culture Change in the Interior Southeast: Depopulation During the Early*

Historic Period. Gainesville: University of Florida Press, 1987.

1668. ———. "Indian Responses to European Contact: The Coosa Example." In *First Encounters: Spanish Explorations in the Caribbean and the United States, 1492–1570,* ed. J. T. Milanich and S. Milbrath, 135–49.

1669.   Sturtevant, William C. "Creek into Seminole." In *North American Indians in Historical Perspective,* ed. E. B. Leacock and N. O. Lurie, 92–128. Prospect Heights, Ill.: Waveland Press, 1988.

1670. ———, ed. *A Creek Source Book.* New York: Garland, 1987.

1671. ———, ed. *A Seminole Source Book.* New York: Garland, 1987.

1672.   "The 'Takinge Upp of Powhatan's Bones': Virginia Indians, 1585–1945." *Virginia Magazine of History and Biography* (special issue) 95, no. 2 (1987): 133–231

1673.   Tanner, Helen Hornbeck. "The Land and Water Communication Systems of the Southeastern Indians." In *Powhatan's Mantle: Indians in the Colonial Southeast,* ed. P. H. Wood, G. A. Waselkov, and M. T. Hatley, 6–20. Lincoln: University of Nebraska Press, 1989.

1674.   Turner, E. Randolph. "Socio-Political Organization Within the Powhatan Chiefdom and the Effects of European Contact, A.D. 1607–1646." In *Cultures in Contact: The Impact of European Contacts on Native American Cultural Institutions, A.D. 1000–1800,* ed. W. W. Fitzhugh, 193–224. Washington, D.C.: Smithsonian Institution Press, 1985.

1675.   Ward, Rufus. "Choctaw Farmsteads in Mississippi, 1830." In *After Removal; The Choctaw in Mississippi,* ed. S. J. Wells and R. Tubby, 33–41. Jackson: University Press of Mississippi, 1985.

1676.   Waselkov, Gregory A. "Indian Maps of the Colonial Southeast." In *Powhatan's Mantle: Indians in the Colonial Southeast,* ed. P. H. Wood, G. A. Waselkov, and M. T. Hatley, 292–343. Lincoln: University of Nebraska Press, 1989.

1677. ———. "Lamhitty's Map." *Southern Exposure* 16 (1988): 23–29. [300 years old]

1678.   Weddle, Robert S., Mary C. Markovsky, and Patricia Galloway, eds. *La Salle, the Mississippi, and the Gulf: Three Primary Docuements.* Translated by Ann Linda Bell and Robert S. Weddle. College Station: Texas A & M University Press, 1987.

1679.   Weisman, Brent Richards. *Like Beads on a String: A Culture History of the Seminole Indians in North Peninsular Florida.* Tuscaloosa: University of Alabama Press, 1989.

1680.   Wells, Samuel J. "The Role of Mixed Bloods in Mississippi Choctaw History." In *After Removal: The Choctaw in Mississippi,* ed. S. J. Wells and R. Tubby, 42–55. Jackson: University Press of Mississippi, 1985.

1681.   Wells, Samuel J., and Roseanna Tubby, eds. *After Removal: The Choctaw in Mississippi.* Jackson: University Press of Mississippi, 1985.

1682.   Wood, Peter H., Gregory A. Waselkov, and M. Thomas Hatley, eds. *Powhatan's Mantle: Indians in the Colonial Southeast.* Lincoln: University of Nebraska Press, 1989.

1683.   Wright, J. Leitch, Jr. *Creeks and Seminoles: Destruction and Regeneration of the Muscogulge People.* Lincoln: University of Nebraska Press, 1986.

7.4   CULTURES OF THE GREAT LAKES AND NORTH-CENTRAL REGION (INCLUDING ADJOINING AREAS OF CANADA)

1684. **Barlow, William, and David O. Powell.** "The Late Dr. Ward of Indiana: Rafinesque's Source of the Walam Olum." *Indiana Magazine of History* 82 (1986): 185–93.

1685. **Boatman, John.** "Historical Overview of the Wisconsin Area: From Early Years to the French, British, and Americans." In *An Anthology of Western Great Lakes Indian History,* ed. D. L. Fixico, 13–68. Milwaukee: American Indian Studies, University of Wisconsin—Milwaukee, 1987.

1686. **Brightman, Robert A.** "Primitivism in Missinippi Cree Historical Consciousness." *Man* 25 (March 1990): 108–48.

1687. ———. "The Windigo in the Material World." *Ethnohistory* 35, no. 4 (1988): 337–79.

1688. **Brown, Jennifer S. H., and Robert Brightman.** *"The Orders of the Dreamed, 1823": George Nelson on Cree and Northern Ojibwa Religion and Myth.* Winnipeg: University of Manitoba Press, 1987.

1689. **Buffalohead, Roger, and Priscilla Buffalohead.** *Against the Tide of American History: The Story of the Mille Lacs Anishinabe.* Cass Lake: Minnesota Chippewa Tribe, 1985.

1690. **Clifton, James A.** *The Pokagons, 1683–1983: Catholic Potawatomi Indians of the St. Joseph Rivery Valley.* Lanham, Md.: University Press of America, 1985.

1691. ———. "The Potawatomi." In *People of the Three Fires,* J. A. Clifton, G. L. Cornell, and J. M. McClurken, 40–74. Grand Rapids, Mich.: Grand Rapids Inter-Tribal Council, 1986.

1692. ———. *The Potawatomi.* New York: Chelsea Press, 1987.

1693. **Driben, Paul.** *Aroland Is Our Home: An Incomplete Victory in Applied Anthropology.* New York: AMS Press, 1986. [Ontario Ojibwa]

1694. ———. "A Death in the Family: The Strategic Importance of Women in Contemporary Northern Ojibwa Society." *Native Studies Review* 6, no. 1 (1990): 83–110.

1695. **Ebbott, Elizabeth.** *Indians in Minnesota.* Edited by J. Rosenblatt. 4th ed. Minneapolis: University of Minnesota Press, 1985.

1696. **Edmunds, R. David.** "Main Poc: Potawatomi Wabeno." *American Indian Quarterly* 9 (1985): 259–72. [A Potawatomi prophet and sorceror in the War of 1812]

1697. **Fixico, Donald L., ed.** *An Anthology of Western Great Lakes Indian History.* Milwaukee: American Indian Studies, University of Wisconsin—Milwaukee, 1987.

1698. **Goddard, Ives.** "Reflections of Historical Events in Some Traditional Fox and Miami Narratives." In *Papers of the Sixteenth Algonquian Conference,* ed. W. Cowan, 47–62. Ottawa: Carleton University Press, 1985.

1699. **Hauser, Raymond E.** "Warfare and the Illinois Indian Tribe During the Seventeenth Century: An Exercise in Ethnohistory." *Old Northwest* 10 (1984/85): 367–87.

1700. **Herring, Joseph B.** *The Enduring Indians of Kansas: A Century and a Half of Acculturation.* Lawrence: University of Kansas Press, 1990.

1701. **Hickerson, Harold.** "The

Chippewas of the Upper Great Lakes: A Study in Sociopolitical Change." In *North American Indians in Historical Perspective,* ed. E. B. Leacock and N. O. Lurie, 169–99. Prospect Heights, Ill.: Waveland Press, 1988.

1702. Holzkamm, Tim E. "Sturgeon Utilization by the Rainy River Ojibwa Bands." In *Papers of the Eighteenth Algonquian Conference,* ed. W. Cowan, 155–63. Ottawa: Carleton University Press, 1987.

1703. Horsman, Reginald. "The Wisconsin Oneidas in the Preallotment Years." In *The Oneida Indian Experience: The Perspectives,* ed. J. Campisi and L. M. Hauptman, 65–82. Syracuse, N.Y.: Syracuse University Press, 1988.

1704. Johnston, Basil. *Ojibway Ceremonies.* Toronto: McClelland and Stewart, 1987; Norman: University of Oklahoma Press, 1987.

1705. ———. *Ojibway Heritage: The Ceremonies, Rituals, Songs, Dances, Prayers, and Legends of the Ojibway.* Toronto: McClelland and Stewart, 1988; Norman: University of Oklahoma Press, 1989.

1706. Keesing, Felix. *The Menomini Indians of Wisconsin: A Study of Three Centuries of Cultural Contact and Change.* 1939. Reprint, Madison: University of Wisconsin Press, 1987.

1707. Kohl, Johann Georg. *Kitchi-Gami: Life Among the Lake Superior Ojibway.* 1860. Repring with a new introduction by Robert E. Bieder and additional translation, St. Paul: Minnesota Historical Society, 1985.

1708. Lytwyn, Victor P. "Ojibwa and Ottawa Fisheries Around Manitoulin Island: Historical and Geographical Perspectives on Aboriginal and Treaty Fishing Rights." *Native Studies Review* 6, no. 1 (1990): 1–30.

1709. McClurken, James. "The Ottawa." In *People of the Three Fires,* ed. J. A. Clifton, G. L. Cornell, and J. M. McClurken, 2–38. Grand Rapids, Mich.: Grand Rapids Inter-Tribal Council, 1986.

1710. ———. "Strangers in Their Own Land." *Grand River Valley Review* 6, no. 1 (1985): 2–26.

1711. Magnaghi, Russell M. "Red Slavery in the Great Lakes Country During the French and British Regime." *Old Northwest* 12 (1986: 201–17.

1712. Mason, Carol I. *Introduction to Wisconsin Indians: Prehistory to Statehood.* Salem, Wisc.: Sheffield Publishing, 1988.

1713. Meyer, Melissa L. "Signatures and Thumbprints: Ethnicity Among the White Earth Anishinaabeg, 1889–1920." *Social Science History* 14, no. 3 (1990): 305–45.

1714. Morris, J. L. *Indians of Ontario.* Ohsweken, Ont.: Irocrafts, 1986.

1715. Murphy, Joseph. *Potawatomie of the West: Origins of the Citizen Band.* Shawnee, Okla.: Citizen Band Potawatomie Tribe, 1988.

1716. Olson, Gordon, ed. *Michigan's Indians.* Grand Rapids, Mich.: Grand Rapids Inter-Tribal Council, 1986.

1717. Ourada, Patricia. *The Menominee.* New York: Chelsea House, 1990.

1718. Pentland, David H. "The Ashkee Indians." In *Papers of the Sixteenth Algonquian Conference,* ed. W. Cowan, 151–60. Ottawa: Carleton University Press, 1985.

1719. Peters, Bernard C. "Moon Names of the Chippewa." *Names* 36 (1988): 51–59.

1720. ———. "Wa-bish-kee-pe-nas and the Chippewa Reverence for Copper." *Michigan Historical Review* 15 (fall 1989): 47–60.

1721. Schmalz, Peter S. *The Ojibwa of Southern Ontario.* Toronto: University of Toronto Press, 1990.

1722. Schorer, C. E., ed. *Indian Tales of C. C. Trowbridge: Collected from Wyandots, Miamis, and Shawanoes.* Brighton, Mich.: Green Oak Press, 1985.

1723. Sugden, John. *The Shawnee in Tecumseh's Time.* Nortoff, West Cermany: Abhandlungen der Volkerkundlichen Arbeitgemeinschaft, 1990.

1724. Vecsey, Christopher. "Grassy Narrows Reserve: Mercury Pollution, Social Disruption, and Natural Resources: A Question of Autonomy." *American Indian Quarterly* 11 (1987): 287–314.

1725. Vennum, Thomas, Jr. *Wild Rice and the Ojibway People.* St. Paul: Minnesouta Historical Society, 1988.

1726. Vizenor, Gerald. "Minnesota Chippewa: Woodland Treaties to Tribal Bingo." *American Indian Quarterly* 13 (winter 1989): 31–57.

1727. Vogel, Virgil J. *Indian Names in Michigan.* Ann Arbor: University of Michigan Press, 1986.

7.5   CULTURES OF THE PLAINS (INCLUDING ADJOINING AREAS OF CANADA)

1728. Albers, Patricia C., and William R. James. "On the Dialectics of Ethnicity: To Be or Not to Be a Santee (Sioux)." *Journal of Ethnic Studies* 14, no. 1 (1986): 1–27.

1729. Anderson, Gary Clayton, and Alan R. Woolworth, *Through Dakota Eyes: Narrative Accounts of the Minnesota Indian War of 1862.* St. Paul: Minnesota Historical Society Press, 1987.

1730. Baird, W. David. *The Quapaws.* New York: Chelsea House, 1989.

1731. Bamforth, Douglas B. *Ecology and Human Organization on the Great Plains.* New York: Plenum Press, 1988.

1732. ———. "Historical Documents and Bison Ecology on the Great Plains." *Plains Anthropologist* 32, no. 115 (1987): 1–16.

1733. Barsh, Russell Lawrence. "Plains Indian Agrarianism and Class Conflict." *Great Plains Quarterly* 7 (1987): 83–90.

1734. Bentley, Christopher H. "The Comanche Shield: Symbol of Identity." In *American Indian Identity: Today's Changing Perspectives,* ed. C. E. Trafzer, 38–49. Publications in American Indian Studies, no. 1. San Diego: San Diego State University, 1985.

1735. Blakeslee, Donald L., and Robert Blasing. "Indian Trails in the Central Plains." *Plains Anthropologist* 33, no. 1 (1988): 17–26.

1736. Bleed, Peter. "Indian and Japanese Swords on the Northern Plains Frontier." *Nebraska History* 68, no. 3 (1987): 112–15. [Photos and essay on swords kept by Plains natives]

1737. Bolz, Peter. "'Life Among the Hunkpapa': A Case Study of German Indian Lore." In *Indians and Europe: An Interdisciplinary Collection of Essays,* ed. C. Feest, 475–90. Aachen, West Germany: Edition Herodot, 1987.

1738. Bray, Kingsley M. "Lone Horn's Peace: A New View of Sioux-Crow Relations, 1851–1858." *Nebraska History* 66, no. 1 (1985): 28–47.

1739. Brink, Jack. *Dog Day in Southern Alberta,* Archaeological Survey of

Alberta, Occasional Paper no. 28. Edmonton: Alberta Culture, Historical Resource Division, 1986.

1740. **Brooks, Robert L.,** and **Robert Bell.** "The Last Prehistoric People: The Southern Plains Villages." *Chronicles of Oklahoma* 67 (1989): 296–319.

1741. **Brownstone, Aaron.** "A New Perspective on the Blackfoot." *Rotunda* 18, no. 2 (1985): 41–45.

1742. **Bruguier, Leonard R.,** ed. *Remember Your Relatives: Yankton Sioux Images, 1851–1904, by Renee S. Flood and Shirley A. Bemie.* Marty, S.Dak.: Marty Indian School, 1985.

1743. **Bullchild, Percy.** *The Sun Came Down: The History of the World as My Blackfeet Elders Told It.* New York: Harper & Row, 1985.

1744. **Callahan, Alice Anne.** *The Osage Ceremonial Dance I'n-Lon-Schka.* Norman: University of Oklahoma Press, 1900.

1745. **Calloway, Colin G.** "'The Only Way Open to Us': The Crow Struggle for Survival in the Nineteenth Century." *North Dakota History* 53, no. 3 (1986): 25–34.

1746. **Christianson, James R.** "The Early Osages—The Ishmaelites of the Savages." *Kansas History* 11 (1988): 2–21.

1747. **Criqui, Orvel A.** "A Northern Cheyenne Called Roman Nose." *Kansas History* 8, no. 3 (1985): 176–85.

1748. **Darnell, Regna.** "Thirty-Nine Postulates of Plains Cree Conversation, 'Power,' and Interaction: A Culture-Specific Model." In *Papers of the Twenty-First Algonquian Conference,* ed. W. Cowan, 89–102. Ottawa: Carleton University Press, 1990.

1749. **De Flyer, Joseph E.** "From

Creation Stories to '49 Songs: Cultural Transactions with the White World as Portrayed in Northern Plains Indian Story and Song." *Studies in American Indian Literatures* 2 (spring 1990): 11–27.

1750. **Dempsey, Hugh A.** *Indian Tribes of Alberta.* Calgary: Glenbow Museum, 1986. [Update of 1979 version]

1751. ———, ed. "Simpson's Essay on the Blackfoot, 1841." *Alberta History* 38, no. 1 (1990): 1–14.

1752. **Dempsey, James.** "Persistence of a Warrior Ethic Among the Plains Indians." *Alberta History* 36, no. 1 (1988): 1–10.

1753. **Dickinson, Samuel D.** "Caddos Moved to the Little Missouri." *Arkansas Historical Quarterly* 49 (autumn 1990): 240–48.

1754. **Dodge, Richard Irving.** *The Plains of North America and Their Inhabitants.* 1877. Reprint, Newark: University of Delaware Press, 1989.

1755. **Duke, Philip.** "The Morning Star Sacrifice of the Skiri Pawnee as Described by Alfred C. Haddon." *Plains Anthropologist* 34, no. 149 (1989): 193–203.

1756. **Dunlay, Thomas.** "Fire and Sword: Ambiguity and the Plains War." In *The American Indian Experience: A Profile, 1524 to the Present,* ed. P. Weeks, 135–52. Arlington Heights, Ill.: Forum Press, 1988.

1757. **Dyck, Paul.** *Brule: The Sioux People of the Rosebud.* Flagstaff, Ariz.: Northland Press, 1985.

1758. **Ellis, Clyde.** "'Truly Dancing Their Own Way': The Modern Revival and Diffusion of the Gourd Dance." *American Indian Quarterly* 14 (1990): 19–34.

1759. **Fowler, Loretta.** *Shared Sym-*

bols, Contested Meanings: Alternative Views of Culture and History in an American Indian Society, the Gros Ventres, 1778–1984. Ithaca, N.Y.: Cornell University Press, 1987.

1760. ———. "'What They Issue You': Political Economy at Wind River." In The Plains Indians of the Twentieth Century, ed. P. Iverson, 187–217. Norman: University of Oklahoma Press, 1985.

1761. Frey, Rodney. The World of the Crow Indians: As Driftwood Lodges. Norman: University of Oklahoma Press, 1987.

1762. Gooderham, George H. "Teddy Yellow Fly." Alberta History 33 (winter 1985): 10–13. [Blackfoot councilor with a Blackfoot mother and Chinese father]

1763. Hamrick, William S. "Redeeming the Earth: Tragic Wisdom and the Plains Indians." Journal of the British Society for Phenomenology 16 (1985): 36–55.

1764. Hanson, Jeffrey. "Age-Set Theory and Plains Indian Age Grading: A Critical Review and Revision." American Ethnologist 15 (1988): 349–64.

1765. Hatton, Orin T. Power and Performance in Gros Ventre War Expedition Songs. Mercury Series Paper, vol. 114. Hull, Queb.: Canadian Museum of Civilization, 1990.

1766. Haynes, John J. The Forgotten People: The Story of the Fort Berthold Indian Mission, 1876–1985. Exeter: [Published by the author,] 1987.

1767. Heidenreich, C. Adrian. "The Native Americans' Yellowstone." Montana 35 (fall 1985): 2–17.

1768. Hickerson, Nancy P. "Jumana: The Missing Link in South Plains History." Journal of the West 31 (October 1990): 5–14.

1769. Hoig, Stan. The Cheyenne. New York: Chelsea House, 1989.

1770. Hoover, Herbert T. The Yankton Sioux. New York: Chelsea House, 1988.

1771. Hoxie, Frederick E. The Crow. New York: Chelsea House, 1989.

1772. Hughes, J. Donald. American Indians in Colorado. Boulder, Colo.: Pruett, 1987.

1773. Hungry Wolf, Adolf, and Beverly Hungry Wolf. Shadows of the Buffalo: A Family Odyssey Among the Indians. Edited by Pat Golblitz. New York: Morrow, 1985.

1774. Iverson, Peter, ed. The Plains Indians of the Twentieth Century. Norman: University of Oklahoma Press, 1985.

1775. Janetski, Joel C. Indians of Yellowstone Park. Salt Lake City: University of Utah Press, 1987.

1776. John, Elizabeth A. H. "An Earlier Chapter of Kiowa History." New Mexico Historical Review 60 (1985): 379–97.

1777. Kavanagh, Thomas. "The Comanche: Paradigmatic Anomaly or Ethnographic Fiction?" Haliska'i 4 (1985): 109–48.

1778. Kidd, Kenneth E. Blackfoot Ethnography. Archaeological Survey of Alberta, Manuscript Series, no. 8. Edmonton: Alberta Culture, Historical Resource Division, 1986.

1779. Linderman, Frank B. Wolf and the Winds. Introduction by Hugh A. Dempsey. Norman: University of Oklahoma Press, 1986. [Gros Ventre]

1780. McCoy, Ronald. Kiowa Memories: Images from Indian Territory, 1880. Santa Fe, N.Mex.: Morning Star Gallery, 1987.

1781. ———. "Plains Indian Shields: A Kiowa Miscellany." *Heritage of the Great Plains* 23 (spring 1990): 2–8.

1782. McDonnell, Janet A. "Sioux Women: A Pictographic Essay." *South Dakota History* 13 (1985): 227–44.

1783. McGinnis, Anthony. *Counting Coups and Cutting Horses: Intertribal Warfare on the Northern Plains, 1738–1889.* Evergreen, Colo.: Cordillera Press, 1990.

1784. Markoe, Glenn E., ed. *The Ogden B. Read Northern Plains Indian Collection.* With Raymond J. DeMallie and Royal B. Hassrick. Burlington, Vt.: Robert Hull Fleming Museum and University of Nebraska Press, 1986.

1785. Mikkelsen, Glen. "Indians and Rodeo." *Alberta History* 35, no. 3 (1987): 13–19.

1786. Milloy, John. *The Plains Cree: Warriors, Traders, and Diplomats, 1790–1870.* Winnipeg: University of Manitoba Press, 1988.

1787. Moore, John. *The Cheyenne Nation: A Social and Demographic History.* Lincoln: University of Nebraska Press, 1987.

1788. ———. "The Dialectics of Cheyenne Kinship: Variability and Change." *Ethnology* 27 (1988): 253–69.

1789. ———. "The Ornithology of Cheyenne Religionists." *Plains Anthropologist* 31, no. 113 (1986): 177–92.

1790. Morgan, George Robert, and Ronald R. Weedon. "Oglala Sioux Use of Medicinal Herbs." *Great Plains Quarterly* 10 (1990): 18–35.

1791. Morris, John, Charles R. Goins, and Edwin C. McReynolds. *Historical Atlas of Oklahoma.* Norman: University of Oklahoma Press, 1986.

1792. Murie, James. *Ceremonies of the Pawnee.* Edited by Douglas Parks. Lincoln: University of Nebraska Press, 1989.

1793. Orser, Charles E., Jr. "Real or Imagined Confusion in Ethnohistorical Research? A Rejoinder to Thurman." *North American Archaeologist* 8 (1987): 317–26.

1794. Paige, Harry W. *Land of the Spotted Eagle: A Portrait of the Reservation Sioux.* Photographs by Don Doll, S.J. Chicago: Loyola University Press, 1987.

1795. Pakes, Fraser J. "Seeing with the Stereotypic Eye: The Visual Image of the Plains Indians." *Native Studies Review* 1, no. 2 (1985): 1–32.

1796. Parks, Douglas R. "The Importance of Language Study for the Writing of Plains Indian History." In *New Directions in American Indian History,* ed. C. G. Calloway, 153–97. Norman: University of Oklahoma Press, 1988.

1797. ———. "Interpreting Pawnee Star Lore: Science or Myth?" *American Indian Culture and Research Journal* 9, no. 1 (1985): 53–65.

1798. Parks, Douglas R., and Waldo R. Wedel. "Pawnee Geography: Historical and Sacred." *Great Plains Quarterly* 5 (1985): 143–76.

1799. Paul, R. Eli. "Faces of the First Nebraskans." *Nebraska History* 69, no. 2 (1985): 50–59.

1800. ———, ed. "Lester Beach Platt's Account of the Battle of Massacre Canyon." *Nebraska History* 67, no. 4 (1986): 381–407. [1873 Sioux-Pawnee battle]

1801. "Plains Indian Cultures." *Great Plains Quarterly* 7 (1987): 67–138.

1802. Pond, Samuel W. *The Dakota*

or Sioux in Minnesota as They Were in 1834. Introduction by Gary Clayton Anderson. St. Paul: Minnesota Historical Society Press, 1986.

1803.   Poole, Dewitt Clinton. *Among the Sioux of Dakota: Eighteen Months' Experience as an Indian Agent, 1869–70.* St. Paul: Minnesota Historical Society, 1988.

1804.   Powers, William K. *War Dance: Plains Indian Musical Performance.* Tucson: University of Arizona Press, 1990.

1805.   Ridington, Robin. "Omaha Survival: A Vanishing Indian Tribe That Would Not Vanish." *American Indian Quarterly* 11, no. 1 (1987): 37–51.

1806.   Riebeth, Carolyn Reynolds. *J. H. Sharp Among the Crow Indians, 1902–1910: Personal Memories of His Life and Friendships on the Crow Reservation in Montana.* El Segundo, Calif.: Upton and Sons, 1985.

1807.   Rollings, Willard. *The Comanche.* New York: Chelsea House, 1989.

1808.   Salinas, Martin. *Indians of the Rio Grande Delta: Their Role in the History of Southern Texas and Northeastern Mexico.* Austin: University of Texas Press, 1990.

1809.   Samarin, William J. "Demythologizing Plains Indian Sign Language History." *International Journal of American Linguistics* 53 (1987): 65–73.

1810.   Schilz, Jodye Lynn Dickson, and Thomas F. Schilz. *Buffalo Hump and the Penateka Comanche.* El Paso: Texas Western Press, 1989.

1811.   Schneider, Mary Jane. *The Hidatsa.* New York: Chelsea House, 1989.

1812.   Schusky, Ernest L. "The Evolution of Indian Leadership on the Great Plains, 1750–1950." *American Indian Quarterly* 10 (1986): 65–82.

1813.   Stead, Robert. "Traditional Lakota Religion in Modern Life." In *Sioux Indian Religion: Tradition and Innovation,* ed. R. J. DeMallie and D. Parks, 211–16. Norman: University of Oklahoma Press, 1987.

1814.   Taylor, Colin. "Catlin's Picture of Iron Horn: An Early Style of Blackfeet Shirt." *Plains Anthropologist* 31, no. 114, pt. 1 (1986): 265–80.

1815.   Theisz, R. D. "The Bad Speakers and the Long Braids: References to Foreign Enemies in Lakota Song Texts." In *Indians and Europe: An Interdisciplinary Collection of Essays,* ed. C. Feest, 427–34. Aachen, West Germany: Edition Herodot, 1987.

1816.   Voget, Fred W. "The Crow Indian Give-Away: A Plains Instrument for Cultural Adaptation and Persistence." *Anthropos* 82, no. 1/3 (1987): 207–14.

1817.   Weltfish, Gene. "The Plains Indians: Their Continuity in History and Their Indian Identity." In *North American Indians in Historical Perspective,* ed. E. B. Leacock and N. O. Lurie, 200–227. Prospect Heights, Ill.: Waveland Press, 1988.

1818.   [Wilson, Gilbert L.] *Buffalo Bird Woman's Garden: Agriculture of the Hidatsa Indians as Told to Gilbert L. Wilson.* New introduction by Jeffrey R. Hanson. St. Paul: Minnesota Historical Society Press, 1987.

1819.   Wilson, Terry P. *The Osage.* New York: Chelsea House, 1988.

1820.   Wunder, John R. *The Kiowa.* New York: Chelsea House, 1989.

7.6   CULTURES
OF THE SOUTHWEST

1821.   Alhstrom, Richard V. N., and Nancy J. Parezo, eds. "Matilda Coxe Stevenson's 'Dress and Adornment of the Pueblo Indians.'" *Kiva* 52, no. 4 (1987): 266–314.

1822.   Bailey, Garrick, and Roberta Glenn Bailey. *A History of the Navajos: The Reservation Years.* Seattle: University of Washington Press; Santa Fe: School of American Research Press, 1986.

1823.   Barber, Clifton E., Alice S. Cook, and Alan Ackerman. "The Influence of Acculturation on Attitudes of Filial Responsibility Among Navajo Youth." *American Indian Quarterly* 9 (1985): 421–32.

1824.   Bean, Lowell John. *Seasons of the Kachina: Proceedings of the California State University Hayward Conference on the Western Pueblos, 1987–88.* Novato, Calif.: Ballena Press, 1989.

1825.   Bee, Robert L. *The Yuma.* New York: Chelsea House, 1989.

1826.   Bodine, John J. "The Taos Blue Lake Ceremony." *American Indian Quarterly* 12 (1988): 91–106.

1827.   Brower, Kenneth. "The Navajo Nation." *Atlantic* 263 (March 1989): 79–83.

1828.   Buskirk, Winfred. *The Western Apache: Living off the Land Before 1950.* Foreword by Morris E. Opler. Norman: University of Oklahoma Press, 1986.

1829.   Cliff, Janet M. "Navajo Games." *American Indian Culture and Research Journal* 14, no. 3 (1990): 1–82.

1830.   Correll, J. Lee. *Through White Men's Eyes: A Contribution to Navajo History.* Tucson: University of Arizona Press, 1988.

1831.   Delaney, Robert W. *The Ute Mountain Utes.* Albuquerque: University of New Mexico Press, 1989.

1832.   Dewar, John. "Old Oraibi, 1934: Hopi Portfolio." *Journal of the Southwest* 31 (1989): 534–48.

1833.   Dobyns, Henry F. *The Pima-Maricopa.* New York: Chelsea House, 1989.

1834.   Dozier, Edward P. "The American Southwest." In *North American Indians in Historical Perspective,* ed. E. B. Leacock and N. O. Lurie, 228–56. Prospect Heights, Ill.: Waveland Press, 1988.

1835.   Elm, Adelaide, and Heather S. Hatch, comps. "'Ready to Serve': Elsie Pugh Herndon Among the Pima and Papago, a Photo Essay." *Journal of Arizona History* 30 (1989): 193–208.

1836.   Faris, James C. *The Nightway: A History and a History of Documentation of a Navajo Ceremonial.* Albuquerque: University of New Mexico Press, 1990.

1837.   Ferg, Alan, ed. *Western Apache Material Culture: The Goodwin and Guenther Collections.* Tucson: University of Arizona Press, 1987.

1838.   Ferguson, T. J., and Richard E. Hart. *A Zuni Atlas.* Norman: University of Oklahoma Press, 1985.

1839.   Ferguson, T. J., and Barbara J. Mills. "Settlement and Growth of Zuni Pueblo: An Architectural History." *Kiva* 52, no. 4 (1987): 243–66.

1840.   Ford, Richard I., ed. *The Ethnographic American Southwest—A Source Book: Southwestern Society in Myth, Clan, and Kinship.* New York: Garland Press, 1985.

1841.   Fowler, Loretta. *The Apache.* New York: Chelsea House, 1989.

1842.   Frisbie, Charlotte. *Navajo Medicine Bundles or Jish: Acquisition,*

Transmission, and Disposition in Past and Present. Albuquerque: University of New Mexico Press, 1987.

1843. "From the Four Corners: Images of the Reservation Utes and Navajos." *Colorado Heritage* 1 (1986): 10–29.

1844. **Gaede, Marnie, Barton Wright,** and **Marc Gaede.** *The Hopi Photographs: Kate Cory, 1905–1914.* La-Canada, N.Mex.: Chaco, 1986.

1845. **Geertz, Amin W.,** and **Michael Lomatuway'ma.** *Children of Cottonwood: Piety and Ceremonialism in Hopi Indian Puppetry.* Lincoln: University of Nebraska Press, 1987.

1846. **Goodman, James.** *The Navajo Atlas: Environments, Resources, People, and History of the Dine Bikeyah.* With the assistance of Mary Goodman. Norman: University of Oklahoma Press, 1986.

1847. **Hall, Thomas D.** *Social Change in the Southwest, 1350–1880.* Lawrence: University of Kansas Press, 1989.

1848. **Harrington, Gwyneth.** "Seri Dreams." *Journal of the Southwest* 30 (1988): 502–21.

1849. **Hickerson, Nancy.** "The Linguistic Position of the Jumano." *Journal of Anthropological Research* 44, no. 3 (1988): 311–26.

1850. **Hills, Jim.** "In Search of the Seris." *Arizona Highways* 65 (January 1989): 38–45.

1851. **Houlihan, Patrick T.** *Lummis in the Pueblos.* Flagstaff, Ariz.: Northland Press, 1986.

1852. **Iliff, Flora Gregg.** *People of the Blue Water: A Record of Life Among the Walapai and Havasupai Indians.* Foreword by Robert C. Euler. Tucson: University of Arizona Press, 1985.

1853. **Iverson, Peter.** "Continuity and Change in Navajo Culture: A Review Essay." *Nex Mexico Historical Review* 62 (1987): 191–200.

1854. ———. *The Navajos.* New York: Chelsea House, 1990.

1855. **James, H. L.** *Acoma: People of the White Rock.* West Chester, Penn.: Schiffer Publishing, 1988.

1856. **Kennedy, John G.** *The Tarahumara.* New York: Chelsea House, 1990.

1857. **King, William R.** "Dionysos Among the Mesas: The Water Serpent Puppet Play of the Hopi Indians." *American Indian Culture and Research Journal* 11, no. 3 (1987): 17–49.

1858. **Kroeber, Clifton B.,** and **Bernard L. Fontana.** *Massacre on the Gila: An Account of the Last Major Battle Between American Indians, with Reflections on the Origin of War.* Tucson: University of Arizona Press, 1986. [Battle of Maricopa Wells, 1857, Quechan and Mohaves versus Maricopas]

1859. **Levi, Jerrold, Raymond Neutra,** and **Dennis Parker.** *Hand Trembling, Frenzy Witchcraft, and Moth Madness: A Study of Navajo Seizure Disorders.* Tucson: University of Arizona Press, 1987.

1860. **Lyon, William H.** "Ednishodi Yazhe: The Little Priest and the Understanding of Navajo Culture." *American Indian Culture and Research Journal* 11, no. 1 (1987): 1–42.

1861. ———. "Gladys Reichard at the Frontiers of Navajo Culture." *American Indian Quarterly* 13 (1989): 137–63.

1862. ———. "History Comes to the Navajos: A Review Essay." *American Indian Culture and Research Journal* 11, no. 3 (1987): 75–92.

1863. **Magnaghi, Russell M.** "Plains Indians in New Mexico: The Genizaro

Experience." *Great Plains Quarterly* 10 (1990): 86–95.

1864.   Melody, Michael E. *The Apache.* New York: Chelsea House, 1989.

1865.   Mindeleff, Victor. *A Study of Pueblo Architecture in Tusayan and Cibola.* 1891. Reprint, with an introduction by P. Nabokov, Washington, D.C.: Smithsonian Institution Press, 1989.

1866.   Morris, C. Patrick. " 'Monster Slayer' Among the Upland Yumans: A Folk Theory on the Evolution of Hunting Cultures." *American Indian Quarterly* 10 (1986): 199–211.

1867.   Moser, Mary Beck. "Seri History (1904): Two Documents." *Journal of the Southwest* 30 (1988): 469–501.

1868.   Nabokov, Peter. *Architecture of Acoma Pueblo: The 1934 Historic American Buildings Survey Project.* Santa Fe, N.Mex.: Ancient City Press, 1986.

1869.   Naranjo, Tito, and Rina Swentzell. "Healing Spaces in the Tewa Pueblo World." *American Indian Culture and Research Journal* 13, no. 3–4 (1989): 257–65.

1870.   Native American Special Issue. *New Mexico Magazine* 67, no. 8 (1989).

1871.   Painter, Muriel Thayer. *With Good Heart: Yaqui Beliefs and Ceremonies in Pescua Village.* Tucson: University of Arizona Press, 1986.

1872.   Patterson, Carol. "Uretsete and Naosete Genesis Myth of Cochiti Pueblo." *Artifact* 26 (1988): 1–24.

1873.   "The Plaza." *El Palacio* 94 (winter 1988): 1–60.

1874.   Poore, Anne V., ed. *Reflections: Papers on Southwestern Culture History in Honor of Charles H. Lange.* Santa Fe: Ancient City Press, 1988.

1875.   Pride, Nigel. *Crow Man's People: Three Seasons with the Navajo.* New York: Constable, 1985.

1876.   Sandweiss, Martha A. *Denizens of the Desert: A Tale in Word and Picture of Life Among the Navajo Indians: The Letters of Elizabeth W. Foster.* Albuquerque: University of New Mexico Press, 1988.

1877.   Smith, Watson. "Kihus at Wupatki." *Journal of Arizona History* 26 (1985): 327–34.

1878.   Spicer, Edward. *People of Pascua.* 1953. Reprint, Tucson: University of Arizona Press, 1988.

1879.   Swentzell, Rina, and Tito Naranjo. "Nurturing: The Gia at Santa Clara Pueblo." *El Palacio* 92 (summer/fall 1986): 35–52.

1880.   Tapahonsio, Luci, Mike Mitchell, and Martha A. Sandweiss. *Sign Language: Contemporary Southwest Native America.* New York: Aperture, 1989.

1881.   Walker, Willard, and Lydia L. Wyckoff. *Hopis, Tewas, and the American Road.* Albuquerque: University of New Mexico Press, 1986. [Mehlville Collection assembled in *1927* on the Hopi Mesas]

1882.   Waters, Frank. "This Sacred Land." *Arizona Highways* 63 (November 1987): 38–45.

1883.   Weber, Stephen A., and P. David Seaman, eds. *Havasupai Habitat: A. F. Whiting's Ethnography of a Traditional Indian Culture.* Tucson: University of Arizona Press, 1985.

1884.   Whiteley, Peter M. *Deliberate Acts: Changing Hopi Culture Through the Oraibi Split.* Tucson: University of Arizona Press, 1988.

1885.   Wilder, Joseph C., ed. "The

Vikita Ceremony." *Journal of the Southwest* 29 (1987): 257–329. [Fine color illustrations of floats and events]

1886. Wyckoff, Lydia L. *Designs and Factions: Politics, Religion, and Ceramics on the Hopi Third Mesa.* Albuquerque: University of New Mexico Press, 1990.

7.7 CULTURES OF CALIFORNIA

1887. Bean, Lowell John. "Indians of Southern California." *Masterkey* 59, no. 2/3 (1985): 32–41.

1888. Bean, Lowell John, and **Lisa Bourgeault.** *The Cahuilla.* New York: Chelsea House, 1989.

1889. Bee, Robert L. *The Yuma.* New York: Chelsea House, 1989.

1890. Bettinger, Robert L. "Native Life in Desert California: The Great Basin and Its Aboriginal Inhabitants." *Masterkey* 59, no. 2/3 (1985): 42–50.

1891. Black, Robert. "Preface." *American Indian Quarterly* 13, no. 4 (1989): v–vi.

1892. Blout, Clinton M., and **Dorothea J. Theodoratus.** "Central California Indians." *Masterkey* 59, no. 2/3 (1985): 22–31.

1893. Buckley, Thomas. "Suffering in the Cultural Construction of Others: Robert Spott and A. L. Kroeber." *American Indian Quarterly* 13 (1989): 437–45.

1894. Dobyns, Henry F. *The Pima-Maricopa.* New York: Chelsea House, 1989.

1895. Downs, James F. "California." In *North American Indians in Historical Perspective,* ed. E. B. Leacock and N. O. Lurie, 289–316. Prospect Heights, Ill.: Waveland Press, 1988.

1896. Felger, Richard Stephen, and **Mary Beck Moser.** *People of the Desert and Sea: Ethnobotany of the Seri Indians.*

Tucson: University of Arizona Press, 1985.

1897. Fernandez, Raul. "Evaluating the Loss of Kinship Structures: A Case Study of North American Indians." *Human Organization* 46 (1987): 1–9.

1898. Giovannetti, Joseph M. "Using Depth Psychology Constructs to Accurately Interpret Native Symbolism: An Examination of the Tolowa 'Catching the White Bird' Myth." *American Indian Quarterly* 13 (1989): 511–27.

1899. Gould, Richard A. "The Indians of Northwest California." *Masterkey* 59, no. 2/3 (1985): 14–21.

1900. Hundley, Norris. "California's Aboriginal Waterscape: Harmony and Manipulation." *California History* 66 (1987): 2–11.

1901. Lalande, Jeff. *First over the Siskiyous: Peter Skene Ogden's 1826–1827 Journey Through the Oregon-California Borderlands.* Portland: Oregon Historical Society Press, 1987.

1902. Maniery, James Gary, and **Dwight Dutschke.** "Northern Miwok at Big Bar: A Glimpse of the Lives of Pedro and Lily O'Connor." *American Indian Quarterly* 13 (1989): 481–95.

1903. Miller, Bruce W. *Chumash: A Picture of Their World.* Los Osos, Calif.: Sand River Press, 1988.

1904. Moratto, Michael J. "The California Culture Area." *Masterkey* 59, no. 2/3 (1985): 4–11.

1905. Nabokov, Peter. "Reconstituting the Chumash: A Review Essay." *American Indian Quarterly* 13 (1989): 535–43.

1906. ———. "The Roundhouse: Giving Life to Community." *News from Native California* 3, no. 1 (1989): 4–9.

1907. Nelson, Bryon. *Our Home For-*

ever: The Hupa Indians of Northern California. Salt Lake City, Utah: Howe Brothers, 1988.

1908. "New Perspectives on California Indian Research." *American Indian Culture and Research Journal* (special issue) 12, no. 2 (1988).

1909. Norton, Jack. "Introduction." *American Indian Quarterly* 13, no. 4 (1988): vii–x.

1910. ———. "Traversing the Bridge of Our Lives." *American Indian Quarterly* 13, no. 4 (1989): 347–58.

1911. ———, ed. "The California Indians." (special issue) *American Indian Quarterly* 13, no. 4 (1989).

1912. Ortiz, Bev. "Mount Diablo as Myth and Reality: An Indian History Convoluted." *American Indian Quarterly* 13 (1989): 457–70.

1913. Parkman, E. Breck. "A Stone for Yontocket." *American Indian Quarterly* 13 (1989): 529–33.

1914. Pilling, Arnold. "Yurok Aristocracy and Great Houses." *American Indian Quarterly* 13 (1989): 421–36.

1915. Shipek, Florence C. *Pushed into the Rocks: Southern California Indian Land Tenure, 1769–1986.* Lincoln: University of Nebraska Press, 1988.

1916. Slagle, Al Logan. "Tolowa Indian Shakers and the Role of Prophecy at Smith River, California." *American Indian Quarterly* 9 (1985): 353–74.

1917. Sutton, Imre. "The Cartographic Factor in Indian Land Tenure: Some Examples from Southern California." *American Indian Culture and Research Journal* 14, no. 2 (1988): 53–81.

1918. Thornton, Russell. "History, Structure, and Survival: A Comparison of the Yuki (Unkomno'n) and Tolowa

(Kush) Indians of Northern California." *Ethnology* 25 (1986): 119–30.

1919. Wilson, Darryl. "Jema-Halo Ti-Wi-Ji (Great Horned Owl)." *American Indian Quarterly* 13 (1989): 497–509.

7.8 CULTURES OF THE GREAT BASIN AND PLATEAU

1920. Ackerman, Lillian A. "The Effect of Missionary Ideals on Family Structure and Women's Roles in Plateau Indian Culture." *Idaho Yesterdays* 31 (spring/summer 1987): 64–73.

1921. Arrington, Leonard J. "A Mormon Apostle Visits the Umatilla and Nez Perce in 1885." *Idaho Yesterdays* 31 (spring/summer 1987): 47–54.

1922. Bailey, Paul. *Ghost Dance Messiah.* Tucson, Ariz.: Westernlore Press, 1986.

1923. Beach, Margery Ann. "The Waptashi Prophet and the Feather Religion: Derivative of the Washani." *American Indian Quarterly* 9 (1985): 325–33.

1924. Bordwell, Constance. "Fort Rock Cave: Monument to the First Oregonians." *Oregon Historical Quarterly* 88 (1987): 117–48.

1925. Brooks, Sheilagh, and **Richard H. Brooks.** "Who Were the Stillwater Marsh People?" *Halcyon* 12 (1990): 63–74.

1926. Bunte, Pamela, and **Robert Franklin.** *From the Sands to the Mountain: Change and Persistence in a Southern Paiute Community.* Lincoln: University of Nebraska Press, 1987.

1927. ———. *The Paiute.* New York: Chelsea House, 1990.

1928. Callaway, Donald G., Joel C. Janetski, and **Omer C. Stewart.** "Ute." In *Great Basin,* ed. W. L.

d'Azevedo, 336–67. Vol. 11 of *Handbook of North American Indians,* ed. W. Sturtevant. Washington, D.C.: Smithsonian Institution, 1986.

1929. **Clemmer, Richard O.** "Differential Leadership Patterns in Early Twentieth Century Great Basin Indian Societies." *Journal of California and Great Basin Anthropology* 11 (1989): 35–49.

1930. **Corless, Hank.** *The Weiser Indians/Shoshoni Peacemakers.* Salt Lake City: University of Utah Press, 1990.

1931. **Crum, Steven J.** "The Ruby Valley Indian Reservation of Northeastern Nevada: 'Six Miles Square.'" *Nevada Historical Society Quarterly* 30 (1987): 1–18.

1932. ———. "The Skull Valley Band of the Gosiute Tribe—Deeply Attached to Their Native Homeland." *Utah Historical Quarterly* 55, no. 3 (1987): 250–67.

1933. ———. "The Western Shoshone People and Their Attachment to the Land: A Twentieth Century Perspective." *Nevada Public Affairs Review* 2 (1987): 15–18.

1934. **d'Azevedo, Warren L.** "Washoe." In *Great Basin,* ed. W. L. d'Azevedo, 466–98. Vol. 11 of *Handbook of North American Indians,* ed. W. Sturtevant. Washington, D.C.: Smithsonian Institution, 1986.

1935. ———, ed. *Great Basin.* Vol. 11 of *Handbook of North American Indians,* ed. W. Sturtevant. Washington, D.C.: Smithsonian Institution, 1986.

1936. **Drake-Terry, Joanne.** *The Same as Yesterday: The Lillooet Chronicle of Theft of Their Lands and Resources.* Lillooet, B.C.: Lillooet Tribal Council, 1989.

1937. **Fahey, John.** *The Kalispel Indi-ans.* Norman: University of Oklahoma Press, 1986.

1938. **Faulk, Odie B.** *The Modoc.* New York: Chelsea House, 1988.

1939. **Fowler, Catherine S.,** ed. *Willard Z. Park's Ethnographic Notes on the Northern Paiute of Western Nevada, 1933–1944,* vol. 1. Salt Lake City: University of Utah Press, 1990.

1940. **Fowler, Catherine S.,** and **Sven Liljebled.** "Northern Paiute." In *Great Basin,* ed. W. L. d'Azevedo, 435–65. Vol. 11 of *Handbook of North American Indians,* ed. W. Sturtevant. Washington, D.C.: Smithsonian Institution, 1986.

1941. **Gortner, Willis A.** *The Martis Indians: Ancient Tribe of the Sierra Nevada.* Woodside, Calif.: Portola Press, 1986.

1942. **Great Basin Foundation.** *Woman, Poet, Scientist: Essays in New World Anthropology Honoring Dr. Emma Louise Davis.* Los Altos, Calif.: Ballena Press, 1985.

1943. **Harper, Kimball T.** "Historical Environments." In *Great Basin,* ed. W. L. d'Azevedo, 51–63. Vol. 11 of *Handbook of North American Indians,* ed. W. Sturtevant. Washington, D.C.: Smithsonian Institution, 1986.

1944. **Hunn, Eugene.** *N'Chi-Wana, "The Big River": Mid-Columbia Indians and Their Land.* Seattle: University of Washington Press, 1990.

1945. **Kelly, Isabel T.,** and **Catherine S. Fowler.** "Southern Paiute." In *Great Basin,* ed. W. L. d'Azevedo, 368–97. Vol. 11 of *Handbook of North American Indians,* ed. W. Sturtevant. Washington, D.C.: Smithsonian Institution, 1986.

1946. **Liljeblad, Sven,** and **Cather-**

ine S. Fowler. "Owens Valley Paiute." In *Great Basin*, ed. W. L. d'Azevedo, 414–34. Vol. 11 of *Handbook of North American Indians*, ed. W. Sturtevant. Washington, D.C.: Smithsonian Institution, 1986.

1947. McPherson, Robert S. "Paiute Posey and the Last White Uprising." *Utah Historical Quarterly* 53, no. 3 (1985): 248–67.

1948. Murphy, Robert F., and Yolanda Murphy. "Northern Shoshoni and Bannock." In *Great Basin*, ed. W. L. d'Azevedo, 284–307. Vol. 11 of *Handbook of North American Indians*, ed. W. Sturtevant. Washington, D.C.: Smithsonian Institution, 1986.

1949. Opler, Marvin. "The Ute and Paiute Indians of the Great Basin Southern Rim." In *North American Indians in Historical Perspective*, ed. E. B. Leacock and N. O. Lurie, 257–88. Prospect Heights, Ill.: Waveland Press, 1988.

1950. Reichwein, Jeffrey C. "Native American Response to Euro-American Contact in the Columbia Plateau of Northwestern North America, 1840 to 1914: An Anthropological Interpretation Based on Written and Pictorial Ethnohistorical Data." In *The Evolution of North American Indians*, ed. D. H. Thomas. New York: Garland Publishing, 1990.

1951. Ruby, Robert H., and John A. Brown. *Dreamer-Prophets of the Columbia Plateau: Smohalla and Skolaskin*. Lincoln: University of Nebraska Press, 1989.

1952. Schuster, Helen H. *The Yakima*. New York: Chelsea House, 1990.

1953. Shimkin, Demitri B. "Eastern Shoshoni." In *Great Basin*, ed. W. L. d'Azevedo, 308–35. Vol. 11 of *Handbook of North American Indians*, ed. W. Sturtevant. Washington, D.C.: Smithsonian Institution, 1986.

1954. Stowell, Cynthia D. *Faces of a Reservation: A Portrait of the Warm Springs Indian Reservation*. Portland: Oregon Historical Society Press, 1987.

1955. Thomas, David H., Lorann S. A. Pendleton, and Stephen C. Cappannari. "Western Shoshoni." In *Great Basin*, ed. W. L. d'Azevedo, 262–83. Vol. 11 of *Handbook of North American Indians*, ed. W. Sturtevant. Washington, D.C.: Smithsonian Institution, 1986.

1956. Trafzer, Clifford E. "The Palouse in Eehish Pah." *American Indian Quarterly* 9 (1985): 169–82.

1957. Trafzer, Clifford E., and Margery Ann Beach. "Smohalla, the Washani, and Religion as a Factor in Northwestern Indian History." *American Indian Quarterly* 9 (1985): 309–24.

1958. Vander, Judith. *Songprints: The Musical Experience of Five Shoshone Women*. Urbana: University of Illinois Press, 1988.

1959. Zigmond, Maurice. "Kawaiisu." In *Great Basin*, ed. W. L. d'Azevedo, 398–411. Vol. 11 of *Handbook of North American Indians*, ed. W. Sturtevant. Washington, D.C.: Smithsonian Institution, 1986.

7.9 CULTURES OF THE NORTHWEST COAST, ALASKA, AND THE ARCTIC (INCLUDING ADJACENT AREAS OF CANADA)

1960. Acheson, Steven R. "Ninstint's Village: A Case of Mistaken Identity." *BC Studies* 67 (autumn 1985): 47–56.

1961. Aoki, Haruo, and Deward E. Walker, Jr. *Nez Perce Oral Narratives*.

Berkeley: University of California Press, 1989.

1962.   **Arima, Eugene,** and John Dewhirst. "Nootkans of Vancouver Island." In *Northwest Coast,* ed. W. Suttles, 391–411. Vol. 7 of *Handbook of North American Indians,* ed. W. Sturtevant. Washington, D.C.: Smithsonian Institution, 1990.

1963.   **Averkieva, Julia.** "The Tlingit Indians." In *North American Indians in Historical Perspective,* ed. E. B. Leacock and N. O. Lurie, 317–42. Prospect Heights, Ill.: Waveland Press, 1988.

1964.   **Bancroft-Hunt, Norman.** *People of the Totem: The Indians of the Pacific Northwest.* Norman: University of Oklahoma Press, 1988.

1965.   **Barbeau, Marius,** and **William Beynon,** comps. *Tsimshian Narratives.* Vol. 1, *Tricksters, Shamans, and Heroes.* Ed. J. J. Cove and G. F. MacDonald. Directorate Paper no. 3. Hull, Queb.: Canadian Museum of Civilization, 1987.

1966.   ———, comps. *Tsimshian Narratives.* Vol. 2, *Trade and Warfare.* Ed. J. J. Cove and G. F. MacDonald. Directorate Paper no. 3. Hull, Queb.: Canadian Museum of Civilization, 1987.

1967.   **Blackman, Margaret B.** "Haida: Traditional Culture." In *Northwest Coast,* ed. W. Suttles, 240–60. Vol. 7 of *Handbook of North American Indians,* ed. W. Sturtevant. Washington, D.C.: Smithsonian Institution, 1990.

1968.   **Boelscher, Marianne.** *The Curtain Within: Haida Social and Mythical Discourse.* Vancouver: University of British Columbia Press, 1988.

1969.   **Boxberger, Daniel L.** *To Fish in Common: The Ethnohistory of Lummi Indian Salmon Fishing.* Lincoln: University of Nebraska Press, 1989.

1970.   **Braund, Stephen.** *The Skin Boats of St. Lawrence Island, Alaska.* Seattle: University of Washington Press.

1971.   **Brody, Hugh.** *Living Arctic: Hunters of the Canadian North.* London: Faber and Faber, 1987.

1972.   **Brown, Jennifer S. H.** "Coastal Manitoba Saulteaux in the Nineteenth Century." In *Papers of the Sixteenth Algonquian Conference,* ed. W. Cowan, 1–8. Ottawa: Carleton University Press, 1985.

1973.   **Bruggman, Maximilien,** and **Peter R. Gerber.** *Indians of the Northwest Coast.* New York: Facts on File, 1989. [Translated from German]

1974.   **Burch, Ernest S., Jr.,** and **Werner Forman.** *The Eskimos.* Norman: University of Oklahoma Press, 1988.

1975.   **Capoeman, Pauline K.,** ed. *Land of the Quinault.* Taholah, Wash.: Quinault Indian Nation, 1990.

1976.   **Carlisle, Robert S.** "Crowfoot's Dying Speech." *Alberta History* 38, no. 3 (1990): 16–17.

1977.   **Carter, Sarah.** "Two Acres and a Cow: 'Peasant' Farming for the Indians of the Northwest, 1889–97." *Canadian Historical Review* 70 (1989): 27–52.

1978.   **Castile, George Pierre.** "The Indian Connection: Judge James Wickersham and the Indian Shakers." *Pacific Northwest Quarterly* 81 (1990): 122–29.

1979.   ———, ed. *The Indians of Puget Sound: The Notebooks of Myron Eells.* Seattle: University of Washington Press, 1985.

1980.   **Codere, Helen.** "Kwakiutl: Traditional Culture." In *Northwest Coast,* ed. W. Suttles, 359–77. Vol. 7 of *Handbook of North American Indians,* ed. W. Sturtevant. Washington, D.C.: Smithsonian Institution, 1990.

1981. Cole, Douglas. *Captured Heritage: The Scramble for Northwest Coast Artifacts.* Seattle: University of Washington Press, 1985.

1982. Cruikshank, Julie. "Getting the Word Right: Perspectives on Naming and Places in Athapaskan Oral History." *Arctic Anthropology* 27 (1990): 52–65.

1983. ———, ed. *Life Lived Like a Story: Life Stories of Three Yukon Native Elders.* With Angela Sidney, Kitty Smith, and Annie Ned. Lincoln: University of Nebraska Press, 1990.

1984. Damas, David, ed. *Arctic.* Vol. 5 of *Handbook of North American Indians,* ed. W. Sturtevant. Washington, D.C.: Smithsonian Institution, 1985.

1985. Dauenhauer, Nora, and Richard Dauenhauer. *Haa Shuka, Our Ancestors: Tlingit Oral Narratives.* Seattle: University of Washington Press, 1987.

1986. De Laguna, Frederica. "Eyak." In *Northwest Coast,* ed. W. Suttles, 119–34. Vol. 7 of *Handbook of North American Indians,* ed. W. Sturtevant. Washington, D.C.: Smithsonian Institution, 1990.

1987. ———. "Tlingit." In *Northwest Coast,* ed. W. Suttles, 203–28. Vol. 7 of *Handbook of North American Indians,* ed. W. Sturtevant. Washington, D.C.: Smithsonian Institution, 1990.

1988. Delhalle, J. C.,. and Albert Luykx. "The Nahuatl Myth of Creation of Humankind: A Coastal Connection." *American Antiquity* 51 (1986): 117–21.

1989. Dunn, John A., and Arnold Booth. "Tsimshian of Metlakatla, Alaska." In *Northwest Coast,* ed. W. Suttles, 294–97. Vol. 7 of *Handbook of North American Indians,* ed. W. Sturtevant. Washington, D.C.: Smithsonian Institution, 1990.

1990. Edwards, G. Thomas, and Carlos A. Schwantes. *Experiences in a Promised Land: Essays in Pacific Northwest History.* Seattle: University of Washington Press, 1986.

1991. Elias, Peter Douglas. *The Dakota of the Canadian Northwest: Lessons for Survival.* Winnipeg: University of Manitoba Press, 1988.

1992. Elmendorf, William W. "Chimakum." In *Northwest Coast,* ed. W. Suttles, 438–40. Vol. 7 of *Handbook of North American Indians,* ed. W. Sturtevant. Washington, D.C.: Smithsonian Institution, 1990.

1993. Fienup-Riordan, Ann. *Eskimo Essays.* New Brunswick, N.J.: Rutgers University Press, 1990.

1994. ———. "Robert Redford, Apanuugpak, and the Invention of Tradition." *Études Inuit/Inuit Studies* 11, no. 1 (1987): 135–48.

1995. Fitzhugh, W. W., and A. Crowell. *Crossroads of Continents: Cultures of Siberia and Alaska.* Washington, D.C.: Smithsonian Institution Press, 1988.

1996. Flannery, Regina, and Mary Elizabeth Chambers. "Each Man Has His Own Friends: The Role of Dream Visitors in Traditional East Cree Belief and Practice." *Arctic Anthropology* 22 (1985): 1–22.

1997. Freed, Stanley, Ruth Freed, and Laila Williamson. "Capitalist Philanthropy and Russian Revolutionaries: The Jesup North Pacific Expedition (1897–1902)." *American Anthropologist* 90 (1988): 7–24.

1998. Gottesfeld, Leslie M. J., and Beverly Sun Anderson. "Gitksan Traditional Medicines: Herbs and Healing." *Journal of Ethnobiology* 8 (1988): 13–33.

1999.   Haberland, Wolfgang. "Nine Bella Coolas in Germany." In *Indians and Europe: An Interdisciplinary Collection of Essays,* ed. C. Feest, 337–74. Aachen, West Germany: Edition Herodot, 1987.

2000.   Hajda, Yvonne. "Southwestern Coast Salish." In *Northwest Coast,* ed. W Suttles, 503–17. Vol. 7 of *Handbook of North American Indians,* ed. W. Sturtevant. Washington, D.C.: Smithsonian Institution, 1990.

2001.   Halpin, Marjorie M., and **Margaret Seguin.** "Tsimshian Peoples." In *Northwest Coast,* ed. W. Suttles, 267–84. Vol. 7 of *Handbook of North American Indians,* ed. W. Sturtevant. Washington, D.C.: Smithsonian Institution, 1990.

2002.   Hamori-Torok, Charles. "Haisla." In *Northwest Coast,* ed. W. Suttles, 306–11. Vol. 7 of *Handbook of North American Indians,* ed. W. Sturtevant. Washington, D.C.: Smithsonian Institution, 1990.

2003.   Hawker, Ronald W. "In the Way of the White Man's Totem Poles: Stone Monuments Among Canada's Tsimshian Indians, 1879–1910." *Markers* 7 (1990): 213–31.

2004.   Heber, Wesley R. "Indians as Ethnics: Chipewyan Ethno-Adaptations." *Western Canadian Anthropologist* 6 (1989): 55–77.

2005.   Helm, June, and **Eleanor Burke Leacock.** "The Hunting Tribes of Subarctic Canada." In *North American Indians in Historical Perspective,* ed. E. B. Leacock and N. O. Lurie, 343–74. 1971. Reprint, Prospect Heights, Ill.: Waveland Press, 1988.

2006.   Hilton, Susanne F. "Haihais, Bella Bella, and Owekeeno." In *Northwest Coast,* ed. W. Suttles, 312–22. Vol. 7 of *Handbook of North American Indians,* ed. W. Sturtevant. Washington, D.C.: Smithsonian Institution, 1990.

2007.   Holm, Bill. "Kwakiutl: Winter Ceremonies." In *Northwest Coast,* ed. W. Suttles, 378–86. Vol. 7 of *Handbook of North American Indians,* ed. W. Sturtevant. Washington, D.C.: Smithsonian Institution, 1990.

2008.   Hughes, Charles C. "The Changing Eskimo World." In *North American Indians in Historical Perspective,* ed. E. B. Leacock and N. O. Lurie, 375–417. Prospect Heights, Ill.: Waveland Press, 1988.

2009.   Inglis, Gordon B., Douglas R. Hudson, Barbara K. Rigsby, and **Bruce Rigsby.** "Tsimshian of British Columbia Since 1900." In *Northwest Coast,* ed. W. Suttles, 285–93. Vol. 7 of *Handbook of North American Indians,* ed. W. Sturtevant. Washington, D.C.: Smithsonian Institution, 1990.

2010.   Inglis, Richard, and **James C. Haggarty.** "Cook to Jewett: Three Decades of Change in Nootka Sound." In *Le Castor Fait Tout: Selected Papers of the Fifth North American Fur Trade Conference, 1985,* ed. B. G. Trigger, T. Morantz, and L. Dechene, 193–222. Montreal: Lake St. Louis Historical Society, 1987.

2011.   Israel, Heinz. "Johann Gottfried Schadow and His Inuit Portraits." In *Indians and Europe: An Interdisciplinary Collection of Essays,* ed. C. Feest, 235–41. Aachen, West Germany: Edition Herodot, 1987.

2012.   Jarvenpa, Robert, and **Hetty Joe Brambach.** "Socio-Spatial Organization and Decision-Making Processes: Observations from the Chipewyan." *American Anthropologist* 90 (1988): 598–618.

2013.   Johnston, Moira. "Canada's

Queen Charlotte Islands: Homeland of the Haida." *National Geographic* 172 (July 1987): 102–27.

2014.   Jorgensen, Joseph G. *Oil Age Eskimos.* Berkeley: University of California Press, 1990.

2015.   Kan, Sergei. "Cohorts, Generations, and Their Culture: The Tlingit Potlatch in the 1980s." *Anthropos* 84 (1989): 405–22.

2016.   ———. "The Nineteenth Century Tlingit Potlatch: A New Perspective." *American Ethnologist* 13 (1986): 191–214.

2017.   ———. "The Sacred and the Secular: Tlingit Potlatch Songs Outside the Potlatch." *American Indian Quarterly* 14 (1990): 355–66.

2018.   ———. *Symbolic Immortality: The Tlingit Potlatch of the Nineteenth Century.* Washington, D.C.: Smithsonian Institution Press, 1989.

2019.   ———, trans. and ed. *Tlingit Indians of Alaska by Anatolii Kamenskii.* 1906. Translated from Russian. Fairbanks: University of Alaska Press, 1986.

2020.   Kaplan, Susan, and **Kristin Barsness.** *Raven's Journey: The World of Alaska's Native People.* Philadelphia: University Museum, 1986.

2021.   Kari, James. *Ahtna Athabaskan Dictionary.* Fairbanks: Alaska Native Language Center, University of Alaska, 1990.

2022.   ———, ed. and trans. *Tatl'Ahwt'Aenn Nenn, the Headwaters People's Country: Narratives of the Upper Ahtna Athabaskans.* Fairbanks: Alaska Native Language Center, University of Alaska, 1986.

2023.   Kendall, Daythal L. "Takelma." In *Northwest Coast,* ed. W. Suttles, 589–92. Vol. 7 of *Handbook of North American Indians,* ed. W. Sturtevant. Washington, D.C.: Smithsonian Institution, 1990.

2024.   Kennedy, Dorothy I. D., and **Randall R. Bouchard.** "Bella Coola." In *Northwest Coast,* ed. W. Suttles, 323–39. Vol. 7 of *Handbook of North American Indians,* ed. W. Sturtevant. Washington, D.C.: Smithsonian Institution, 1990.

2025.   ———. "Northern Coast Salish." In *Northwest Coast,* ed. W. Suttles, 441–52. Vol. 7 of *Handbook of North American Indians,* ed. W. Sturtevant. Washington, D.C.: Smithsonian Institution, 1990.

2026.   Kenyon, W. A. *History of James Bay, 1610–1680: A Study in Historical Archaeology.* Toronto: Royal Ontario Museum, 1986.

2027.   Kew, J. E. Michael. "Central and Southern Coast Salish Ceremonies Since 1900." In *Northwest Coast,* ed. W. Suttles, 476–80. Vol. 7 of *Handbook of North American Indians,* ed. W. Sturtevant. Washington, D.C.: Smithsonian Institution, 1990.

2028.   Kirk, Ruth. *Transition and Change on the Northwest Coast: The Makah, Nuu-Chah-Nulth, Southern Kwakiutl, and Nuxalk.* Seattle: University of Washington Press, 1986

2029.   Krause, Michael E. "Kwalhioqua and Clatskanie." In *Northwest Coast,* ed. W. Suttles, 530–32. Vol. 7 of *Handbook of North American Indians,* ed. W. Sturtevant. Washington, D.C.: Smithsonian Institution, 1990.

2030.   Leacock, Eleanor. "The Innu Bands of Labrador." In *Native People, Native Lands: Canadian Indians, Inuit, and Métis,* ed. B. A. Cox, 92–106. Ottawa: Carleton University Press, 1988.

2031.   Leland, Donald. "Paths out of

Slavery on the Aboriginal North Pacific Coast of North America." *Slavery and Abolition* 10 (December 1989): 1–22.

2032. MacDonald, George F. *Chiefs of the Sea and Sky: Haida Heritage Sites of the Queen Charlotte Islands.* Vancouver: University of British Columbia Press, 1989.

2033. McDonald, James A. "The Marginalization of the Tsimshian Cultural Ecology: The Seasonal Cycle." In *Native People, Native Lands: Canadian Indians, Inuit, and Métis,* ed. B. A. Cox, 199–218. Ottawa: Carleton University Press, 1988.

2034. ———. "Su-Sit-Aatk." *Rotunda* 21, no. 2 (1988): 19–25.

2035. McGregor, Roy. *Chief: The Fearless Vision of Billy Diamond.* Toronto: Penguin, 1989. [James Bay Cree]

2036. McIlwraith, Thomas F. "At Home with the Bella Coola Indians." *BC Studies* 75 (autumn 1987): 43–60.

2037. Marr, Carolyn J. "Taken Pictures: On Interpreting Native American Photographs of the Southern Northwest Coast." *Pacific Northwest Quarterly* 80 (1989): 52–61.

2038. Miller, Jay, and **William Seaberg.** "Athapaskans of Southwestern Oregon." In *Northwest Coast,* ed. W. Suttles, 580–88. Vol. 7 of *Handbook of North American Indians,* ed. W. Sturtevant. Washington, D.C.: Smithsonian Institution, 1990.

2039. Milliker, Rebecca. "Alaska's Lost Heritage: The Unprecedented Flowering of Drama, Dance, and Song in the Nineteenth Century Potlatch of the North Pacific Coast Indians." *Journal of Popular Culture* 21 (1987): 63–76.

2040. Mishler, Craig. "Athabascan Indian Fiddling: A Musical History." *Alaska* 53, no. 11 (1987): 47–51.

2041. Murray, Paul E. "Recollections of an Eskimo Triumph: A Cultural Analysis." *Anthropos* 83 (1988): 153–60.

2042. Neils, Selma. *The Klickitat Indians.* Portland, Oreg.: Binford & Mort Publishing, 1985.

2043. Nicandri, David L. *Northwest Chiefs.* Tacoma: Washington State Historical Society, 1985.

2044. Oliver, Ethel Ross. *Journal of an Aleutian Year.* Seattle: University of Washington Press, 1988.

2045. Oswalt, Wendell H. *Bashful No Longer: An Alaskan Eskimo Ethnohistory, 1778–1988.* Norman: University of Oklahoma Press, 1990.

2046. Perry, Richard J. "Matrilineal Descent in a Hunting Context: The Athapaskan Case." *Ethnology* 28 (1989): 33–51.

2047. Porter, Frank. *Coast Salish Tribes.* New York: Chelsea House, 1990.

2048. Powell, James V. "Quileute." In *Northwest Coast,* ed. W. Suttles, 431–37. Vol. 7 of *Handbook of North American Indians,* ed. W. Sturtevant. Washington, D.C.: Smithsonian Institution, 1990.

2049. Preston, Richard J. "The View from the Other Side of the Frontier: East Cree Historical Nations." In *Papers of the Twenty-First Algonquian Conference,* ed. W. Cowan, 313–28. Ottawa: Carleton University Press, 1990.

2050. Renker, Ann M., and **Erna Gunter.** "Makah." In *Northwest Coast,* ed. W. Suttles, 422–30. Vol. 7 of *Handbook of North American Indians,* ed. W. Sturtevant. Washington, D.C.: Smithsonian Institution, 1990.

2051. Reynolds, Brad. "Athapaskans

Along the Yukon." *National Geographic* 177 (February 1990): 44–69.

2052. **Ridington, Robin.** "Knowledge, Power, and the Individual in Subarctic Hunting Societies." *American Anthropologist* 90 (1988): 98–110.

2053. **Ruby, Robert H., and John A. Brown.** *A Guide to the Indian Tribes of the Pacific Northwest.* Norman: University of Oklahoma Press, 1986.

2054. **Ruppert, James.** "The Russians Are Coming, the Russians Are Dead: Myth and Historical Consciousness in Two Contact Narratives." *Studies in American Indian Literatures* 2 (Spring 1990): 1–10.

2055. **Seaberg, William, and Jay Miller.** "Tillamook." In *Northwest Coast,* ed. W. Suttles, 560–67. Vol. 7 of *Handbook of North American Indians,* ed. W. Sturtevant. Washington, D.C.: Smithsonian Institution, 1990.

2056. **Sharp, Henry S.** "Giant Fish, Giant Otters, and Dinosaurs: 'Apparently Irrational Beliefs' in a Chippewyan Community." *American Ethnologist* 14 (1987): 226–35.

2057. ———. "Shared Experience and Magical Death: Chipewyan Explanations of a Prophet's Decline." *Ethnology* 25 (1986): 257–70.

2058. ———. *The Transformation of Big Foot: Maleness, Power and Belief Among the Chipewyan.* Washington, D.C.: Smithsonian Institution Press, 1988.

2059. **Silverstein, Michael.** "Chinookans of the Lower Columbia." In *Northwest Coast,* ed. W. Suttles, 533–46. Vol. 7 of *Handbook of North American Indians,* ed. W. Sturtevant. Washington, D.C.: Smithsonian Institution, 1990.

2060. **Smith, D. M.** "Big Stone Foundations: Manifest Meaning in Chipewyan Myths." *Journal of American Culture* 8 (spring 1985): 73–77.

2061. **Smith, James G. E.** "The Western Woods Cree: Anthropological Myth and Historical Reality." *American Ethologist* 14 (1987): 434–48.

2062. **Stearns, Mary Lee.** "Haida Since 1960." In *Northwest Coast,* ed. W. Suttles, 261–66. Vol. 7 of *Handbook of North American Indians,* ed. W. Sturtevant. Washington, D.C.: Smithsonian Institution, 1990.

2063. **Stenbaek, Marianne.** "Forty Years of Cultural Change Among the Inuit in Alaska, Canada, and Greenland: Some Reflections." *Arctic* 40 (1987): 300–309.

2064. **Suquamish Museum.** *The Eyes of Chief Seattle.* Seattle: University of Washington Press, 1985.

2065. **Suttles, Wayne.** "Central Coast Salish." In *Northwest Coast,* ed. W. Suttles, 453–75. Vol. 7 of *Handbook of North American Indians,* ed. W. Sturtevant. Washington, D.C.: Smithsonian Institution, 1990.

2066. ———. *Coast Salish Essays.* Seattle: University of Washington Press, 1987.

2067. ———, ed. *Northwest Coast.* Vol. 7 of *Handbook of North American Indians,* ed. W. Sturtevant. Washington, D.C.: Smithsonian Institution, 1990.

2068. **Suttles, Wayne, and Barbara Lane.** "Southern Coast Salish." In *Northwest Coast,* ed. W. Suttles, 485–502. Vol. 7 of *Handbook of North American Indians,* ed. W. Sturtevant. Washington, D.C.: Smithsonian Institution, 1990.

2069. **Tepper, Leslie M.,** ed. *The In-*

terior Salish Tribes of British Columbia: A Photographic Collection. Mercury Series Paper, vol. III. Hull, Queb.: Canadian Museum of Civilization, 1987; University of Chicago Press, 1988.

2070. **Thompson, Judy.** *Pride of the Indian Wardrobe: Northern Athapaskan Footwear.* Toronto: University of Toronto Press, 1990.

2071. **Tollefson, Kenneth D.** "The Snoqualmie: A Puget Sound Chiefdom." *Ethnology* 26 (1987): 121–36.

2072. **Trafzer, Clifford E.** *The Chinook.* New York: Chelsea House, 1990.

2073. **Webster, Gloria Cranmer.** "Kwakiutl Since 1980." In *Northwest Coast,* ed. W. Suttles, 387–90. Vol. 7 of *Handbook of North American Indians,* ed. W. Sturtevant. Washington, D.C.: Smithsonian Institution, 1990.

2074. **Whitehead, Peter J. P.** "Earliest Extant Painting of Greenlanders." In *Indians and Europe: An Interdisciplin-ary Collection of Essays,* ed. C. Feest, 141–59. Aachen, West Germany: Edition Herodot, 1987.

2075. **Wyatt, Victoria.** *Images from the Inside Passage: An Alaskan Portrait by Winter and Pond.* Seattle: University of Washington Press, 1989.

2076. **Zenk, Henry B.** "Alseans." In *Northwest Coast,* ed. W. Suttles, 568–71 Vol. 7 of *Handbook of North American Indians,* ed. W. Sturtevant. Washington, D.C.: Smithsonian Institution, 1990.

2077. ———. "Kalapuyans." In *Northwest Coast,* ed. W. Suttles, 547–53. Vol. 7 of *Handbook of North American Indians,* ed. W. Sturtevant. Washington, D.C.: Smithsonian Institution, 1990.

2078. ———. "Siuslawans and Coosans." In *Northwest Coast,* ed. W. Suttles, 572–79. Vol. 7 of *Handbook of North American Indians,* ed. W. Sturtevant. Washington, D.C.: Smithsonian Institution, 1990.

VIII

The Métis in Canada and the United States

2079. **Andrews, Gerry.** *Métis Outpost: Memoirs of the First Schoolmaster at the Métis Settlement of Kelly Lake, B.C., 1923–1925.* Victoria, B.C.: Pencrest Publications, 1985.

2080. **Barkwell, Lawrence J., David N. Gray, David N. Chartrand, Lyle N. Longclaws, and Ron H. Richard.** "Devalued People: The Status of the Métis in the Justice System." *Canadian Journal of Native Studies* 9 (1989): 141–50.

2081. **Brown, Jennifer S. H.** "Diverging Identities: The Presbyterian Métis of St. Gabriel Street." In *The New Peoples: Being and Becoming Métis in North America,* ed. J. Peterson and J. S. H. Brown, 195–206. Lincoln: University of Nebraska Press, 1985.

2082. ———. "The Métis: Genesis and Rebirth." In *Native People, Native Lands: Canadian Indians, Inuit, and Métis,* ed. B. A. Cox, 136–47. Ottawa: Carleton University Press, 1988.

2083. **Burt, Larry W.** "In a Crooked Piece of Time: The Dilemma of the Montana Cree and the Métis." *Journal of American Culture* 9 (1986): 45–51.

2084. **Coates, K. S., and W. R. Morrison.** "More Than a Matter of Blood: The Federal Government, the Churches, and the Mixed Blood Populations of the Yukon and the Mackenzie River Valley, 1890–1950." In *1885 and After: Native Society in Transition,* ed. F. L. Barron and J. B. Waldram, 253–77. Regina, Sask.: Canadian Plains Research Center, University of Regina, 1986.

2085. **Crawford, John C.** "What Is Michif? Language in the Métis Tradition." In *The New Peoples: Being and Becoming Métis in North America,* ed. J. Peterson and J. S. H. Brown, 231–41. Lincoln: University of Nebraska Press, 1985.

2086. **Daniels, Dorothy.** "Métis Identity: A Personal Perspective." *Native Studies Review* 3, no. 2 (1987): 7–16.

2087. **Dickason, Olive P.** "From 'One Native' in the Northeast to 'New Nation' in the Northwest: A Look at the Emergence of the Métis." In *The New Peoples: Being and Becoming Métis in North America,* ed. J. Peterson and J. S. H. Brown, 19–36. Lincoln: University of Nebraska Press, 1985.

2088. **Douaud, Patrick C.** *Ethnolinguistic Profile of the Canadian Métis.* Canadian Ethnology Service, Paper no. 99. Ottawa: National Museums of Canada, 1985.

2089.   **Driben, Paul.** *We Are Métis: The Ethnography of a Halfbreed Community in Northern Alberta.* New York: AMS Press, 1985.

2090.   **Dunsenberry, Verne.** "Waiting for the Day That Never Comes: The Dispossessed Métis of Montana." In *The New Peoples: Being and Becoming Métis in North America,* ed. J. Peterson and J. S. H. Brown, 119–36. Lincoln: University of Nebraska Press, 1985.

2091.   **Edmunds, R. David.** "'Unacquainted with the Laws of the Civilized World': American Attitudes Toward the Métis Communities in the Old Northwest." In *The New Peoples: Being and Becoming Métis in North America,* ed. J. Peterson and J. S. H. Brown, 185–93. Lincon: University of Nebraska Press, 1985.

2092.   **Flanagan, Thomas.** "Métis Aboriginal Rights: Some Historical and Contemporary Problems." In *The Quest for Justice: Aboriginal Peoples and Aboriginal Rights,* ed. M. Boldt and J. A. Long, 230–45. Toronto: University of Toronto Press, 1985).

2093.   **Flanagan, Thomas** and **J. Foster,** eds. "The Métis Past and Present." *Canadian Ethnic Studies* (special issue) no. 17, 2 (1985).

2094.   **Foster, John E.** "Paulet Paul: Métis or 'House Indian' Folk Hero?" *Manitoba History* 9 (spring 1985): 2–7.

2095.   ———. "The Plains Métis." In *Native Peoples: The Canadian Experience,* ed. R. B. Morrison and R. C. Wilson, 375–403. Toronto: McClelland and Stewart, 1986.

2096.   ———. "Some Questions and Perspectives on the Problems of Métis Roots." In *The New Peoples: Being and Becoming Métis in North America.* ed. J. Peterson and J. S. H. Brown, 73–91.

Lincoln: University of Nebraska Press, 1985.

2097.   **Gallagher, Brian.** "A Reexamination of Race, Class, and Society in Red River." *Native Studies Review* 4, no. 1/2 (1988): 25–68.

2098.   **Gorham, Harriet.** "Families of Mixed Descent in the Western Great Lakes Region." In *Native People, Native Lands: Canadian Indians, Inuit, and Métis,* ed. B. A. Cox, 37–55. Ottawa: Carleton University Press, 1988.

2099.   **Harrison, Julia D.** "Métis: A Glenbow Museum Exhibition." *American Indian Art Magazine* 11 (spring 1986): 54–59.

2100.   ———. *Métis: People Between Two Worlds.* Seattle: University of Washington Press, 1985.

2101.   **Hatt, Ken.** "Ethnic Discourse in Alberta: Land and the Métis in the Ewing Commission." *Canadian Ethnic Studies* 17 (1985): 64–79.

2102.   **Judd, Carol M.** "Moose Factory Was Not Red River: A Comparison of Mixed-Blood Experiences." In *Explorations in Canadian Economic History: Essays in Honor of Irene M. Spy,* ed. D. Cameron, 251–68. Ottawa: University of Ottawa Press, 1985.

2103.   **Lederman, Anne.** "Old Indian and Métis Fiddling in Manitoba: Origins, Structure, and Question of Syncretism." *Canadian Journal of Native Studies* 8 (1988): 205–30.

2104.   **Lee, David.** "The Métis Militant Rebels of 1885." *Canadian Ethnic Studies* 21 (1989): 1–19.

2105.   **Long, John S.** "Treaty No. 9 and Fur Trade Company Families: Northeastern Ontario's Halfbreeds, Indians, and Métis." In *The New Peoples: Being and Becoming Métis in North Ameri-*

ca, ed. J. Peterson and J. S. H. Brown, 137–62. Lincoln: University of Nebraska Press, 1985.

2106. **McNab, David T.** "Métis Participation in the Treaty-Making Process in Ontario: A Reconnaissance." *Native Studies Review* 1, no. 2 (1985): 57–79.

2107. **Madill, Dennis F. K.** "Riel, Red River, and Beyond: New Developments in Métis History." In *New Directions in American Indian History,* ed. C. G. Calloway, 49–78. Norman: University of Oklahoma Press, 1988.

2108. **Miller, J. R.** "From Riel to the Métis." *Canadian Historical Review* 69 (1988): 1–20.

2109. **Nicks, Trudy.** "Mary Anne's Dilemma: The Ethnohistory of an Ambivalent Identity." *Canadian Ethnic Studies* 17 (1985): 103–14.

2110. **Nicks, Trudy,** and **Kenneth Morgan.** "Grande Cache: The Historic Development of an Indigenous Alberta Métis Population." In *The New Peoples: Being and Becoming Métis in North America,* ed. J. Peterson and J. S. H. Brown, 163–81. Lincoln: University of Nebraska Press, 1985.

2111. **Payment, Diane.** "Batoche After 1885: A Society in Transition." In *1885 and After: Native Society in Transition.* ed. F. L. Barron and J. B. Waldram, 178–87. Regina, Sask.: Canadian Plains Research Center, University of Regina, 1986.

2112. ———. *"The Free People— Otipemisiswak": Batoche, Saskatchewan, 1870–1930.* Studies in Archaeology, Architecture, and History, no. 0821-1027. Ottawa: National Historic Parks and Sites, 1990.

2113. **Peterson, Jacqueline.** "Many Roads to Red River: Métis Genesis in the Great Lakes Region, 1680–1815." In *The New Peoples: Being and Becoming a Métis in North America,* ed. J. Peterson and J. S. H. Brown, 37–71. Lincoln: University of Nebraska Press, 1985.

2114. **Peterson, Jacqueline,** and **Jennifer S. H. Brown,** eds. *The New Peoples: Being and Becoming Métis in North America.* Lincoln: University of Nebraska Press, 1985.

2115. **Purich, Donald.** *The Métis.* Toronto: James Lorimar and Co., 1988.

2116. **Rivard, Ron.** "The Métis and Social Science." *Native Studies Review* 3, no. 2 (1987): 1–6.

2117. **Sawchuck, Joe.** "The Métis, Non-status Indians, and the New Aboriginality: Government Influence on Native Political Alliances and Identity." *Canadian Ethnic Studies* 17 (1985): 135–46.

2118. **Sprenger, Herman.** "The Métis Nation: Buffalo Hunting Versus Agriculture in the Red River Settlement, 1810–1870." In *Native People, Native Lands: Canadian Indians, Inuit, and Métis,* ed. B. A. Cox, 120–35. Ottawa: Carleton University Press, 1988.

2119. **Spry, Irene M.** "The Métis and Mixed-Bloods of Rupert's Land Before 1870." In *The New Peoples: Being and Becoming Métis in North America,* ed. J. Peterson and J. S. H. Brown, 95–118. Lincoln: University of Nebraska Press, 1985.

2120. **Stanley, George F. G.,** gen. ed. *The Collected Writings of Louis Riel.* 5 vols. Edmonton: University of Alberta Press, 1985.

2121. **Trask, Kerry A.** "Settlement in a Half-Savage Land: Life and Loss in the Métis Community of La Baye." *Michigan Historical Review* 15 (spring 1989): 1–27.

2122.   **Van Kirk, Sylvia.** "'What if Mama Is an Indian?' The Cultural Ambivalence of the Alexander Ross Family." In *The New Peoples: Being and Becoming a Métis in North America,* ed. J. Peterson and J. S. H. Brown, 207–17. Lincoln: University of Nebraska Press, 1985.

2123.   **Weaver, Sally M.** "Federal Policy-Making for Métis and Non-status Indians in the Context of Native Policy." *Canadian Ethnic Studies* 17 (1985): 80–102.

IX
Biographies of American Indians

2124. **Abbott, Devon I.** "Ann Florence Wilson: Matriarch of the Cherokee Female Seminary." *Chronicles of Oklahoma* 67 (1990): 426–47.

2125. **Abler, Thomas S.** "Governor Blacksnake as a Young Man? Speculation on the Identity of Trumbull's 'The Young Sachem.'" *Ethnology* 34 (1987): 329–51.

2126. ———, ed. *Chainbreaker: The Revolutionary War Memoirs of Governor Blacksnake, as Told to Benjamin Williams.* Lincoln: University of Nebraska Press, 1989. [Seneca autobiography as told to another Seneca]

2127. **Agogino, George.** "Oscar Howe: Sioux Artist." *Plains Anthropologist* 32, no. 116 (1987): 197–202.

2128. **Alexander, Ruth Ann.** "Elaine Goodale Eastman and the Failure of the Feminist Protestant Ethic." *Great Plains Quarterly* 8 (1988): 89–101.

2129. **Amchan, Arthur J.** *The Most Famous Soldier in America: A Biography of Lt. Gen. Nelson A. Miles, 1839–1925.* Alexandria, Va.: Amchan, 1989.

2130. **Anderson, Gary Clayton.** "Joseph Renville and the Ethos of Biculturalism" In *Being and Becoming Indian: Biographical Studies of North American Frontiers,* ed. J. A. Clifton, 59–81. Chicago: Dorsey Press, 1989.

2131. ———. *Little Crow: Spokesman for the Sioux.* St. Paul: Minnesota Historical Society Press, 1986.

2132. **Assu, Harry.** *Assu of Cape Mudge: Recollections of a Coastal Indian Chief.* With Joy Inglis. Vancouver: University of British Columbia Press, 1989.

2133. **Avanyu Publishing.** *J. B. Moore, United States Licensed Indian Trader.* Albuquerque: University of New Mexico Press, 1988.

2134. **Baird, W. David.** *A Creek Warrior for the Confederacy: The Autobiography of Chief G. W. Grayson.* Norman: University of Oklahoma Press, 1988.

2135. **Bangert, Buckley.** "Uncompahgre Statesman: The Life of Ouray." *Journal of the Western Slope* 1 (1986): 1–76.

2136. **Becker, Marshall J.** "Hannah Freeman: An Eighteenth-Century Lenape Living and Working Among Colonial Farmers." *Pennsylvania Magazine of History and Biography* 114 (April 1990): 249–69.

2137. **Beninato, Stefanie.** "Pope, Pose-yemu, and Naranjo: A New Look at Leadership in the Pueblo Revolt of

1680." *New Mexico Historical Review* 64 (1990): 417–36.

2138.   Berkhove, Lawrence I. "Introduction to 'Pahenit, Prince of the Land of Lakes.'" *Nevada Historical Society Quarterly* 31 (1988): 19–86.

2139.   Black Elk, Wallace H., and William S. Lyon. *Black Elk: The Sacred Ways of a Lakota.* New York: Harper & Row, 1990.

2140.   Black-Rogers, Mary. "Dan Raincloud: 'Keeping Our Indian Way.'" In *Being and Becoming Indian: Biographical Studies of North American Frontiers,* ed. J. A. Clifton, 226–48. Chicago: Dorsey Press, 1989.

2141.   Boehme, Sarah E. "The North and Snow: J. H. Sharp in Montana." *Montana* 40 (autumn 1990): 32–47.

2142.   Brandt, Penny S. "A Letter of Dr. John Sibley, Indian Agent: Annotated." *Louisiana History* 29 (1988): 365–87.

2143.   Bremer, Richard G. *Indian Agent and Wilderness Scholar: The Life of Henry Rowe Schoolcraft.* Mt. Pleasant: Clarke Historical Library, Central Michigan University, 1987.

2144.   Brito, Sylvester S. *The Way of a Peyote Roadman.* New York: Peter Lang, 1989.

2145.   Brower, Kenneth. "Grey Owl." *Atlantic* 265 (January 1990): 74–84.

2146.   Brown, Jennifer S. H. "A. I. Hallowell and William Berens Revisited." In *Papers of the Eighteenth Algonquian Conference,* ed. W. Cowan, 17–27. Ottawa: Carleton University Press, 1987.

2147.   ———. "'A Place in Your Mind for Them All': Chief William Berens." In *Being and Becoming Indian:*
Biographical Studies of North American Frontiers, ed. J. A. Clifton, 204–25. Chicago: Dorsey Press, 1989.

2148.   Bruce, Michael L. "'Our Best Men Are Fast Leaving Us': The Life and Times of Robert M. Jones." *Chronicles of Oklahoma* 66 (1988): 294–305.

2149.   Brugge, David M. "Henry Chee Dodge: From the Long Walk to Self-Determination." In *Indian Lives: Essays on Nineteenth- and Twentieth-Century Native American Leaders,* ed. L. G. Moses and R. Wilson, 91–114. Albuquerque: University of New Mexico Press, 1985.

2150.   Brumble, H. David, III. "Albert Hensley's Two Autobiographies and the History of American Indian Autobiography." *American Quarterly* 37 (1985): 702–18.

2151.   ———. "Sam Blowsnake's Confessions: Crashing Thunder and the History of American Indian Autobiography." *Canadian Review of American Studies* 16, no. 3 (1985): 272–82.

2152.   ———. "Social Scientists and American Indian Autobiographers: Sun Chief and Gregorio's 'Life Story.'" *Journal of American Studies* 20, no. 2 (1986): 273–90.

2153.   Buerger, Geoffrey. "Eleazer Williams: Elitism and Multiple Identity on Two Frontiers." In *Being and Becoming Indian: Biographical Studies of North American Frontiers,* ed. J. A. Clifton, 114–36. Chicago: Dorsey Press, 1989.

2154.   Burchfield, Chris. "The Sweet, Sad Song of Yellow Bird, California's Confederate Cherokee." *Californians* 8 (1990); 3–21.

2155.   Calloway, Colin G. "Simon Girty: Interpreter and Intermediary." In *Being and Becoming Indian: Biographical Studies of North American Frontiers,* ed. J.

A. Clifton, 38–58. Chicago: Dorsey Press, 1989.

2156. **Carlson, Pamela McGuire,** and **E. Breck Parkman.** "An Exceptional Adaptation: Carrillo Ynitia." *California History* 65 (1986): 238–47.

2157. **Carter, Harvey Lewis.** *The Life and Times of Little Turtle: First Sagamore of the Wabash.* Urbana: University of Illinois Press, 1987.

2158. **Chance, Laura L.** "Indian Portraits." *Queen City Heritage* 48 (summer 1990); 42–48.

2159. **Clark, Jerry E.,** and **Martha Ellen Webb.** "Susette and Susan LaFlesch: Reformer and Missionary." In *Being and Becoming Indian: Biographical Studies of North American Frontiers,* ed. J. A. Clifton, 137–59. Chicago: Dorsey Press, 1989.

2160. **Clark, Robert A.** *The Killing of Crazy Horse.* Lincoln: University of Nebraska Press, 1988.

2161. **Clifton, James A.** "Leopold Pokagon: Transformative Leadership on the St. Joseph River Frontier." *Michigan History* 69 (September 1985): 17–23.

2162. ———, ed. *Being and Becoming Indian: Biographical Studies of North American Frontiers.* Chicago: Dorsey Press, 1989.

2163. **Colbert, Thomas B.** "Elias Cornelius Boudinot: The Indian Orator and Lecturer.: *American Indian Quarterly* 13 (1989); 149–60.

2164. **Covington, James W.** "Billy Bowlegs, Sam Jones, and the Crisis of 1849." *Florida Historical Quarterly* 68 (1990): 299–311.

2165. **Crowder, James L., Jr.** "Osage Aviator: The Life and Career of Major General Clarance L. Tinker." *Chronicles of Oklahoma* 65 (1988): 400–431.

2166. **Crum, Steven J.** "Henry Roe Cloud, a Winnebago Indian Reformer: His Quest for American Indian Higher Education." *Kansas History* 11 (1988): 171–84.

2167. **DeArmond, Robert N.** "Saginaw Jake: Navy Hostage, Indian Policeman, Celebrity." *Alaska History* 5 (spring 1990): 23–33.

2168. **De Quille, Dan.** "Pahnenit, Prince of the Land of Lakes." *Nevada Historical Society Quarterly* 31 (1988): 87–118.

2169. **Derounian, Kathryn Zabelle.** "The Publication, Promotion, and Distribution of Mary Rowlandson's Indian Captivity Narrative in the Seventeenth Century." *Early American Literature* 23 (1988): 239–61.

2170. **Diedrich, Mark.** *Famous Chiefs of the Eastern Sioux.* Minneapolis: Coyote Press, 1987.

2171. **Diffendal, Ann P.** "Fred 'Bright-Star' Murree: Pawnee Roller Skater." *Nebraska History* 70 (1989): 158–63.

2172. **Dinges, Bruce J.** "Leighton Finley: A Forgotten Soldier of the Apache Wars." *Journal of Arizona History* 29 (1988): 163–84.

2173. **Duffek, Karen.** *Bill Reid: Beyond the Essential Form.* Vancover: University of British Columbia Press, 1986.

2174. **Duncan, Kunigunde.** *Blue Star: The Story of Corabelle Fellows, Teacher at Dakota Missions, 1884–1888.* St. Paul: Minnesota Historical Society Press, 1990.

2175. **Edmunds, R. David.** "Black Hawk." *Timeline* 5 (1988): 24–27.

2176. ———. "The Thin Red Line: Tecumseh, the Prophet, and Shawnee Resistance." *Timeline* 4 (1988): 2–19.

2177. **Ellis, Clyde.** "'Our Ill Fated Relative: John Rollins Ridge and the Cherokee People." *Chronicles of Oklahoma* 68 (1990): 360–75.

2178. **Ellis, Richard N.** "Luther Standing Bear: 'I Would Raise Him to Be an Indian.'" In *Indian Lives: Essays on Nineteenth- and Twentieth-Century Native American Leaders,* ed. L. G. Moses and R. Wilson, 139–58. Albuquerque: University of New Mexico Press, 1985.

2179. **Gardner, Robert G.** "Duncan O'Bryant: Missionary to Georgia Cherokees." *Baptist History and Heritage* 22 (April 1987): 27–37.

2180. **Godbold, Stanley, Jr.,** and **Russell U. Malte.** *Confederate Colonel and Cherokee Chief: The Life of William Holland Thomas.* Knoxville: University of Tennessee Press, 1990.

2181. **Green, Gretchen.** "Molly Brant, Catharine Brant, and Their Daughters: A Study in Acculturation." *Ontario History* 81 (1989): 235–50.

2182. **Grumet, Robert S.** "Taphow: The Forgotten 'Sakemau and Commander in Chief of All Those Indians Inhabiting Northern New Jersey.'" *Bulletin of the Archaeological Society of New Jersey* 43 (1988): 23–28.

2183. **Gunderson, Robert G.** "Chief Tomah's Reply: A Pacific Footnote on the Folklore of Tecumseh." *Indiana Magazine of History* 86 (1990): 311–14.

2184. **Hacker, Margaret Schmidt.** *Cynthia Ann Parker: The Life and the Legend.* El Paso: Texas Western Press, 1990.

2185. **Halpin, Marjorie.** *Jack Schadbolt and the Coastal Indian Image.* Vancouver: University of British Columbia Press, 1986.

2186. **Hardorff, Richard G.** *The Oglala Lakota Crazy Horse: A Preliminary Genealogical Study and an Annotated Listing of Primary Sources.* Mattituek, N.Y.: J. M. Carroll and Co., 1985.

2187. **Hauck, Philomena,** and **Kathleen Snow.** *Famous Indian Leaders.* Calgary: Detselig Enterprises, 1989.

2188. **Hauptman, Laurence M.** "Designing Woman: Minnie Kellogg, Iroquois Leader." In *Indian Lives: Essays on Nineteenth- and Twentieth-Century Native American Leaders,* ed. L. G. Moses and R. Wilson, 159–88. Albuquerque: University of New Mexico Press, 1985.

2189. **Herring, Joseph B.** "Kenekuk, the Kickapoo Prophet: Acculturation Without Assimilation." *American Indian Quarterly* 9 (1985): 295–307.

2190. **Hoig, Stan.** "Diana, Tiana, or Tulihina? The Myth and Mystery of Sam Houston's Cherokee Wife." *Chronicles of Oklahoma* 64 (1986): 53–59.

2191. **Hollow, Robert C., Jr.** "Sitting Bull: Artifact and Artifake." *North Dakota History* 54, no. 3 (1987): 3–14.

2192. **Humins, John H.** "Squanto and Massasoit: A Struggle for Power." *New England Quarterly* 60 (1987): 54–70.

2193. **Irons, Angie.** "Big Bow—Terror of the Plains." *True West* 34, no. 7 (1987): 38–43.

2194. **Jennings, Francis.** "Brother Miquon: Good Lord!" In *The World of William Penn,* ed. R. S. Dunn and M. M. Dunn, 195–214. Philadelphia: University of Pennsylvania Press, 1986.

2195. **Johnson, David L.,** and **Raymond Wilson.** "Gertrude Simmons Bonin, 1876–1938: 'Americanize the First Americans.'" *American Indian Quarterly* 12 (1988): 27–40.

2196. **Johnson, Helen S.** "Chief of the Creek Nation." *North Florida Living*

5 (1985): 24–26. [Alexander McGillivray]

2197.   Johnson, Thomas H. "Maud Clairmont: Artist, Entrepreneur, Cultural Mediator." In *Being and Becoming Indian: Biographical Studies of North American Frontiers,* ed. J. A. Clifton, 249–75. Chicago: Dorsey Press, 1989.

2198.   Jones, Lawrence T., III. "Cynthia Ann Parker and Pease Ross— The Forgotten Photographs." *Southwestern Historical Quarterly* 93 (1990): 379–84.

2199.   Knight, Wilfred. *Red Fox: Stand Watie and the Confederate Indian Nations During the Civil War Years in Indian Territory.* Glendale, Calif.: Arthur C. Clark Co., 1988.

2200.   Littlefield, Daniel F., Jr. *The Life of Okah Tubee.* Lincoln: University of Nebraska Press, 1988.

2201.   Lockwood, Patricia. "Judge John Martin: First Chief Justice of the Cherokees." *Chronicles of Oklahoma* 64 (summer 1986): 61–74.

2202.   Lubick, George M. "Peterson Zah: A Progressive Outlook at a Traditional Style." In *Indian Lives: Essays on Nineteenth- and Twentieth-Century Native American Leaders,* ed. L. G. Moses and R. Wilson, 189–216. Albuquerque: University of New Mexico Press, 1985.

2203.   Lurie, Nancy. *North American Indian Lives.* Milwaukee: Milwaukee Public Museum, 1985.

2204.   McCartney, Martha W. "Cockacoeske, Queen of Pamunkey: Diplomat and Suzeraine." In *Powhatan's Mantle: Indians in the Colonial Southeast,* ed. P. H. Wood, G. A. Waselkov, and M. T. Hatley, 173–95. Lincoln: University of Nebraska Press, 1989.

2205.   McClurken, James M. "Au-gustin Hamlin, Jr.: Ottawa Identity and the Politics of Ottawa Resistance." In *Being and Becoming Indian: Biographical Studies of North American Frontiers,* ed. J. A. Clifton, 82–111. Chicago: Dorsey Press, 1989.

2206.   McCoy, Ronald. "Hopi Artist Fred Kabotie (1900–1986)" *American Indian Art Magazine* 15 (autumn 1990): 40–49.

2207.   ———. "Nampeyo: Giving the Artist a Name." In *Indian Lives: Essays on Nineteenth- and Twentieth-Century Native American Leaders,* ed. L. G. Moses and R. Wilson, 43–59. Albuquerque: University of New Mexico Press, 1985.

2208.   McElroy, Ann. "Oopeeleeka and Mina: Contrasting Responses to Modernization of Two Bafflin Island Inuit Women." In *Being and Becoming Indian: Biographical Studies of North American Frontiers,* ed. J. A. Clifton, 290–318. Chicago: Dorsey Press, 1989.

2209.   Madsen, Brigham D. *Chief Pocatello, the "White Plume."* Salt Lake City: University of Utah Press, 1986.

2210.   Mathes, Valerie Sherer. "Dr. Susan LaFlesche Picotte." In *Indian Lives: Essays on Nineteenth- and Twentieth-Century Native American Leaders,* ed. L. G. Moses and R. Wilson, 61–90. Albuquerque: University of New Mexico Press, 1985.

2211.   Mattison, David. "Sitting Bull in Canada." *History of Photography* 14 (1988): 121–24.

2212.   Menta, John. "The Strange Case of Nepaupunk: Warrior or Criminal?" *Journal of the New Haven Colony Historical Society* 33, no. 2 (1987): 3–17.

2213.   Meredith, Howard L. *Bartley Milam: Principal Chief of the Cherokee Na-*

tion. Muscogee, Okla.: Indian University Press (Bacone College), 1985.

2214. **Miller, Jay.** "Mourning Dove: The Author as Cultural Mediator." In *Being and Becoming Indian: Biographical Studies of North American Frontiers,* ed. J. A. Clifton, 160–82. Chicago: Dorsey Press, 1989.

2215. **Moses, L. G.** "'The Father Tells Me So!' Wovoka, the Ghost Dance Prophet." *American Indian Quarterly* 9 (1985): 335–51.

2216. ———. "James Mooney and Wovoka: An Ethnologist's Visit with the Ghost Dance Prophet." *Nevada Historical Society Quarterly* 30 (1987): 131–46.

2217. **Moses, L. G.,** and **Raymond Wilson,** eds. *Indian Lives: Essays on Nineteenth- and Twentieth-Century Native American Leaders.* Albuquerque: University of New Mexico Press, 1985.

2218. **Norcini, Marilyn.** "The Education of a Native American Anthropologist: Edward P. Dozier (1916– 1971)." Master's thesis, University of Arizona, 1988.

2219. **Paul, Andrea.** "Buffalo Bill and Wounded Knee: The Movie." *Nebraska History* 71, no. 3 (1990): 182– 90.

2220. **Poten, Constance J.** "Robert Yellowtail: The New Warrior." *Montana* 39 (summer 1989): 36–41.

2221. **Ramsey, Jack C., Jr.** *Sunshine on the Prairie: The Story of Cynthia Ann Parker.* Austin, Tex.: Eakin Press, 1990.

2222. **Roberts, Charles.** "A Choctaw Odyssey: The Life of Lesa Phillip Roberts." *American Indian Quarterly* 14 (1990): 259–76.

2223. **Robertson, Pauline D.,** and **R. L. Robertson.** *Quanah: A Pictorial History of the Last Comanche Chief.* Amarillo, Tex.: Paramount Publishing, 1985.

2224. **Roebuck, Field.** "Richards Fields—Cherokee Chief." *True West* 34, no. 3 (1987): 18–23.

2225. **Rollings, Willard.** "D'Arcy McNickle." In *Historians of the American Frontier,* ed. J. R. Wiender, 408–25. New York: Greenwood Press, 1988.

2226. **Ronnow, Gretchen.** "John Milton Oskison, Cherokee Journalist: A Singer of the Semantics of Power." *Native Press Research Journal* 4 (1987): 1–14.

2227. **Roscoe, Will.** "'That Is My Road': The Life and Times of a Crow Berdache." *Montana* 40 (winter 1990): 46–55.

2228. **Ruppert, James.** *D'Arcy McNickle.* Boise, Idaho: Boise State University, 1988.

2229. **Sadler, Carl K.** "Jim Thorpe's 100th Birthday: A Pictoral Tribute." *Chronicles of Oklahoma* 65 (1987): 90–97.

2230. **Smith, Annick.** "The Two Frontiers of Mary Ronan." *Montana* 39 (winter 1989): 28–33.

2231. **Smith, Donald B.** "From Sylvester Long to Chief Buffalo Child Long Lance." In *Being and Becoming Indian: Biographical Studies of North American Frontiers,* ed. J. A. Clifton, 183–203. Chicago: Dorsey Press, 1989.

2232. ———. *From the Land of Shadows: The Making of Grey Owl.* Saskatoon: Western Producer Prairie Books, 1990.

2233. ———. *Sacred Feathers: The Reverend Peter Jones (Kahkewaquonaby) and the Mississauga Indians.* Lincoln: University of Nebraska Press, 1987.

2234. **Smith, P. David.** *Ouray, Chief of the Utes.* Ouray, Colo.: Wayfinder Press, 1986.

2235. Sonnichsen, C. L. "From Savage to Saint: A New Image for Geronimo." *Journal of Arizona History* 27 (1986): 5–34.

2236. ———. "The Remodeling of Geronimo." *Arizona Highways* 62 (September 1986): 2–11.

2237. Stahl, Robert J. "Joe True: Convergent Needs and Assumed Identity." In *Being and Becoming Indian: Biographical Studies of North American Frontiers,* ed. J. A. Clifton, 276–89. Chicago: Dorsey Press, 1989.

2238. Sweeney, Edwin R. "I Had Lost All: Geronimo and the Carrasco Massacre of 1851." *Journal of Arizona History* 27 (1986): 35–52.

2239. Turpin, Solveig A. "The End of the Trail: An 1870s Plains Combat Autobiography in Southwest Texas." *Plains Anthropologist* 34, no. 144, pt. 1 (1989): 105–9. [Rock art]

2240. Tyman, James. *Inside Out: An Autobiography of a Native Canadian.* Saskatoon: Fifth House, 1989.

2241. Unrau, William E. "Charles Curtis: The Politics of Allotment." In *Indian Lives: Essays on Nineteenth- and Twentieth-Century Native American Leaders,* ed. L. G. Moses and R. Wilson, 113–38. Albuquerque: University of New Mexico Press, 1985.

2242. ———. *Mixed-Bloods and Tribal Dissolution: Charles Curtis and the Quest for Indian Identity.* Lawrence: University of Kansas Press, 1989.

2243. Vernon, H. A. "Maris Bryant Pierce: The Making of a Seneca Leader." In *Indian Lives: Essays on Nineteenth- and Twentieth-Century Native American Leaders,* ed. L. G. Moses and R. Wilson, 19–42. Albuquerque: University of New Mexico Press, 1985.

2244. Vestal, Stanley. *Sitting Bull, Champion of the Sioux: A Biography.* 1932. Reprint, Norman: University of Oklahoma Press, 1989.

2245. Walter, Albert E. "George Walter: Friend of the Apaches." *Journal of Arizona History* 27 (1986): 91–144.

2246. Young, David, Grant Ingram, and Lise Swartz. *Cry of the Eagle: Encounters with a Cree Healer.* Toronto: University of Toronto Press, 1989.

2247. Zanger, Martin N. "Pierre Parquette, Winnebago Mixed-Blood: Profiteer or Tribal Spokesman?" In *An Anthology of Western Great Lakes Indian History,* ed. D. L. Fixico, 297–351. Milwaukee: American Indian Studies, University of Wisconsin—Milwaukee, 1987.

X
Social Life and Relationships

10.1 SOCIAL TRADITIONS AND SOCIAL CONDITIONS IN INDIAN COMMUNITIES

2248. Anders, Gary C. "Social and Economic Consequences of Federal Indian Policy: A Case Study of the Alaska Natives." *Economic Development and Social Change* 37 (1989): 285–303.

2249. Champagne, Duane. "American Bureaucratization and Tribal Governments: Problems of Institutionalization at the Community Level." Comments by Peter Iverson. In *The Impact of Indian History on the Teaching of United States History: Papers and Commentary from the 1986 Conference at Los Angeles,* 175–232. D'Arcy McNickle Center for the History of the American Indian, Occasional Papers in Curriculum, no. 5. Chicago: Newberry Library, 1987.

2250. ———. *American Indian Societies: Strategies and Conditions of Political and Cultural Survival.* Cultural Survival, Report no. 32. Cambridge, Mass.: Cultural Survival, 1989.

2251. Clark, Orville, Clifford Abbott, Amos Christjohn, and **Marie Hinton.** "Recollections of the Oneida Language Revival, 1972–85, by Participants of the Program." In *The Oneida Indian Experience: Two Perspectives,* ed. J.

Campisi and L. M. Hauptman, 139–44. Syracuse, N.Y.: Syracuse University Press, 1988.

2252. Dallas Inter-Tribal Center. "Native Americans: A Southern Survey." *Southern Exposure* 13 (1985): 94–108.

2253. DeLong, Julie. "The Fort Apache Indian Reservation." *Arizona Highways* 65 (June 1989): 18–33.

2254. Edmunds, R. David. "Antelope and the Engineers: Challenge and Change in the Indian Communities." In *American Indian Identity: Today's Changing Perspectives,* ed. C. E. Trafzer, 8–16. Publications in American Indian Studies, no. 1. San Diego: San Diego State University, 1985.

2255. Farr, William E. *The Reservation Blackfeet, 1885–1945: A Photographic History of Cultural Survival.* Introduction by James Welch. Seattle: University of Washington Press, 1985.

2256. Fixico, Donald L. "From Indians to Cowboys: The Country Western Trend." In *American Indian Identity: Today's Changing Perspectives,* ed. C. E. Trafzer, 17–27. Publications in American Indian Studies, no. 1. San Diego: San Diego State University. 1985.

2257. Fixico, Michelene. "The Road to Middle Class Indian America." In

American Indian Identity: Today's Changing Perspectives, ed. C. E. Trafzer, 50–63. Publications in American Indian Studies, no. 1, San Diego: San Diego State University. 1985.

2258. Fulton, William. "Indian Bingo: High Stakes Fundraising." *Grantsmanship Center News* 13, no. 2 (1985): 13–19.

2259. Gidley, M. *With One Sky Above Us: Life on an American Indian Reservation at the Turn of the Century.* Seattle: University of Washington Press, 1985.

2260. Harkin, Michael. "Mortuary Practices and the Category of Person Among the Heiltsuk." *Arctic Anthropology* 27 (1990): 87–108.

2261. Harrigan, Stephen. "The Lost Tribe." *Texas Monthly* 17 (February 1989): 68–75, 116–43. [Comanches today]

2262. Hatton, Orin T. *Power and Performance in Gros Ventre War Expedition Songs.* Mercury Series Paper, vol. 114. Hull, Queb.: Canadian Ethnology Service, 1990.

2263. Hauser, Raymond E. "The *Berdache* and the Illinois Indian Tribe During the Last Half of the Seventeenth Century." *Ethnohistory* 37, no. 1 (1990): 45–65.

2264. Heizer, Robert. "Indian Servitude in California." In *History of Indian-White Relations,* ed. W. Washburn, 414–16. Vol. 4 of *Handbook of North American Indians,* ed. W. Sturtevant. Washington, D.C.: Smithsonian Institution Press, 1988.

2265. Hodge, Felicia. "Disabled American Indians: A Special Population Requiring Special Considerations." *American Indian Culture and Research Journal* 13, no. 3–4 (1989): 83–104.

2266. Iverson, Peter. "Cowboys, Indians, and the Modern West." *Arizona and the West* 28 (1986): 107–44.

2267. Jett, Stephen C. "Cultural Fusion in Native-American Architecture: The Navajo Hogan." In *A Cultural Geography of North American Indians,* ed. T. E. Ross and T. G. Moore, 243–58. Boulder, Colo.: Westview Press, 1987.

2268. Jorgensen, Joseph G., R. Mc-Cleary, and **S. McNabb.** "Social Indicators in Native Village Alaska." *Human Organization* 14 (1985): 2–17.

2269. Kawashima, Yashuhide. "Indian Servitude in the Northeast." In *History of Indian-White Relations,* ed. W. Washburn, 404–6. Vol. 4 of *Handbook of North American Indians,* ed. W. Sturtevant. Washington, D.C.: Smithsonian Institution Press, 1988.

2270. Knack, Martha C. "Indian Economies, 1950–80." In *Great Basin,* ed. W. L. d'Azevedo, 573–91. Vol. 11 of *Handbook of North American Indians,* ed. W. Sturtevant. Washington Smithsonian Institution, 1986.

2271. La Polin, Armand S., ed. *Native American Voluntary Organizations.* New York: Greenwood Press, 1987.

2272. Lees, William B. "Dakota Acculturation During the Early Reservation Period: Evidence from the Deerfly Site (39L M39), South Dakota." *Plains Anthropologist* 30, no. 108 (1985): 103–21.

2273. Liebow, Edward B. "Category or Community? Measuring Urban Indian Social Cohesion with Network Sampling." *Journal of Ethnic Studies* 16, no. 4 (1989): 67–100.

2274. Lounsbury, Floyd. "Recollections of the Works Progress Administration's Oneida Language and Folklore Project, 1938–1941." In *The Oneida Indian Experience: Two Perspectives,* ed. J. Campisi and L. M. Hauptman, 131–34.

Syracuse, N.Y.: Syracuse University Press, 1988.

2275.   **Lurie, Nancy O.** "Recollections of an Urban Indian Community: The Oneidas of Milwaukee." In *The Oneida Indian Experience: Two Perspectives,* ed. J. Campisi and L. M. Hauptman, 101–7. Syracuse, N.Y.: Syracuse University Press, 1988.

2276.   **McClurken, James M.** "Boundaries of the Reservation: Social, Political, and Geographical Considerations for Defining the Limits of the Keweenaw Bay Chippewa Reservation." *Native Studies Review* 6, no. 2 (1990): 65–80.

2277.   **McKee, Jesse O.** "The Choctaw: Self Determination and Socioeconomic Development." In *A Cultural Geography of North American Indians,* ed. T. E. Ross and T. G. Moore, 173–90. Boulder, Colo.: Westview Press, 1987.

2278.   **McLuhan, T. C.** "Dream Tracks: The Railroad and the American Indian." *Arizona Highways* 63 (June 1987): 4–9.

2279.   **McPherson, Robert S.** "Ricos and Pobres: Wealth Distribution on the Navajo Reservation in 1915." *New Mexico Historical Review* 60 (1985): 415–34.

2280.   **Miller, David Reed.** "Shared Reservations: The Contest of Representations." *Journal of Ethnic Studies* 17 (1989): 123–31.

2281.   **Miller, Virginia.** "The Changing Role of the Chief on a California Indian Reservation." *American Indian Quarterly* 13, no. 4 (1989): 447–55.

2282.   **Novak, Steven J.** "The Real Takeover of the BIA: The Preferential Hiring of Indians." *Journal of Economic History* 50 (1990): 639–54.

2283.   **O'connor, Nancy Fields,** comp. *Fred D. Miller: Photographer of the Crows.* Missoula: University of Montana/ Carnan Vid Film, 1985.

2284.   **Ourada, Patricia K.** "Indians in the Work Force." *Journal of the West* 25 (April 1986): 52–58.

2285.   **Peak, Ken,** and **Jack Spencer.** "Crime in Indian Country: Another 'Trail of Tears.'" *Journal of Criminal Justice* 15 (1987): 485–94.

2286.   **Rhodes, Terrel.** "The Urban American Indian." In *A Cultural Geography of North American Indians,* ed. T. E. Ross and T. G. Moore, 259–74. Boulder, Colo.: Westview Press, 1987.

2287.   **Robinson, Patricia.** "Language Retention Among Canadian Indians: A Simultaneous Equations Model with Dichotomous Endogenous Variables." *American Sociological Review* 50 (August 1985): 515–29.

2288.   **Sandefur, Gary D.** "American Indian Migration and Economic Opportunities." *International Migration Review* 20 (spring 1986): 55–68.

2289.   **Schroeder, Albert,** and **Omer Stewart.** "Indian Servitude in the Southwest." In *History of Indian-White Relations,* ed. W. Washburn, 410–13. Vol. 4 of *Handbook of North American Indians,* ed. W. Sturtevant. Washington, D.C.: Smithsonian Institution Press, 1988.

2290.   **Shkilnyl, Anastasia M.** *A Poison Stronger Than Love: The Destruction of an Ojibwe Community.* Foreword by Kai Erikson. New Haven, Conn.: Yale University Press, 1985.

2291.   **Theisz, R. D.** "Song Texts and Their Performers: The Centerpiece of Contemporary Lakota Identity Formulation." *Great Plains Quarterly* 7 (1987): 116–44.

2292. **Trafzer, Clifford E.,** ed. *American Indian Identity: Today's Changing Perspectives.* Publications in American Indian Studies, no. 1. San Diego: San Diego State University, 1985.

2293. **Waddell, Jack O.** "Malhiot's Journal: An Assessment of Chippewa Alcohol Behavior in the Early Nineteenth Century." *Ethnohistory* 32, no. 3 (1985): 246–68.

2294. **Williams, Walter L.** *The Spirit and the Flesh: Sexual Diversity in American Indian Culture.* Boston: Beacon Press, 1986.

2295. **Wood, Peter H.** "Indian Servitude in the Southeast." In *History of Indian-White Relations,* ed. W. Washburn, 407–9. Vol. 4 of *Handbook of North American Indians,* ed. W. Sturtevant. Washington, D.C.: Smithsonian Institution Press, 1988.

2296. **Young, R. A.,** and **Peter McDermott.** "Employment Training Programs and Acculturation of Native Peoples in Canada's Northwest Territories." *Arctic* 41 (1988): 195–202.

10.2   EDUCATION

2297. **Abbott, Devon I.** "'Commendable Progress': Acculturation at the Cherokee Female Seminary." *American Indian Quarterly* 11 (1987): 187–201.

2298. ———. "History of the Cherokee Female Seminary: 1851–1910." Ph.D. dissertation, Texas Christian University, 1989.

2299. **Adams, David W.** "Before Columbus: Toward an Ethnohistory of Indian Education." *History of Education Quarterly* 28 (spring 1988): 95–105.

2300. ———. "From Bullets to Boarding Schools: The Educational Assault on the American Indian Identity." In *The American Indian Experience: A Pro-*

file, 1524 to the Present, ed. P. Weeks, 218–39. Arlington Heights, Ill.: Forum Press, 1988.

2301. **Agnew, Brad.** "A Legacy of Education." *Chronicles of Oklahoma* 63 (1985): 128–47.

2302. **Barman, Jean, Yvonne Herbert,** and **Don McCaskill,** eds. *Indian Education in Canada.* Vol. 1, *The Legacy.* Vancouver: University of British Columbia Press, 1987.

2303. ———, eds. *Indian Education in Canada.* Vol. 2, *The Challenge.* Vancouver: University of British Columbia Press, 1987.

2304. **Bearinger, David.** "To Lead and to Serve: Presenting the Story of Indian Education at Hampton Institute." *History News* 45 (September/October 1990): 18–20.

2305. **Beck, Nicholas.** "The Vanishing Californians: The Education of Indians in the Nineteenth Century." *Southern California Quarterly* 69 (1987): 33–50.

2306. **Browne, Duana Bell.** "Learning Styles and Native Americans." *Canadian Journal of Native Education* 17, no. 1 (1990): 23–35.

2307. **Coleman, Michael C.** "Motivations of Indian Children at Missionary and U.S. Government Schools, 1860–1918: A Study Through Published Reminiscences." *Montana* 40 (winter 1990): 30–45.

2308. ———. "The Responses of American Indian Children to Presbyterian Schooling in the Nineteenth Century: An Analysis Through Missionary Sources." *History of Education Quarterly* 27 (winter 1987): 473–97.

2309. **Crum, Steven J.** "Bizzell and Brandt: Pioneers in Indian Studies,

1929–37." *Chronicles of Oklahoma* 66 (1988): 178–91.

2310. **Easton, Jerry.** "A Special Salute: Phoenix Indian School." *Arizona Highways* 65 (May 1989): 4–13.

2311. **Ellis, Howard.** "From the Battle in the Classroom to the Battle for the Classroom." *American Indian Quarterly* 11 (1987): 255–64.

2312. **Franco, Jere.** "Howard Billman and the Tucson Indian School, 1888–1894." *Social Science Journal* 26 (1989): 143–60.

2313. **Garmhauson, Winona.** *History of Indian Arts Education in Santa Fe: The Institute of American Indian Arts with Historical Background, 1890–1962.* Santa Fe, N.Mex.: Sunstone Press, 1988.

2314. **Gollnick, William A.** "Educational Development for the Oneida Reservation: The Oneida Tribal School and Beyond." In *The Oneida Indian Experience: Two Perspectives,* ed. J. Campisi and L. M. Hauptman, 177–82. Syracuse, N.Y.: Syrcause University Press, 1988.

2315. **Haig-Brown, Celia.** *Resistance and Renewal: Surviving the Indian Residential School.* Vancouver: Tillacum, 1988.

2316. **Hale, Duane K.** "The American Indian Institute, University of Oklahoma." *History News* 45 (May/June 1990): 8–16.

2317. **Hill, Norbert.** "Educating the Next Generation of Oneidas." In *The Oneida Indian Experience: Two Perspectives,* ed. J. Campisi and L. M. Hauptman, 153–56. Syracuse, N.Y.: Syracuse University Press, 1988.

2318. **Hyer, Sally.** *One House, One Voice, One Heart: Native American Education at the Santa Fe Indian School.* Santa Fe: Museum of New Mexico Press, 1990.

2319. **James, Thomas.** "Rhetoric and Resistance: Social Science and Community Schools for Navajos in the 1930s." *History of Education Quarterly* 28 (winter 1988): 599–626.

2320. **Johnston, Basil.** *Indian School Days.* Toronto: Key Porter Books, 1988; Norman: University of Oklahoma Press, 1989.

2321. **Kinchloe, Teresa Scott.** "South Louisiana Houma Indians' Struggle for Educational Parity." *Southern Studies* 26 (fall 1987): 295–303.

2322. **King, Wilma.** "Multicultural Education at Hampton Institute—The Shawnees: A Case Study, 1900–1923." *Journal of Negro Education* 57 (fall 1988): 524–35.

2323. **Knack, Martha C.** "Philene T. Hall, Bureau of Indian Affairs Field Matron: Planned Culture Change of Washaki Shoshone Women." *Prologue* 22 (summer 1990): 151–67.

2324. **Lomawaima, Kimberly Tsianina.** "Oral Histories from Chilocco Indian Agricultural School, 1920–1940." *American Indian Quarterly* 11 (1987): 241–54.

2325. ———. "'They Call It Prairie Light': Oral Histories from Chilocco Indian Agricultural Boarding School, 1920–1940." Ph.D. dissertation, Stanford University, 1989.

2326. **McCarthy, T. L.** "The Rough Rock Demonstration School: A Case History with Implications for Educational Evaluation." *Human Organization* 46 (1987): 103–14.

2327. **McClellan, E. Fletcher.** "Implementation and Policy Reformulation of the Title I of the Indian Self-Determination and Education Assistance Act of 1975–80." *Wicazo Sa Review* 4 (spring 1990): 45–55.

2328. Makofsky, Abraham. "Experience of Native Americans at a Black College: Indian Students at Hampton Institute, 1878–1923." *Journal of Ethnic Studies* 17, no. 3 (1989): 31–46.

2329. Molin, Paulette Fairbanks. "'Training the Hand, the Head, and the Heart': Indian Education at Hampton Institute." *Minnesota History* 51 (1988): 82–98.

2330. Monaghan, E. Jennifer. "She Loved to Read in Good Books: Literacy and the Indians of Martha's Vineyard, 1643–1725." *History of Education Quarterly* 30 (winter 1990): 493–521.

2331. Quick, Bob. "Santa Fe Indian School: A Native American Perspective." *Humanities* 11 (November/December 1990): 24–27.

2332. Reyhner, John, and Jeanne Eder. *A History of Indian Education.* Billings: Eastern Montana College, 1989.

2333. Roberts, Charles. "The Cushman Indian Trades School and World War I." *American Indian Quarterly* 11 (1987): 221–39.

2334. Robertson, Rosalie M. "Oneida Educational Planning: Assessing Community Needs Today." In *The Oneida Indian Experience: Two Perspectives,* ed. J. Campisi and L. M. Hauptman, 157–76. Syracuse, N.Y.: Syracuse University Press, 1988.

2335. Scott-Brown, Joan. "The Short Life of St. Dunsten's Calgary Indian Industrial School, 1896–1907." *Canadian Journal of Native Education* 14, no. 1 (1987): 41–49.

2336. Snively, Gloria. "Traditional Native Indian Beliefs, Cultural Values, and Science Instruction." *Canadian Journal of Native Education* 17, no. 1 (1990): 44–59.

2337. Stevenson, Winona. "Prairie Indians and Higher Education: An Historical Overview, 1976–1977." In *Hitting the Books: The Politics of Educational Retrenchment,* ed. Terry Witherspoon, 215–34. Toronto: Garamond Press, 1990.

2338. Szasz, Margaret Connell. *Indian Education in the American Colonies, 1607–1783.* Albuquerque: University of New Mexico Press, 1988.

2339. ———. "Listening to the Native Voice: American Indian Schooling in the Twentieth Century." *Montana* 39 (summer 1989): 42–53.

2340. Szasz, Margaret Connell, and Carmelita Ryan. "American Indian Education." In *History of Indian-White Relations,* ed. W. Washburn, 284–300. Vol. 4 of *Handbook of North American Indians,* ed. W. Sturtevant. Washington, D.C.: Smithsonian Institution Press, 1988.

2341. Trennert, Robert A., Jr. *The Phoenix Indian School: Forced Assimilation in Arizona, 1891–1935.* Norman: University of Oklahoma Press, 1988.

2342. ———. "Selling Indian Education at World's Fairs and Expositions, 1893–1904." *American Indian Quarterly* 11 (1987): 203–20.

2343. Utley, Robert M., ed. *Battlefield and Classroom: Four Decades with the American Indian, 1867–1904.* 1964. Reprint, Lincoln: University of Nebraska Press, 1987.

2344. Whitecap, Leah. "The Education of Children in Pre-European Plains America." *Canadian Journal of Native Education* 15, no. 2 (1988): 33–40.

2345. Wright, Bobby. "'For the Children of the Infidels'? American Indian Education in Colonial Colleges." *American Indian Culture and Research Journal* 14, no. 3 (1988): 1–14.

10.3   FAMILIES AND
FAMILY LIFE

2346.   Gilman, Carolyn, and **Mary Jane Schneider.** *The Way to Independence: Memories of a Hidatsa Indian Family, 1840–1920.* St. Paul: Minnesota Historical Society Press, 1987.

2347.   Moore, John, and **Gregory Campbell.** "An Ethnohistorical Perspective on Cheyenne Demography." *Journal of Family History* 14, no. 1 (1989): 17–42.

2348.   Petershoare, Lillian. "Tlingit Adoption Practices Past and Present." *American Indian Culture and Research Journal* 9, no. 2 (1985): 1–32.

2349.   Sandefur, Gary D., and **Arthur Sakamoto.** "American Indian Household Structure and Income." *Demography* 25, no. 1 (1988): 71–80.

2350.   Smith, Sherry L. "Beyond Princess and Squaw: Army Officers' Perceptions of Indian Women." In *The Women's West,* ed. S. Armitage and E. Jameson, 63–75. Norman: University of Oklahoma Press, 1987.

10.4   WOMEN AND
WOMEN'S EXPERIENCE

2351.   Armitage, Susan, and **Elizabeth Jameson,** eds. *The Women's West.* Norman: University of Oklahoma Press, 1987.

2352.   Babcock, Barbara A. "'A New Mexican Rebecca': Imagining Pueblo Women." *Journal of the Southwest* 32 (1990): 400–437.

2353.   Braund, Kathryn E. Holland. "Guardians of Tradition and Handmaidens to Change: Women's Roles in Creek Economic and Social Life During the Eighteenth Century." *American Indian Quarterly* 14 (1990): 239–50.

2354. "Contemporary Issues in Native American Health." *American Indian Culture and Research Journal* (special issues) 13, no. 3–4 (1989).

2355.   Crow Dog, Mary, and **Richard Erdoes.** *Lakota Woman.* New York: Grove Weidenfeld, 1990.

2356.   Dearborn, Mary V. *Pocahontas's Daughters: Gender and Ethnicity in American Culture.* New York: Oxford University Press, 1986. [Pocahontas as a symbol]

2357.   Fiske, Jo-Anne. "Fishing Is Women's Business: Changing Economic Roles of Carrier Women and Men." In *Native People, Native Lands: Canadian Indians, Inuit, and Métis,* ed. B. A. Cox, 186–98. Ottawa: Carleton University Press, 1988.

2358.   Harris, Betty L. "Ethnicity and Gender in the Global Periphery: A Comparison of Basotho and Navajo Women." *American Indian Culture and Research Journal* 14, no. 4 (1990): 15–38.

2359.   Kestler, Frances Roe. *The Indian Captivity Narrative: A Woman's View.* New York: Garland Press, 1990.

2360.   Kidwell, Clara Sue, ed. "Special Tenth Anniversary Issue on American Indian Women." *Creative Woman* 8, no. 3 (1987).

2361.   Knack, Martha. "Contemporary Southern Paiute Women and the Measurement of Women's Economic and Political Status." *Ethnology* 28 (1989): 233–48.

2362.   Koester, Susan. "'By the Words of Thy Mouth Let Thee Be Judged': The Alaska Native Sisterhood Speaks." *Journal of the West* 27 (April 1989): 35–44.

2363.   Medicine, Beatrice. "Indian Women and the Renaissance of Traditional Religion." In *Sioux Indian Reli-*

gion: Tradition and Innovation, ed. R. J. DeMallie and D. Parks, 159–71. Norman: University of Oklahoma Press, 1987.

2364. **Perrone, Bobette, H. Henriette Stockel, and Victoria Krueger.** *Medicine Women, Curanderas, and Women Doctors.* Norman: University of Oklahoma Press, 1989.

2365. **Powers, Marla N.** *Oglala Women: Myth, Ritual, and Reality.* Chicago: University of Chicago Press, 1986.

2366. **Schilz, Thomas F., and Jodye Lynn Dickson Schilz.** "Amazons, Witches, and 'Country Wives': Plains Indian Women in Historical Perspective." *Annals of Wyoming* 59 (1987): 48–56.

2367. **Young, M. Jane.** "Women, Reproduction, and Religion in Western Puebloan Society." *Journal of American Folklore* 100 (October/December 1987): 435–45.

10.5 DEMOGRAPHY (INCLUDING INTERMARRIAGE), HEALTH, AND MEDICINE

2368. **Abbott, Devon I.** "Medicine for the Rosebuds: Health Care at the Cherokee Female Seminary, 1876–1909." *American Indian Culture and Research Journal* 14, no. 1 (1988): 59–72.

2369. **Becker, Marshall J.** "The Moravian Mission in the Forks of the Delaware: Reconstructing the Migration and Settlement Patterns of the Jersey Lenape During the Eighteenth Century Through Documents in the Moravian Archives." *Unitas Fratrum* 21/22 (1987): 83–172.

2370. **Boyun, William.** "Health Care: An Overview of the Indian Health Care Service." *American Indian Law Review* 14 (1989): 241–68.

2371. **Brod, Rodney L., and Ronald LaDue.** "Political Mobilization and Conflict Among Western Urban and Reservation Indian Health Service Programs." *American Indian Culture and Research Journal* 13, no. 3/4 (1989): 171–214.

2372. **Brown, William R., Jr.** "Comancheria Demography, 1805–1830." *Panhandle-Plains Historical Review* 59 (1986): 8–14.

2373. **Campbell, Gregory R.** "The Changing Dimension of Native American Health: A Critical Understanding of Contemporary Native American Health Issues." *American Indian Culture and Research Journal* 13, no. 3/4 (1989): 1–20.

2374. ———. "The Political Epidemiology of Infant Mortality: A Health Crisis Among Montana American Indians." *American Indian Culture and Research Journal* 13, no. 3/4 (1989): 105–48.

2375. ———, ed. "Contemporary Issues in Native American Health." *American Indian Culture and Research Journal* (special issue) 13, no. 3/4 (1989).

2376. ———, ed. "Plains Indian Historical Demography and Health." *Plains Anthropologist* 34, no. 144, pt. 2 (1989).

2377. **Carter, Kent.** "Wantabees and Outalucks: Searching for Indian Ancestors in Federal Records." *Chronicles of Oklahoma* 66 (1988): 94–104.

2378. **Claymore, Betty J., and Marian A. Taylor.** "AIDS—Tribal Nations Face the Newest Communicable Disease: An Aberdeen Area Perspective." *American Indian Culture and Research Journal* 13, no. 3/4 (1989): 21–32.

2379. **Clow, Richmond L.** "Tribal Populations in Transition: Sioux Reservations and Federal Policy." *South Dakota History* 19 (1989): 362–91.

2380. Crosby, Alfred W. *Ecological Imperialism: The Biological Expansion of Europe, 900–1900.* Cambridge: Cambridge University Press, 1986.

2381. Decker, Jody F. "Tracing Historical Diffusion Patterns: The Case of the 1780–1792 Smallpox Epidemic Among the Indians of Western Canada." *Native Studies Review* 4, no. 1/2 (1988): 1–24.

2382. Deuschle, Kurt W. "Cross-Cultural Medicine: The Navajo Indians as Case Exemplar." *Daedelus* 115 (1986): 175–84.

2383. Dickson, Gerri. "Iskwew: Empowering Victims of Wife Abuse." *Native Studies Review* 5, no. 1 (1989): 115–36.

2384. Dobyns, Henry, Dean Snow, Kim Lanphear, and David Henige. "Commentary on Native American Demography." *Ethnohistory* 36, no. 3 (1989): 285–307.

2385. Dufour, Rose. "The Etiology of Otitis Media Among Inuit Children: An Anthropological Approach." *Native Studies Review* 5, no. 1 (1989): 71–78.

2386. Dyck, Lillian E. "Are North American Indians Biochemically More Susceptible to the Effects of Alcohol?" *Native Studies Review* 2, no. 2 (1986): 85–96.

2387. Farkas, Carol, Carole Howe, Ilze Kalnius, Reva Jewell, and Sheila Sovell. "Explanatory Models of Health During Pregnancy: Native Women and Non-native Health Care Providers in Toronto." *Native Studies Review* 5, no. 1 (1989): 79–96.

2388. Farkas, Carol, and Gord Johnston. "'Food—A Balance to Life': A Response to the Food and Nutrition Needs of Native Men in Toronto." *Native Studies Review* 5, no. 1 (1989): 137–44.

2389. Finley, Britt. "Social Network Differences in Alcohol Use and Related Behaviors Among Indian and Non-Indian Students, Grades 6–12." *American Indian Culture and Research Journal* 13, no. 3/4 (1989): 33–48.

2390. Forbes, Jack D. *Black Africans and Native Americans: Color, Race, and Caste in the Evolution of Red-Black Peoples.* New York: Blackwell, 1988.

2391. ———. "Undercounting Native Americans: The 1980 Census and the Manipulation of Racial Identity in the United States." *Storia Nordamericana* 5, no. 1 (1988): 5–49.

2392. ———. "Undercounting Native Americans: The 1980 Census and the Manipulation of Racial Identity in the United States." *Wicazo Sa Review* 4 (spring 1990): 2–26.

2393. Frost, Richard H. "The Pueblo Indian Smallpox Epidemic in New Mexico, 1898–1899." *Bulletin of the History of Medicine* 64 (fall 1990): 417–45.

2394. Gagnon, Yvon. "Physicians' Attitudes Toward Collaboration with Traditional Healers." *Native Studies Review* 5, no. 1 (1989): 175–87.

2395. Gonzales, Ellice B. "Tri-racial Isolets in a Bi-racial Society: Poospatuck Ambiguity and Conflict." In *Strategies for Survival: American Indians in the Eastern United States,* ed. F. W. Porter III, 113–37. Westport, Conn.: Greenwood Press, 1986.

2396. Gray, John S. "The Story of Mrs. Picotte-Galpin, a Sioux Heroine: Eagle Woman Learns About White Ways and Racial Conflict, 1820–1868." *Montana* 36 (spring 1986): 2–21.

2397.   Gregory, David. "Traditional Indian Healers in Northern Manitoba: An Emerging Relationship with the Health Care System." *Native Studies Review* 5, no. 1 (1989): 163–74.

2398.   Grondin, Jacques. "Social Support and Decision-Making: The Inuit in the Biomedical System." *Native Studies Review* 5, no. 1 (1989): 17–40.

2399.   Grumet, Robert S. "Strangely Decreased by the Hand of God: A Documentary Appearance-Disappearance Model for Munsee Demography, 1630–1801." *Journal of Middle Atlantic Archaeology* 5 (1989): 129–45.

2400.   Hann, John H. "Demographic Patterns and Changes in Mid-Seventeenth Century Timucua and Apalachee." *Florida Historical Quarterly* 64 (1986): 371–92.

2401.   Henige, David. "Primary Source by Primary Source? On the Role of Epidemics in New World Depopulation." *Ethnohistory* 33, no. 3 (1986): 293–314.

2402.   ———. "Their Numbers Become Thick: Native American Historical Demography as Expiation." In *The Invented Indian: Cultural Fictions and Government Policies,* ed. J. A. Clifton, 169–92. New Brunswick, N.J.: Transaction Publishers, 1990.

2403.   Hurtado, Albert L. "California Indian Demography, Sherburne F. Cook, and the Revision of American History." *Pacific Historical Review* 59 (1989): 323–43.

2404.   Jackson, Robert H. "Patterns of Demographic Change in the Missions of Central Alta California." *Journal of California and Great Basin Anthropology* 9, no. 2 (1987): 251–72.

2405.   Joe, Jennie, and Dorothy Lone Wolf Miller. "Barriers and Surviv-al: A Study of an Urban Indian Health Care Center." *American Indian Culture and Research Journal* 13, no. 3–4 (1989): 233–56.

2406.   Johnston, Susan. "Epidemics: The Forgotten Factor in Seventeenth Century Native Warfare in the St. Lawrence Region." In *Native People, Native Lands: Canadian Indians, Inuit, and Métis,* ed. B. A. Cox, 14–31. Ottawa: Carleton University Press, 1988.

2407.   Justice, James. "Twenty Years of Diabetes on the Warm Springs Indian Reservation, Oregon." *American Indian Culture and Research Journal* 13, no. 3/4 (1989): 49–82.

2408.   Kopp, Judy. "Crosscultural Contacts: Changes in the Diet and Nutrition of the Navajo Indians." *American Indian Culture and Research Journal* 10, no. 4 (1986): 1–30.

2409.   Larson, Clark Spencer, et al. "Beyond Demographic Collapse: Biological Adaptation and Change in Native Populations of La Florida." In *Columbian Consequences,* vol. 2, *Archaeological and Historical Perspectives on the Spanish Borderlands East,* ed. D. H. Thomas, 409–28. Washington, D.C.: Smithsonian Institution Press, 1990.

2410.   McIntire, Elliot. "Early Twentieth Century Hopi Population." In *A Cultural Geography of North American Indians,* ed. T. E. Ross and T. G. Moore, 275–98. Boulder, Colo.: Westview Press, 1987.

2411.   McNabb, Steven. "Native Health Status and Native Health Policy: Current Dilemmas at the Federal Level." *Arctic Anthropology* 27 (1990): 20–35.

2412.   Meister, Gary W. "Methods of Evaluating the Accuracy of Census Reports as Ethnohistorical Demographic

Data: A Brief Assessment of Pima and Maricopa Populations." In *Ethnohistory: A Researcher's Guide,* ed. D. Wiedman, 77–106. Williamsburg, Va.: College of William and Mary, 1986.

2413.   Numbers, Ronald L., ed. *Medicine in the New World: New Spain, New France, and New England.* Knoxville: University of Tennessee Press, 1987.

2414.   O'Neil, John D., and **James B. Waldram.** "Native Health Research in Canada: Anthropological and Related Approaches." *Native Studies Review* 5, no. 1 (1989): 1–16.

2415.   Pearcy, Thomas L. "The Control of Smallpox in New Spain's Northern Borderlands." *Journal of the West* 29 (July 1990): 90–98.

2416.   Perdue, Theda. "Cherokee Women and the Trail of Tears." *Journal of Women's History* 1, no. 1 (1989): 14–30.

2417. ———. "Southern Indians and the Cult of True Womanhood." In *The Web of Southern Social Relations,* ed. W. J. Fraser, R. F. Saunders, Jr., and J. L. Wakelyn. Athens: University of Georgia Press, 1985.

2418.   Peyser, Joseph L. "It Was Not Smallpox: The Miami Deaths of 1732 Reexamined." *Indiana Magazine of History* 81 (1985): 159–69.

2419. ———. "Smallpox or 'Subtle Poison'? The Miami Debacle Reexamined." In *Proceedings of the Tenth Meeting of the French Colonial Historical Society,* ed. P. P. Boucher, 165–78. Lanham, Md.: University Press of America, 1985.

2420.   Ramenofsky, Ann F. "The Introduction of European Disease and Aboriginal Population Collapse." *Mississippi Archaeologist* 20 (1985): 2–18.

2421. ———. *Vectors of Death: The Archaeology of European Contact.* Albuquerque: University of New Mexico Press, 1988.

2422.   Reff, Daniel T. *Depopulation and Culture Change in Northwestern New Spain, 1518 to 1764.* Salt Lake City: University of Utah Press, 1990.

2423. ———. "Disease Episodes and the Historical Record: A Reply to Dobyns." *American Anthropologist* 91 (1989): 174–75.

2424. ———. "The Introduction of Smallpox in the Greater Southwest." *American Anthropologist* 89 (1987): 704–8.

2425. ———. "Old World Diseases and the Dynamics of Indian and Jesuit Relations in Northwestern New Spain, 1520–1660." In *Ejidos and Regions of Refuge in Northwestern Mexico,* ed. N. R. Crumrine and P. C. Weigand, 4–6, 85–94. Anthropological Research Papers of the University of Arizona, no. 46. Tucson: University of Arizona, 1987.

2426.   Ross, Thomas E. "The Lumbees: Population Growth of a Nonreservation Indian Tribe." In *A Cultural Geography of North American Indians,* ed. T. E. Ross and T. G. Moore, 297–312. Boulder, Colo.: Westview Press, 1987.

2427.   Sempowski, Martha L. "Differential Mortuary Treatment of Seneca Women: Some Social Influences." *Archaeology of Eastern North America* 14 (1986): 35–44.

2428.   Sherley-Spiers, Sandra K. "Dakota Perceptions of Clinical Encounters with Western Health-Care Providers." *Native Studies Review* 5, no. 1 (1989): 41–52.

2429.   Smith, Marvin. *Archaeology of Aboriginal Culture Change in the Interior Southeast: Depopulation During the Early*

Historic Period. Ripley P. Bullen Monographs in Anthropology and History. Gainesville: University Press of Florida, 1987.

2430.   **Snow, Dean R., and Kim M. Lanphear.** "European Contact and Indian Depopulation in the Northeast: The Timing of the First Epidemics." *Ethnohistory* 35, no. 1 (1988): 15–33.

2431.   **Snow, Dean R., and William A. Starna.** "Sixteenth-Century Depopulation: A View from the Mohawk Valley." *American Anthropologist* 91 (1989): 142–49.

2432.   **Speck, Dara Culhane.** "The Indian Health Transfer Policy: A Step in the Right Direction or Revenge of the Hidden Agenda?" *Native Studies Review* 5, no. 1 (1989): 187–214.

2433.   **Spiess, A. E., and B. D. Spiess.** "New England Pandemic of 1616–1622: Cause and Archaeological Implication." *Man in the Northeast* 34 (1987): 71–83.

2434.   **Stannard, David E.** "Disease and Infertility: A New Look at the Demographic Collapse of Native Populations in the Wake of Western Contact." *Journal of American Studies* 24 (1990): 325–50. [Focus on Hawaii]

2435.   **Taylor, Timothy L.** "Determinants of Primary Medical Care Use Among Urban American Indians." *American Indian Culture and Research Journal* 13, no. 3/4 (1989): 215–23.

2436.   **Thornton, Russell.** *American Indian Holocaust and Survival: A Population History Since 1492.* Norman: University of Oklahoma Press, 1987.

2437.   ———. *The Cherokees: A Population History.* Lincoln: University of Nebraska Press, 1990.

2438.   ———. "Nineteenth Century Cherokee History." *American Sociological Review* 50 (February 1985): 121–27.

2439.   ———. *We Shall Live Again: The 1870 and 1890 Ghost Dance Movements as Demographic Revitalization.* Cambridge: Cambridge University Press, 1986.

2440.   **Trennert, Robert A.** "Indian Sore Eyes: The Federal Campaign to Control Trachoma in the Southwest, 1910–1940." *Journal of the Southwest* 32 (1990): 121–49.

2441.   **Trimble, Michael K.** *An Ethnohistorical Interpretation of the Spread of Smallpox in the Northern Plains Utilizing Concepts of Disease Ecology.* 1979. University of Nebraska Reprints in Anthropology, no. 33. Lincoln: University of Nebraska Press, 1986.

2442.   **Ubelaker, Douglas.** "North American Indian Population Size, A.D. 1500 to 1985." *American Journal of Physical Anthropology* 77 (1988): 289–94.

2443.   **Upham, Steadman.** "Smallpox and Climate in the American Southwest." *American Anthropologist* 88 (1986): 115–28.

2444.   **Venables, Robert W.** "The Cost of Columbus: Was There a Holocaust?" *Northeast Indian Quarterly* 7 (1990): 29–36.

2445.   **Waldram, James B.** "Native People and Health Care in Saskatoon." *Native Studies Review* 5, no. 1 (1989): 97–114.

2446.   **Waldram, James B., and John D. O'Neil, eds.** "Native Health Research in Canada." *Native Studies Review* (special issue) 5, no. 1 (1990).

2447.   **Wiedman, Dennis.** "Adiposity or Longevity: Which Factor Accounts for the Increase of Type II Diabetes Mellitus when Populations Acculturate to an Industrial Technology." *Medical Anthropology* 11, no. 3 (1989): 237–53.

2448. ———. "Big and Little Moon Peyotism as Health Care Delivery Systems." *Medical Anthropology* 12, no. 4 (1990): 371–87.

2449. ———. "Oklahoma Cherokee Technological Development and Diabetes Mellitus." In *Encounters with Biomedicine: Case Studies in Medical Anthropology,* ed. H. Baer, 43–71. New York: Gordon and Breach Scientific Publishing, 1987.

2450. Wood, Peter H. "The Changing Population of the Colonial South: An Overview by Race and Region, 1685–1790." In *Powhatan's Mantle: Indians in the Colonial Southeast,* ed. P. H. Wood, G. A. Waselkov, and M. T. Hatley, 35–103. Lincoln: University of Nebraska Press, 1989.

2451. ———. "The Impact of Smallpox on the Native Population of the Eighteenth Century South." *New York State Journal of Medicine* 87 (1987): 30–36.

2452. Young, T. K., and R. I. Casson. "The Decline and Persistence of Tuberculosis in a Canadian Indian Population: Implication for Control." *Canadian Journal of Public Health* 79 (1988): 302–8.

10.6   IMAGES AND STEREOTYPES OF AMERICAN INDIANS

2453. Albers, Patricia, and William James. "Illusion and Illumination: Visual Images of American Indian Women in the West." In *The Women's West,* ed. S. Armitage and E. Jameson, 35–50. Norman: University of Oklahoma Press, 1987.

2454. ———. "Images and Reality: Post Cards of Minnesota's Ojibway People, 1900–1980." *Minnesota History* 49 (1985): 229–40.

2455. Aleiss, Angela. "Hollywood Addresses Postwar Assimilation: Indian/White Attitudes in *Broken Arrow.*" *American Indian Culture and Research Journal* 11, no. 1 (1987): 67–79.

2456. Anderson, Karen. "As Gentle as Little Lambs: Images of Huron and Montagnais-Naskapi Women in the Writings of the Seventeenth Century Jesuits." *Canadian Review of Sociology and Anthropology* 25 (1988): 560–76.

2457. Berkhofer, Robert F., Jr. "White Conceptions of Indians." In *History of Indian-White Relations,* ed. W. Washburn, 522–47. Vol. 4 of *Handbook of North American Indians,* ed. W. Sturtevant. Washington, D.C.: Smithsonian Institution Press, 1988.

2458. Blackman, Margaret B. "Studio Indians: Cartes de Visite of Native People in British Columbia, 1862–1872." *Archivaria* 21 (1985/86): 68–86.

2459. Blair, John G. "Buffalo Bill and Sitting Bull: The Wild West as a Media Event." In *The American West as Seen by Europeans and Americans,* ed. R. Kroes, 262–81. Amsterdam: Free University Press, 1989.

2460. Borsanyi, Laszlo. "The Emerging Dual Image of Native North Americans During the Nineteenth Century in Hungary." In *Indians and Europe: An Interdisciplinary Collection of Essays,* ed. C. Feest, 287–96. Aachen, West Germany: Edition Herodot, 1987.

2461. Brand, Stewart. "Indians and the Counterculture, 1960s–1970s." In *History of Indian-White Relations,* ed. W. Washburn, 570–72. Vol. 4 of *Handbook of North American Indians,* ed. W. Sturtevant. Washington, D.C.: Smithsonian Institution Press, 1988.

2462.   Clerici, Naila. "Native Americans in Columbus's Home Land." In *Indians and Europe: An Interdisciplinary Collection of Essays,* ed. C. Feest, 415–26. Aachen, West Germany: Edition Herodot, 1987.

2463.   Colin, Susi. "The Wild Man and the Indian in Early Sixteenth Century Book Illustration." In *Indians and Europe: An Interdisciplinary Collection of Essays,* ed. C. Feest, 5–36. Aachen, West Germany: Editio Herodot, 1987.

2464.   Conrad, Rudolf. "Mutual Fascination: Indians in Dresden and Leipzig." In *Indians and Europe: An Interdisciplinary Collection of Essays,* ed. C. Feest, 455–73. Aachen, West Germany: Edition Herodot, 1987.

2465.   Diedrich, Maria. "The Characterization of Native Americans in the Antebellum Slave Narrative." *CLA Journal* 31 (1988): 414–35.

2466.   Dippie, Brian W. *Catlin and His Contemporaries: The Politics of Patronage.* Lincoln: University of Nebraska Press, 1990.

2467.   Duffek, Karen. "It's Native: Where Do You Put It? A Northwest Coast Perspective." *Native Studies Review* 3, no. 2 (1987): 61–70.

2468.   Ewers, John C. "Charlie Russell's Indians." *Montana* 37 (summer 1987): 36–53.

2469.   Feest, Christian. "The Indian In Non-English Literature." In *History of Indian-White Relations,* ed. W. Washburn, 582–86. Vol. 4 of *Handbook of North American Indians,* ed. W. Sturtevant. Washington, D.C.: Smithsonian Institution Press, 1988.

2470.   ———. "Pride and Prejudice: The Pocahontas Myth and the Pamunkey." In *The Invented Indian: Cultural Fictions and Government Policies,* ed. J. A.

Clifton, 49–70. New Brunswick, N.J.: Transaction Publishers, 1990.

2471.   Fiedler, Leslie. "The Indian in Literature in English." In *History of Indian-White Relations,* ed. W. Washburn, 573–81. Vol. 4 of *Handbook of North American Indians,* ed. W. Sturtevant. Washington, D.C.: Smithsonian Institution Press, 1988.

2472.   Fiorentino, Daniele. "'Those Red-Brick Faces': European Press Reactions to the Indians of Buffalo Bill's Wild West Show." In *Indians and Europe: An Interdisciplinary Collection of Essays,* ed. C. Feest, 403–14. Aachen, West Germany: Edition Herodot, 1987.

2473.   Green, Rayna. "The Indian in Popular American Culture." In *History of Indian-White Relations,* ed. W. Washburn, 587–606. Vol. 4 of *Handbook of North American Indians,* ed. W. Sturtevant. Washington, D.C.: Smithsonian Institution Press, 1988.

2474.   Hagan, William T. "Full Blood, Mixed Blood, Generic, and Ersatz: The Problem of Indian Identity." *Arizona and the West* 27 (1985): 309–26.

2475.   Hanson, Jeffrey R., and Linda P. Rouse. "Dimensions of Native American Stereotyping." *American Indian Culture and Research Journal* 11, no. 4 (1987): 33–58.

2476.   Harrison, Julia. "The Great White Coverup." *Native Studies Review* 3, no. 2 (1987): 47–60.

2477.   Hirschfelder, Arlene B. "Unlearning Indian Stereotypes." *Halcyon* 12 (1990): 49–62.

2478.   "Images of Great Lakes Indians by Paul Kane, 1845 to 1848." *Native Studies Review* 6, no. 1 (1990): 111–18.

2479.   "Images of the Treaty Process,

1871–1950." *Native Studies Review* 6, no. 2 (1990): 89–114.

2480. Jojola, Ted. "American Indian Stereotypes." *Northeast Indian Quarterly* 7 (1990): 26–28.

2481. Jones, Eugene H. *Native Americans as Shown on the Stage, 1753–1916.* Metuchen, N.J.: Scarecrow Press, 1988.

2482. Letay, Miklos. "'Redskins at the Zoo': Sioux Indians in Budapest." In *Indians and Europe: An Interdisciplinary Collection of Essays,* ed. C. Feest, 375–81. Aachen, West Germany: Edition Herodot, 1987.

2483. Lewis, James R. "Assessing the Impact of Indian Captivity on the Euro-American Mind: Some Critical Issues." *Connecticut Review* 11 (summer 1989): 14–26.

2484. Marsden, Michael, and Jack Nachbar. "The Indian in the Movies." In *History of Indian-White Relations,* ed. W. Washburn, 607–16. Vol. 4 of *Handbook of North American Indians,* ed. W. Sturtevant. Washington, D.C.: Smithsonian Institution Press, 1988.

2485. Mason, Peter. "Seduction from Afar: Europe's Inner Indians." *Anthropos* 82 (1987): 581–601.

2486. Matijasic, Thomas D. "Reflected Values: Sixteenth-Century Europeans View the Indians of North America." *American Indian Culture and Research Journal* 11, no. 2 (1987): 31–50.

2487. Napier, Rita G. "Across the Big Water: American Indians' Perceptions of Europe and Europeans, 1887–1906." In *Indians and Europe: An Interdisciplinary Collection of Essays,* ed. C. Feest, 383–401. Aachen, West Germany: Edition Herodot, 1987.

2488. Pakes, Fraser J. "'But Is It In-dian?' — Indian and Non-Indian Interpretation of Plains Indian Art." *Native Studies Review* 3, no. 2 (1987): 27–46.

2489. Porter, Joseph C. *Paper Medicine Man: John Gregory Bourke and His American West.* Norman: University of Oklahoma Press, 1986.

2490. Powers, William. "The Indian Hobbyist Hovement in North America." In *History of Indian-White Relations,* ed. W. Washburn, 557–61. Vol. 4 of *Handbook of North American Indians,* ed. W. Sturtevant. Washington, D.C.: Smithsonian Institution Press, 1988.

2491. Regular, Keith. "On Public Display." *Alberta History* 34, no. 1 (1986): 1–10.

2492. Riegler, Johanna. "'Tame Europe' and the 'Mysteries of Wild America'": Viennese Press Coverage of American Indian Shows, 1886–1898." *European Reviews of Native American Studies* 1 (1988): 17–20.

2493. Simard, Jean-Jacques. "White Ghosts, Red Shadows: The Reduction of North-American Natives." In *The Invented Indian: Cultural Fictions and Government Policies,* ed. J. A. Clifton, 333–70. New Brunswick, N.J.: Transaction Publishers, 1990.

2494. Sullivan, Sherry. "Indians in American Fiction: 1820–1850: An Ethnohistorical Perspective." *CLIO* 15 (1986): 239–57.

2495. Taylor, Colin. "The Indian Hobbyist Movement in Europe." In *History of Indian-White Relations,* ed. W. Washburn, 562–69. Vol. 4 of *Handbook of North American Indians,* ed. W. Sturtevant. Washington, D.C.: Smithsonian Institution Press, 1988.

2496. Trennert, Robert A., Jr. "Fairs, Expositions, and the Changing Image of Southwestern Indians, 1876–

1904." *New Mexico Historical Review* 62 (1987): 147–50.

2497.   **Trenton, Patricia.** *Native Americans: Five Centuries of Changing Images.* New York: H. N. Abrams, 1989.

2498.   **Vaughan, Alden T.** "Shakespeare's Indian: The Americanization of Caliban." *Shakespeare Quarterly* 39 (1988): 137–53.

2499.   **Williams, Daniel E.** "Until They Are Contaminated by Their More Refined Neighbors: The Images of the Native Americans in Carver's Travels Through the Interior and Its Influence on the Euro-American Imagination." In *Indians and Europe: An Interdisciplinary Collection of Essays,* ed. C. Feest, 195–214. Aachen, West Germany: Edition Herodot, 1987.

XI

Environments: Physical and Spiritual

11.1 AGRICULTURE

2500. **Barsh, Russell L.** "Plains Indian Agrarianism and Class Conflict." *Great Plains Quarterly* 7 (1987): 83–90.

2501. **Carter, Sarah.** *Lost Harvests: Prairie Indian Reserve Farmers and Government Policy.* Montreal: McGill-Queens University Press, 1990.

2502. **Coutts, Robert.** "The Role of Agriculture in an English Speaking Halfbreed Economy: The Case of St. Andrews, Red River." *Native Studies Review* 4, no. 1/2 (1988): 67–94.

2503. **Fredericks, John, III.** "Indian Lands: Financing Indian Agriculture: Mortgaged Indian Lands and the Federal Trust Responsibility." *American Indian Law Review* 14 (1989): 105–34.

2504. **Holzkamm, Tim E.** "Ojibwa Horticulture in the Upper Mississippi and Boundary Waters." In *Acts of the Seventeenth Algonquian Conference,* ed. W. Cowan, 143–54. Ottawa: Carleton University Press, 1986.

2505. **Hurt, R. Douglas.** *Indian Agriculture in America, Prehistory to the Present.* Lawrence: University of Kansas Press, 1987.

2506. **McGuire, Thomas R.** "Illusions of Choice in the Indian Irrigation Service: The Akchin Project and an Epilogue." *Journal of the Southwest* 30 (1988): 200–221.

2507. **Nabhan, Gary Paul.** *Enduring Seeds: Native American Agriculture and Wild Plant Conservation.* San Francisco: North Point Press, 1989.

2508. ————. "Invisible Erosion: The Rise and Fall of Native Farming." *Journal of the Southwest* 30 (1988): 552–72.

2509. **Nespor, Robert P.** "From War Lance to Plow Share: The Cheyenne Dog Soldiers as Farmers, 1879–1930s." *Chronicles of Oklahoma* 65 (1987): 42–75.

2510. **Wilson, John P.** "The Southern Apaches as Farmers, 1630–1870." In *Reflections: Papers on Southwestern Culture History in Honor of Charles H. Large,* ed. A. V. Poore, 79–90. Santa Fe, N.Mex.: Ancient City Press, 1988.

11.2 VISUAL ARTS

2511. **Anderson, Marcia,** and **Kathy Hussy-Arnton.** "Ojibwe Bandolier Bags in the Collection of the Minnesota Historical Society." *American Indian Art Magazine* 11 (1986): 36–45.

2512. **Anderson, William L.** "Cherokee Clay from Duche to Wedgwood: The Journal of Thomas Griffiths." *North*

Carolina Historical Review 63 (1986): 477–510.

2513. "A. V. Thomas Photographs Concerning the 1910 Treaty Five Adhesions." *Native Studies Review* 3, no. 1 (1987): 95–116.

2514. Babcock, Barbara A. "At Home, No Women Are Storytellers: Potteries, Stories, and Politics in Cochiti Pueblo." *Journal of the Southwest* 30 (1988): 356–89.

2515. Bataille, Gretchen. "Ethnography, Film, and American Indian Arts." *North Dakota History* 53 (spring 1985): 142–49.

2516. Batkin, Jonathan. "Master Potters of San Ildefonso and Cochiti Pueblos." *American Indian Art Magazine* 12 (autumn 1987); 28–37.

2517. Bernstein, Bruce. "Weaver's Talk: The Language of Baskets and the Meaning of Aesthetic Judgments: The Patwin of Central California." In *The Art of Native American Basketry: A Living Legacy,* ed. F. W. Porter III, 213–26. New York: Greenwood Press, 1990.

2518. Blackard, David M. "Patchwork and Palmettos: Seminole/Miccosukee Folk Art Since 1820." *American Indian Art Magazine* 15 (spring 1990): 66–84.

2519. Blackman, Margaret B. "Visual Ethnohistory: Photographs in the Study of Culture History." In *Ethnohistory: A Researcher's Guide,* ed. D. Wiedman, 137–66. Williamsburg, Va.: College of William and Mary, 1986.

2520. Blomberg, Nancy J. *Navajo Textiles: The William Randolph Hearst Collection.* Tucson: University of Arizona Press, 1988.

2521. Bol, Marsha Clift. "Lakota Women's Artistic Strategies in Support of the Social System." *American Indian Culture and Research Journal* 9, no. 1 (1985): 33–51. [Costume change]

2522. Brasser, Ted J. "In Search of Métis Art." In *The New Peoples: Being and Becoming Métis in North America,* ed. J. Peterson and J. S. H. Brown, 221–29. Lincoln: University of Nebraska Press, 1985.

2523. Coe, Ralph T. *Lost and Found Traditions: Native American Art, 1965–1985.* Seattle: University of Washington Press, 1986.

2524. Cohodas, Marvin. "Washoe Basketweaving: A Historical Outline." In *The Art of Native American Basketry: A Living Legacy,* ed. F. W. Porter III, 153–86. New York: Greenwood Press, 1990.

2525. Conn, Richard. *A Persistent Vision: Art of the Reservation Days.* Denver: Denver Art Museum and University of Washington Press, 1986.

2526. Dauber, Kenneth. "Pueblo Pottery and the Politics of Regional Identity." *Journal of the Southwest* 32 (1990): 576–96.

2527. Davis, Barbara A. *Edward S. Curtis: The Life and Times of a Shadow Catcher.* Foreword by Bill Holm. San Francisco: Chronicle, 1985.

2528. Denton, Joan Frederick. "Kiowa Murals: 'Behold I Stand in Good Relation to All Things.'" *Southwest Art* 14 (July 1987): 68–75.

2529. Duncan, Kate C. *Northern Athapaskan Art: A Beadwork Tradition.* Seattle: University of Washington Press, 1989.

2530. Eisenhart, Linda L. "Hupa, Karok, and Yurok Basketry." In *The Art of Native American Basketry: A Living Legacy,* ed. F. W. Porter III, 241–66. New York: Greenwood Press, 1990.

2531. **Ewers, John C.** *Hair Pipes in Plains Indian Adornment.* Ohswehen, Ont.: Irocrafts, 1986.

2532. ———. *Plains Indian Sculpture: A Traditional Art from America's Heartland.* Washington, D.C.: Smithsonian Institution Press, 1986.

2533. **Gordon, Beverly.** "Souvenirs of Niagara Falls: The Significance of Indian Whimsies." *New York History* 67 (1986): 389–409.

2534. **Gordon, Joleen.** "Micmac Indian Basketry." In *The Art of Native American Basketry: A Living Legacy,* ed. F. W. Porter III, 17–44. New York: Greenwood Press, 1990.

2535. **Grumet, Robert S.** *Out of the Mists: Northwest Coast Indian Art and Culture.* New York: IBM Gallery of the Arts and Sciences and the Museum of the American Indian, Heye Foundation, 1985.

2536. **Heilbron, Bertha L.,** ed. *With Pen and Pencil on the Frontier in 1851: The Diary and Sketches of Frank Blackwell Mayer.* Foreword by Thomas O'Sullivan. St. Paul: Minnesota Historical Society, 1986.

2537. **Hill, Rick.** "Seneca Art in Transition." *Turtle Quarterly* 1, no. 1 (1986): 4–6.

2538. **Houston, Alma.** *Anthology of Inuit Art.* Winnipeg: Watson and Dwyer, 1988.

2539. **Hudson, Raymond L.** "The Influence of Attu Weavers on Aleut Basketry." In *The Art of Native American Basketry: A Living Legacy,* ed. F. W. Porter III, 335–44. New York: Greenwood Press, 1990.

2540. **Hultgren, Mary Lou.** "American Indian Collection of the Hampton University Museum." *American Indian Art Magazine* 13 (winter 1987): 32–39.

2541. **Idiens, Dale.** "Northwest Coast Artifacts in the Perth Museum and Art Gallery: The Colin Robertson Collection." *American Indian Art Magazine* 13 (winter 1987): 46–53.

2542. **Ivory, Carol S.** "Northwest Coast Uses of Polynesian Art." *American Indian Culture and Research Journal* 9, no. 4 (1985): 49–66.

2543. **Jasper, Cynthia R.** "Change in Ojibwa (Chippewa) Dress, 1820–1980." *American Indian Culture and Research Journal* 12, no. 4 (1988): 17–38.

2544. **Jensen, Doreen,** and **Polly Sargent.** *Robes of Power: Totem Poles on Cloth.* Vancouver: University of British Columbia Press, 1987.

2545. **Johnston, Thomas F.** "Community History and Environment as Wellspring of Inupiaq Eskimo Songtexts." *Anthropos* 83 (1988): 161–71.

2546. **Jonaitis, Aldona.** *Art of the Northern Tlingit.* Seattle: University of Washington Press, 1986.

2547. ———. *From the Land of the Totem Poles: The Northwest Coast Indian Art Collection at the American Museum of Natural History.* New York: American Museum of Natural History Press, 1988.

2548. **Kelso, Carl, Sr.** "The Frontiers of Edward Curtis." *Missouri Historical Review* 83 (July 1989): 429–97.

2549. **Kenagy, Suzanne G.** "Eight Indians: Contemporary Indian Art at the Southwest Museum." *American Indian Art Magazine* 13 (winter 1987): 54–64.

2550. **Kent, Kate Peck.** *Navajo Weaving: Three Centuries of Change.* Seattle: University of Washington Press, 1985.

2551. King, J. C. H. "Tradition in Native American Art." In *The Arts of the North American Indian*, ed. E. L. Wade, 65–92. New York: Hudson Hills, 1986.

2552. Kramer, Barbara. "Nampeyo, Hopi House, and the Chicago Land Show." *American Indian Art Magazine* 14 (winter 1988): 46–53.

2553. Laforet, Andrea. "Regional and Personal Style in Northwest Coast Basketry." In *The Art of Native American Basketry: A Living Legacy*, ed. F. W. Porter III, 281–98. New York: Greenwood Press, 1990.

2554. Lee, Molly. "Objects of Knowledge: The Communicative Aspect of Baleen Baskets." In *The Art of Native American Basketry: A Living Legacy*, ed. F. W. Porter III, 319–34. New York: Greenwood Press, 1990.

2555. Loeb, Barbara. "Crow Beadwork: The Resilience of Cultural Values." *Montana* 40 (autumn 1990): 48–59.

2556. Mack, Jeanne M. "Changes in Cahuilla Coiled Basketry." In *The Art of Native American Basketry: A Living Legacy*, ed. F. W. Porter III, 227–40. New York: Greenwood Press, 1990.

2557. McMullen, Ann. "Many Motives: Change in Northeastern Native Basket Making." In *The Art of Native American Basketry: A Living Legacy*, ed. F. W. Porter III, 45–78. New York: Greenwood Press, 1990.

2558. Marr, Carolyn J. "Continuity and Change in the Basketry of Western Washington." In *The Art of Native American Basketry: A Living Legacy*, ed. F. W. Porter III, 267–80. New York: Greenwood Press, 1990.

2559. ———. "Taken Pictures: On Interpreting Native American Photographs of the Southern Northwest Coast." *Pacific Northwest Quarterly* 80 (1989): 52–61.

2560. Miller, G. Lynette. "Basketry of the Northwestern Plateaus." In *The Art of Native American Basketry: A Living Legacy*, ed. F. W. Porter III, 135–52. New York: Greenwood Press, 1990.

2561. "Native Art History in Canada." *Journal of Canadian Studies* 21, no. 4 (1987): 3–94.

2562. "Navajo Pottery." *Plateau* (special issue) 58, no. 2 (1987).

2563. Neuerburg, Norman. "The Alta California Indians as Artists Before and After Contact." In *Columbian Consequences*, vol. 1, *Archaeological and Historical Perspectives on the Spanish Borderlands West*, ed. D. H. Thomas, 467–80. Washington, D.C.: Smithsonian Institution Press, 1989.

2564. Payne, Richard W. "Medicine and Music: Whistles of Eastern Oklahoma Indians." *Chronicles of Oklahoma* 68 (1990): 424–33.

2565. Penny, David W. "The Origins of an Indigenous Ontario Arts Tradition: Ontario Art from the Laker Archaic Through the Woodland Periods, 1500 B.C.–A.D. 600." *Journal of Canadian Studies* 21, no. 4 (1987): 37–54.

2566. Phillips, Ruth B. "Jasper Grant and Edward Walsh: The Gentleman-Soldier as Early Collector of Great Lakes Indian Art." *Journal of Canadian Studies* 21, no. 4 (1987): 56–71.

2567. ———. "Souvenirs from North America: The Miniature as Image of Woodland Indian Life." *American Indian Art Magazine* 14 (spring 1989): 52–63.

2568. Porter, Frank W., III. "American Indian Baskets in the Middle Atlantic Region: Material Survival and

Changing Function." *Material Culture* 17 (1985): 25–45.

2569. ———. "Basketry of the Middle Atlantic and Southeast." In *The Art of Native American Basketry: A Living Legacy,* ed. F. W. Porter III, 79–105. New York: Greenwood Press, 1990.

2570. ———, ed. *The Art of Native American Basketry: A Living Legacy.* New York: Greenwood Press, 1990.

2571. **Powell, Peter J.** *To Honor the Crow People: Crow Indian Art from the Gallatin Collection of American Indian Art.* Lincoln: University of Nebraska Press, 1988.

2572. **Roscoe, Will.** "We'Wha and Klah: The American Indian Berdache as Artist and Priest." *American Indian Quarterly* 12 (1988): 127–50.

2573. **Running, John.** *Honor Dance: Native American Photographs.* Reno: University of Nevada Press, 1985.

2574. **Samuel, Cheryl.** *Raven's Tail: Northern Geometric Style Weaving.* Vancouver: University of British Columbia Press, 1987.

2575. **Sands, Kathleen M., and Allison Sekaquaptewa Lewis.** "Seeing with a Native Eye: A Hopi Film on Hopi." *American Indian Quarterly* 14 (1990): 387–96.

2576. **Schneider, Mary Jane.** "Plains Indians Basketry: Techniques and Uses." In *The Art of Native American Basketry: A Living Legacy,* ed. F. W. Porter III, 107–34. New York: Greenwood Press, 1990.

2577. **Schuster, Helen H.** "Tribal Interpretations of Wyoming Rock Art: Some Problematic Considerations." *Archaeology in Montana* 28, no. 2 (1987): 25–43.

2578. **Schwarz, Gregory.** *Patterns of Life, Patterns of Art: The Rahr Collection of Native American Art.* Hanover, N.H.: University Press of New England for the Hood Museum, Dartmouth College, 1987.

2579. **Silberman, Arthur.** "Watonga's Day in the Sun, or Trickster Comes to Town." *Chronicles of Oklahoma* 66 (1989): 374–91.

2580. **Szabo, Joyce M.** "Captive Artists and Changing Messages: The Paloheimo Drawing Books at the Southwest Museum." *Masterkey* 62, no. 1 (1988): 14–21. [Howling Wolf and Zoton drawings from Fort Marion]

2581. **Tanner, Clara Lee.** "Southwestern Indian Basketry." In *The Art of Native American Basketry: A Living Legacy,* ed. F. W. Porter III, 187–214. New York: Greenwood Press, 1990.

2582. **Tooker, Elisabeth.** "Fabrics of the Iroquois: The Lewis H. Morgan Collection for the New York State Museum." *Expedition* 28 (1986): 29–34.

2583. **Torrence, Gaylord.** "A Mesquakie Drawing." *Palimpsest* 69 (1988): 64–68.

2584. **Torrence, Gaylord, and Robert Hobbs.** *Art of the Red Earth People: The Mesquakie of Iowa.* Seattle: University of Washington Press, 1989.

2585. **Troccoli, Joan Carpenter.** "J. H. Sharp: Between Past and Present in the Art of the West." *Persimmon Hill* 16 (winter 1990): 8–15.

2586. **Turpin, Solveig A.** "Rock Art of the Despoblado." *Archaeology* 41 (September/October 1988): 50–55.

2587. **Vastokas, Joan M.** "Native Art as Art History: Meaning and Time from Unwritten Sources." *Journal of Canadian Studies* 21, no. 4 (1986/87): 7–36.

2588.   Wade, E. L., ed. *The Arts of the North American Indian.* New York: Hudson Hills, 1986.

2589.   Walton, Anne, John C. Ewers, and Royal B. Hassrick. *After the Buffalo Were Gone: The Louis Warren Hill, Sr., Collection of Indian Art.* Seattle: University of Washington Press, 1985.

2590.   Weber, Ronald L. "Tlingit Basketry, 1750–1950." In *The Art of Native American Basketry: A Living Legacy,* ed. F. W. Porter III, 299–318. New York: Greenwood Press, 1990.

2591.   Wheeler, Pauline. "Masks: Artist Pauline Wheeler Interprets the Ceremonial Art of the Northwest Coast Indians." *Beaver* 66 (August/September 1986): 16–21.

2592.   Whiteford, Andrew Hunter. *Southwestern Indian Baskets: Their History and Their Makers.* Santa Fe, N.Mex.: School of American Research Press, 1988.

2593.   Young, M. Jane. "Images of Power and the Power of Images: The Significance of Rock Art for Contemporary Zunis." *Journal of American Folklore* 98 (January 1985): 3–48.

11.3   RELIGION

2594.   Albanese, Catherine L. *Native Religion in America: From the Algonkian Indians to the New Age.* Chicago: University of Chicago Press, 1990.

2595.   Amiotte, Arthur. "The Lakota Sun Dance: Historical and Contemporary Perspectives." In *Sioux Indian Religion: Tradition and Innovation,* ed. R. J. DeMallie and D. Parks, 79–89. Norman: University of Oklahoma Press, 1987.

2596.   Barney, Gerald D. *Mormons, Indians, and the Ghost Dance Religion of 1890.* Lanham, Md.: University Press of America, 1986.

2597.   Bean, Lowell, John. *Seasons of the Kachina: Proceedings of the California State University, Hayward Conferences on the Western Pueblos, 1987–1988.* Novato, Calif.: Ballena Press, 1989.

2598.   Bierhorst, John. *The Mythology of North America.* New York: Morrow, 1985.

2599.   Brightman, Robert A. "Toward a History of Indian Religion: Religious Changes in Native Societies." In *New Directions in American Indian History,* ed. C. G. Calloway, 223–49. Norman: University of Oklahoma Press, 1988.

2600.   Brown, Ian W. "The Calumet Ceremony in the Southeast and Its Archeological Manifestations." *American Antiquity* 54 (1989): 311–31.

2601.   Capeci, Dominic L., Jr., and Jack C. Knight. "Reactions to Colonialism: The North American Ghost Dance and East African Maji-Maji Rebellions." *Historian* 52 (1990): 584–601.

2602.   Castile, George Pierre. "The Indian Connection: Judge James Wickersham and the Indian Shakers." *Pacific Northwest Quarterly* 81 (1990): 142–49.

2603.   d'Azevedo, Warren L. *Straight with the Medicine: Narratives of Washoe Followers of the Tipi Way as Told to Warren L. d'Azevedo.* Berkeley: Heyday Books, 1985.

2604.   DeMallie, Raymond J. "Lakota Belief and Ritual in the Nineteenth Century." In *Sioux Indian Religion: Tradition and Innovation,* ed. R. J. DeMallie and D. Parks, 25–43. Norman: University of Oklahoma Press, 1987.

2605.   DeMallie, Raymond, J., and Douglas Parks, eds. *Sioux Indian Religion: Tradition and Innovation.* Norman: University of Oklahoma Press, 1987.

2606. Dooling, D. M., and Paul Jordan Smith, eds. *I Become Part of It: Sacred Dimensions in Native American Life.* New York: Parabola Books, 1989.

2607. Dugan, Kathleen Margaret. *The Vision Quest of the Plains Indians: Its Spiritual Significance.* Lewiston, Ont.: Edwin Mellen Press, 1985.

2608. Erdoes, Richard. *Crying for a Dream: The World Through Native American Eyes.* Santa Fe, N.Mex.: Bear and Co., 1990.

2609. Fehrer-Elson, Catherine. *Children of the Sacred Ground: America's Last Stand?* Flagstaff, Ariz.: Northland Publishing, 1988.

2610. Gill, Sam. "Mother Earth: An American Myth." In *The Invented Indian: Cultural Fictions and Government Policies,* ed. J. A. Clifton, 129–44. New Brunswick, N.J.: Transaction Publishers, 1990.

2611. ———. *Mother Earth: An American Story.* Chicago: University of Chicago Press, 1987.

2612. ———. *Native American Religious Action: A Performance Approach to Religion.* Columbia: University of South Carolina Press, 1987.

2613. Good, Diane L. "Sacred Bundles: History Wrapped up in Culture." *History News* 45 (July/August 1990): 13–14, 27.

2614. Goodman, Linda J. "Mescalero Apache Medicine Men: An Aid to Living a Fine Life." *El Palacio* 95 (fall/winter 1989): 30–37.

2615. Goodwin, Derek V. "Raiders of the Sacred Sites." *New York Times Magazine,* 7 December 1986, 65–70.

2616. Griffin-Pierce, Trudy. "Cosmological Order as a Model for Navajo Philosophy." *American Indian Culture and Research Journal* 12, no. 4 (1988): 1–16.

2617. Grimes, Ronald L. "Desecration of the Dead: An Inter-religious Controversy." *American Indian Quarterly* 10 (1986): 305–18.

2618. Grobsmith, Elizabeth S. "The Impact of Litigation on the Religious Revitalization of Native American Inmates in the Nebraska Department of Corrections." *Plains Anthropologist* 34, no. 144, pt. 1 (1989): 135–48.

2619. Harrod, Howard. *Renewing the World: Plains Indian Religion and Morality.* Tucson: University of Arizona Press, 1987.

2620. Hecht, Robert A. "Taos Pueblo and the Struggle for Blue Lake." *American Indian Culture and Research Journal* 13, no. 1 (1989): 53–77.

2621. Hittman, Michael. *Wovoka and the Ghost Dance.* Yerington, Nev.: Yerington Paiute Tribe, 1990.

2622. Kehoe, Alice B. "Primal Gala: Primitivists and Plastic Medicine Men." In *The Invented Indian: Cultural Fictions and Government Policies,* ed. J. A. Clifton, 193–210. New Brunswick, N.J.: Transaction Publishers, 1990.

2623. Klesert, Anthony L., and Michael Andrews. "The Treatment of Human Remains on Navajo Lands." *American Antiquity* 53 (1988): 310–20.

2624. Lawrence, Elizabeth A. "'That by Means of Which People Live': Indians and Their Horses' Health." *Journal of the West* 27 (January 1988): 7–15.

2625. Lewis, James R. "Shamans and Prophets: Continuities and Discontinuities in Native American New Religions." *American Indian Quarterly* 14 (1988): 221–28.

2626. Lewis, Thomas H. "The Contemporary Yuwipi." In *Sioux Indian Religion: Tradition and Innovation,* ed. R. J. DeMallie and D. Parks, 173–87. Norman: University of Oklahoma Press, 1987.

2627. **Loftin, John D.** "Anglo-American Jurisprudence and the Native American Tribal Quest for Religious Freedom." *American Indian Culture and Research Journal* 13, no. 1 (1989): 1–52.

2628. **Looking Horse, Arval.** "The Sacred Pipe in Modern Life." In *Sioux Indian Religion: Tradition and Innovation,* ed. R. J. DeMallie and D. Parks, 67–73. Norman: University of Oklahoma Press, 1987.

2629. **McCoy, Ron.** "Naalye he Bahoogan: Where the Past Is the Present." *Arizona Highways* 63 (June 1987): 10–15.

2630. **McLoughlin, William G.** "Ghost Dance Movements: Some Thoughts on Definition Based on Cherokee History." *Ethnohistory* 37, no. 1 (1990): 25–44.

2631. **Malotki, Ekkehart, and Michael Lomatuway'ma.** *Maasaw: Profile of a Hopi God.* Lincoln: University of Nebraska Press, 1987.

2632. ———. *Stories of Maasaw, a Hopi God.* Lincoln: University of Nebraska Press, 1987.

2633. **Martin, Elizabeth.** "The Peyote Religion—Factors Aiding and Limiting Its Diffusion." *Saskatchewan Indian Federated College Journal* 3 (1987): 5–20.

2634. **Mazzola, Lars Charles.** "The Medicine Wheel: Center and Periphery." *Journal of Popular Culture* 22 (1988): 63–74.

2635. **Michaelson, Robert S.** "American Indian Religious Freedom Litigation: Promise and Perils." *Journal of Law and Religion* 13, no. 1 (1985): 47–76.

2636. **Miller, Jay.** *Shamanic Odyssey: The Lushootseed Salish Journey to the Land of the Dead.* Menlo Park, Calif.: Ballena Press, 1988.

2637. **Morrison, Kenneth M.** "Baptism and Alliances: The Symbolic Mediations of Religious Syncretism." *Ethnohistory* 37, no. 4 (1990): 416–37.

2638. **O'Brien, Patricia J.** "Morning Star Sacrifice: Contradiction or Dualism?" *Plains Anthropologist* 32, no. 115 (1987): 73–76.

2639. **Owsley, Frank L., Jr.** "Prophet of War: Josiah Francis and the Creek War." *American Indian Quarterly* 9 (1985): 273–94.

2640. **Paper, Jordan.** *Offering Smoke: The Sacred Pipe and Native American Religion.* Moscow: University of Idaho Press, 1988.

2641. **Payne, Richard W.** "Medicine and Music: Whistles of Eastern Oklahoma Indians." *Chronicles of Oklahoma* 68 (1990): 424–33.

2642. **Powell, Peter J.** "Power for New Days." In *The Plains Indians of the Twentieth Century,* ed. P. Iverson, 249–64. Norman: University of Oklahoma Press, 1985.

2643. **Powers, William K.** *Beyond the Vision: Essays on American Indian Culture.* Norman: University of Oklahoma Press, 1987.

2644. ———. *Sacred Language: The Nature of Supernatural Discourse in Lakota.* Norman: University of Oklahoma Press, 1987.

2645. **Ravesloot, John C.** "On the Treatment and Reburial of Human Remains: The San Xavier Bridge to Project, Tucson, Arizona." *American Indian Quarterly* 14 (1990): 35–50.

2646. Sanborn, Geoff. "Unfencing the Range: History, Identity, Property, and Apocalypse in *Lame Deer—Seeker of Visions.*" *American Indian Culture and Research Journal* 14, no. 4 (1990): 39–57.

2647. Schlesier, Karl. *The Wolves of Heaven: Cheyenne Shamanism, Ceremonies, and Prehistoric Origins.* Norman: University of Oklahoma Press, 1987

2648. Spider, Emerson, Sr. "The Native American Church of Jesus Christ." In *Sioux Indian Religion: Tradition and Innovation,* ed. R. J. DeMallie and D. Parks, 189–209. Norman: University of Oklahoma Press, 1987.

2649. Steinmetz, Paul B., S.J. *Pipe, Bible, and Peyote Among the Oglala Lakota.* 1980. Reprint, Knoxville: University of Tennessee Press, 1989.

2650. Stewart, Omer C. *Peyote Religion.* Norman: University of Oklahoma Press, 1987.

2651. Sullivan, Lawrence, ed. *Native American Religions.* New York: Macmillan, 1989.

2652. Talamantez, Ines M. "Use of Dialogue in the Reinterpretation of American Indian Religious Traditions: A Case Study." *American Indian Culture and Research Journal* 9, no. 2 (1985): 33–48.

2653. Tooker, Elisabeth. "On the Development of the Handsome Lake Religion." *Proceedings of the American Philosophical Society* 133 (1989): 35–50.

2654. Trafzer, Clifford E., ed. *American Indian Prophets: Religious Leaders and Revitalization Movements.* Newcastle, Calif.: Sierra Oaks Publishing Co., 1986.

2655. Vecsey, Christopher. "The Story and Structure of the Iroquois Con-

federacy." *Journal of the American Academy of Religion* 54 (1986): 79–106.

2656. ——, ed. *Religion in Native North America.* Moscow: University of Idaho Press, 1990.

2657. Wiedman, Dennis. "The Staff, Fan, Rattle, and Drum: Artistic and Spiritual Expressions of Oklahoma Peyotists." *American Indian Art Magazine* 10 (summer 1985): 38–45.

2658. Wiedman, Dennis, and **Candace Green.** "Early Kiowa Peyote Ritual (Haugooan)." *American Indian Art Magazine* 13 (autumn 1989): 32–41.

2659. Wright, Barton. *Kachinas of the Zuni.* Flagstaff, Ariz.: Northland Press, 1985.

11.4   LAND-USE PHILOSOPHIES
        AND PRACTICES

2660. Albers, Patricia C., and **Jeanne Kay.** "Sharing the Land: A Study in American Indian Territoriality." In *A Cultural Geography of North American Indians,* ed. T. E. Ross and T. G. Moore, 47–91. Boulder, Colo.: Westview Press, 1987.

2661. Ball, Georgiana. "The Monopoly System of Wildlife Management of the Indians and the Hudson's Bay Company in the Early History of British Columbia." *BC Studies* 66 (summer 1985): 37–58.

2662. Caduto, Michael J., and **Joseph Bruchac.** *Keepers of the Earth: Native American Stories, with Environmental Activities for Children.* Golden, Colo.: Fulcrum, 1988.

2663. Callicott, J. Baird. "American Indian Land Wisdom." In *The Struggle for the Land: Indigenous Insight and Industrial Empire in the Semiarid World,* ed. P. A. Olson, 255–72. Lincoln: University of Nebraska Press, 1990.

2664. ———. "American Indian Land Wisdom? Sorting Out the Issues." *Journal of Forest History* 33 (1989): 35–42.

2665. **Clemmer, Richard O.** "The Piñon-Pine: Old Ally or New Pest? Western Shoshone Indians Versus the Bureau of Land Management in Nevada." *Environmental Review* 9, no. 2 (1985): 131–49.

2666. **Cornell, George L.** "The Influence of Native Americans on Modern Conservationists." *Environmental Review* 9, no. 2 (1985): 104–17.

2667. ———. "Native American Perceptions of the Environment." *Northeast Indian Quarterly* 7 (1990): 3–13.

2668. **Cronon, William,** and **Richard White.** "Ecological Change and Indian-White Relations." In *History of Indian-White Relations,* ed. W. Washburn, 417–29. Vol. 4 of *Handbook of North American Indians,* ed. W. Sturtevant. Washington, D.C.: Smithsonian Institution Press, 1988.

2669. ———. "Indians and the Land." *American Heritage* 37, no. 5 (1986): 19–25.

2670. **Cummins, Bryan.** "Attawapiskat Cree Land Use and State Intervention." In *Papers of the Twenty-First Algonquian Conference,* ed. W. Cowan, 100–103. Carleton University Press, 1990.

2671. **Curry-Roper, Janel M.** "Cultural Change and the Houma Indians: A Historical and Ecological Examination." In *A Cultural Geography of North American Indians,* ed. T. E. Ross and T. G. Moore, 227–42. Boulder, Colo.: Westview Press, 1987.

2672. **Eliades, David K.** "Two Worlds Collide: The European Advance into North America." In *A Cultural Geography of North American Indians,* ed. T. E. Ross and T. G. Moore, 33–46. Boulder, Colo.: Westview Press, 1987.

2673. **Feit, Harvey A.** "Waswapini Cree Management of Land and Wildlife: Cree Ethno-ecology Revisited." In *Native People, Native Lands: Canadian Indians, Inuit, and Métis,* ed. B. A. Cox, 75–91. Ottawa: Carleton University Press, 1988.

2674. **Getches, David H.** "A Philosophy of Permanence: The Indians' Legacy for the West." *Journal of the West* 29 (July 1990): 54–68.

2675. **Janke, Ronald A.** "The Loss of Indian Lands in Wisconsin, Montana, and Arizona." In *A Cultural Geography of North American Indians,* ed. T. E. Ross and T. G. Moore, 127–48. Boulder, Colo.: Westview Press, 1987.

2676. **Kaiser, Rudolf.** "'A Faith Gospel, Almost': Chief Seattle's Speech, American Origins and European Reception." In *Indians and Europe: An Interdisciplinary Collection of Essays,* ed. C. Feest, 505–26. Aachen, West Germany: Edition Herodot, 1987.

2677. **Klesert, Anthony L.,** and **Alan S. Downer,** eds. *Preservation on the Reservation: Native Americans, Native American Lands, and Archaeology.* Navajo Nation Papers in Anthropology, no. 26. Window Rock, Ariz.: Historic Preservation Department, Navajo Nation, 1990.

2678. **Levine, Richard.** "Indians, Conservation, and George Bird Grinnell." *American Studies* 28 (fall 1987): 41–55.

2679. **McNab, Miriam.** "What Evidence Is There That Western Indians Were Conservationists?" *Native Studies Review* 1, no. 1 (1985): 96–107.

2680. **Mason, Carol I.** "A Sweet Small Something: Maple Sugaring in the New World." In *The Invented Indian: Cultural Fictions and Government Policies,* ed. J. A. Clifton, 91–107. New Brunswick, N.J.: Transaction Publishers, 1990.

2681.   M'Gonigle, R. Michael. "Native Rights and Environmental Sustainability: Lessons from the British Columbia Wilderness." *Canadian Journal of Native Studies* 8 (1988): 108–30.

2682.   Notzke, Claudia. "Indian Land in Southern Alberta." In *A Cultural Geography of North American Indians,* ed. T. E. Ross and T. G. Moore, 107–26. Boulder, Colo.: Westview Press, 1987.

2683.   Romeo, Stephanie. "Concepts of Nature and Power: Environmental Ethic of the Northern Ute." *Environmental Review* 9, 2 (1985): 150–70.

2684.   Schwarz, Douglas O. "Plains Indian Influences on the American Environmental Movement: Ernest Thompson Seton and Ohiyesa." In *The Struggle for the Land: Indigenous Insight and Industrial Empire in the Semiarid World,* ed. P. A. Olson, 273–88. Lincoln: University of Nebraska Press, 1990.

2685.   Shapcott, Catherine. "Environmental Impact Assessment and Resource Management, a Haida Case Study: Implications for Native People of the North." *Canadian Journal of Native Studies* 9 (1989): 55–84.

2686.   Stoffle, Richard W., David B. Halmo, Michael L. Evans, and John E. Olmstead. "Calculating the Cultural Significance of American Indian Plants: Paiute and Shoshone Ethnobotany at Yucca Mountain, Nevada." *American Anthropologist* 92 (1990): 416–32.

2687.   Tanner, Adrian. "The Significance of Hunting Territories Today." In *Native People, Native Lands: Canadian Indians, Inuit, and Métis,* ed. B. A. Cox, 60–74. Ottawa: Carleton University Press, 1988.

2688.   Weil, Richard H. "The Loss of Lands Inside Indian Reservations." In *A Cultural Geography of North American Indians,* ed. T. E. Ross and T. G. Moore, 149–72. Boulder, Colo.: Westview Press, 1987.

2689.   West, G. James. "Early Historic Vegetation Change in Alta California: The Fossill Evidence." In *Columbian Consequences,* vol. 1, *Archaeological and Historical Perspectives on the Spanish Borderlands West,* ed. D. H. Thomas, 333–48. Washington, D.C.: Smithsonian Institution Press, 1989.

2690.   Williamson, Ray. *Living the Sky: The Cosmos of the American Indian.* Norman: University of Oklahoma Press, 1987.

XII
Indian History and
the Historians of Native America

12.1 HISTORIOGRAPHY AND THEORETICAL COMMENTARIES

2691. **Ames, Michael M.** "A New Indian History for Museums." *Native Studies Review* 3, no. 2 (1987): 17–26.

2692. **Ames, Michael M., and Claudia Haagen.** "A New Native Peoples History for Museums." *Native Studies Review* 4, no. 1/2 (1988): 119–28.

2693. **Ballas, Donald J.** "Historical Geography and American Indian Development." In *A Cultural Geography of North American Indians,* ed. T. E. Ross and T. G. Moore, 15–32. Boulder, Colo.: Westview Press, 1987.

2694. **Barreiro, Jose.** "View from the Shore—Toward an Indian Voice in 1992." *Northeast Indian Quarterly* (Columbus quincentenary issue) 7 (1990): 4–20.

2695. **Barsh, Russell L.** "Are Anthropologists Hazardous to Indians' Health?" *Journal of Ethnic Studies* 15, no. 4 (1988): 1–38.

2696. ———. "Contemporary Marxist Theory and Native American Reality." *American Indian Quarterly* 12 (1988): 187–212.

2697. **Bernard, H. R.** "The Power of Print: The Role of Literacy in Preserving Native Cultures." *Human Organization* 44 (1985): 88–93.

2698. **Bush, Clive.** "Cultural Reflections in American Linguistics from Whitney to Sapir." *Journal of American Studies* 22 (1988): 185–214.

2699. **Campbell, Gregory.** "Ethics and Writing Native American History: A Commentary About *People of the Sacred Mountain.*" *American Indian Culture and Research Journal* 11, no. 1 (1987): 81–96.

2700. **Churchill, Elizabeth.** "The Blackfoot Elders Project: Linking People and Objects in Museum Research." *Native Studies Review* 3, no. 2 (1987): 71–86.

2701. **Clifton, James A.** "The Political Rhetoric of Indian History." *Annals of Iowa* 49 (summer/fall 1987): 101–10.

2702. ———, ed. *The Invented Indian: Cultural Fictions and Government Policies.* New Brunswick, N.J.: Transaction Publishers, 1990.

2703. **Cronon, William.** "Revisiting the Vanishing Frontier: The Legacy of Frederick Jackson Turner." *Western Historical Quarterly* 18 (1987): 157–76.

2704. **Darnell, Regna.** *Edward Sapir: Linguist, Anthropologist, Humanist.* Berkeley: University of California Press, 1989.

2705. **Dippie, Brian W.** "The Winning of the West Reconsidered." *Wilson Quarterly* 14, no. 3 (1990): 71–85.

2706. **Donald, Leland.** "Liberty, Equality, Fraternity: Was the Indian Really Egalitarian?" In *The Invented Indian: Cultural Fictions and Government Policies,* ed. J. A. Clifton, 145–68. New Brunswick, N.J.: Transaction Publishers, 1990.

2707. **Dulaney, William L.** "Native American Press Association: The Working Press and American Indian Studies." *Native Press Research Journal* 1 (1986): 2–5.

2708. **Feest, Christian.** "Europe's Indians." In *The Invented Indian: Cultural Fictions and Government Policies,* ed. J. A. Clifton, 313–32. New Brunswick, N.J.: Transaction Publishers, 1990.

2709. **Feraca, Stephen E.** *Why Don't They Give Them Guns? The Great American Indian Myth.* Lanham, Md.: University Press of America, 1990.

2710. **Fiorentino, Daniele.** "Recovering Time and Space: Ethnohistory, History, and Anthropology and the Current Debate on American Indian History." *Storia Nordamericana* 5, no. 1 (1988): 101–15.

2711. **Fixico, Donald L.** "Indian and White Interpretations of the Frontier." In *Native Views of Indian-White Historical Relations,* ed. D. L. Fixico, 7–20. D'Arcy McNickle Center for the History of the American Indian, Occasional Papers in Curriculum, no. 7. Chicago: Newberry Library, 1989.

2712. ———, ed. *Native Views of Indian-White Historical Relations.* D'Arcy McNickle Center for the History of the American Indian, Occasional Papers in Curriculum, no. 7. Chicago: Newberry Library, 1989.

2713. ———, ed. *Native Voices in the City: The Chicago American Indian Oral History Project.* D'Arcy McNickle Center for the History of the American Indian, Occasional Papers in Curriculum, no. 6. Chicago: Newberry Library, 1987.

2714. **Fogelson, Raymond D.** "The Context of American Indian Political History: An Overview and Critique." In *The Struggle for Political Autonomy: Papers and Comments from the Second Newberry Conference on Themes in American Indian History,* 8–21. D'Arcy McNickle Center for the History of the American Indian, Occasional Papers in Curriculum, no. 11. Chicago: Newberry Library, 1989.

2715. ———. "The Impact of Indian History on U.S. History and Culture: A Final Look and Glance at the Bearing of Bering Straits on Native American History." In *The Impact of Indian History on the Teaching of United States History: Papers and Commentary from the 1986 Conference at Los Angeles,* 233–62. D'Arcy McNickle Center for the History of the American Indian, Occasional Papers in Curriculum, no. 5. Chicago: Newberry Library, 1987.

2716. ———. "Interpretation of the American Indian Psyche: Some Historical Notes." In *Social Contexts of American Ethnology, 1840–1984,* ed. J. Helm, 4–27. Proceedings of the American Ethnological Society, Monograph Series 1984. Washington, D.C.: American Anthropological Association, 1985.

2717. ———. "Night Thoughts on Native American Social History." Comments by Richard White and David Hackett Fischer. In *The Impact of Indian History on the Teaching of United States History: Proceedings of the 1984 Chicago Conference, Sessions 3–4,* 67–89. D'Arcy McNickle Center for the History of the American Indian, Occasional Papers in

Curriculum, no. 3. Chicago: Newberry Library, 1985.

2718. ———. "Summary." In *The Struggle for Political Autonomy: Papers and Comments from the Second Newberry Conference on Themes in American Indian History,* 171–77. D'Arcy McNickle Center for the History of the American Indian, Occasional Papers in Curriculum, no. 11. Chicago: Newberry Library, 1989.

2719. **Green, Michael D.** "Final Comments." In *The Struggle for Political Autonomy: Papers and Comments from the Second Newberry Conference on Themes in American Indian History,* 178–83. D'Arcy McNickle Center for the History of the American Indian, Occasional Papers in Curriculum, no. 11. Chicago: Newberry Library, 1989.

2720. **Hall, Thomas D.** "Historical Sociology and Native American Methodological Problems." *American Indian Quarterly* 13 (1989): 233–37.

2721. **Halpern, Katherine S.,** and **R. Landman.** *Applied Anthropologist and Public Servant: The Life and Work of Philleo Nash.* Washington, D.C.: American Anthropological Association, 1989.

2722. **Hampton, Carol M.** "Why Write History? A Caddo Grandmother's Perspective." *Creative Woman* 8, no. 3 (1987): 13–14.

2723. **Helm, June,** ed. *Social Contexts of American Ethnology, 1840–1984.* Proceedings of the American Ethnological Society, Monograph Series 1984. Washington, D.C.: American Anthropological Association, 1985.

2724. **Higham, John.** "Paleface and Redskin in American Indian Historiography: A Comment." *Journal of Interdisciplinary Studies* 16 (summer 1985): 11–16.

2725. **Hinsley, C. M.** "Hemispheric Hegemony in Early American Anthropology, 1841–1851: Reflections on John Lloyd Stephens and Lewis Henry Morgan." In *Social Contexts of American Ethnology, 1840–1984,* ed. J. Helm, 28–40. Proceedings of the American Ethnological Society, Monograph Series 1984. Washington, D.C.: American Anthropological Association, 1985.

2726. **Hoxie, Frederick E.** "Humored, Oppresed, or Ignored? American Indian History from an International Perspective." *Storia Nordamericana* 5, no. 1 (1988): 89–100.

2727. ———. "The Indians Versus the Textbooks: Is There Any Way Out? *Perspectives* 23, no. 4 (1985): 18–22.

2728. ———. "The Problems of Indian History." *Social Science Journal* 25 (1988): 389–99.

2729. **Iverson, Peter.** "Environmental History and Native Americans: A Comment." In *Environmental History: Critical Issues in Comparative Perspective,* ed. K. E. Bailes, 288–92. Lanham, Md.: University Press of America, 1985.

2730. ———. "Plains Indians and Australian Aborigines in the Twentieth Century." In *The Struggle for the Land: Indigenous Insight and Industrial Empire in the Semiarid World,* ed. P. A. Olson, 171–85. Lincoln: University of Nebraska Press, 1990.

2731. **Jacobs, Wilbur.** "Sherburne Friend Cook: Rebel-Revisionist (1896–1974)." *Pacific Historical Review* 54 (1985): 191–99.

2732. **Jennings, Francis.** "Anthony F. C. Wallace: An Ethnohistorical Pioneer." *Ethnohistory* 37, no. 4 (1990): 438–44.

2733. ———. "Francis Parkman: A Brahmin Among Untouchables." *Wil-*

liam and Mary Quarterly 42 (1985): 305–28.

2734.   Kehoe, Alice B. "The Ideological Paradigm in Traditional American Ethnology." In *Social Contexts of American Ethnology, 1840–1984,* ed. J. Helm, 41–49. Proceedings of the American Ethnological Society, Monograph Series 1984. Washington, D.C.: American Anthropological Association, 1985.

2735.   Keller, Robert H. "Hostile Language: Bias in Historical Writing About American Indian Resistance." *Journal of American Culture* 9 (winter 1986): 9–23.

2736.   ———. "Lac La Croix: Rumor, Rhetoric, and Reality in Indian Affairs." *Canadian Journal of Native Studies* 8 (1988): 59–72.

2737.   Kelly, Lawrence C. "Why Applied Anthropology Developed When It Did: A Commentary on People, Money, and Changing Times, 1930–1945." In *Social Contexts of American Ethnology, 1840–1984,* ed. J. Helm, 122–38. Proceedings of the American Ethnological Society, Monograph Series 1984. Washington, D.C.: American Anthropological Association, 1985.

2738.   Kenzer, Martin, ed. *Carl O. Sauer: A Tribute.* Corvallis: Oregon State University Press, 1987.

2739.   Key, Mary Ritchie, and Henry R. Hoeningswald, eds. *General and Amerindian Ethnolinguistics: In Remembrance of Stanley Newman.* New York: Mouton de Gruyter, 1989.

2740.   Koerner, Konrad. "Toward a History of Americanist Linguistics." In *Acts of the Twentieth Algonquian Conference,* ed. W. Cowan, 179–92. Ottawa: Carleton University Press, 1989.

2741.   Lankford, George E. "Losing the Past: Draper and the Ruddell Indian Captivity." *Arkansas Historical Quarterly* 49 (autumn 1990): 214–39.

2742.   Leeds-Hurwitz, Wendy. "The Committee on Research in Native American Languages." *Proceedings of the American Philosophical Society* 129 (1985): 129–60.

2743.   Lestringant, Frank. "The Myth of the Indian Monarchy: An Aspect of the Controversy Between Thevet and Levy (1575–1585)." In *Indians and Europe: An Interdisciplinary Collection of Essays,* ed. C. Feest, 37–60. Aachen, West Germany: Edition Herodot, 1987.

2744.   Lewis, G. Malcolm. "Misinterpretation of Amerindian Information as a Source of Error on Euro-American Maps." *Annals of the Association of American Geographers* 77, no. 4 (1987): 542–63.

2745.   Luebke, Frederich C., Frances W. Kaye, and Gary E. Moulton, eds. *Mapping the North American Plains: Essays in the History of Cartography.* Norman: University of Oklahoma Press, 1987.

2746.   Lurie, Nancy. "Relations Between Indians and Anthropologists." In *History of Indian-White Relations,* ed. W. Washburn, 548–56. Vol. 4 of *Handbook of North American Indians,* ed. W. Sturtevant. Washington, D.C.: Smithsonian Institution Press, 1988.

2747.   McIntosh, Kenneth W. "Geronimo's Friend: Angie Debo and the New History." *Chronicles of Oklahoma* 66 (1988): 164–77.

2748.   Mariani, Giorgio. "Was Anybody More of an Indian Than Karl Marx? The 'Indian Metropolitani' and the 1977 Movement." In *Indians and Europe: An Interdisciplinary Collection of Essays,* ed. C. Feest, 585–97. Aachen, West Germany: Edition Herodot, 1987.

2749. Martin, Calvin, ed. *The American Indian and the Problem of History.* New York: Oxford University Press, 1987.

2750. Merrell, James H. "Some Thoughts on Colonial Historians and American Indians." *William and Mary Quarterly* 46 (1989): 94–111.

2751. Meyer, Melissa, and Russell Thornton. "Indians and the Numbers Game: Quantitative Methods in Native American History." In *New Directions in American Indian History,* ed. C. G. Calloway, 5–48. Norman: University of Oklahoma Press, 1988.

2752. Mohawk, John. "Discovering Columbus: The Way Here." *Northeast Indian Quarterly* 7 (1990): 37–46.

2753. "Native Peoples, Museums, and Heritage Resource Management." *Native Studies Review* (special issue) 3, no. 2 (1987).

2754. Nichols, Roger L. "Historians and Indians." In *American Frontier and Western Issues: A Historiographical Review,* ed. R. L. Nichols, 149–78. Westport, Conn.: Greenwood Press, 1986.

2755. Palmer, Stanley, and Dennis Reinhartz, eds. *Essays on the History of North American Discovery and Exploration.* College Station: Texas A & M University Press, 1988.

2756. Paton, Pat. "Ruth Underhill Remembered: A Backward Glance into the Life of a Noted Anthropologist." *Colorado Heritage* 1 (1985): 14–20.

2757. Pilling, Arnold. "Dating Photographs." In *Ethnohistory: A Researcher's Guide,* ed. D. Wiedman, 167–226. Williamsburg, Va.: College of William and Mary, 1986.

2758. Preston, Richard J. "The View from the Other Side of the Frontier: East Cree Historical Notions." In *Papers of the Twenty-First Algonquian Conference,* ed. W. Cowan, 313–28. Ottawa: Carleton University Press, 1990.

2759. Price, John A. "Native Studies." In *Interdisciplinary Approaches to Canadian Society: A Guide to the Literature,* ed. A. J. Artibise, 117–47. Montreal: McGill-Queens University Press, 1990.

2760. Quinn, William W., Jr. "Public 'Ethno'history? or, Writing Tribal Histories at the Bureau of Indian Affairs." *Public Historian* 10 (1988): 71–79.

2761. Ray, Arthur J. "Moose Factory: Heritage Planning in a Northern Community." *Native Studies Review* 3, no. 2 (1987): 99–122.

2762. Red Horse, John, Troy Johnson, and Diane Weiner. "Commentary: Cultural Perspectives on Research Among American Indians." *American Indian Culture and Research Journal* 13, no. 3–4 (1989): 267–71.

2763. Richer, Stephen. "Fieldwork and the Commodification of Culture: Why the Natives Are Restless." *Canadian Review of Sociology and Anthropology* 25 (1988): 406–20.

2764. Robbins, Peggy. "A Walk of Injustice." *Pennsylvania Heritage* 14 (1988): 32–37.

2765. Ronda, James P. "'A Chart in History': Indian Cartography and the Lewis and Clark Expedition." In *Mapping the North American Plains: Essays in the History of Cartography,* ed. F. C. Luebke, F. W. Kaye, and G. E. Moulton, 81–91. Norman: University of Oklahoma Press, 1987.

2766. Rowan, Madeline Bronsdon. "Native Indian Youth in Museums: Success in Education at the U. B. C. Museum of Anthropology." *Native Studies Review* 3, no. 2 (1987): 87–98.

2767. Sheehan, Bernard W. "The Problem of Moral Judgments in History." *South Atlantic Quarterly* 84, no. 1 (1985): 37–50.

2768. Sheridan, Thomas E. "How to Tell the Story of a 'People Without History': Narrative Versus Ethnohistorical Approaches to the Study of the Yaqui Indians Through Time." *Journal of the Southwest* 30 (1988): 168–81.

2769. Shipley, William, ed. *In Honor of Mary Haas: From the Haas Festival Conference on Native Linguistics.* Berlin: Mouton de Gruyter, 1988.

2770. Sider, Gerald. "When Parrots Learn to Talk and Why They Can't: Domination, Deception, and Self-Deception in Indian-White Relations." *Comparative Studies in Society and History* 29 (1987): 3–23.

2771. Simmons, William S. "Culture Theory in Contemporary Ethnohistory." *Ethnohistory* 35, no. 1 (1988): 1–14.

2772. ———. "Frank Speck and 'The Old Mohegan Indian Stone Cutter.'" *Ethnohistory* 32, no. 2 (1985): 155–63.

2773. Stannard, David E. "The Invisible People of Early American History." *American Quarterly* 39 (1987): 649–55.

2774. Taylor, Colin. "William Blackmore: A Nineteenth Century Englishman's Contribution to American Indian Ethnology." In *Indians and Europe: An Interdisciplinary Collection of Essays,* ed. C. Feest, 321–35. Aachen, West Germany: Edition Herodot, 1987.

2775. Tedlock, Dennis. "Scholarship, Politics, and Dialogic Anthropology." Reply by Arnold Krupat. *American Indian Culture and Research Journal* 9, no. 4 (1985): 67–84.

2776. Tough Frank, ed. "Advocacy Research and Native Studies." *Native Studies Review* (special issue) 6, no. 2 (1990).

2777. *Towards a Quantitative Approach to American Indian History: Papers and Commentaries from a Research Conference Held at the Newberry Library, February 19–21, 1987.* D'Arcy McNickle Center for the History of the American Indian, Occasional Papers, no. 8. Chicago: Newberry Library, 1987.

2778. Trafzer, Clifford E. "The Earth, Animals, and Academics: The Walla Walla Council and Plateau Indians of the Northwest." In *Native Views of Indian-White Historical Relations,* ed. D. L. Fixico, 119–28. D'Arcy McNickle Center for the History of the American Indian, Occasional Papers in Curriculum, no. 7. Chicago: Newberry Library, 1989.

2779. Trautman, Thomas R. *Lewis Henry Morgan and the Invention of Kinship.* Berkeley: University of California Press, 1987.

2780. Trigger, Bruce G. "Evolutionism, Relativism, and Putting Native People into Historical Context." *Culture* 6, no. 2 (1986): 65–79.

2781. van Gestel, Allan. "When Fictions Take Hostages." In *The Invented Indian: Cultural Fictions and Government Policies,* ed. J. A. Clifton, 291–314. New Brunswick, N.J.: Transaction Publishers, 1990.

2782. Walker, Ernest G. "Indian Involvement in Heritage Resource Development: A Saskatchewan Example." *Native Studies Review* 3, no. 2 (1987): 123–32.

2783. Warren, Dave. "American Indians and the Columbus Quincentenary." *Northeast Indian Quarterly* 7 (1990): 21–25.

2784. **White, Richard.** "American Indians and the Environment." *Environmental Review* 9 (1985): 101–3.

2785. ————, eds. "American Indian Environmental History." *Environmental Review* (special issue) 9, no. 2 (1985).

2786. **Wickwire, Wendy C.** "James A. Teit: His Contribution to Canadian Ethnomusicology." *Canadian Journal of Native Studies* 8 (1988): 183–204.

2787. **Wiedman, Dennis.** "The Anthropological Use of Historic Documents." In *Ethnohistory: A Researcher's Guide,* ed. D. Wiedman, vii–xx. Williamsburg, Va.: College of William and Mary, 1986.

2788. **Willson, Margaret E.** "Oral History Interviews: Some History and Practical Suggestions." In *Ethnohistory: A Researcher's Guide,* ed. D. Wiedman, 253–74. Williamsburg, Va.: College of William and Mary, 1986.

2789. **Zanjani, Sally S.** "The Indian Massacre That Never Happened." *Nevada Historical Society Quarterly* 31 (1988): 119–49.

12.2   TEACHING

2790. **Brindin, Judith A., and Mary C. Bradford.** *The Native People of the Northeast Woodlands: An Educational Resource Publication.* New York: Museum of the American Indian, Heye Foundation, 1990.

2791. **Cameron, Ian.** "Student Achievement Among Native Students in British Columbia." *Canadian Journal of Native Education* 17, no. 1 (1990): 36–43.

2792. **Charles, Jim.** "For the Sake of a Fad: The Misrepresentation of American Indians and Their Literature in High School Literature Anthologies." *Journal of Ethnic Studies* 15, no. 2 (1987): 131–40.

2793. **Clark, Carter Blue.** "America's First Discipline: American Indian Studies." In *American Indian Identity: Today's Changing Perspectives,* ed. C. E. Trafzer, 77–84. Publications in American Indian Studies, no. 1. San Diego: San Diego State University, 1985.

2794. **Helms, Mary.** *Ulysses' Sail: An Ethographic Odyssey of Power, Knowledge, and Geographical Distance.* Princeton, N.J.: Princeton University Press, 1988.

2795. **Hurtado, Albert L.** "Public History and the Native American." *Montana* 40 (spring 1990): 58–69.

2796. *The Impact of Indian History on the Teaching of United States History: Proceedings of the 1984 Chicago Conference, Sessions 1–2.* D'Arcy McNickle Center for the History of the American Indian, Occasional Papers in Curriculum, no. 2. Chicago: Newberry Library, 1985.

2797. *The Impact of Indian History on the Teaching of United States History: Proceedings of the 1984 Chicago Conference, Sessions 3–4.* D'Arcy McNickle Center for the History of the American Indian, Occasional Papers in Curriculum, no. 3. Chicago: Newberry Library, 1985.

2798. *The Impact of Indian History on the Teaching of United States History: Papers and Commentary from the 1985 Conference at the Smithsonian Institution, Washington, D.C.* D'Arcy McNickle Center for the History of the American Indian, Occasional Papers in Curriculum, no. 4. Chicago: Newberry Library, 1986.

2799. *The Impact of Indian History on the Teaching of United States History: Papers and Commentary from the 1986 Conference at Los Angeles.* D'Arcy McNickle Center for the History of the American Indian, Occasional Papers in Curriculum, no. 5. Chicago: Newberry Library, 1987.

2800. Jaimes, M. Annette. "American Indian Studies: Toward an Indigenous Model." *American Indian Culture and Research Journal* 11, no. 3 (1987): 1–16.

2801. Musser, Louise S., and Evelyn B. Freeman. "Teaching Young Students About Native Americans." *Social Studies* 80 (1989): 5–10.

2802. Richter, Daniel K. "A Framework for Pennsylvania Indian History." *Pennsylvania History* 57 (1990): 236–61.

2803. *Teaching American Indian History: A Selection of Course Outlines.* D'Arcy McNickle Center for the History of the American Indian, Occasional Papers in Curriculum, no. 10. Chicago: Newberry Library, 1988.

2804. Vogel, Virgil J. "The Blackout of Native American Cultural Achievements." *American Indian Quarterly* 11 (1987): 11–35.

12.3   REVIEW ESSAYS

2805. Axtell, James. "Europeans, Indians, and the Age of Discovery in American History Textbooks." *American History Review* 92, no. 3 (1987): 621–32.

2806. Berlo, Janet Catherine. "Recent Scholarship on Northwest Coast Indian Art." *American Indian Quarterly* 10 (1986): 119–25.

2807. Climont, Karl E. "A Review and Comments on Indian Histories." *American Indian Culture and Research Journal* 9, no. 1 (1985): 66–72.

2808. Dippie, Brian W. "'Only One Truth': Assimilation and the American Indian." *Canadian Review of American Studies* 16, no. 1 (1985): 31–39.

2809. Hedren, Paul L. "Paper Medicine Man and the Renaissance in Frontier Military History: A Review Essay." *New Mexico Historical Review* 62 (1987): 95–104

2810. Hoxie, Frederick E. "Positively Paternal." *Reviews of American History* 13 (1985): 386–94. [Of Prucha, *The Great Father*]

2811. Iverson, Peter. "Hohokam, Hoover Dam, Hayden: Indians, Water, and Power in the West." *American Indian Quarterly* 12 (1988): 329–32.

2812. Jaenen, Cornelius J. "Assessing Early Native-European Contact." *Journal of Canadian Studies* 23, no. 1–2 (1988): 243–48.

2813. Kuester, Martin. "American Indians and German Indians: Perspectives of Doom in Cooper and May." *Western American Literature* 22 (1988): 217–22.

2814. Martin, Calvin. "The Covenant Chain of Friendship, Inc.: America's First Great Real Estate Agency." *Reviews in American History* 13 (1985): 14–22. [Of Jennings, *Ambiguous Iroquois Empire*]

2815. Merrell, James H. "High Priests and Missionaries: James Axtell— *After Columbus: Essays in the Ethnohistory of Colonial North America*." *Reviews in American History* 17 (1989): 177–78.

2816. Miller, David Reed. "Excursions in Siouan Sociology." *American Indian and Culture Research Journal* 9 (1985): 49–57. [Of R. H. Barnes, *Two Crows Denies It*]

2817. Moulton, Gary E. "On Reading Lewis and Clark: The Last Twenty Years." *Montana* 38 (summer 1988): 28–39.

2818. Perdue, Theda. "John Ross and the Cherokee." *Georgia Historical Quarterly* 70 (1986): 456–76.

2819. Ray, Arthur J., and Arthur

Roberts. "Approaches to the Ethnohistory of the Subarctic: A Review of the *Handbook of North American Indians: Subarctic*." *Ethnohistory* 32, no. 3 (1985): 270–80.

2820.   **Richter, Daniel K.** "Up the Cultural Stream: Three Recent Works in Iroquois Studies." *Ethnohistory* 32, no. 4 (1985): 363–69.

2821.   **Riding In, James.** "Scholars and Twentieth-Century Indians: Reassessing the Recent Past." In *New Directions in American Indian History*, ed. C. G. Calloway, 127–49. Norman: University of Oklahoma Press, 1988.

2822.   **Salisbury, Neal.** "Francis Jennings and the State of American Indian History." *Reviews in American History* 17 (1989): 378–83.

2823.   **Simmons, William S.** "Anthropology, History and the North American Indian: A Review Article." *Comparative Studies in Society and History* 27 (1985): 174–83.

2824.   **Trigger, Bruce G.** "Ethnohistory: The Unfinished Edifice." *Ethnohistory* 33, no. 3 (1986): 253–67.

2825.   ———. "The Historians' Indian: Native Americans in Canadian Historical Writing from Charlevoix to the Present." *Canadian Historical Review* 67 (1986): 315–42.

2826.   **White, Richard.** "Race Relations in the American West." *American Quarterly* 38 (1986): 396–416.

2827.   ———. "Simple Stories of a Complicated People, or Complicated Stories for a Simple People?" *Montana* 37 (winter 1986): 66–70. [Of Slotkin, *The Fatal Environment*]

2828.   **Young, Mary.** "Will the Real Winner Please Stand Up?" *Reviews in American History* 15 (1987): 1–7.

12.4   TRAVELERS' ACCOUNTS AND OTHER FIRST-PERSON SOURCES

2829.   **Altherr, Thomas L.** "The Pajarito or Cliff Dwellers' National Park Proposal, 1900–1920." *New Mexico Historical Review* 60 (1985): 271–94.

2830.   **Avellaneda, Ignacio.** *Los Sobrevivientes de la Florida: The Survivors of the de Soto Expedition.* Research Publications of the P. K. Younge Library of Florida History, no. 2. Gainesville: University of Florida Libraries, 1990.

2831.   **Boden, E. A.** "Letter to Premier T. C. Douglas from E. A. Boden." *Native Studies Review* 3, no. 2 (1987): 134–35.

2832.   **Erasmus, Bill.** "Notes for an Address by Bill Erasmus, President of the Dene Nation, on the Signing of the Agreement-In-Principle with the Government of Canada, Fort Rae, Denendeh, September 5, 1988." *Native Studies Review* 4, no. 1/2 (1988): 203–10.

2833.   **Fulton, E. D.** "Lubicon Lake Land Claim 'Discussion Paper,' by E. D. Fulton, February 1987." *Native Studies Review* 4, no. 1/2 (1988): 183–202.

2834.   **Gehring, Charles T.,** and **Robert S. Grumet.** "Observations of the Indians from Jasper Danckaerts's Journal, 1679–1680." *William and Mary Quarterly* 44 (1987): 104–40.

2835.   **Gertler, Franklin S.,** and **Peter W. Hutchins,** eds. "R{egina} v. Sioui." *Native Studies Review* 6, no. 2 (1990): 115–94.

2836.   **Grumet, Robert S.** *New World Encounters: Jasper Danckaerts's View of Indian Life in Seventeenth Century Brooklyn.* New York: Brooklyn Historical Society, 1986.

2837. **Keller, Robert H.** "A Rocky Mountain Expedition in Process in Washington State, 1864: William Crawford's Journey to Middle Park." *Essays and Monographs in Colorado History* 5 (1987): 53–65.

2838. **King, J. C. H.** "A Family of Botocudos Exhibiting on Bond Street, in 1822." In *Indians and Europe: An Interdisciplinary Collection of Essays,* ed. C. Feest, 243–75. Aachen, West Germany: Edition Herodot, 1987.

2839. **Lincoln, Kenneth.** *The Good Red Road: Passages into Native America.* Assisted by Al Logan Slagle. San Francisco: Harper and Row, 1987.

2840. **Manitoba Métis Foundation.** "Position Paper on Child Care and Family Services (May 15, 1982)." *Native Studies Review* 2, no. 1 (1986): 125–40.

2841. **Mulvey, Christopher.** "Among the Sag-a-noshes: Ojibwa and Iowa Indians with George Catlin in Europe, 1843–1848." In *Indians and Europe: An Interdisciplinary Collection of Essays,* ed. C. Feest, 253–75. Aachen, West Germany: Edition Herodot, 1987.

2842. "Notes on Indian Council at Treaty Rock, Beren's River, Lake Winnipeg, Man., 12th July 1890."

Native Studies Review 3, no. 1 (1987): 117–28.

2843. **Padron, F. M.,** and **A. M. Topping,** eds. and trans. *Journal of Don Francisco Saavedra de Sangronis During the Commission He Had in His Charge from 25 June 1780 Until the 20th of the Same Month 1783.* Gainesville: University of Florida Press, 1989. [Upper Creeks]

2844. **Paull, Andrew.** "Letter to Premier T. C. Douglas from Andrew Paull." *Native Studies Review* 3, no. 2 (1987): 136–38.

2845. **Rusinowa, Izabella.** "Indians in the Reports of Polish Travelers of the Second Half of the Nineteenth Century." In *Indians and Europe: An Interdisciplinary Collection of Essays,* ed. C. Feest, 297–306. Aachen, West Germany: Edition Herodot, 1987.

2846. **Stone, E. L.** "Health and Disease at the Norway House Indian Agency, 1926." *Native Studies Review* 5, no. 1 (1989): 237–56.

2847. **Wall, Dr.** "Report of the Medical Services to Indians Located Along the Line of the Canadian National Railways from Cochrane, Ontario, to La Tuque, Quebec, June to October, 1926, by Dr. Wall." *Native Studies Review* 5, no. 1 (1989): 257–74.

XIII
Native American Literatures

13.1 TRADITIONAL TEXTS

2848. **Altherr, Thomas L.** "Tombo-Chiqui: or, The American Savage: John Cleland's Noble Savage Satire." *American Indian Quarterly* 9 (1985): 411–20.

2849. **Basso, Keith.** *Western Apache Language and Culture: Essays in Linguistic Anthropology.* Tucson: University of Arizona Press, 1990.

2850. **Bergsland, Knut,** and **Moses L. Dirks,** ed. *Unangam Ungiikangin Kayux Tunsangin, Unangam Uniikangis Ama Tunzangis: Aleut Tales and Narratives, Collected 1909–1910 by Waldemar Jochelson.* Fairbanks: Alaska Native Language Center, University of Alaska, 1990.

2851. **Bowen, Deborah.** "Squaring the Circle: The Problem of Translation in 'The Temptation of Little Bear.'" *Canadian Literature* 117 (1988): 62–70.

2852. **Brant, Beth,** ed. *The Gathering of Spirit: A Collection by North American Indians.* Ithaca, N.Y.: Firebrand Books, 1988.

2853. **Bruchac, Joseph.** *The Faithful Hunter: Abenaki Stories.* Greenfield Center, N.Y.: Greenfield Review Press, 1988.

2854. ———. *Return of the Sun: Native American Tales from the Northeast Woodlands.* Freedom, Calif.: Crossing Press, 1989.

2855. ———. *The Wind Eagle and Other Abenaki Stories.* Greenfield Center, N.Y.: Greenfield Review Press, 1985.

2856. **Clements, William M.** *Native American Folklore in Nineteenth Century Periodicals.* Athens, Ohio: Swallow Press, 1986.

2857. **Danielson, Linda L.** "Storyteller: Grandmother Spider's Web." *Journal of the Southwest* 30 (1988): 325–55.

2858. **Edmonds, Margot,** and **Ella E. Clark.** *Voices of the Winds: Native American Legends.* New York: Facts on File, 1989.

2859. **Erdoes, Richard.** *Crying for a Dream: The World Through Native American Eyes.* Santa Fe, N.Mex.: Bear and Co., 1990.

2860. **Gibbons, Byrd.** "Tricksters and Earthdivers: Tradition as Vision in Native American Publications." *Native Press Research Journal* 2 (1986): 1–4.

2861. **Goddard, Ives,** and **Kathleen J. Bragdon.** *Native Writings in Massachusetts.* Philadelphia: American Philosophical Society, 1988.

2862. **Hamell, George R.** "Strawberries, Floating Islands, and Rabbit Captains: Mythical Realities and European Contact in the Northeast During the Sixteenth and Seventeenth Centuries." *Journal of Canadian Studies* 21, no. 4 (1987): 72–94.

2863.   Harkin, Michael. "History, Narrative, and Temporality: Examples from the Northwest Coast." *Ethnohistory* 35, no. 2 (1988): 99–130.

2864.   Karney, Beulah. *Old Father's Long Journey.* San Andreas, Calif.: CLC Press, 1985.

2865.   Karpan, Robin, and Arlene Karpan. "Saskatchewan Indians Tell Their Own Story." *History News* 45 (May/June 1990): 19–21.

2866.   McLoughlin, William G., and Walter H. Conser, Jr. " 'The First Man Was Red'—Cherokee Responses to the Debate over Indian Origins, 1760–1860." *American Quarterly* 41, no. 3 (1989): 243–64.

2867.   Maud, Ralph. "The Henry Tale–Franz Boas Collaboration on Tsimshian Mythology." *American Ethnologist* 16 (1989): 158–62.

2868.   Moore, Patricia J., and Angela Wheelock. *Wolverine Myths and Visions: Dene Traditions from Northern Alberta.* Lincoln: University of Nebraska Press, 1989.

2869.   Niatum, Duane, ed. *Harper's Anthology of Twentieth Century Native American Poetry.* New York: Harper and Row, 1988.

2870.   Parks, Douglas R. *Traditional Narratives of the Arikara Indians.* Vol. 3, *Stories of Alfred Morsette;* vol. 4. *Stories of Other Narrators.* Lincoln: University of Nebraska Press, 1990. [Volumes 1 and 2 are in Arikara, with an audiocassette]

2871.   Rice, J. "Akicita of the Thunder: Horses in Black Elk's Vision." *Melus* 14, no. 1 (1985): 5–14.

2872.   Robinson, Harry. *Write It on Your Heart: The Epic World of an Okanagan Storyteller.* Edited by Wendy Wickwire. Vancouver: Talonbooks, 1989.

2873.   Rustige, Rona, comp. *Tyendinaga Tales.* Montreal: McGill-Queens University Press, 1988.

2874.   Spresser, James Clarance. "Fantasy Theme Analysis as Applied to the Oglala Sioux Indian Text *Black Elk Speaks.*" *Journal of American Culture* 8 (fall 1985): 75–78.

2875.   Stott, Jon C. "Form, Content, and Cultural Values in Three Inuit (Eskimo) Survival Stories." *American Indian Quarterly* 10 (1986): 213–26.

2876.   Tedlock, Dennis. "The Witches Were Saved: A Zuni Origin Story." *Journal of American Folklore* 101 (July 1988): 314–20.

2877.   Williams, Angeline, Leonard Bloomfield, and John D. Nichols, eds. *The Dog's Children: Anishinaabe Texts.* Winnepeg: University of Manitoba Press, 1990.

2878.   Worchester, Don. *A Visit from Father and Other Tales of the Mohave.* College Station: Texas A & M Press, 1989.

2879.   Zitkala-Sa. *American Indian Stories.* 1921. Reprint, with a foreword by Dexter Fisher, Lincoln: University of Nebraska Press, 1985.

2880.   ———. *Old Indian Legends.* 1901. Reprint, with foreword by Agnes M. Picotte, Lincoln: University of Nebraska Press, 1985.

13.2   MODERN TEXTS

2881.   Aoki, Haruo. "Footnote to History: Chief Joseph's Words." *Idaho Yesterdays* 33 (fall 1989): 16–21.

2882. Johnson, E. Pauline. *The Moccasin Maker.* Reprint, with an introduction, annotation, and bibliography by A. LaVonne Brown Ruoff, Tucson: University of Arizona Press, 1987.

2883. Littlefield, Mary Wood. "Cherokee Publishing in Arkansas, 1859–1880." *Native Press Research Journal* 3 (1986): 11–20.

2884. Marmon, Lee. "Laguna Portfolio." *Journal of the Southwest* 30 (1988): 317–24.

2885. Miller, Jay, ed. *Mourning Dove: A Salishan Autobiography.* Lincoln: University of Nebraska Press, 1990.

2886. Nelson, Dean. "Akwesasne Notes: Endurance of a Native Voice." *Native Press Research Journal* 2 (1986): 5–8.

2887. Swann, Brian, and Arnold Krupat. *I Tell You Now: Autobiographical Essays by Native American Writers.* Lincoln: University of Nebraska Press, 1987.

13.3 CRITICAL COMMENTS AND LITERARY HISTORIES

2888. Ainsworth, Linda. "History and Imagination: Gerald Vizenor's *The People Named the Chippewa.*" *American Indian Quarterly* 9 (1985): 49–54.

2889. Allen, Paula Gunn. *The Sacred Hoop: Recovering the Feminine in American Indian Traditions.* Boston: Beacon Press, 1986.

2890. ———. "Special Problems in Teaching Leslie Marmon Silko's *Ceremony.*" *American Indian Quarterly* 14 (1990): 379–86.

2891. Antell, Judith A. "Momaday, Welch, and Silko: Expressing the Feminine Principle Through Male Alienation." *American Indian Quarterly* 12 (1988): 213–20.

2892. Ballinger, Franchot. "Living Sideways: Social Themes and Social Relationships in Native American Trickster Tales." *American Indian Quarterly* 13 (1989): 15–30.

2893. ———. "Sacred Reversals: Trickster in Gerald Vizenor's *Earthdivers: Tribal Narratives on Mixed Descent.*" *American Indian Quarterly* 9 (1985): 55–60.

2894. Beidler, Peter G. "The Indian Half-Breed in Turn-of-the-Century Short Fiction." *American Indian Culture and Research Journal* 9, no. 1 (1985): 1–14.

2895. Blackburn, Alexander. "The New Age of Frank Waters." *Journal of the Southwest* 30 (1988): 535–44.

2896. Blumenthal, Susan. "Spotted Cattle and Deer: Spirit Guides and Symbols of Endurance and Healing in *Ceremony.*" *American Indian Quarterly* 14 (1990): 367–78.

2897. Brown, Parker B. "The Historical Accuracy of the Captivity Narrative of Doctor John Knight." *Western Pennsylvania Historical Magazine* 70 (1987): 53–67.

2898. Bruchac, Joseph. "The Many Roots of Song: Influences on Native American Literature, Past and Present." *North Dakota Quarterly* 53 (spring 1985): 28–35.

2899. ———. "Storytelling and Native American Writing." *Halcyon* 12 (1990): 25–42.

2900. Coltelli, Laura. "Native American Literature and Mainstream American Literature, 1968–1988: A Bibliographical Evaluation." *Storia Nordamericana* 5, no. 1 (1988): 187–211.

2901. ———. *Native American Literatures.* Forum 1. Pisa, Italy: Servizio Editoriale Universitario, 1989.

2902. Gish, Robert F. "Word Medicine: Storytelling and Magic Realism in James Welch's *Fool's Crow.*" *American Indian Quarterly* 14 (1990): 349–54.

2903.   Gleason, William "'Her Laugh an Ace': The Function of Humor in Louise Erdrich's *Love Medicine.*" *American Indian Culture and Research Journal* 11, no. 3 (1987): 51–74.

2904.   Greene, David L. "New Light on Mary Rowlandson." *Early American Literature* 20 (1985): 24–38.

2905.   Haseltine, Patricia. "The Voices of Gerald Vizenor: Survival Through Transformation." *American Indian Quarterly* 9 (1985): 31–48.

2906.   Hegeman, Susan. "Native American 'Texts' and the Problem of Authenticity." *American Quarterly* 41, no. 2 (1989): 265–83.

2907.   Hirsch, Bernard A. "'The Telling Which Continues': Oral Tradition and the Written Word in Leslie Marmon Silko's *Storyteller.*" *American Indian Quarterly* 12 (1988): 1–26.

2908.   Jahner, Elaine A. "Cultural Shrines Revisited." *American Indian Quarterly* 9 (1985): 23–30. [Gerald Vizenour]

2909.   ———. "History and the Imagination of Loss." *Storia Nordamericana* 5, no. 1 (1988): 147–66. [John Joseph Matthews and historical writing]

2910.   Keady, Maureen. "Walking Backwards into the Fourth World: Survival of the Fittest in *Bearheart.*" *American Indian Quarterly* 9 (1985): 61–66.

2911.   Kestler, Francis Roe, comp. *The Indian Captivity Narrative: A Woman's View.* New York: Garland, 1990.

2912.   Krupat, Arnold. *The Voice in the Margin: Native American Literature and the Canon.* Berkeley: University of California Press, 1989.

2913.   LaBorwit, Melanie. "Folklore and Native American Traditions." *North Dakota History* 56 (1989): 10–15.

2914.   Lincoln, Kenneth. "Historical Slippage and Indian Humor Today." *Storia Nordamericana* 5, no. 1 (1988): 167–84.

2915.   ———. "The Literary Presence of Native American History." In *The Impact of Indian History on the Teaching of United States History: Papers and Commentary from the 1986 Conference at Los Angeles,* 111–74. D'Arcy McNickle Center for the History of the American Indian, Occasional Papers in Curriculum, no. 5. Chicago: Newberry Library, 1987.

2916.   ———. "Tai-Me to Rainy Mountain: The Makings of American Indian Literature." *American Indian Quarterly* 10 (1986): 101–17.

2917.   MacCarthy, William B. "Folklore of Cultural Contact: The American Indian Example." *Mid-America Folklore* 16 (1990): 1–68.

2918.   McKenzie, James. "'Lipsha's Good Road Home': The Revival of Chippewa Culture in *Love Medicine.*" *American Indian Culture and Research Journal* 10, no. 3 (1986): 53–64.

2919.   Manly, Kathleen, and Paul Rea. "An Interview with Simon Ortiz." *Journal of the Southwest* 31 (1989): 362–78.

2920.   Maristuen-Rodakowski, Julie. "The Turtle Mountain Reservation in North Dakota: Its History as Depicted in Louise Erdrich's *Love Medicine* and *Beet Queen.*" *American Indian Culture and Research Journal* 14, no. 3 (1988): 33–48.

2921.   Michaels, Walter Benn. "The Vanishing American." *American Literary History* 2 (summer 1990): 220–41.

2922. Molyneaux, Brian. "Floating Islands: The Micmac Vision of Sailing Ships." *Rotunda* 18, no. 1 (1985): 6–13.

2923. Nelson, Robert M. "Place and Vision: The Function of Landscape in *Ceremony*." *Journal of the Southwest* 30 (1988): 281–316.

2924. Orestano, Francesca, "Dickens on the Indians." In *Indians and Europe: An Interdisciplinary Collection of Essays,* ed. C. Feest, 277–86. Aachen, West Germany: Edition Herodot, 1987.

2925. Owens, Louis. "The 'Map of the Mind': D'Arcy McNickle and the American Indian Novel." *Western American Literature* 19 (winter 1985): 275–83.

2926. ———. "The Red Road to Nowhere: D'Arcy McNickle's *The Surrounded* and 'The Hungry Generations.'" *American Indian Quarterly* 13 (1989): 239–48.

2927. Petrone, Penny. *Native Literature in Canada: From Oral Tradition to the Present.* Don Mills, Ont.: Oxford University Press, 1990.

2928. Purdy, John Lloyd. "'He Was Going Along': Motion in the Novels of James Welch." *American Indian Quarterly* 14 (1990): 133–46.

2929. ———. *Word Ways: The Novels of D'Arcy McNickle.* Tucson: University of Arizona Press, 1990.

2930. Rice, Julian. *Lakota Storyteller: Black Elk, Ella Deloria, and Frank Fools Crow.* American University Studies, Series 21, Regional Studies, no. 3. New York: Peter Lang, 1989.

2931. Ruoff, A. Lavonne Brown. "Gerald Vizenor: Compassionate Trickster." *American Indian Quarterly* 9, no. 1 (1985): 67–74.

2932. ———. "The Survival of Tradition: American Indian Oral and Written Narrative." *Massachusetts Review* 27 (1986): 274–93.

2933. Sevillano, Mando. "Interpreting Native American Literature: An Archetypal Approach." *American Indian Culture and Research Journal* 10, no. 1 (1986): 1–12.

2934. Siekminshi, Greg. "The Puritan Captivity Narrative and the Politics of the American Revolution." *American Quarterly* 42 (1990): 35–56.

2935. Silberman, Robert. "Gerald Vizenor and *Harold of Orange*: From Word Cinemas to Real Cinema." *American Indian Quarterly* 9 (1985): 5–22.

2936. Stineman, Esther L. "Mary Austin Rediscovered." *Journal of the Southwest* 30 (1988): 545–51.

2937. Strong, Pauline Turner. "Captive Images." *Natural History* 94, no. 12 (1985): 50–57

2938. Sullivan, Sherry. "The Literary Debate over 'the Indian' in the Nineteenth Century." *American Indian Culture and Research Journal* 9, no. 1 (1985): 13–31.

2939. Swan, Edith E. "Healing via the Sunwise Cycle in Silko's *Ceremony*." *American Indian Quarterly* 12 (1988): 313–28.

2940. ———. "Laguna Symbolic Geography and Silko's *Ceremony*." *American Indian Quarterly* 12 (1988): 229–49.

2941. Tsosie, Rebecca. "Surviving the War by Singing the Blues: The Contemporary Ethos of American Indian Political Poetry." *American Indian Culture and Research Journal* 10, no. 3 (1986): 25–52.

2942. Vizenor, Gerald. "Bone Courts: The Rights and Narrative Representation of Tribal Bones." *American Indian Quarterly* 10 (1986): 319–32.

2943. ———. *Crossbloods, Bone Courts, Bingo, and Other Reports.* Minneapolis: University of Minnesota Press, 1990.

2944. ———. *Narrative Choice: Postmodern Discourse on Native American Indian Literature.* Albuquerque: University of New Mexico Press, 1989.

2945. ———. "Trickster Discourse." *American Indian Quarterly* 14 (1990): 277–88.

2946. Vogel, Dan. *Indian Origins and the Book of Mormon: Religious Solutions from Columbus to Joseph Smith.* Salt Lake City, Utah: Signature Books, 1986. [Summarizes literature and folklore that influenced the Book of Mormon]

2947. Weigle, Marta. "Creator and Procreation, Cosmogony and Childbirth—Reflections on Ex Nihilo, Earth Diver, and Emergence Mythology." *Journal of American Folklore* 100 (October/December 1987): 426–34.

2948. Wiget, Andrew O. *Native American Literature.* Boston: Twayne, 1985.

2949. ———, ed. *Critical Essays on Native American Literature.* Philadelphia: G. K. Hall, 1985.

2950. Wolfart, H. Christopher. "The Beginnings of Algonquian Lexicography." *Proceedings of the American Philosophical Society* 132 (1988): 119–47.

2951. Wong, Hertha. "Contemporary Native American Autobiography: N. Scott Momaday's *The Way to Rainy Mountain.*" *American Indian Culture and Research Journal* 14, no. 3 (1988): 15–32.

Index

Note: In this index ass't. is the abbreviation for assistant; comm. for comments by; comp. for compiled by; ed. for edited by; intro. for introduction by; trans. for translated by

Buecker, Thomas R.: 607(ed.), 608, 609(ed.)
Buerger, Geoffrey: 2153
Buffalo: 193, 1100, 1732, 1773, 2118
Buffalo Bill: 602, 2219, 2459, 2472
Buffalo Bird Woman: 1818
Buffalo Child Long Lance, Chief: 2231
Buffalohead, Priscilla: 1689, 1690, 1691, 1692
Buffalohead, Roger: 1689, 1690, 1691, 1692
Buffalo Hump: 1810
Bullard, Normie: 31
Bullchild, Percy: 1743
Bullen, Ripley P.: 2429
Bundy, David: 1353
Bunte, Pamela: 1926, 1927
Burch, Ernest S., Jr.: 1974
Bureau of Indian Affairs: 756, 1378, 2282, 2323, 2760
Burley, David V.: 194(ed.)
Burnat, Jim: 874
Burnett, Barbara A.: 167
Burns, Robert: 1162
Burrows, James K.: 1064
Burt, Larry W.: 777, 778, 2083
Burton, Bruce: 221
Burton, Lloyd: 1356
Bushnell, Amy Turner: 275, 1121
Bushy Run: 374
Business: 602, 686, 976
Buskirk, Winfred: 1828
Byington, Cyrus: 1159, 1167
Byrne, Kevin: 127

Caddo: 1610, 1628, 1642, 1645, 1652, 1753, 2722
Cadue, Ken, Sr.: 862
Caduto, Michael J.: 1519, 2662
Cahokia: 137, 155, 156
Cahuilla: 1888, 2556
Calendars: 155
Calgary: 886
Caliban: 2498
California: 71, 97, 213, 245, (see ch. 3.3), 458, 516,

518, 556, 1125, 1171, 1202, 1225, 1234, 1279, 1312, 1313, 1379, (see ch. 7.7), 2264, 2281, 2305, 2403, 2404, 2517, 2563
Callahan, Alice Anne: 1744
Callaway, Donald G.: 1928
Callicott, J. Baird: 2663, 2664
Calloway, Colin G.: 32(ed.), 58(ed.), 450, 451, 452, 453, 454, 610, 992(ed.), 1006, 1267(ed.), 1520, 1521, 1522, 1745, 1796(ed.), 2107(ed.), 2155, 2599(ed.), 2751(ed.), 2821(ed.)
Calumet: 126, 450, 2600, 2628, 2640, 2649
Calusa: 1036
Cameron, D.: 261(ed.), 2102(ed.)
Cameron, Ian: 2791
Camp, Gregory S.: 611
Campaigns: 583, 626
Campbell, Gregory R.: 2347, 2373, 2375(ed.), 2376(ed.), 2699
Campbell, Richard D.: 1523
Campeau, Lucien: 1122
Campisi, Jack: 455, 455(ed.), 495(ed.), 807, 1252, 1253, 1286(ed.), 1524, 1525(ed.), 1542(ed.), 1561, 1592(ed.), 1703(ed.), 2251(ed.), 2274(ed.), 2275(ed.), 2314, 2317, 2334
Canada (Lovelace v. Canada): 1394
Canada: 268, 605, 761, 792, 1055, 1108, 1110, 1261, 1394, 1396, 1413, 1427, 1455, 1476, 1487, 1506 (see ch. 7.5, 7.9 and ch. 8), 2211, 2240, 2287, 2296, 2302, 2381, 2387, 2388, 2414, 2445, 2446, 2452, 2458, 2561, 2565, 2661, 2681, 2682, 2759, 2766, 2786, 2791, 2825, 2832, 2842, 2847, 2865, 2868, 2927

Canadian-American Pacific Treaty: 605
Canandaigua: 1252
Canary Islands: 288
Cannibalism: 1501
Capeci, Dominic L., Jr.: 2601
Capoeman, Pauline K.: 1975(ed.)
Cappannari, Stephen C.: 1955
Cardy, Michael: 1526
Caribbean: 286, 325, 336, 1041
Carleton (governor): 571
Carlisle, Robert S.: 1976
Carlisle, Ronald C.: 117
Carlson, Catherine C.: 1123
Carlson, Leonard: 963
Carlson, Pamela McGuire: 2156
Carlson, Richard G.: 1527(ed.)
Carolinas: 314, 318, 391, 1037
Carr, L. G.: 379(ed.)
Carrasco, David: 1497
Carrasco Massacre: 2238
Carrico, Richard L.: 276, 456
Carrier: 144, 2357
Carriker, Robert C.: 168
Carroll, George H.: 457
Carroll, Jane Lamm: 1254
Carroll, John M.: 612(ed.)
Carson, Mary Eisenman: 1240
Carter, Harvey Louis: 2157
Carter, Kent: 617, 2377
Carter, Max L.: 1164
Carter, Nancy Carol: 1357
Carter, Sarah: 875, 876, 877, 1977, 2501
Cartography: 86, 1917, 2745, 2765
Carver: 2499
Cash, Joseph: 716
Cassells, E. Steve: 195
Casson, R. I.: 2452
Castellano, Marlene Brant: 1528
Castile, George Pierre: 1978, 1979(ed.), 2602
Castillo, Edward D.: 277, 278(trans., ed.), 458
Cataldo, Joseph M., S.J.: 1163

Patterson, E. Palmer: 1092, 1214

Patterson, Lisa: 412

Patterson-Rudolph, Carol: 185

Patwin: 2517

Pauguset: 1603

Pauketat, Timothy: 156

Paul, Andrea: 2219

Paul, Paulet: 2094

Paul, R. Eli: 157, 608, 609(ed.), 1799, 1800(ed.)

Paull, Andrew: 2844

Pawnee: 603, 608, 1218, 1755, 1792, 1797, 1798, 2171

Paxton Boy: 434

Payment, Diane: 2111, 2112

Payne, Richard W.: 2564, 2641

Peace: 380, 417, 454, 497, 559, 560, 599, 1930

Peak, Ken: 2285

Pearcy, Thomas L.: 2415

Pearson, Bruce L.: 1575

Pease, Margaret: 1215

Peebles, Christopher S.: 158

Pemberton, Richard, Jr.: 1434

Pendleton, Lorann S. A.: 1955

Pendergast, James F.: 159, 264

Penn, William: 2194

Pennsylvania: 117, 357, 1508, 1548, 2802

Penny, David W.: 125, 2565

Penobscot: 1251

Pentagoet: 255

Pentland, David H.: 1718

Pequot: 132, 366, 393, 420, 1007, 1253, 1524, 1547, 1559, 1589, 1593

Perdue, Theda: 551, 552, 553, 554, 555, 1574, 1657, 1658, 2416, 2417, 2818

Perrone, Bobette: 2364

Perry, Richard J.: 2046

Pershing, John (general): 767

Perth Museum and Art Gallery: 2541

Perttula, Timothy K.: 1093

Peters, Bernard C.: 1719, 1720

Peters, Russell M.: 1575

Petershoare, Lillian: 2348

Peterson, J.: 2085(ed.), 2087(ed.), 2090(ed.), 2091(ed.), 2096(ed.), 2105(ed.), 2110(ed.), 2113(ed.), 2119(ed.), 2122(ed.), 2532(ed.)

Peterson, Jacqueline: 21(ed.), 2113, 2114(ed.)

Peterson, John E., II: 1435

Peterson, John H., Jr.: 55(ed.)

Peterson, Susan C.: 1216, 1299

Peterson, Thomas F.: 1300

Petosky, John: 1301

Petroglyphs: 140, 185

Petrone, Penny: 2927

Pettit, Norman: 1142(ed.)

Peyer, Bernd C.: 843

Peyote: 1285, 1429, 2144, 2448, (see ch. 11.3)

Peyser, Joseph L.: 265, 266, 2418, 2419

Pfeiffer, Ida: 674

Phelps, Glenn A.: 1302

Philip's Grant: 563

Phillips, George: 556

Phillips, Ruth B.: 2566, 2567

Philp, Kenneth R.: 844, 845, 846

Phoenix Indian School: 2310, 2341

Photography: 124, 643, 1598, 1835, 1844, 2037, 2069, 2199, 2255, 2283, (see ch. 11.2)

Pick-Sloan Plan: 748

Picotte, Agnes M.: 2880(foreword)

Picotte, Susan La Flesche: 2210

Picotte-Galpin, Mrs.: 2396

Pictographs: 362, 1782

Pictures: 1795, 1876, 1950, 2223, 2229, (see ch. 11.2)

Pierce, Maris Bryant: 2243

Pierce, Richard: 239

Pilgrims: 371

Pillar, James R.: 1217

Pilling, Arnold: 1914, 2757

Pima: 699, 1833, 1835, 1894, 2412

Pima-Maricopa: 1833, 1894

Pima-Papago: 1157, 1835

Pimeria Alta: 291

Plains Indians: 1863, 2366, 2376, 2488, 2531, 2532, 2576, 2607, 2619, 2684, 2730

Plant life: (see ch. 11.1), 2686, 2689

Plateau Indians: 1064, 1920, 2778

Platt, Lester Beach: 1800

Plaza: 1873

Pleistocene: 212

Plymouth Colony: 1011

Pocahontas: 1662, 2356, 2470

Pocatello, Chief: 522, 2209

Poetry: 31, 2941

Point, Nicholas, S.J.: 1161

Point Barrow: 218

Pointing, J. Rick: 928

Point Pleasant: 436

Pokagon, Leopold: 2161

Pokagon, Simon: 1256

Pokagon: 1690

Poland: 673, 2845

Polhemus, Richard: 1638

Politics: (see ch. 3), 987, 1026, 1036, 1147, 1190, 1345, 1398, 1471, 1474, 1509, 1531, 1674, 1760, 1886, 2357, 2374, 2466, 2514, 2526, 2701, 2714, 2718, 2719, 2775, 2941

Polynesia: 2542

Polzer, Charles W.: 340(ed.), 341(ed.)

Pomedli, Michael: 1143

Pomerance, Bernard: 677

Pommersheim, Frank: 1436, 1437

Ponca: 667, 668

Pond, Samuel W.: 1802

Pontiac: 376

Poole, Dewitt Clinton: 1803

Poore, Anne V.: 1874(ed.), 2510(ed.)

Poor Man, Mercy: 1245

Poospatuck: 2395

Pope: 2137

Popular culture: 2455, 2473, 2481, 2484, (see ch. 11.2)

Population: 179, 213, (see ch. 3), 1081, 1328, 1337, 1599,